# Adventuring in
# Australia

# Adventuring in Australia

NEW SOUTH WALES
NORTHERN TERRITORY
QUEENSLAND
SOUTH AUSTRALIA
TASMANIA
VICTORIA
WESTERN AUSTRALIA

**Second Edition**

*ERIC HOFFMAN*

SIERRA CLUB BOOKS • SAN FRANCISCO

Copyright © 1990, 1999 by Eric Hoffman

Second Edition

Published by Sierra Club Books, in conjunction with Random House, Inc.

LIBRARY OF CONGRESS CATALOGING-IN-PUBLICATION DATA
Hoffman, Eric.
    Adventuring in Australia: New South Wales, Northern Territory, Queensland, South Australia, Tasmania, Victoria, Western Australia/ by Eric Hoffman.—[Rev.]
        p.        cm.
    Includes bibliographical references and index.
    ISBN 0-87156-961-2 (alk. paper)
    1. Natural areas—Australia Guidebooks.    2. Wilderness areas—Australia Guidebooks.    3. National parks and reserves—Australia Guidebooks.
    4. Australia Guidebooks.    I. Title.
    QH77.A8H64    2000        333.78'0994—dc21        99-40331

State maps by Carolyn Poucher. Urban maps courtesy of the Australian Tourist Commission.

Printed in the United States of America on acid-free recycled paper

For the joy known as Sherry Edensmith

# Acknowledgments

This book would not have been possible without the efforts of others. Foremost among those who helped me with my task were Alasdair McGregor, Joc and Robyn S. Schmiechen, Jonathan Day, Elizabeth Dolan, Daryl Hudson, Corina Ammann, Charesse Tokley, Suzanne Noakes, Delia Nicholls, Leigh Sorenson, Sophie Dounoukos, Penny Clegg, Jodie Cox, Sharna Quest, Morea Grosvenor, Robyn Grosvenor, Pauline Hedger, Margaret Sparrow, Mike Smith, Julie Averay, Roger and Clyde Haldane, Karen Stotz, Leanne Henderson, and Linda Zaklikowski.

# Contents

# PART I

# Overview

# Why Visit Australia?

To me Australia is the most attractive contradiction on earth. On one hand there's the familiar—a slightly irreverent English-speaking culture. On the other, there's the unfamiliar—a natural world unlike anywhere else on earth. Australia is the island continent. The total isolation from Gondwanaland that began 225 million years ago has allowed creatures and plants to evolve on their own, as if on another planet.

Australia is proof that you don't have to leave earth to find alien life: numbats, wombats, quolls, Tasmanian devils, dibblers, bilbies, bandicoots, echidnas, platypuses, lyrebirds, and palm cockatoos are for the most part unknown outside of Australia. The complex breadth of Australian wildlife and its many evolutionary peculiarities will intrigue, amuse, and confuse you.

Australia has more than 500 national parks spread throughout the country. It has hundreds of quaint little one- and two-pub towns and long drives between them where the amount of traffic can be tabulated on your fingers. It is a land where getting to a name on a map is still an adventure. It has thousands of idyllic and often empty drive-up beaches bordered by rain forests, deserts, savannahs, or bush. And one of its top regions is beneath the sea. On the waters around the Great Barrier Reef you can snorkel and scuba dive among countless varieties of colorful fish that dance and glide over unimaginable configurations and colors of coral.

There is the Top End, with its primeval Kakadu National Park, featuring the Arnhem Land escarpment containing prolific amounts of Aboriginal rock art dating back at least 20,000 years. Offshore from Darwin are the fabulous self-governing Tiwi people, who've survived the European onslaught and now sell wood carvings and Bima wear cloth to tourists to supplement their hunter-gatherer culture. There's the timeless Red Centre, famous for Uluru (Ayers Rock) but also possessing striking desert parks—where in the morning and evening the sun's rays cause the red rock gorges to glow. If you're up to it, the Centre's where you can climb onto the back of a camel and head off for a week without people. Then there's the rugged Kimberley with Coke-bottle-shaped boab trees, galleries with Aboriginal art, and a spectacular coastline that is as remote and unique as anywhere on earth. Or there are the lush tropics and island paradises along the Queensland coast, where you can river-raft under a rain forest canopy. There's the green and peaceful New England plateau, preserved in parks and farmland, and excellent for car camping, birding, horseback riding, and day walks. There's the Flinders Ranges with its dusty towns made of sandstone brick, where rare yellow-footed rock wallabies dart up near-vertical cliffs and stare down at you through the limbs of giant river red gums filled with screeching parrots. In the southeast there are snow-covered alpine areas excellent for cross-country skiing, hiking, and horseback riding. There's Tasmania, a different world again, a walker's paradise, rich in temperate rain forest and alpine highlands.

Australia is home to the world's oldest culture. The people now collectively known as Aborigines have lived in Australia for at least 40,000 years and quite possibly much longer. Today the Dreamtime culture is in its death throes as a pure culture. But the Australian government has finally shown strong interest in preserving what is left, and there may be enough surviving Aborigines to preserve their heritage. Any trip to Australia should include trying to understand this system of living that worked for thousands of years and was unraveled in a mere two hundred. Ageless Dreamtime stares back at you in ochre paintings and rock carvings and in today's Aborigines, who play their didgeridoos and gather at corroborees. Aboriginal art, with its distinctive characteristics, can be purchased throughout Australia. I'll never forget the time I spent in the Gammon Ranges with Aboriginal Heritage Ranger Clifford Coultard and on Melville Island with the Tiwi people—places you can go and people you can meet.

When it's time to come in from the Outback and wash off the dust, you can retreat to the shiny cities of Sydney, Adelaide, Brisbane, Melbourne, Hobart, and Perth, which are delightful places. Australians complain about rising crime rates, but compared to U.S. cities they're decades behind. The cities are generally clean, vibrant, and committed to the arts.

There's something refreshing about the Australians. At the risk of overgeneralizing, I'll say that they usually take a stranger at face value, assume the best is yet to come, and share values that include common sense and a live-and-let-live attitude—on the whole, a straightforward, fun-loving society.

Australians often refer to their nation as the "lucky country." Australia *is* a lucky country: well managed, safe, sane, away from the world's trouble spots, underpopulated, and possessing the most unique natural heritage of any continent. There is one danger in visiting Australia—you may want to move there.

# What's Special About This Book

*Adventuring in Australia* was the first Australia-wide travel guide focused on the Outback and outdoor activities. Since the first edition many other publications have come forth. This edition of *Adventuring in Australia* is an expansion and updating of the original work. You'll find many other travel books that center their coverage on the cities and treat parks and wildlife superficially. By and large this book looks at Australia from the other way around. You can use this book to find a tour package or you can use it as a do-it-yourself guide.

The overriding focus in every state was to locate the best natural heritage areas and to find specific outdoor activities in them. This required visiting more than 200 national parks, covering the entire continent, and visiting major island groups. It included recording unique qualities of flora and fauna, walking trails, visiting Aboriginal art sites, snorkeling, scuba diving, adventure sailing, camel trekking, bird-watching, wildlife spotlighting, horseback riding, canoeing, river rafting, 4WD driving, and sitting at the back of a tourist bus.

This book is a firsthand account of the 60,000 kilometers on land and in the air that I covered. I enlisted the support of the Australian

Tourist Commission, state-run tourism departments, park service personnel, adventure outfitters, outdoor educators, environmental groups, leading adventurers, museum curators, zoo staffs, leading wildlife biologists, the publishers and writers of *Australian Geographic, Landscape,* and *Australian Natural History,* Aborigines, friends, and friends of friends. I traveled by canoe, rubber raft, aluminum dinghy, speedboat, bareboat yacht, retired 12-meter Americas Cup contender, "big cat," ferry, horse, camel, car, bus, train, helicopter, airplanes of various vintages, including sea planes and gliders—and on foot.

I came away knowing I hadn't seen everything, but confident I'd surveyed the country's most intriguing Outback regions more thoroughly than most comprehensive publications to date. My focus was simple: if I liked what I experienced and it could be duplicated by people buying this book, I included it. If I didn't like something or thought it was too dangerous to recommend (like the Franklin River in Tasmania), I omitted it or explained my concern. Considerable culling took place. In some cases I found highly promoted areas not worth the time and expense. For example, Wave Rock in Western Australia is best appreciated in a photograph, not in person. In this regard I continually made value judgments that also extended to tour operators. Of dozens of adventure tours, I only mentioned the ones that in my estimation provide good value. I judged the quality of the interaction: Was it authentic? Did it deliver what it claimed? Did it actively involve the participant? For example, I nearly went stir-crazy on the transcontinental railroad that links Perth to Sydney—too long and too boring. The passengers were generally well past retirement age and making use of transportation vouchers. The train's passage literally scared wildlife out of sight. On the other hand, I enjoyed a 120-kilometer camel trek through the Flinders Ranges, sailing and camping with the Haldane brothers in the Thorny Passage, and cross-country skiing in the Victorian Alps with Graeme Stoney as much as anything I've ever done. These were new experiences in new environments. My senses were stimulated. There was exertion and suspense. I felt this same euphoria in a light aircraft on the Cape York and Cobourg Peninsulas and while buzzing the Bungle Bungles and in sailing in the Whitsundays, along the forbidding shore of Macquarie Harbour in Tasmania, and in the remote Kimberley—not just sailing but sailing in wild and alien-looking places.

The basics of the capital cities are covered, but so are ways that allow you to break off the beaten track. Even in the cities the emphasis is on activity and the outdoors. There are, for example, beach reviews in Sydney, Adelaide, Perth, Broome, and Darwin, describing the type of beach: windsurfing, bodysurfing, safe swimming, nude bathing, turtle rookeries, family picnicking, or camping. This book is about *adventuring* in Australia. It still tells you where to find the tourist bus, but suggests you'll get more out of your visit Down Under by striking out on your own.

# Basic Travel Information and Contacts

## Climate

There are two things to remember about the climate: Australia's seasons are opposite the Northern Hemisphere's, and Australia is generally warmer than North America. June through August is winter. September through November is spring. December through February is summer. March through May is fall. The farther north you go, the less seasonal variation. Forty percent of the country is in the tropics and heavily influenced by monsoons. In this northern area, which includes Broome, Darwin, and Cairns, there are two seasons: wet and dry. Both are hot. The wet is humid as well as hot and occurs from December through March, though it can fluctuate from year to year. The wet season is a beautiful time in the north, but it is also uncomfortably hot, and ground transportation is often difficult or impossible because of flooding and torrential rains. The dry season, April through November, is the best time to visit the northern latitudes.

The center of the country is usually too hot for comfortable outdoor activities during the summer. However, spring, winter, and fall are often ideal, with cool nights and warm, comfortable days.

The south has distinct seasons. Winters are cold and temperatures are often below freezing in the mountain areas of New South Wales, Victoria, Tasmania, South Australia, and the southwest of Western Australia. Snow is common in the southern Great Dividing Range, which includes the area around Victoria commonly called the Victorian Alps. Tasmania is the coolest area in Australia and is subject to sudden and potentially dangerous shifts in weather that may dive from 80°F to freezing in a matter of minutes, any time of the year.

Weather is reported in degrees Celsius, which can be mystifying to someone familiar only with Fahrenheit. (I found the weather reporting reliable.) Here's a conversion table that should help:

| Celsius | Fahrenheit |
|---------|-----------|
| 0 | 32 |
| 5 | 41 |
| 10 | 50 |
| 20 | 68 |
| 30 | 86 |
| 40 | 104 |

## Passport and Visa Requirements

You will need a passport and visa to enter Australia. In the United States, your nearest large post office can fill you in on how to get a passport. Allow 60 days for processing. In Canada, there are 28 regional passport offices. If you have trouble finding a regional office, contact Canadian Passport Office, Department of Foreign Affairs and International Trade, Ottawa, ON, KIA 0G3, phone 613-994-3500; http://www.dfait-maeci.gc.ca/passport. Allow 30 days' lead time. For a visa, mail or take your valid passport to the nearest Australian consulate. Besides the passport you'll need an extra passport photo and will have to fill out a one-page form. In person, the visa can be issued on the spot. By mail allow 30 days. There is no cost, and the visa is good for 6 months. *Don't* rely on a travel agent to handle any of these requirements. Misunderstanding or ignorance can result in your not being allowed to board your plane, since airlines are required by law to see a valid passport and visa before issuing a seat. Should you lose your passport, report it to the nearest consulate or the local police. Replacement time is much faster if you can produce a photocopy of the original passport or a birth certificate. On your return expect a $A27 ($US18.90) departure tax, though this may become a tax of the past if some Aussie lawmakers get their way.

## Health Regulations and Health Services

There are no unusual health problems in Australia that haven't been encountered in North America. AIDS and all other sexually transmitted diseases exist in Australia. Use good judgment and condoms. No vaccinations are needed for entering Australia from the United States. If you're entering Australia from countries or zones that have been designated "infected" or "endemic zones" by the Aussie government, requirements may be different.

The average Australian enjoys excellent health care for minimal cost, but this does not extend to foreigners. For medical aid be prepared to pay steep costs. The Australian government suggests you have adequate health insurance for overseas trips before you leave home. Drugstores, by the way, are called chemists.

## Holidays

Holiday seasons can affect the quality of your stay in Australia. All of Australia seems to take to their cars during major holidays. Christmas (Chrissie) is the worst. It coincides with a school holiday and lasts two weeks in most places. There are other school holidays in May, August, and September that fall on slightly different dates in the various states. There is a move to bring about national agreement on all major holidays—horrors! Check into school holidays in the area you plan to visit and book in advance if your travel plans fall on those holidays.

## Key Information in the United States

The Australian Tourist Commission (ATC) distributes free literature with a whole range of listings that include state-run tour offices, tour companies, and transportation throughout Australia. Ask for the book *Australian Vacation Planner*. Contact Australian Tourist Commission in the United States, phone 805-755-2000; fax 805-775-4448.

# International Air Carriers

Qantas Airways is Australia's international carrier. Their safety record is exemplary. I've found their service good and their fares competitive. They've recently been allowed to include domestic legs on their international tickets. United, Singapore, and Air New Zealand are active carriers to Australia from the United States as well and are usually very competitive in their pricing. Several U.S. airlines besides United also serve Australia. Check with your travel agent for the best deal. Buying far in advance often brings savings. Fares fluctuate greatly, the high being in Australian summer, centered around December, and the low in Australian winter, centered around July. For example, in 1998, from December 1 to February 28 fares were in the $US1,600 range for advance excursion fares, and the same ticket cost $US1,300 from April 1 to September 30.

Domestic tickets in Australia are expensive, so try to avoid them. Instead, inquire about "stopover routing" or "multistop ticketing" from your international carrier. After reading *Adventuring in Australia,* you'll know which capitals suit your interests. Qantas flies to Sydney, Melbourne, Brisbane, Townsville, Cairns, Adelaide, Darwin, and Perth. Also check into reciprocal partnerships between carriers that will allow you to use two or more airlines on the same ticketing. By cutting the best possible deal on your airfare before you leave North America, you'll know your biggest expense from the outset.

| | |
|---|---|
| Qantas Airways (Canada and United States) | 800-227-4500 |
| United Airlines | 800-241-6522 |
| Singapore Airlines | 800-742-3333 |
| Air New Zealand | 800-262-1234 |
| Canadian Airlines | 800-655-1177 |

United States contact for coach booking in Australia (see specific sections for names of Australian coach companies):

| | |
|---|---|
| Greyhound (U.S.) | 800-231-2222 |
| (Canada) | 800-661-8747 |

United States contact for Australian Railways:

| | |
|---|---|
| Railways of Australia | 800-524-2420 |

## Travel Options and Strategies in Australia

The gateway cities for international flights are Sydney, Melbourne, Adelaide, Perth, Brisbane, Townsville, Cairns, Darwin, and Hobart. These cities are the hubs for ground travel and internal air flights, with Sydney possessing the busiest and most extensive travel network. A multistop international air ticket will allow you to work out of several of these areas on a single trip to Australia. Good-quality paved roads link the capital cities and the perimeter of the country. The paving of Stuart Highway in the 1980s connected Adelaide to Alice Springs and Darwin. There are numerous paved highways throughout eastern Australia, but dirt is the surface you'll find in many of the remote areas described in this book. Weather conditions, driving ability, floods, avoiding night driving, willingness to abide by safety advice, limitations of car insurance, and time should be carefully considered before driving great distances outside the cities. Petrol usually runs around $A.80¢ per liter ($A2.15 per gallon).

All major towns are interconnected by domestic air service (which is generally expensive) and coachlines. Perth, Adelaide, Alice Springs, Melbourne, Sydney, Brisbane, and Cairns are linked by good-quality rail service—the most inexpensive and slowest way to travel. Rent-a-car and rent-a-van or -motorhome companies are plentiful throughout the continent. Most companies deliver vehicles to airports. Prices usually start at $A70 a day in the competitive large cities but are higher in remote areas. Four-wheel-drives run about $A130 a day. Ask about the Austrailpass for train travel within Australia (buy the pass in Australia, and remember to bring your passport).

| Days | Cost of Austrailpass |
|------|----------------------|
| 8    | $A280                |
| 15   | 575                  |
| 22   | 810                  |
| 29   | 1,045                |

Details on transportation (including acquiring road maps) are provided in the coverage of transportation hubs in each state. Because of Australia's size and somewhat limited Outback system of roads, optimum travel involves flying to a particular region, adventuring there, and then flying on to the next region. As stated, you can usually save money by purchasing a ticket from an international airline that stops at transportation hubs rather than at a domestic airline in Australia.

For tourist information, look for a sign with a white dotted "i" on a blue background. You'll find them all over Australia, even in small towns.

## Phones

The number of digits in a phone number may vary from six to ten. Some nationwide commercial numbers are only six digits and have no area code. Most residential and small-business phone numbers are preceded by a two-digit area code with the first digit always being 0. The 0 is dropped from the number when dialing from overseas. Australia's country code is 61.

## Accommodations

Hotels and motels are generally the same quality as in the United States and about the same price. Unless indicated otherwise, expect a clean room, your own bathroom, adequate heat, tea- and coffee-making facilities, a television, a phone, and often a refrigerator. Air-conditioning is common in moderate- and high-priced accommodations. If fans are advertised, there's usually no air-conditioning. Motels are a relatively new phenomenon in Australia, so they're generally new and as aesthetically unattractive as their North American counterparts.

The authentic Aussie accommodation is an old pub-hotel with a wide veranda. Many of the most impressive ones are in small towns.

On-site vans in caravan parks are usually a good deal, often about $A40 a night. The camps have a common shower and laundry facilities. Most also allow car campers with tents.

Farmhouse stays and bed-and-breakfast homes are usually moderately priced and a convenient way to meet Australians. Youth hostels and YMCAs are also found in transportation hubs and some outlying areas. Holding a YHA membership makes you eligible for reduced fare and transportation costs. If you are a YHA member, always mention it during ticketing. Campgrounds are plentiful throughout Australia but not near some of the large cities.

Accommodation information is provided throughout the book, in particularly great detail in the sections on Sydney, Melbourne, Adelaide, Hobart, Alice Springs, Perth, Cairns, Brisbane, Darwin, and some of the more remote areas.

## Electricity

Australia operates on 240/250-volt 50-cycle alternating current (AC). Big hotels have 110 conversions that won't fry electric appliances from the United States. Otherwise you must pack a converter and have a three-prong adapter of the Australian type to put on your appliances. Beware of "cheap" adapters sold in the United States. They fry after a couple of days of use. The Stepdown Auto Transformer made by Todd Systems (Yonkers, N.Y.) is one adapter that does work.

## Restaurants and Food

The selection and variety of restaurants are as good as anywhere in the world in the big cities. Meat, seafood, and fresh fruit are especially abundant. Vegetarian restaurants are easy to find in the big cities (with the exception of Brisbane) and are usually nonexistent in the Outback. Restaurants, bistros, take-aways, U.S. fast-food places, and roadhouses provide prepared foods—though in the case of many roadhouses the selection is often limited to stale junk food. Lunches and dinners are served everywhere. Breakfast, though, is often hard to find. Most travelers eat breakfast at their hotel or motel, make it themselves, or wait until lunch. A continental breakfast in Australia usually includes fruit, cold cereal, toast or biscuits, juice, and tea or coffee. A full breakfast includes meat, eggs, fruit, and so on, and is generally quite filling. Markets with fresh produce and seafood are common in the larger cities. Specific eateries and markets are listed in the coverage of major transportation hubs and in that of some outlying areas.

## Banking Hours

Banking hours are 10:00 A.M. to 3:00 P.M. Monday through Thursday and to 5 P.M. on Friday. Beware, though, of Australia's holiday-filled calendar, which can come as a surprise when you try to push through a locked bank door. Before the advent of the ATM, banking hours stranded many a traveler who ran low on cash.

## Shopping Hours

Shopping hours are traditionally 8:30 to 5:30 Monday through Friday, and 8:30 to 4:00 on Saturday. This, however, is changing. Many stores stay open until 9:00 P.M. in the large cities.

## Tipping

Tipping is not customary in Australia, other than $A1 per bag for hotel bellhops, but this too is changing. Waiters and waitresses will usually accept a tip. If you do tip, about 10 percent is enough.

## Currency, Exchange Rate, ATMs, and Credit Cards

Australian paper currency is color coded—each denomination comes in a different color. They're called notes, not bills. The Australian dollar ($A) has been valued at around 70 cents to the U.S. dollar for most of the past ten years. This favorable exchange translates to roughly 30 percent more buying power for the U.S. against the Aussie dollar. (*Note:* All dollar amounts in this book are given in Australian dollars unless otherwise stated.) So the damage to your pocketbook is about 30 percent less than it initially appears—in other words, a $A100 hotel bill is about $US70. Or, put differently, $US1.00 is worth $A1.43 in Australia. Keep in mind, though, that exchange rates change daily.

Traveler's checks are generally easy to cash in major cities but a bit mystifying to some bankers and businesses in small towns. In fact, on more than one occasion my traveler's check was refused by a bank and by restaurants in small towns. Some banks charge $A5 per check for a $US20 traveler's check! Wespac proved to be reliable in not charging throughout Australia. Wespac has a red logo that is unmistakable and easy to see as one passes down a main street.

I used a Visa credit card in every state in Australia and even paid for petrol in extremely remote roadhouses. In 60,000 kilometers of road travel I came across only one roadhouse that wouldn't accept a Visa card. Visa was also acceptable in restaurants, at hotels, and for car rentals. MasterCard has about as much acceptance as Visa. Most other cards have limited acceptance. Most city businesses post the cards they accept. *Note:* Keep in mind that in the event of a dispute with a car company (for example, the amount that should be paid for a chipped windshield, dents, or worse), the company can charge the amount it wants to your card regardless of your objections. ATMs are firmly established in Australia. You can withdraw money from your U.S. account from any large city in Australia. You will be charged $A4 per withdrawal.

## Disclaimer

Though the author has attempted to report all costs associated with visiting and staying in Australia accurately, prices continually change. The prices reflected here are those obtained during the revision of this book and may not be accurate at the time the book is published. Neither the author nor the publisher assumes any responsibility for inaccuracies due to changes in prices or errors from sources.

## Aussie Law and You

Australia is a representative democracy. In general, the relationship between the citizenry and law enforcement is respectful and much like that in North America and Europe. Foremost for ruining your stay in Australia is drinking and driving: above 0.05 percent on a random breath analysis means a stiff fine and possible jail time. All of Australia has gone whole hog in putting an end to drinking and driving. I've seen fifty motorists stopped in a single check and can say that the police are friendly, efficient, and uncompromising. If you flunk, your vacation will end. Double-talk and being a foreigner won't help. Also, don't operate a vehicle without fastening your seat belt, unless you're willing to pay a stiff fine.

Driving on the left side of the road can be nerve-racking. The close calls I've had always occur after a couple of weeks, when my concentration falters and I find my right-side preference still firmly in control in my subconscious. Try to stay alert and to practice defensive driving. The biggest danger occurs when you have to make an emergency move and your "right-hand" reflex grabs hold. If you are involved in an automobile accident involving another driver or are arrested, contact the U.S. consulate nearest you for help in determining your rights.

Smoking is banned in many forms of public transport. On the Sydney trains, railroad police give citations to anyone who dares chance it. Ask for nonsmoking rooms. Most hotels have them.

Australian customs regulations are strict in regard to potentially dangerous agricultural pests and illegal drugs.

## Metric Measurement

During the 1970s, when the United States was talking about converting to the metric system, Australia actually did it. You'll meet plenty of Aussies (generally older) who still talk inches and miles, but the country is officially metric, and all signpost distances, market scales, tides, and rainfalls are reported in metric measurements, though some shops will talk both pounds and kilos. The distances in this book are reported in kilometers because that's all you'll see on road signs and speedometers. Though it's not exact, I always keep in mind that 100 kilometers is roughly 60 miles (more exactly, 62 miles) when calculating distance and speed in my head. Rounding off allows you to figure fuel needs and travel time without pencil and paper. Here are the common conversions you'll need:

### Length and Distance:

1 kilometer (km) = 0.62 miles, or 1.61 km = 1 mile
1 meter (m) = 1.09 yards (yd), or 1 yd = 0.917 m
1 centimeter (cm) = 0.394 inch, or 2.54 cm = 1 inch
### Volume:

1 liter (l) = 0.264 gallons, or 3.79 l = 1 gallon
1 liter (l) = .91 quart, or 1.1 l = 1 quart
### Weight:

1 kilogram (kg) = 2.20 pounds (lb), or 0.454 kg = 1 lb
1 gram (g) = 0.0353 ounce, or 1 ounce = 28.3 g
### Area:

1 hectare (ha) = 2.47 acres, or 1 acre = 0.404 ha

# Basic Facts About Australia

## Size

Australia is 7,686,884 square kilometers, which is roughly the same as the United States minus Alaska. From east to west, it is 3,278 kilometers; from north to south, it measures 2,643 kilometers, about the distance from San Francisco to Chicago.

## Geography

Australia is an island continent located in the Southern Hemisphere and surrounded by the Indian, Southern, and South Pacific Oceans and the Coral, Arfura, Tasman, and Timor Seas. Even though approximately 40 percent of Australia lies in the tropics, it's the world's driest and flattest continent. The Great Dividing Range, which extends the length of the east coast, is the continent's foremost mountain system. Mount Kosciusko (2,228 meters) is its highest point. The continent's primary river system, the Murray-Darling, irrigates 80 percent of Australia's arable land.

## The Government

Australia is an independent nation but, as in Canada, the queen of England is formally the queen of Australia. The government is based on the English parliamentary model. Voting is compulsory throughout Australia, and the head of the majority party becomes the prime minister. The constitution has been in effect since 1901. State governments are also parliamentary. The federal capital, Canberra, is a separate entity and, like Washington, D.C., does not belong to any state. Australia is divided into seven states. From the largest to the

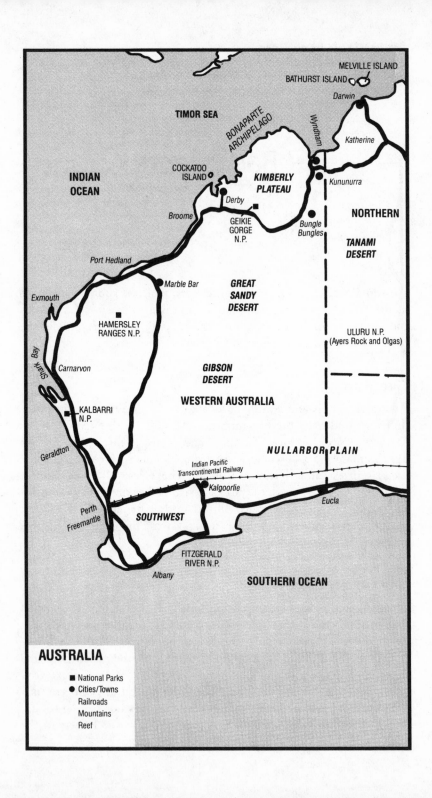

MELVILLE ISLAND
BATHURST ISLAND
Darwin
Wyndham
Katherine

TIMOR SEA

BONAPARTE
ARCHIPELAGO

INDIAN
OCEAN

COCKATOO
ISLAND
KIMBERLY
PLATEAU
Kununurra

Derby
Broome
NORTHERN

GEIKIE
GORGE
N.P.
Bungle
Bungles

Port Hedland

TANAMI
DESERT

Exmouth
Marble Bar
GREAT
SANDY
DESERT

HAMERSLEY
RANGES N.P.

ULURU N.P.
(Ayers Rock and Olgas)

Carnarvon
GIBSON
DESERT

Shark Bay

KALBARRI
N.P.
WESTERN AUSTRALIA

Geraldton
NULLARBOR PLAIN

Indian Pacific
Transcontinental Railway

Kalgoorlie
Eucla

Perth
Freemantle
SOUTHWEST

FITZGERALD
RIVER N.P.

Albany
SOUTHERN OCEAN

**AUSTRALIA**

■ National Parks
● Cities/Towns
   Railroads
   Mountains
   Reef

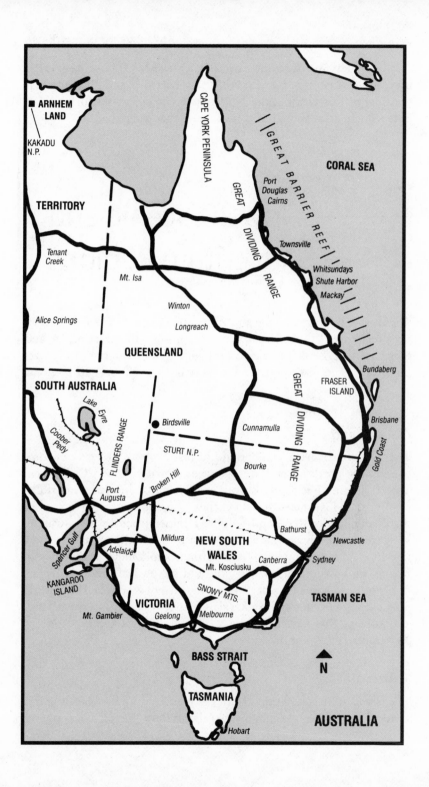

smallest, they are: Western Australia, Queensland, Northern Territory, South Australia, New South Wales, Victoria, and Tasmania. At the time of this writing, the Northern Territory wasn't formally an independent state though it is heading in that direction.

# Top 20 Scenic and Adventure Regions

These are my favorite scenic and adventure regions—listed in order of my preference. I suggest that you read through the descriptions and then choose those that coincide with your greatest interests and travel plans. All, of course, are treated in more detail in the specific sections.

## The Wet Tropics

### Queensland

The wet tropics are a wonderland of lush tropical greenery encompassing the north coastal area between Townsville and Cooktown. Towering rain forests, mist-shrouded tablelands, dramatic waterfalls, sugarcane fields, shell-strewn beaches, fringing reefs, easy access to the Great Barrier Reef, and wildlife oddities (such as tree-dwelling kangaroos, platypuses, and cassowaries) make the area extremely inviting. Activities include river rafting, snorkeling, scuba diving, hiking, and swimming. When you add in the Daintree rain forest north of Cairns, the tropical mountain town of Kuranda, the pristine jungle-covered Hinchinbrook Island, user-friendly Fitzroy Island, and others, the wet tropics is a must in any itinerary. April to November is the best time to visit.

## Tasmania

The island state is separated from the mainland by Bass Strait and is a world apart from mainland Australia in flora, fauna, and topography. Tasmania possesses the most extensive temperate rain forests in the world and also alpine highlands that are as alien looking as they are striking. Giant ferns, trees found only in "Tassie," and Tasmanian devils are some of the island's unique natural features. The island is a walker's paradise, especially the area around Cradle Mountain and Lake Saint Clair. The weather can be as violent as this island's history, which is encapsulated in the extensive ruins of the Port Arthur penal settlement. The Battery Point area in Hobart is a charming place to stay. November to April usually has the best weather, but there are no guarantees in Tasmania. Skiing occurs from June to September.

## The Top End
### Northern Territory

The Top End is the heart of Australia's tropical monsoon environment. Kakadu National Park near Darwin is Australia's answer to the Serengeti. It has vast wetlands teeming with more than 200 species of birds, many of them unseen outside of Australia. You'll see immense saltwater crocodiles, sea eagles, brolgas, jabirus, parrots, wallabies, water buffaloes, and, if you're lucky, the legendary black wallaroo. But for many the main draw is the concentration of Aboriginal art galleries, which hold the richest cache of easily accessible Aboriginal art. Nearby Arnhem Land is a last bastion of Aboriginal culture. Bathurst and Melville Islands are home to the wonderful Tiwi and provide visitors an opportunity to interact with a viable pre-European culture in Australia. Bargain prices for their world-renowned artwork is an extra incentive for visiting the islands. Newly formed Litchfield National Park and the Cobourg Peninsula are remote and exotic places. May, June, and July are the best months to visit the Top End.

## Lord Howe Island
### New South Wales

It might seem that it would be taking a chance to recommend an island only 11 kilometers in length and two hours' flying time from Sydney as one of the top 20 places to visit in Australia. But in the case of Lord Howe Island, there's no risk at all. This World Heritage Area has something for everyone, providing you're vaguely interested in nature. The island's 7 million years of isolation has allowed unique plants and animals to evolve. The parallels to the Galápagos Islands as natural theater of evolution are everywhere, only Lord Howe is a lush green tropical island situated at the convergence of two immense marine ecosystems. Under the surface are both tropical- and temperate-water fishes in prolific numbers. Both snorkelers and scuba divers can anticipate an unforgettable experience. On the island's surface are beautiful beaches, dramatic topography, many species of birds found nowhere else, and a trail system that winds to summits of twin peaks while passing through palm forests and ferns found only here. Most people come for the solitude. Lord Howe is well managed by locals, who don't allow more than 400 visitors at a time onto the island to stay in low-key, affordable accommodations. Besides walking, the main means of transportation is bicycle. The locals have kept the large, glitzy resorts that plague other island paradises in Australia off of Lord Howe. Lord Howe is in a class by itself for maintaining an understated, timeless ambience in a remarkable and bountiful setting.

## The Great Barrier Reef
### Queensland

The Great Barrier Reef is under increasing pressure from tourism but it is still worthy of its status as the "seventh wonder of the world." Its immense 2,000-kilometer length and environmental safeguards have allowed it to withstand a marked increase in human use. The new technology of "big cats" (large, high-powered, aluminum cata- marans capable of carrying a hundred passengers at 30 knots; also known as "fast cats") makes the best of the outer reef affordable and reachable for day tourists, who can now snorkel in the best areas far from the mainland. Combining the reef and the Whitsunday Islands may be your best bet. There are more than 2,500 reefs making up the Great Barrier Reef. You'll find 1,400 kinds of colorful fish and 400 kinds of corals, plus dozens of island paradises—some of them slickly advertised, expensive and exclusive retreats, others moder- ately priced, and still others entirely free if you don't mind setting up a tent and packing in your water and food. The southern reef can be visited year-round. April to November is the best time to visit the northern reef.

## The Kimberley
### Western Australia

Without the help of an adventure travel outfit, the Kimberley is probably the most difficult region to reach in Australia. Because much of it can only be reached by boat, light plane, or 4WD, the Kimberley is my choice for the top pure adventure area in Australia. The dramatic coastline with towering solid rock cliffs and rivers pouring off them into the sea is spectacular. The boab trees are peculiar, and the Wandjina Aboriginal art is mysterious. The most hospitable inland areas consist of million-acre cattle stations, some of which welcome visitors. Geikie Gorge and the Bungle Bungles are every bit as spectacular as Uluru (Ayers Rock) and the rest of the Red Centre. The region's top town, Broome, is too popular for its own good but remains charming. April to November is the best time to visit. Avoid the wet, which usually runs December to March.

## Kangaroo Island
### South Australia

Though it's changing, Kangaroo Island is pristine Australia before the onslaught of feral predators that eliminated the small wallabies and ground birds on the mainland. And, because Aboriginals hadn't been hunting here when Europeans first landed, the wildlife is practically tame—this characteristic of nonchalance toward people still prevails, making wildlife approachable. For the nature lover Kangaroo Island has it all. Take your camera and plenty of film, because you'll see koalas, rare Cape Barren geese, kangaroos, cat-sized tammar wallabies, Australian sea lions, New Zealand fur seals, emus, and goannas with almost guaranteed certainty. Look a little harder and you'll see about a dozen kinds of parrots, echidnas, platypuses, sea eagles, and maybe even a deadly tiger snake. Nature and living things abound here. Under the water, scuba divers report visibility of 200 meters, which gives you a respectful distance and reaction time should the area's top predator, the great white shark, suddenly appear. If you like wildlife, go to Kangaroo Island. You won't be disappointed. September to May is the best time to visit, though year-round is usually okay.

## The Cape York Peninsula
### *Queensland*

Cape York Peninsula is rivaled only by the Kimberley as Australia's most unique truly wild area. The peninsula's southern area around Cape Tribulation and Port Douglas is the stepping-off place to the northern Great Barrier Reef, including Lizard Island. The area also possesses the magnificent Daintree rain forest. The tiny town of Laura can be reached via a grueling dirt road or by light aircraft. This is the heart of Quinkan Country, known for its postcontact Aboriginal art sites and its authentic Aboriginal corroborees. Farther north, at the tip, is a unique enclave, with plants and animals from New Guinea and life-forms indigenous only there (for example, cuscuses and palm cockatoos). Cape York has immense wilderness parks, cattle stations, and Aboriginal reserves. For the most part it is a place suited for those who relish the rigors of a bona fide expedition. Roads are impassable in the wet. Light aircraft are fairly expensive but reliable year-round and practical. Visit May to November.

## Brisbane and Environs
### *Queensland*

In a day's drive in every direction from Brisbane there's an astounding variety of natural beauty. West of Brisbane is Carnarvon Gorge, which could pass for Sir Arthur Conan Doyle's *Lost World*. To me, it rates as one of the top three national parks in Australia. To the south is Lamington National Park, a highlands rain forest park and the best walker's park in Queensland. North of Brisbane is the great "sandy region," which includes Fraser Island—typified by perched lakes, rain forests, dingoes, wild horses, and miles of beaches. North of Fraser Island, but still within a day's drive of Brisbane, is Bundaberg, the stepping-off place for Lady Musgrave Island, the best of the southern Great Barrier Reef. With the exception of Carnarvon

Gorge (don't go in June, July, or August), the area can be visited year-round.

## Thorny Passage and the Joseph Banks Islands
### *South Australia*

This is a destination that offers true adventure-sailing, with appeal to both the gonzo-style adventurer and those who appreciate subtlety in nature. The Joseph Banks Islands are about 40 kilometers east of Port Lincoln, South Australia, and the Thorny Passage is about 20 kilometers to the southeast. All totaled, there are 70 islands, ranging in size from 2 to 200 acres. I wandered through these islands for a week on a sailboat as a guest of the Haldane family, who pioneered the tuna fisheries here. What looked like a series of similar islands turned out to be a study in contrasts. We went ashore on Owens Island and sunbathed on huge granite slabs alongside a colony of Australian sea lions while small parrots flitted around us, noisily chattering. On Thistle Island we watched white-breasted sea eagles hunt and Pearson Island rock wallabies bound down the beach, with huge breakers crashing around them. Hopkins Island featured thousands of muttonbird nests that were being marrauded by oversized, extremely venomous black tiger snakes. The snakes feast on eggs and chicks for about three weeks and then live off what they've eaten for the rest of the year. We fished for our dinner and savored the sunsets. The first challenge is getting here. May to September is the best time to visit.

## The Red Centre
### *Northern Territory*

The Red Centre is known for Uluru (Ayers Rock), the Olgas (Kata Tjuta), and Alice Springs. Despite the daily follow-the-leader air-conditioned coach caravans to Uluru, it still rates as a spiritual experience, especially if you time your visit after the morning arrivals and departures of the tour buses. Uluru is best reached from rapidly growing Alice Springs, which is also the stepping-off place to a half-dozen excellent desert national parks. If red-rock gorges, ghost gums, camel treks, and desert wildlife appeal to you, the Red Centre will take you about a week to get to know and enjoy. Hot-air ballooning and glider rides also go on here. April to October is the optimum time to visit.

## Adelaide and Barossa Valley Wineries
### South Australia

Often Adelaide is forgotten by tourists because of the drawing power of Sydney and Melbourne, which is too bad. Adelaide is a beautiful city, with its sturdy and attractive sandstone homes, wide streets, and impressive Gothic churches. The city is intelligently laid out, surrounded by parklands, close to calm-water beaches that are user-friendly, and a relaxing place to spend time. Adelaide is civilized and sane; the pace is right. There are many good wine-growing areas in Australia, but the nearby Barossa Valley is in a class by itself when it comes to the European tradition that started here in 1842. You just don't find grand châteaus like Château Yaldara anywhere else. The unforgettable accommodations and broad variety of wines from more than 50 wineries make the Barossa a must for any serious connoisseur. In the nearby hills there are historic sheep stations, such as Bungaree, where you can spend a night in the shearer's quarters. Visit September to May ideally, though year-round is usually okay.

## The Flinders Ranges
### South Australia

The Flinders Ranges, a dramatically jagged escarpment, includes Wilpena Pound, historic sandstone towns, Aboriginal communities, and the heart of the Heysen Trail and other walking tracks. The ranges contain two top-quality national parks: Flinders Ranges and Gammon Ranges, the latter the stronghold of the attractive yellow-footed rock wallaby. There are good camel treks in the region. The entire region is stereotypical Australia—huge river red gums, homesteads, one-pub towns, sheep stations, and wildlife. It was made famous by Hans Heysen, perhaps Australia's best-known landscape artist. Spring is usually marked with a bursting forth of greenery and wildflowers. The Flinders are reached from Adelaide or Port Augusta. Temperatures from April to October are reasonable.

# Alpine Australia
## Victoria

Alpine Australia may not fit into your preconception of Australia, but winter in Australia brings more snow-covered ground than in the Swiss Alps. Australia's alpine area includes immense Mount Kosciusko National Park in New South Wales and the "Victorian Alps," which are the most dominant geographic feature in Victoria. Both New South Wales and Victoria have developed good-quality downhill ski areas; however, the cross-country skiing has the most to offer. The scenery is often dominated by twisted snow gums and sharp ridgelines unfamiliar to European and American skiers. It's also the top place in mainland Australia to hike during the summer months, especially in Victoria, where the trails and parks are well developed. Adventure travel opportunities include cross-country skiing and horseback outings with the likes of Graeme Stoney, one of the crack horsemen in the *Man from Snowy River* films. By traveling to alpine Australia from Melbourne, you can include spectacular Wilsons Promontory, the Otways and coastal parks, including the penguin "parade," and the wildlife-rich Grampians. March to November is the best time for walkers, June through August for skiers.

# Hinchinbrook Island
## Queensland

Located in Queensland's wet tropics just offshore from Cardwell, Hinchinbrook Island has just about everything a naturalist or tourist trying to avoid glitzy resorts would want. As you approach in a small boat, Hinchinbrook looks like the lost island from a *Jurassic Park* or *King Kong* movie. It is both forbidding and inviting. Its highest rampart, 1,213-meter high Mount Bowen, is usually shrouded in mist. The island's steep slopes are covered in deep green tropical forests, and around the base are creeks flowing into the sea, virginal beaches, and mangroves. The island is immense, and all 39,350 hectares of it

are committed to national park. With mountains to climb, rain forest and beach walks of a day or more, boat and footpath wilderness
camping, and a chance to be entirely secluded, the island is an adventure in itself. There is a wealth of marine and bird life to occupy your
curiosity. Or maybe you'd rather just sit on a foredune under a huge
shade tree and read a novel, knowing nobody will be coming your
way all day, except for a curious pied oystercatcher or an osprey.
Hinchinbrook may not have the underwater world of the Whitsundays, Lizard Island, or Lord Howe Island, but it has more than they
do on most other counts. Hinchinbrook is a gem.

## The Southwest
### Western Australia

The Southwest near Perth possesses an astounding array of 8,000
species of flowering plants every spring, many of them indigenous
only to that region. Aside from the flowers there are massive karri
trees and jarrah and grass-tree forests and empty beaches. Numerous
parks and small towns with good road access make the Southwest
particularly well suited for car camping. North of Perth is Monkey
Mia, the only place in the world where wild dolphins come to shore
and greet people on a regular basis. Perth is a friendly, clean, restau-
rant-rich city, with the best city beaches in Australia. Rottnest Island,
the home of the quokka, is a ferry ride from the city. And, if you're a
"yachtie," there's Fremantle. September and October are usually best
for the spring bloom.

## Whitsunday Islands
### Queensland

My only reservation in recommending the Whitsundays is that there
are too many high-end resorts whose idea of paradise appears to be
$A400 a night. Still, with the combination of beauty, good weather,
a protective reef to the seaward, personal safety, and recreational
activities, the Whitsundays are arguably the best tropical island paradise in the world. There are 10 major resorts and 160 islands on the
stretch of coast where the Whitsundays are center stage. The islands
are continental in origin, rather than created by reefs; thus they are
heavily vegetated, beautiful, rich green forms that appear to be float-

ing in an azure sea. The colors and panorama are stunning. There is island camping and there are a few reasonably priced hotels. Enjoying the Whitsundays and remaining solvent may require homework and the willingness to resist promotional gimmickry, but it will be worth it. The weather is nearly always perfect. Sailing, snorkeling, scuba diving, parasailing, hiking, fishing, "sunbaking," photography, and relaxation are all possible in a couple of days, but stay a week if you can afford it.

## New England
### New South Wales

North of Sydney is New England, a green highlands area possessing a half dozen rugged parks rich in subalpine and temperate rain forests, waterfalls, woodlands, and wildlife. There are coastal and mountain parks. Rafting the Nymbodia River, bushwalking, and horseback riding are popular. The university town of Armidale is a culturally alive hub in the area, and there are quaint mountain towns. New England can be visited year-round. Its abundant wildlife includes lyrebirds, wallabies, pademelons, brush turkeys, and parrots. The Hunter Valley, which is New South Wales's top wine-growing district, and the dramatic Warrumbungles are near New England.

## Outback Desert Parks
### New South Wales

This is a vast area in the Outback centered around mineral-rich Broken Hill. The area contains many historic sheep stations that have been incorporated into a series of parks. Each park has a different emphasis. Lake Mungo National Park possesses 40,000-year-old remnants of Aboriginal culture and lunette formations. Kinchega National Park may have the greatest concentration of large kangaroos in Australia, along with abundant bird life. Mootwingee National Park is rich in Aboriginal art and dryland parrot species and has high densities of wedge-tailed eagles. Sturt National Park teems with large red kangaroos and emus, whose numbers are governed by the severity of the perpetual drought. April to September is the most temperate period.

## Sydney

### New South Wales

Sydney may be the most visitor-friendly port city in the world, and it possesses the visual cues the world recognizes as Australia: the Sydney Opera House, the Sydney Harbour Bridge, a quaint and hyperactive ferry service, sandstone buildings from the convict era, and wonderful beaches. Sydney reminds me of San Francisco, only Sydney has warm-water beaches, a better harbor, and suburbs landscaped with subtropical plants. The national parks north, south, and west of the city are easily reached by public transport. Sydney's unending cultural events demand at least a four-day stay, and Sydney is ready for you year-round.

# Five Top Treks in Australia

One of the joys of researching this book was getting to know the terrain. If you're a hiker, consider hiking in Australia. There are plenty of stimulating treks throughout the island continent. Here are five worth considering.

## Overland Track

Without a doubt, the consensus favorite is the Overland Track in Tasmania. This is a mostly alpine walking track that connects Cradle Mountain to Lake Saint Clair in a distance of about 70 kilometers. It is an environment filled with plants and geological formations seen nowhere else. It's pristine, often crisp, boggy in places, wild, and stunning. Pack for all kinds of weather: People have perished due to sudden storms. Expect snow and bright sunshine in the same day. Watch out for the leeches and respect the brush-tailed possums' ingenuity in getting to your food during the night. For conditions and details, phone 03-6492-1133.

## Thorsborne Trail

This is a 32-kilometer hike down the east side of Hinchinbrook Island. You may not see another person as you walk behind pristine beaches, cut inland through low rain forest, and cross numerous creeks—some with pools suitable for swimming—but inquire first about saltwater crocodiles on the island. You're likely to see ospreys, egrets, parrots, and tropical pigeons. The trail starts at George Point at the island's only resort and ends in Mission Bay. Get oriented at the resort and tell the park service in Cardwell about your plans. The hike takes between three and four days to complete at a leisurely pace. For conditions and details, phone 07-0688-801.

## Heysen Trail

This is an ambitious 1,200-kilometer trail that stretches from Adelaide to above the Flinders. It is hiked in sections and rarely walked in its entirety. The 55-kilometer stretch between Parachilna and Wilpena Pound is popular. It cuts through picturesque red-rock gorges lined with huge river red gums. Water is a problem year-round, and excessive temperatures can become life threatening. Check the weather and get an accurate map that shows water sources. You're likely to see wedge-tailed eagles, white corellas, galahs, budgies (like in the pet shop, but green in the wild), bearded-dragon lizards, euro and red kangaroos, and, with a little luck, the colorful and agile yellow-footed rock wallaby. I rode a camel through much of this area and enjoyed the vast vistas and the congregations of all living things around the water holes in the gorges. Set aside three to four days for the Parachilna section. There are 15 maps of various portions of the Heysen Trail. For conditions and details about this section and other sections, phone 08-8416-6677.

## Great South-West Walk

This is an ambitious trail made largely by a volunteer effort. It starts near Portland, Victoria, and heads westward along the coast. In all it takes in 235 kilometers, though there are many places to bail out along the way. The trail is a gargantuan loop over fairly flat terrain that cuts through Lower Glenelg National Park and passes by numerous bays and through forests, heathland, and foredunes. There are numerous watercourses and lakes and there is a great deal of bird life en route. Expect to see Australia's beautiful iridescent blue fairy wrens, Willy-wagtails (*Rhipidura leucophrys*), galahs, corellas, and a wide assortment of shorebirds, as well as ospreys and sea eagles. Eastern gray kangaroos and wallabies are plentiful along portions of the trail. This is a walk with few natural hazards. If you want to do the whole thing, set aside two weeks. There are several sections that can be completed in a day to 3 days. Phone the Tourist Information Centre in Portland, Victoria. Phone 03-5523-2671.

## Frenchmans Cap

Truth be told, despite it's smallest-state status, Tasmania has the best wilderness hiking. Frenchmans Cap is a dramatic peak that stands high against the sky in Tasmania's nearly impenetrable temperate rain forests in the Franklin and Gordon Rivers catchments. The area is so rugged that once you enter the Gordon River to raft it, there are no other trails out until you float out the other end days later. The entire region is dramatic and untamed. Though Frenchmans Cap is only 1,443 meters high, it is often dusted with snow because of the southern lattitude and the occasional blast from Antarctica that comes this far north. The hike covers 50 kilometers round-trip and requires you to pull yourself across rivers by hand in a litter suspended from a cable. (It's easy, if you don't look down.) The walk is rugged, with plenty of ups and downs. The vegetation is bright green and some of it only indigenous to Tasmania. People have lost their lives on this trek because of sudden shifts in weather that they were ill-prepared to withstand. Set aside two to four days. Always be prepared in Tasmania. Phone 03-6471-7122.

# Flora and Fauna

## Monotremes

In 1798, scientists at the British Museum opened a box sent by colleagues in Australia. It contained the furry pelt of a creature with webbed feet, a flat tail like a beaver's, a long bill like a duck's, and various appendages and anatomical curiosities that made it unlike anything they had ever seen before.

The reaction was immediate disbelief: the scientists dismissed the specimen as a fake, the clever ruse of irreverent Australian colonials. Today, the pelt is still in the museum's collection, complete with scalpel marks where the skeptical scientists tried to locate the stitchery that attached the bill to the body. The animal, it turns out, was no fake but the creature now commonly known as the duck-billed platypus.

The platypus belongs to a group of mammals called *monotremes* (single vent) that lay eggs instead of live young—a distinction it shares only with the echidna, a small anteater found throughout Australia. A monotreme nurses its young and therefore is considered a mammal. In some circles the platypus is considered the missing link between reptiles and mammals—a primitive transition.

The platypus's most curious appendage—its bill—is anything but primitive, however. It contains 750,000 highly evolved sensory cells connected to the animal's brain and ranks among the most sophisticated food-locating sensory organs in the animal world. A platypus actually closes its eyes and ears when submerged and allows its bill to direct its underwater navigation and hunting activities. Dr. Tom Grant, a world expert on the platypus, says, "The platypus is the Australian mammal of all time." Grant is right on two counts: the platypus is a paradox that defies classification, and a recent fossil find puts its longevity at 100 million years, meaning it once paddled about ponds frequented by huge dinosaurs. The story of the platypus illustrates how long Australian mammals have evolved on their own.

I found platypuses relatively easy to spot in river systems the entire length of eastern Australia. But you have to be willing to get up at the crack of dawn to catch this busy nocturnal paddler before it beds down in its burrow. Watching them dive and feed on the surface is pure delight.

## Marsupials

The rest of Australia's 230 mammals are no less interesting than the paradoxical platypus. The predominant mammal form is the marsupial—an animal that gives birth to an incomplete embryo that is tiny, naked, and lacking rear legs. This unfinished offspring survives by fixing itself to a teat in a protective pouch, where it develops. By contrast, *placental* mammals like you, me, and the family dog are born complete, with all appendages in place, and must only grow to maturity.

Australia's many marsupials are often categorized into carnivores, omnivores, and herbivores. It's a surprise for most people to learn that there are nearly 40 species of marsupial carnivores in Australia. In the distant past there was even a marsupial lion! Most of today's marsupial predators are fairly small creatures about the size of a rat (but handsomer) with bushy tails and large ears and eyes. The antechinus is best known for its fanatical copulating, which results in exhaustion and death for the males. Also among the pint-sized carnivores are such rarities as the dibblers, mulgaras, and kowaris.

The larger marsupial predators are visually interesting. The quoll, a spotted, weasel-shaped animal the size of a small cat, is definitely something new to look at. They are often called native cats, tiger cats, and tiger quolls. The most attractive one is the spotted-tailed quoll, which I found plentiful after dark around Cradle Mountain Lodge in Tasmania. Quolls of one kind or another are nocturnal hunters that occur around Australia's coastal areas, but not in the arid interior.

The Tasmanian devil is the biggest surviving marsupial predator. It is restricted to Tasmania and is relatively easy to find at night around Cradle Mountain Lodge and other areas. Devils are unforgettable, small-dog-sized creatures that spend much of the night screaming, bluffing, and nipping at other devils congregating on animal carcasses. Although their screams can be unnerving, the creatures pose little threat to people. They are slow and clumsy, but possess extremely strong jaws that allow them to break open bones to extract marrow. The Tasmanian devil has had a few close calls with extinction but is plentiful now, which can't be said for its bigger cousin, the thylacine.

The thylacine (or Tasmanian tiger or wolf) was plentiful when Europeans settled Tasmania, but every expert I've talked to now considers it extinct—despite the occasional unverifiable sighting. Its disappearance marks the end to an entire family of large marsupial predators that once roamed all of Australia. The handsome, striped numbat, now restricted to the southwest in Western Australia, may follow the thylacine. Its numbers are declining rapidly for unknown reasons.

The omnivorous (plant- and meat-eating) marsupials consist of bandicoots and bilbies. Like most Australian mammals, they are nocturnal, but unlike many ground-dwelling marsupials, bandicoots and bilbies travel on all fours and run instead of bound. They are cat-sized animals characterized by long slender snouts and, in some species, oversized ears. As a group they're not faring well, largely because of feral predators.

The herbivorous (plant-eating) marsupials are a large and diverse group. Perhaps the most loved is the koala, the tree-dwelling creature that sleeps about 20 hours a day. There's no getting around its teddy bear cuteness. Koalas are fairly plentiful. The Lone Pine Sanctuary near Brisbane, the Taronga Zoo in Sydney, and the Healsville Sanctuary near Melbourne are excellent places to see them in captivity. In the wild, the Grampians, French's Island State Park, Port Macquarie, and Kangaroo Island are top koala-viewing areas. Despite their relative abundance, there is reason for concern about their future. World-renowned expert Dr. Frank Carrick of the University of Queensland explains, "For reasons that aren't entirely understood, some populations have quit reproducing while others have very low reproductive rates."

A koala relative, the unperturbable wombat, seems to be hanging on in fairly good shape. Wombats are handsome 50-pound burrowing marsupials. Like koalas, they are compact and round, which contributes to their cuteness rating. Wombat habitat is unmistakable because of their huge tunnel systems that look like a gigantic gopher has been at work. The hairy-nosed wombat is common in parts of the Nullarbor Plain and the Eyre Peninsula, and the common wombat inhabits Tasmania, parts of Victoria, New South Wales, and pockets in South Australia.

When you think of the North American possum, which looks like an overgrown rat, the idea of getting excited about possums may seem ridiculous. It's anything but when you see the selection of possums in Australia. Counting their close relatives, the cucuses and gliders, there are more than 20 kinds of possums in Australia. They range in size from the tiny pygmy possums to some the size of a small dog. There is also great variety in color, habitat, diet, and appearance, but they generally have a handsome furry face, large round eyes, a bushy tail, and a round body. They are mischievous, with the ability to ingratiate themselves with people. In the Sydney suburbs, wild ring-tailed possums often get the same treatment as the family dog.

The gliders are my favorite members of the possum family. These animals, which range from squirrel- to cat-sized, glide between trees on outstretched limbs connected to loose skin, like flying squirrels. The silver color phase of the greater glider and the bushy tailed squirrel glider are among the most endearing animals in Australia. Gliders are relatively common in parks in the eastern states. They are nocturnal and can be located with flashlights, usually after you hear them squabbling over territorial rights to a particular tree.

The last group of marsupial herbivores is by far the most populous, most diverse, and best known. This is the group of *macropods* (big feet), which refers to their large hind legs. The biggest member of this group is the red kangaroo, which can stand six feet tall and weigh 180 pounds. Gray and euro (wallaroo) kangaroos are nearly as big. The smallest is the nabarlek, which usually weighs about half a pound. In between these extremes are around 40 kinds of macropods, including wallabies, potoroos, pademelons, and bettongs.

It would be hard to imagine a national park or wild area without macropods. Kinchega and Sturt National Parks in New South Wales are heavily populated with the large kangaroo species. Gammon Ranges National Park in South Australia has findable populations of the colorful and courageous yellow-footed rock wallaby, my favorite wallaby. You can spend hours watching them flash across precipitous rock faces. The Adelaide Zoo has a healthy captive population. Tammar wallabies, found on Kangaroo Island, are also entertaining and easy to approach in places where they've grown used to people.

Whip-tailed wallabies are perhaps the fastest and most fun to watch streak across an open area. They're found in the northeast, specifically in Carnarvon Gorge, but may be spotted any place where there are broken woodlands. If you're going to spend time in the parks, a field guide will allow you to identify the "macropod of the moment."

## Placentals

In Australia, *placental* mammals larger than mice are mostly nonnative creatures that have wreaked havoc on native species. Though nobody really knows for sure, there are an estimated 80,000 feral dromedary camels in the Centre and probably as many brumbies (wild horses) and donkeys in pockets around the country. In the north there are huge herds of Asian water buffalo, particularly in Arnhem Land. The Northern Territory is a stronghold for these larger feral animals. Rabbit plagues have subsided, but they left a heavy scar in native ecosystems. Feral pigs are rampant in the eastern third of the continent. But probably the feral animals most devastating to native species have been the red foxes and "house" cats that are found throughout the continent. The foxes are descendants of a hunting club's release near Melbourne in 1893. The cats have hybridized to bobcat-sized creatures in many regions. The wild dog known as the dingo is the enigma among the placental mammals. It was on the continent when the Europeans arrived and is thought to have arrived some 10,000 years ago. Scientists believe that the dingo eliminated the thylacines and Tasmanian devils from the mainland. Dingoes are much persecuted by humans but, like the coyote in the United States, they are very adept at surviving. Dingoes are easily photographed around Uluru, the nearby gorge parks, and on Fraser Island—places where they've enjoyed protection.

## Birds: Cockatoos to Kookaburras

Australia is known for the beauty, variety, and color of its birds. Because of strict export laws, many of the most dramatic species have rarely appeared outside Australia. There are more than 730 species filling an incredible number of niches. By comparison there's about the same number of species in the United States and about 900 in Europe. But while there's parity in numbers, there's no contest when it comes to glitter, variety, and sheer entertainment value. Any time spent in the Aussie bush will be punctuated with flashes of color and a wide range of sounds, many of them unlike any bird sounds in other parts of the world.

The parrots are probably the most striking and unmistakable of the birds you'll see. Of these, the cockatoo family is the biggest and most entertaining. In their respective habitats you'll see large numbers of sulfur-crested, red-tailed black, little corella, and galah cockatoos. I've seen flocks of little corellas in the thousands in South Australia and the Northern Territory. Less common but findable are pink Major Mitchell cockatoos, an arid-land bird found in the Centre, and the gang gang cockatoo, found in the Alps in Victoria. The Major Mitchell is perhaps the prettiest parrot in the world. One of the rarest birds in Australia is the striking palm cockatoo found on the tip of Cape York.

Parrots are found through the Southern Hemisphere, but cockatoos are only found in Australia. The middle-sized parrots like the rainbow lorikeet, king parrot, and crimson rosella are particularly colorful. I've even seen the bright red crimson rosellas while I was sliding along on cross-country skis in the Victorian Alps.

Many of the parrot species are particularly delightful because of their flocking behavior. Budgerigars, which Americans know as budgies or parakeets, often appear in a swirling mass that twists and turns, one moment exposing the bright green bellies of each bird in the flock, the next showing the dark wing tops—a kaleidoscope of moving frantic feathers. A flock of corellas will sometimes look like a great white twister as the flock descends into a stand of river red gums for the night. The crescendo of their screeching is so loud you won't be able to hear a person who is standing next to you.

The honeyeaters are the most populous family, with 65 members—no wonder, since in Australia something is always flowering.

Australia's ostrichlike flightless emu and cassowary are the two biggest birds on the continent. Both stand eye to eye with a person. The emu shares the Australian coat of arms with the kangaroo and is found throughout Australia away from urban centers. It's easily found in the desert parks of New South Wales and the Grampians in Victoria. The cassowary lives in the wet tropical rain forests and comes equipped with a permanently affixed calcified helmet.

The wedge-tailed eagle is common throughout Australia. It is a majestic golden-brown raptor similar in appearance to the golden

eagle found in North America, but a "wedgie" has a characteristic tri-
angularly shaped tail that is unmistakable in flight. Wedgies are common along roads in the interior, where they live the easy life by
scavenging road kills with the always present magpies. Mootwingee
National Park in New South Wales may be wedgie heaven. I saw
dozens in Mootwingee, along with huge flocks of corellas and budgies.

The white-breasted sea eagle is Australia's other dramatic eagle.
This is one of the flashiest eagles in the world. The bird does high-
altitude acrobatics during courting that can be witnessed on Kangaroo Island, Tasmania, and other suitable coastal habitats. It's also
very adept at snatching fish from the sea.

There is a wide selection of other raptors in Australia, including
peregrine, brown, and gray falcons and ospreys, harriers, kites, and
kestrels. In coastal tropics you may think you've seen a bald eagle,
when it's a brahminy kite. Kites of one kind or another are as common as sparrows in the Top End. There's also a barking owl that
barks the night away, and the tawny frogmouth, a nighttime predator with a huge wide bill that gives it a froglike appearance.

Two species of lyrebird live in Australia. This fern-gully forest
dweller imitates every sound within its hearing: the calls of other
birds, car doors shutting, and, on one occasion, the closing whistle of
a logging camp. They look somewhat like peacocks and put on an
impressive display during courting that can be seen at the Healsville
Sanctuary in Victoria or, if you're adept enough to draw close, in the
parks of New England.

The kingfisher family is led by the clown of feathers, the laughing
kookaburra. There's no mistaking a kookaburra's laugh—it sounds
like laughter from the inner wards of an insane asylum. The kookaburra is a compact, pigeon-sized white, blue, and gray bird with a
somewhat large head and straight daggerlike beak. They're loved in
Australia because of their laugh and because they eat poisonous
snakes. In some national parks (Carnarvon and Grampians) they
have been known to snatch a sandwich from a person's hand while
flying at full throttle.

The other kingfishers aren't as loud as the laughing kookaburra or
as mischievous, but they're more colorful. There's the blue-winged
kookaburra, which lives mainly in the tropics. There's the yellow-
billed kingfisher, which is mostly bright gold and is found on the tip
of Cape York. There are half a dozen other colorful kingfishers; the
flashiest one, gold underneath and iridescent blue on top, is the buff-

breasted paradise kingfisher, found along river courses in the wet tropics in Queensland.

Australia's waterfowl also sport striking color schemes. Black swans are native to Australia and are quite common in river mouths and protected estuaries from Tasmania to Perth. Other dramatically marked waterfowl include: huge white Australian pelicans, which fish in flotilla fashion; the once endangered green-billed Cape Barren geese; pied, pygmy, and magpie geese; and zebra-marked radjah shelducks and whistling ducks. Leading the long list of waders are a wide variety of egrets, stiltlike brolgas, and jabirus and spoonbills.

Nearly two dozen finch species occur in Australia. Zebra finches, which are sold in pet shops in the United States, are common throughout Australia, but the flashiest finches are the gouldian and crimson finches of the tropical north.

The wrens come in incredible violets and blues. If you see a splendid fairy wren, which is common in the Grampians, you'll know it. The bird is a rich iridescent blue.

Fairy (or little) penguins are a major tourist attraction on Phillip Island near Melbourne. These plucky little penguins are common on the islands and rocky portions of the southern Australian coast.

There are many splendid bird sanctuaries in Australia. Standouts during my travels were Kakadu National Park, Northern Territory; Kangaroo Island and the Coorong, South Australia; Little Desert National Park and the Grampians, Victoria; the wet tropics and Cape York, Queensland; and Mootwingee and Kinchega National Parks in New South Wales. See the coverage of Sydney's Australian Museum for information about buying bird books. More detailed coverage of birds is provided in the descriptions of each region and national park.

## Flora

Australia is a botanical wonderland. The island continent has more species of plants than the United States, Canada, and Greenland combined. The same millions of years of isolation that produced Australia's maverick animals created thousands of unique plants. Nobody knows for sure, but there are at least 20,000 kinds of plants living in Australia and most of them are found only there. In the southwest near Perth there are a reported 8,000 species of flowering plants. The most diverse plant region in the United States is California, which has about 7,500 native plants.

Plants in Australia tend to be bushes, most of them flowering bushes. Some of them are known in North America because of their flowers, drought resistance, and poor-soil tolerance. For example, bottlebrush is common along freeways in California and is easily identified by its red bottle-brush-shaped flowers—but in Australia the plant we know as "the" bottlebrush is just one of thirty kinds of bottlebrush. Some kinds have green flowers, others purple.

There are dramatic regional differences as you move from the wet tropics in Queensland to the alpine areas in Tasmania, from the spinifex country in South Australia to the boab trees of the Kimberley. The forests are primarily limited to the wetter areas relatively near the coast.

There are 600 different kinds of eucalyptus. The tallest are the giant 100-meter swamp gums (all eucalyptus are called gum trees), which rival the California redwoods as the world's tallest tree. There are also multistemmed arid-land mallees that rarely exceed 2 meters. There's the gnarled and twisted snow gum, which survives above the snowline because it creates its own "antifreeze." And then there's the red-flowering gum that explodes in a veneer of red flowers every spring and can't tolerate temperature even near freezing.

If you're confident you can identify an acacia when you see one, don't bet on it. In Australia there are 600 species of acacias. They're commonly called wattles and are abundant throughout the island continent and take on many forms. The golden wattle—which is just that, pure gold when in bloom—is Australia's national flower and appears on its coat of arms.

Within Australia there are isolated areas where plants have been evolving in their own direction. The Nullarbor Plain and the western deserts have isolated the southwest near Perth as a unique botanical area with literally thousands of flowering plants, many of them native only to that region. Tasmania has its own collection of temperate rain forest and alpine species, including Huon and King Billy pines. The wet tropics are literally an explosion of vegetation and contain some of the world's oldest plants, such as *Idiospermum australiense,* which is the only living member of its family anywhere.

Banksias are another unique group of plant. The genus *Banksia* is named after Sir Joseph Banks, Captain Cook's botanist, who brought the first banksia sprigs back to Europe. There are more than 50 species. Some are trees, others are bushes. Most of them produce huge cylindrical flowers up to 15 centimeters long that often hang like Christmas tree ornaments. Depending on the species, banksia colors range from purple to green, red, orange, and yellow.

The Proteaceae family is found in Australia, South Africa, and South America, but the lion's share of about 600 species live in Australia. The distribution of the family is evidence of the link between South America, Australia, and Africa. The bright red waratah is the state flower of New South Wales.

Besides these colorful plants, there's the king fern, with its 3.5-meter fronds. There are also primitive species of palms, and grass trees that have been growing since the time of Christopher Columbus. But probably the weirdest-looking tree is the baobob, which is called the boab in Australia. The Australian version's trunk is Coke-bottle shaped and the color of steel. The tree lives in the Kimberley, and Aborigines claim it never dies from natural causes. Near Derby a huge boab tree has become a tourist attraction because it was hollowed out and used to hold Aboriginal prisoners earlier in this century. The tree is still alive.

Another common tree is the she-oak (not an oak), which has wispy pendulous branches and needlelike leaves. She-oaks are found throughout Australia. Pandanus and zamia palms are two of the more common palms, though there are many species in the tropics. There is also a great variety of mangrove species and figs, with the Moreton Bay fig possibly the most prominent. Paperbarks, with their unmistakable flaky bark, occur in swampy areas. In arid belts you'll see mulgas, scraggly one-trunked trees—the last trees before the heart of the treeless Nullarbor Plain.

The areas I found most striking botanically were the wet tropics, Queensland; Tasmania; the Top End, Northern Territories; and the Southwest, Western Australia, during the major bloom in September and October. You'll find more detail by turning to the coverage of the respective regions.

## Reptiles

If you suffer from reptile phobia, hold someone's hand while you continue reading. Australia is chock-full of reptiles: about 240 species of lizards, 140 species of snakes, 2 species of crocodiles, and 12 species of freshwater turtles. Saltwater turtles come ashore during nesting activities.

Unfortunately for all you nervous Nellies, the Elapidae family of snakes provides Australia with more than its fair share of extremely poisonous snakes (see "Knowing the Nasties," below). The saltwater crocodile has also been getting bad press for gulping down a few too many Australians in recent years. Venomous snakes and salties should not be taken lightly.

After the nasties, things pick up a bit. There is a healthy collection of constrictors, mostly middle-sized pythons. Some of these are encouraged to stay around stations for pest control. One even has the reassuring name of children's python.

Most visitors find lizards more to their liking. The monitor group supplies Australia with its famous goannas, which are big and harmless. Goannas are "bush tucker" to Aborigines and taste something like chicken. In some areas goannas are used to nonpredatory people and are quite tame. Keep in mind, though, that they don't bother to separate food from fingers if you try to hand-feed them—and they have a strong bite. The meter-long sand goanna is everywhere; the 2-meter perentie goanna is a little more difficult to find, but it's by far the most impressive lizard. It lives in the Centre. The dragon lizards include thorny devil to frilled lizards. The devil is covered by bumps and thorns and looks like a version of the North American horned toad. The frilled lizard runs around with its own Elizabethan collar trying to look bigger than it is. Water dragons, found in Sydney suburbs and the tropics, are perhaps the most entertaining. They seem to plop into the water the moment you dive into an idyllic rain forest swimming hole. But they're trying to avoid you, not trying to make you into a meal. Australia also has a great variety of skinks and geckos.

If you suffer from reptile phobia keep in mind that in all my travels in Australia I only saw one live poisonous snake on the mainland—and it was going the other way. Goannas may act fearless, which can be unnerving, but if one plods in your direction it's probably only because it's conditioned to handouts. If you're trying to finish a meal, you can keep it at bay by tossing something edible in its direction. There's only one reptile I fear: the saltwater crocodile, because its only criterion for a meal is catching it. The rest of the 400 kinds of reptiles would rather run than fight—that is, as long as you don't step on them. That's the key to peaceful coexistence with reptiles. Don't step on them.

## Knowing the Nasties

In the Australian lexicon the nasties are animals that can do you some harm. There's no shortage of creatures that qualify, but unlike on other continents, where tooth and claw pose the real or imagined threat, in Australia deadly poisons seem to be the defense of preference. Australian coastal waters possess the blue-ringed octopus, sea snakes, stonefish, and box jellyfish—each capable of killing a person, but easily avoided. (I discuss these creatures and other marine menaces in detail in the coverage of the Great Barrier Reef.)

On land, poisonous snakes, mostly from the Elapidae family, create a formidable list: tiger, taipan, brown, king brown, yellow-bellied black, red-bellied black, copperhead, and death adder are the best known of the deadliest. There are 12 species that pack a fatal bite and a hundred species with venom of some kind. The taipan wins top honors in the deadliest group because it often strikes three to four times in the blink of an eye, which assures that venom hits home in one of the bites. The one weakness in these snakes' lethal bite is that their fangs are relatively short and often do not penetrate farther than clothing. Sometimes no poison is injected in a bite that does penetrate the skin—but don't count on it.

Besides the snakes there's the funnel-web spider, the deadliest spider in the world. It occurs in Sydney, but it is a reclusive creature content to sit at the bottom of its funnel web, set up for passing insects. Even the lovable platypus packs venom. Male platypuses have venomous spurs on their hind legs that are potent enough to kill a dog, if one should be quick enough to snare a platypus from a pool.

The potential of these creatures is the bad news. The good news is that your chances of being bitten are extremely slim. Chances are, you'll be lucky even to see a poisonous creature, let alone get close enough to be bitten. During my 60,000 kilometers on the ground in Australia, which included countless hikes, swims, night walks, bush bashes, and camp-outs, I came across one poisonous snake on the mainland. However, for safety's sake, assume that any snake you come across is poisonous, which means you should walk the other way and not kill it. The regional distribution of poisonous snakes and their appearances can be learned by visiting the Australian Museum in Sydney or like institutions in other parts of the country. Antivenins have been developed and are kept at hospitals.

The rule for not getting bitten is simple: don't step on snakes or allow them to use your sleeping bag. Look before you step and don't blindly put your hand anywhere. The National Parks and Wildlife Service adds the following written advice: "Snakes are shy and will nearly always attempt to escape. Most snake bites occur in limbs when a snake is handled or stepped on. When bushwalking wear appropriate clothes, including heavy shoes or boots with thick socks. Snakes are often active at night. Carry a torch [flashlight] when walking at night." In case of a bite, the National Parks and Wildlife Service advises: "Keep the victim calm. Immediately apply a firm, broad bandage over the bite and as much of the limb as possible. The bandage should be applied as strongly as you would for a sprained wrist. Put the limb in a splint to entirely immobilize it. If it's safe to do so, kill the snake, stick it in a bag, and take it to the hospital with the victim for the purpose of identification. If possible, give the hospital advance warning that a snakebite victim is en route. Minimize the victim's movement to slow the circulation." Poisons take from 30 minutes to 2 hours to work. Identification of the snake is important because venoms are blood and nerve poisons and doctors need to know which antivenin to use, since application of an antivenin is not risk-free.

The other menaces of note are saltwater crocodiles and sharks. Saltwater crocodiles have consumed seven Australians and one American in recent years. Every victim was swimming or wading in croc-infested water. Saltie habitat extends from north of Broome across the top of Australia and down the eastern seaboard as far as Cardwell. The name *saltwater crocodile* is deceiving, because though they can live in salt water, they usually live in freshwater swamps near the coast and can occur in river systems far inland from the coast. If you're in croc habitat, assume there are crocodiles unless an authority tells you differently. The species is protected and is increasing in numbers and reclaiming its historic haunts. Pay attention to signs and vary your habits if you camp near watercourses in the tropical north. Salties are quick and very aggressive. Large adults weigh over a ton and measure 7 meters, which makes the American alligator look like a pet-store lizard in comparison. Australia's other crocodile, the smaller freshwater croc (with the pointed snout), is considered safe to swim with as long as you don't touch it. They generally occur farther inland than salties, often above waterfalls and rapids, which separate them from salties.

Sharks are associated with the Australian coastline. There have been two deaths due to shark attacks in Australia in recent years. Both occurred in South Australia, which is a stronghold for great white sharks (known as white pointers in Australia). In many areas there are shark nets. Ask about sharks before snorkeling or diving. In general, sharks aren't much of a problem in the Great Barrier Reef, especially in the areas "fast cat" operators take you. There's more detail on sharks in the coverage on the Great Barrier Reef.

If you're interested in poisonous snakes, selected islands in the Thorny Passage (South Australia) are the stronghold of the tiger snake.

# The Aborigines: The First People

The first people did not come to Australia when the much celebrated sailing ships from England, packed to the gunnels with social discards, arrived in 1788—the year that started English settlement. The English social experiment of deportation amounted to putting in place a labor force to settle a new and strange land that blossomed into one of the great stories of human migration and settlement—for people of European ancestry.

But these weren't the first people in Australia, and they weren't even the first Europeans. The first people came much earlier. Experts disagree on exactly when, but somewhere between 20,000 and 40,000 years ago is seen as a safe bet. Some scientists have postulated that human occupation actually started 100,000 years ago. These original inhabitants may have arrived in waves with the coming and going of ice ages and land bridges connecting Australia to New Guinea and beyond. For example, the emergence of the dingo as a predator didn't occur until 10,000 years ago. It is thought to have arrived with one of the human migrations from the north. Any way you slice it, the first Australians were surviving here so long ago they predate all traces of civilization collectively known today as Western civilization. When Neanderthals were hunting giant bison, mastodons, and one another for food in Europe, Australia had already been occupied for tens of thousands of years.

Today these first Australians are known by the collective term *Aborigine,* a name that was foreign to the Aborigines themselves. When European settlement began, it is estimated that something like 500,000 Aborigines lived in Australia. They had common cultural beliefs, generally went about naked, used similar tools, and had dark brown skin, yet they were not entirely homogenous. It has been estimated that there were at least 650 tribal-clan groupings and around 300 different dialects in 1788, the year that the preceding 20,000 years of human occupation and way of living would begin to unravel forever.

Aborigines living at opposite ends of the continent never met, nor was it likely that groups living just 50 kilometers apart met often. However, it has been established that there were trade routes that crisscrossed Australia in matrixes covering hundreds of kilometers. These routes moved necessities from one group to another, and they also were the conduit for ideas and beliefs. There were seasonal gatherings of regional groups known as corroborees, where kinship business, trade, dancing, music, and storytelling took place.

Aborigines were generally hunter-gatherers who survived in the harshest environment imaginable. They were spiritual people and unfaltering pragmatists. Knowing the land and the creatures dwelling on it was mandatory for survival. In order to avoid inbreeding within kinships, they developed intricately worked out social beliefs. Each group adapted to their environment and knew the land they were born onto so well that features in their landscape were named and carried "sacred" significances. Extracting food through hunting and gathering took up much of their time, but they still had time to pursue spiritual beliefs, kinship rituals, and other cultural practices that were the underpinning of social structure among all Aborigines.

Central to spiritual beliefs are Dreaming stories, known as Dreamtime. Aborigines have shared some of them with me; in the telling, the stories reminded me of Greek mythology, though when I suggested this to two Aborigines I befriended in the Flinders Ranges they shrugged and shook their heads. One said, "We believe longer than the Greeks." There is pride about Dreaming.

In Dreaming stories there are historical accounts, universal truths, and a deep understanding of the way creatures behave. Imparting tradition, understanding, and ways to survive are part of what Dreaming stories do for their people. Dreaming informs the next generation. In Dreaming stories all things have a spiritual identity. A large boulder sitting on a hill may be a sleeping serpent or a transformed giant kangaroo figure who happens to be occupying the form of the rock. Dreaming extends to all things living and nonliving, including the stars, water, geological formations, and all creatures. The central figure or creator may be a different form, sometimes a kind of superman, but most often is a serpent with incredible powers. Interestingly, some Dreaming stories that may sound like exaggerations or highly imaginative tales are historical accounts of something that happened thousands of years ago and was preserved, through telling, from generation to generation. The Dreaming stories in central Australia explain a series of large meteors that plummeted to earth thousands of years ago. Other Dreaming stories tell of hunting gigantic wombats and kangaroos, which in fact once existed and went extinct during the time Aborigines have occupied Australia. In other instances Dreaming stories identify an entity that is unique to the region, such as "Lightning Man" in the Kakadu area, where lightning storms are a common phenomenon. The most sacred Dreaming stories are those tied closely to secret and sacred initiation rituals that boys undergo to enter manhood.

Aboriginal Australia saw the coming and going of foreign visitors before the British arrived and stayed. Macassars, from what is now Indonesia, plied the water along the north coast, harvesting sea slugs for markets in China. Dutchman Abel Tasman showed up in Tasmania in 1640, and other Dutch vessels landed in that century. The weirdest contact was in 1629, when the Dutch ship *Batavia* ran aground in Western Australia and several sailors mutinied, then hacked to death most of the passengers and crew before they were captured and hanged or dumped on the mainland to fend for themselves. The first Europeans to live in Australia were most likely two of these mutineers, whose final fate will never be known. *Islands of Angry Ghosts,* by Hugh Edwards, recounts this bizarre event. All of this early contact didn't change things for the Aborigines.

European settlement spelled disaster to Aboriginal Australia. In the 1790s, only a couple of years after the First Fleet had arrived, the young British officer Watkin Trent described the sudden death of local Aborigines due to what appeared to be smallpox. This pattern occurred throughout coastal Australia. When Europeans moved into an area, the Aborigines, with no immunity to the unfamiliar European diseases, often perished. Whole groups disappeared without direct European contact, as disease spread from one Aboriginal group to another through trading and kinship contacts.

As European settlement increased and spread, conflict arose. In Tasmania, Europeans conducted "black drives," hunting Aborigines with dogs and shooting them on sight. Eventually only a handful of Tasmanian Aborigines survived; they were moved to an isolated island. Today there are no Aborigines from Tasmania.

Slaughtering Aborigines on a whim, because of racial hatred, or just to take their land went unpunished until well into this century. The Aborigines who were not killed huddled around missions, which, under the guise of helping, worked to demoralize and strip the Aborigines of their beliefs. For a time Aboriginal women were sterilized by decree and children were taken from their families and educated elsewhere to bring about their desired acculturation into an English belief system. Missionizing and forced removal from their ancestral lands deprived Aborigines of their dignity and their culture. Without their land, their spiritual world and cultural traditions were taken. The results of these policies were devastating. Once they had had their sense of home torn from them, alcoholism further eroded the Aborigines.

Today about 300,000 Aborigines live in Australia, which is about 1 percent of the total population. The blatant prejudice that extended into the 1960s in government policies has gone through a transformation. The two best known national parks, Uluru and Kakadu, now belong to the Aboriginal people, who hire and fire their superintendents and bank the revenues the parks produce. Many young Australians of European descent have actively worked to better the plight of Aborigines in health issues and land rights. By and large, today's Australian society is respectful toward what's left of the Aboriginal culture. Aboriginal art, which dates back some 20,000 years, is encouraged and marketed around the world. Aboriginal musicians, such as David Hudson, play the eerie-sounding traditional didgeridoo and sing traditional songs; their tapes and CDs have made them wealthy. There are Aborigine soccer stars and Aborigines who are superintendents of national parks. But social problems caused by the ruthless period of European settlement have taken a huge toll. There are proportionally more Aboriginals in Australian jails than any other ethnic group, and social consequences as a result of alcohol and drug use is still a significant problem.

In 1993 Australia's High Court handed down the famous Mabo Decision, which got the attention of all of Australia. The Court honored the contention of a group of Torres Strait islanders that they, not the government, were the rightful owners of tracts of federal land. The islanders were able to prove occupation and ownership that predated English settlement. Now similar cases await interpretation by the High Court. The results could change Australian land ownership in ways that were unimaginable even ten years ago. Understandably, agrarian and mining interests are challenging the direction of the Court. The issue of "land rights" is now a hotly contested issue that has not run its course.

In the meantime, the lasting testimony of what was left behind by Aboriginal culture is in the rock art and music that exists in different forms throughout Australia. The most appreciative book cataloging rock art is *Australia's Greatest Rock Art,* by Grahame L. Walsh. This monumental undertaking, with beautiful color photographs and carefully worded identification and analysis, is a scholarly work written in straightforward fashion for anyone who can read.

In *Adventuring in Australia,* especially in the coverage of Kakadu National Park, Cape York Peninsula, and the Kimberley, I attempt to lead you to rich rock art sites. I also spend time identifying and locating outlets for art produced by Aboriginal communities that is marketed in Australia's large cities. The coverage of Aboriginal art galleries in Sydney is as extensive as that in any travel book in print.

Aboriginal music is also marketed in Australia in the form of tapes and CDs. I met the young Aboriginal musician David Hudson in northern Queensland in 1987. He had the idea of touring Australia and recording traditional music as well as contemporary Aboriginal music. Today, in Sydney and throughout the country, David Hudson's music is purchased by Australians and foreigners alike in an astounding volume.

The legacy of the Aborigines lives on in what wasn't extinguished.

# PART II

# New South Wales

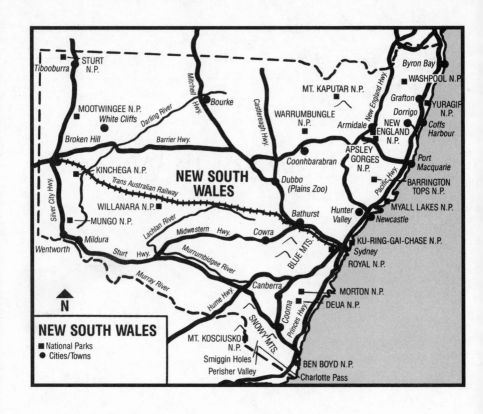

# Overview

In 1770, in full view of suspicious Aborigines, Captain James Cook planted the Union Jack near what is today Sydney's international airport. He named the land New South Wales and started back to England (with a detour caused by shipwrecking himself on the Great Barrier Reef). A decade later, Britain lost the U.S. colonies that had been a dumping ground for felons, impoverished petty offenders, and political undesirables. Now hordes of convicts languished in rotting hulks on English waterways. Finally, Lord Sydney, the home secretary, decided that New South Wales would be a suitable place to send convict labor to start a new colony.

On May 13, 1787, the First Fleet sailed from Portsmouth, England, to New South Wales. After eight months at sea, the understocked fleet carrying 736 convicts of both sexes found its way into "the finest natural harbour in the world," which is how Arthur Phillip, the fleet's commander and the colony's first governor, referred to what is now Sydney's harbor. The tent city was named after the home secretary, and so began the settlement of white people in Australia.

One of Arthur Phillip's first public acts was to lecture the male convicts against straying into the women convicts' quarters. He harangued them on their questionable moral character and on the virtues of marriage and threatened to shoot men found in the women's quarters at night. Phillip knew his role was to provide order and decorum for the society he was to create. History has judged him as an extraordinary pragmatist whose decisions successfully set into motion uninterrupted European settlement in Australia against tremendous odds.

Despite the passage of 200 years, Sydney still has embedded in her character the combination of irreverence, daring, frontier spirit, and English wit and formality brought by those who laid the first stones against their will and the "custodians of civilization" who watched over them. The near absence of women and the comradeship between soldiers and convicts evolved into matesmanship and an egalitarian ethic.

Take the famous Sydney Opera House. Where else would civic fathers choose a radical architectural design for something so traditional as opera and finance it with lottery money? This single structure combines Australians' love of the arts and passion for gambling with their desire for architectural excellence.

Today New South Wales is home to more than 5.4 million Australians and is the most populous, economically diverse, and productive state in Australia. The tent city of Sydney is now the state's capital, one of the world's busiest seaports, and the multifaceted economic and cultural hub for the entire country. The city's population exceeds 3.3 million people, of many nationalities and every race. Yes, Australia is shedding its "whites only" image. Personal freedom and a "live and let live" attitude are strong in Sydney.

The frontier spirit is alive in the remote parts of the state and alluded to by city dwellers, but for the most part New South Wales, and the rest of Australia, is a highly urbanized society. Most Australians would be more at home in San Francisco, London, or New York than in the Outback. Officials at Sydney's Taronga Zoo estimate that fewer than 5 percent of Australians have ever seen a platypus in the wild, even though it's relatively common. And, though matesmanship is alive and well, women now outnumber men, and the last decade has seen tremendous growth in women entering professional schools and casting off traditional roles.

For the visitor with a naturalist's bent, New South Wales has a great deal to offer: the largest alpine area in Australia, a superb Outback rich in wildlife and tradition, the lush subtropical rain forests of New England, and striking coastal scenery. Much of it is protected in scores of national parks, and much of it is virtually uninhabited.

However you slice up New South Wales, there's no getting around Sydney. Sydney is hardly a naturalist's dream, but it is the historical starting place, and because it is the busiest transportation hub for the state and the nation, odds are that you'll pass through it. It's your good luck that Sydney is a dynamic and attractive city.

# Sydney

Sydney is a wonderful, multifaceted city. I remember in particular one sunny day on a harbor ferry. The ferry purred past flashy racing yachts, past impeccably landscaped houses lining both sides of Mosman Bay, past people fishing on Cremorne Point, past historic Fort Deninson (reinforced in the last century to repel the Russians—who never came), past the soaring Harbour Bridge and the glistening tile-coated Sydney Opera House, to the heart of the city at Circular Quay, where the gangplank was dropped. On a balmy night the same ride can be a romantic excursion on calm, black water surrounded by the radiant twinkle of the millions of lights that define the city and bathe the Opera House and Harbour Bridge in luminous splendor.

Highlights include the Taronga Zoo, where you can marvel at platypuses, wombats, koalas, multitudes of native parrots, and the comical kookaburra, among other delights. At the Australian Museum, the English formality of Sydney asserts itself when students from the nearby prestigious Sydney Grammar, in their British-style school uniforms, feverishly take notes as a curator lectures.

Sydney has its casual side, too. During weekend races the "gambling" ferry follows the "Flying Squadron" around the harbor. Odds and money change as fast as the superquick, high-tech sailboats alter their courses or dump their acrobatic crews in the drink. On the beaches a conservatively attired family of six is apt to lunch on meat pies alongside a half dozen topless sunbathing women. (Nobody stares.) On the weekends speakers take to soapboxes in the Domain park to espouse any and every view.

At dawn, jogging in the Royal Botanical Gardens beneath huge Morton Bay figs filled with screeching cockatoos and mynah birds, it'll seem like there's no city at all. Then, strolling through the fashionable residential districts of Vaucluse and iron-lace-rich Paddington will convince you that Sydneysiders take a back seat to nobody when it comes to good taste. In the tidy semitropical northern sub-

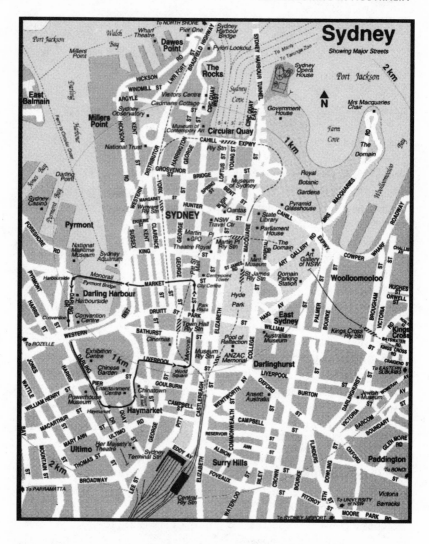

urbs, rainbow lorikeets swipe the family cat's food off the porch, and chattery disputes between brush-tailed possums and the high-frequency squeaks of flying foxes (bats) can awaken you in the night. To the overseas visitor with a naturalist's eye, even the suburbs are a rich repository for Australia's unique wildlife.

I fell in love with Sydney, both for what was new and unfamiliar and for its similarities with my favorite U.S. city, San Francisco. The social milieu is much the same. On balance Sydney is a top contender for the friendliest port city in the world. It's where most for-eigners begin and end their stay in Australia. It's a great place to spend a few days before shoving off to the limitless natural riches of Australia.

## The Weather

This is the Southern Hemisphere, so the seasons are reversed. The wettest months are June and July, while the driest are November to February. February (the end of summer) is usually the least com-fortable month because of the high humidity. Seasonal average temperatures are: December–February (summer): 73°F; March–May (fall): 62°F; June–August (winter): 51°F; and September–November (spring): 58°F.

## The Airport

After 12 or more hours of jetting through a half dozen or more time zones, you'll be tired and slightly disoriented when you get to Sydney (Kingsford Smith) Airport. Situated on Botany Bay, the airport is ten kilometers from central Sydney. There are no flights allowed in or out of Kingsford Smith between 11:00 P.M. and 6:00 A.M., which means you'll arrive when transportation to and from the airport is running on all cylinders.

### Customs

As your plane descends you'll be given agricultural declaration forms. Fill them out and don't lose them. Collecting your luggage and clearing customs takes anywhere from 20 to 90 minutes, depending on the volume of international passengers. If other jumbo jets are deplaning, you can save time by hustling down the ramp to the customs lines. Have your passport, visa, and filled-out agricul-tural declaration papers at the ready.

### Getting to the City Center and Internal Travel in Sydney

You've just flown for 12 hours and you're tired and a little irritable. How do you get to your hotel, and how do you get around in this immense unfamiliar city? The answer is that it's pretty easy, if you stay out of rental cars, at least at the beginning. Sydney is a difficult city to figure out, especially while you're driving on the other, unfamiliar side of the road. Why torture yourself when there's an easier way?

*Airport Bus.* Outside the airport, at the curb, the first thing to look for is the big yellow-and-green bus that has "Airport Express" inscribed on its side. There are actually two buses with slightly different routes. The 300 bus runs to and from Circular Quay at 10-minute intervals and the 350 bus runs to and from Kings Cross at 20-minute intervals. The buses head for accommodation areas and transportation hubs. These are the only scheduled direct routes Sydney Bus Service offers from the airport to the city's center, a distance of 8 kilometers. If you don't see one immediately, rest assured that it will come soon. If you're confused as to which of the two buses will take you closest to your destination, simply tell the driver where you want to go and heed his advice. The Airport Express operates every day of the year from 5:00 A.M. to 11:00 P.M. The buses also travel between the international and domestic terminals. You don't need a reservation and can board the bus by simply waving it down anywhere along its route. You can get off it anywhere too. One-way fare costs $A6. Private bus systems offer the same service; with Kingsford Smith Airport Coach, you must give an hour's notice before you wish to return to the airport. The fare is comparable.

*Taxis.* Sydney has no scarcity when it comes to taxis, though they respond more slowly to calls on Fridays and before holidays. RSL Taxi, phone 02-9581-1111; Taxis Combined Services, phone 02-9332-8888; Premier Taxis, phone 13-10-17. You'll meet a lot of people who just moved to Sydney from many points on the globe driving taxis. Cabs are metered. Wear the seat belt; it is the law. A cab from the airport to downtown will cost about $A20; it could be double this to go to the north shore. If the traffic is horrible, consider the bus. The meter in a cab keeps running even when you're stopped.

*Water Taxis.* So much of what goes on in Sydney is along the waterfront, it only makes sense that there are water taxis. Most companies are on call 24 hours a day. Water taxis will pick you up and deliver you and take you sightseeing. They are, however, expensive; a water-taxi trip across the harbor costs about $A30, and a sightseeing outing for an hour can be $A170. Try Water Taxis Combined, phone 02-9810-5010.

*Public Transportation.* The Sydney Transit Authority does a good job at the formidable task of overseeing an immense transportation system. There are three interlocking components: CityRail, Sydney Buses, and Sydney Ferries. City trains extend far out into the suburbs and become subterranean subway trains only as they enter the heart of the city. Central Station is the hub of this system. The bus system is also extensive and generally efficient and punctual. You can travel miles and miles on city buses. The ferry system connects the harbor at 50 wharves spread along the meandering shoreline of the harbor. The three systems are synchronized, so that you can jump off a bus or a train at Circular Quay and run up a gangplank onto a ferry for a ride to Mossman on the northern shore. When you reach Mossman's wharf, a bus will be waiting to hustle you up to Mossman's swank shops and delis. For a direct line to the transit authority for questions about schedules, phone 13-15-00. Fares are inexpensive, but the best deal for a tourist is the Travel Pass. For $A21 dollars, you get unlimited use of trains, buses, and ferries for seven days. You are given an electronically coded pass that is inserted into a scanner on each transport conveyance you board. The scanner approves your pass or, if its time has expired, rejects it—at which point the driver will sell you a ticket. There is also the Sydney Pass, which is more expensive but allows more use of high-speed ferries, harbor cruises, and transportation farther afield.

The Sydney Transit Authority's Sydney Explorer, Bondi Bay Explorer, and Voyages of Discovery services are explained in detail on pages 62–66. The CityRail system can take you across town for about $A1. CityRail is fast and efficient and seems to never sleep. It starts each day at 4:00 A.M. and ends at 2:30 A.M. The ferry system is centered at Circular Quay's six jetties. The ferries are also efficient. The standard ferries are comfortable double-decker crafts with areas to sit outside. Visit the Ferry Information Centre opposite Jetty 4, phone 02-9207-3170. You can pick up fares and learn about cruises sponsored by the Sydney Transit Authority. The ferries run from 5:00 A.M. to midnight. If you're looking for a "ferry ride," consider the ferry to the Taronga Zoo or Mossman (nice eateries and shopping) or the fast cat to Manly (shops, cheap eats, and nice beaches). Short trips cost about $A4. If you plan on splurging on ferry travel you can reduce your fares by purchasing either the Ferry Ten Pass, which gives you ten rides for $A21, or the Day Pass, which for $A13 allows you unlimited use of ferries and buses for a day.

*Car Rentals*. There are not many intelligent reasons to rent a car in downtown Sydney once you're aware of the interlocking train, ferry, and bus system, which is further enhanced by taxis. If you must, or if you're headed outside of the city, there are numerous rental-car companies to consider. Avis, Budget, Dollar, Hertz, and Thrifty have booths in the international airport. They also have city offices. For Avis, phone 02-9357-2000; Budget, 02-9339-8888; Hertz, 02-9360-6621; Thrifty, 02-9380-5399. For undermarket rentals try Ascot, 02-9317-2111 and Bayswater Car Rental, 02-9360-3622. For camper vans try Maui, 02-9555-2700, or North Australia Rentals, 02-9316-8663. Cars rent for about $45 a day if you take them for a week or longer. A distinction is often made between stick-shift and automatic-transmission cars. Automatics generally cost more. It's always "ouch" for one-day rentals, which are often around $A100. Vans and campers rent for between $A70 and $A120. If you're going to the bush make sure your insurance is good when you drive on dirt roads. I had an unpleasant experience once in which the policy was suddenly voided because I had traveled on dirt. Watch the small print. When in doubt, visit with the National Roads and Motorists' Association, for everything from road maps to insurance coverage and emergency services; phone 13-11-11.

## Information Sources

Understanding the phone system is helpful. The area code for Sydney and most of New South Wales is 02. You don't have to dial 02 if you are phoning from within this area code. If you're phoning from outside Australia, drop the 0. The country code is 61.

The Sydney Visitors Centre, 106 George Street, The Rocks, has maps, some Sydney bus, train, and water transportation information, brochures on hotels and eateries, and a helpful staff. Phone 02-9255-1788; fax 02-9241-5010. Nearby, at 110 George Street, in historic Cadman's Cottage, is the National Parks and Wildlife Centre. This information outlet has brochures on specific parks throughout New South Wales, as well as bird books, plant books, bushwalking books, and handouts on everything from wombats to squirrel gliders and flying foxes. There are also good-quality posters and postcard photos of wildlife and dramatic scenery; phone 02-9247-8861. If you're planning on touring the national parks on your own, I recommend that you purchase *Gregory's Touring the*

*National Parks of New South Wales,* which is accurate and offers a matter-of-fact series of written sketches of each park and reserve.

The Sydney Information Kiosk located on Martin Place, between Elizabeth and Castlereagh Streets, dispenses information of a general nature. The kiosk sits atop the subway station, so it is often a convenient source of information; phone 02-9235-2424. The National Roads and Motorists Association (NRMA) headquarters, at 151 Clarence Street, has piles of driving information on everything from car insurance to routes, as well as detailed road maps and camper and van guides to Australia; phone 02-9892-0355. The Youth Hostel Membership Centre, 422 Kent Street, is the place to go to straighten out your youth hostel membership and get a directory to what's available in Sydney (see "Accommodations"); phone 02-9261-1111 or E-mail yha@yhansw.org.au. The center is near Town Hall and the city train station. One of the most valuable tourist services is provided by the Australian Travel Specialists. They handle bookings for every major tour in Sydney (and most minor ones, too). Phone them and tell them what you want to do and they'll tell you what is available and for what price: 02-9555-2700. From anywhere in Australia, call toll-free: 1-800-355-537. Their Web site is www .hestravel.com; E-mail them at quayside@ozemail.com.au.

At any News Agency outlet (at all transportation hubs and on many city street corners), you can get a copy of *Day Tour and Sightseeing, Sydney Attractions, Sydney Events, This Week in Sydney,* or the *Sydney Tourist Guide. Out and About in Sydney,* by Taffy Davis, is a good guidebook, but it's a little sparse for the bare-bones traveler.

To get started from the United States or Canada, contact Tourism New South Wales, 13737 Fiji Way, Suite C-10, Marina Del Rey, CA 90291; phone 310-301-6573; E-mail tourismaswla@earthlink.net.

Most hotels and youth hostels are closely aligned with travel and tourism. If you feel a little flat-footed about your options, talk to the people behind the desk in the lobby. Some of the best tips I've received have come from hotel personnel. And if you have a special interest, be it canoeing, scuba diving, jazz music, surf or clothing-optional beaches, or where to find the native fuchsia (*Epacris loniflora*) during its glorious bloom, try the phone book. You'll find garden clubs, birding clubs, hiking groups, and groups with a wide spectrum of interests, many of which will be pleased to offer guidance to a foreign traveler. Yes, it's entirely possible to start an adventure with a phone book.

## Adventure Travel

Visit the Sydney Visitors Centre, 106 George Street; phone 02-9255-1788. There are videos and brochures describing the remotest parts of New South Wales as well as city parks and points of interest.

### Outdoor Equipment and Advice

High-quality outdoor equipment got a later start in Australia than in the United States, but selected outlets now sell products from all over the world. Paddy Pallin's Adventure Equipment is a reliable source for excellent equipment throughout most of Australia. The Sydney store is located 69 Liverpool Street, and many of the employees are knowledgeable about the remotest and most scenic parts of Australia. In the Sydney area, other Paddy Pallin's stores can be found in Miranda at 527 Kingsway and in Parramatta at 61 Macquarie Street.

## Sydney Discovery Tours

For the out-of-town visitor the Sydney Transit Authority's Discovery Tours give visitors easy access to what Sydney has to offer. The Sydney Explorer Service is the best way to get a hassle-free glimpse of the main sights in Sydney. The Sydney Explorer stops at 22 points of interest in an 18-kilometer loop through Sydney. The service allows you to get off at a point of interest and reboard later. Along the way you'll get the benefit of the driver's commentary (the quality varies greatly from driver to driver). The buses run at 15-minute intervals from 8:40 A.M. to 5:25 P.M. Buy your ticket ($A22) from the driver or at the Sydney airport, Circular Quay, CityRail, or the Queen Victoria Building. Circular Quay is a convenient starting place, or use the nearest stop by your hotel. The buses are red with large white lettering.

### The Sydney Explorer Tour

Stops marked with an asterisk (*) are discussed in "Things to Do on Your Own," below.

> *Stop 1:* Circular Quay. This is where you board harbor cruises (see below) or catch the ferries to the Taronga Zoo or Manly (see "Things to Do on Your Own," below).
> *Stop 2:* The Sydney Opera House.*

*Stop 3:* The Royal Botanical Gardens.*

*Stop 4:* The State Library and the Mint.

*Stop 5:* Mrs. Macquarie's Chair. This stop is named after the wife of one of Sydney's early governors. She came here to take in the view, which includes the harbor, the Opera House, and the Harbour Bridge, all from inside the Royal Botanical Gardens.

*Stop 6:* The Art Gallery of New South Wales.* This is a top-quality gallery with visiting exhibits as well as a permanent collection of many of Australia's best-known artists. The Domain*—the park across Art Gallery Road from the gallery—is where crowds gather on weekends to listen to soapbox oratory.

*Stop 7:* The Hard Rock Cafe.

*Stop 8:* Kings Cross. This area is known for its strip joints, prostitutes (not conspicuous), fast foods, pastry shops, the dinner show of Les Girls (female impersonators), good restaurants, hostel-like accommodations, and a few high-priced hotels. It's sleepy during the day and comes alive at night.

*Stop 9:* MacLeay Street. This area is at the end of Kings Cross and is a stopping place primarily because of the El Alamein Fountain, the Kings Cross Wax Works, and the café restaurants. It's a convenient lunch or snacking area.

*Stop 10:* The Elizabeth Bay House. This is a Regency mansion that was built in 1832. The grand old home is entirely restored and is an example of the finest colonial architecture.

*Stop 11:* Potts Point. This is an area in transition from stately homes to Bohemia. I stayed in the Chateau Sydney hotel here and found it peaceful, but relatively uninspiring. My guess is that this stop is to accommodate hotels in the area.

*Stop 12:* Woolloomooloo Bay.

*Stop 13:* Wynard Station and Martin Place.

*Stop 14:* The Queen Victoria Building, Sydney Tower, Planet Hollywood.*

*Stop 15:* The Australian Museum.* A block away, on College Street, is Saint Mary's, a full-blown stone-masoned Gothic cathedral. Hyde Park, across the street, is where you'll find the Anzac Memorial and Pool of Remembrance for Australia's war dead. Chess with figures as large as children is played in the park.

*Stop 16:* The Central Station. This is an important train terminal that can deliver you to most places in the city, the suburbs, the Blue Mountains, and throughout New South Wales. The terminal agents can book trips to anywhere in Australia, including the Indian Pacific train that crosses the entire continent. The station has extensive shops and restaurants underground.

*Stop 17:* Chinatown, Paddy's Market, and the Sydney Entertainment Centre. Chinatown has a great number of good restaurants. Also in the area are Paddy's Market and the Sydney Entertainment Centre. Paddy's is a huge stall-type market that runs full tilt on the weekends—it's a great place to stock up on necessities. You can buy everything from fresh prawns to outlandish T-shirts to live parrots (which can't be taken out of the country!). The Entertainment Centre can seat 12,000 people for concert performances.

*Stop 18:* Darling Harbour, Maritime Museum.*

*Stop 19:* Powerhouse Museum.*

*Stop 20:* Sydney Aquarium.*

*Stop 21:* Campbell's Point.*

*Stop 22:* The Rocks Visitors Centre.*

## Bondi Bay Explorer

The Bondi Bay Explorer is similar to the Sydney Explorer except the bus is silver and blue, not red, and rather than a city tour, the Bondi Bay Explorer's circuitous route runs from Circular Quay to popular bays and beaches around Sydney, with a few stops at historic houses and gardens. Buses leave every 15 minutes, and passengers can get off at any stop and catch a later bus when they want to resume the tour. The bus passes through some of Sydney's most upscale neighborhoods, and the beaches include both calm-water bay beaches, suitable for children, and ocean beaches that have big wave action for bodysurfers and board surfers. The Bondi Bay Explorer service runs the same hours as the Sydney Explorer and costs the same. After its first pickup at Circular Quay, the Bondi Bay Explorer travels to Kings Cross, Top of the Cross, Rushcutters Bay, Double Bay, Rose Bay Ferry, Rose Bay Convent, Vaucluse Bay, Watson's Bay, the Gap Park, Bondi Beach, Bronte Beach, Coogee Beach, Royal Randwick Racecourse, Sydney Cricket Ground and Football Stadium, Oxford Street, Hyde Park, and Martin Place. (See "The Beaches" on page 81.)

## Voyages of Discovery

Voyages of Discovery is the third service provided by the Sydney Transit Authority aimed at showing off Sydney to newcomers, this time via a ferry boat. It is my firm belief that a visitor hasn't really experienced Sydney until they've traveled on its ferries. For a brief three weeks Sydney's harbor is generally user-friendly, with smooth water and warm weather. Riding on the open deck of a ferry with the breeze in your face is a fun experience. I commuted from Circular Quay to Mossman every evening and found it a delightful, contemplative, and invigorating experience. Ferries run throughout the day from Circular Quay to 50 wharves around Sydney. (See "Getting Around in Sydney.") Voyages of Discovery, however, operates outside of the regularly scheduled ferries and is a service provided for visitors wanting to enjoy a ferry ride and see Sydney from the water. Often the ferries in use are the older models with charm and long service histories, such as the *Lady Wakehurst*. Not to worry: they are well maintained, were designed for Sydney Harbour, and have excellent safety records.

The Voyages of Discovery program changes from time to time, but over the years there have been three basic cruises lasting between one and two hours each. The cruises are narrated and have onboard food and beverages. The three cruises are the Morning Harbour Cruise, the Afternoon Harbour Cruise, and the Harbour Lights Cruise.

The Morning Harbour Cruise is a one-hour affair that passes Shark and Clarke Islands, the Opera House, the Royal Botanic Gardens, and Fort Denison. You can see beautiful harborside homes and waterfront gardens and cruise under the Sydney Harbour Bridge. The Morning Harbour Cruise costs $A12 for an adult, less for children. It leaves Circular Quay at 10:00 and 11:15.

The Afternoon Harbour Cruise also leaves from Circular Quay and lasts 90 minutes. The ferry journeys down the center of the harbor toward the open ocean at Sydney Heads, where it travels north inside the heads to the less populated areas in Middle Harbour. The ferry passes by the Opera House, some of Sydney's most fashionable waterside conclaves, and harbor beaches at Elizabeth Bay, Double Bay, Rose Bay, and Watson's Bay. This cruise departs Circular Quay at 1:00 P.M. on weekdays and at 1:30 P.M. on weekends. It often runs longer on the weekends. An adult ticket costs $A16.

The Harbour Lights Cruise is my favorite. It last about 90 minutes and is worth every minute of it. Sydney is spectacular from the water at night, when the city is fully lighted. The ferry ride usually begins too late to catch the sunset, which can be spectacular. As night comes over the city, Sydney glitters and floodlights illuminate the Opera House, the Sydney Harbour Bridge, and other historically significant buildings. The light show is enhanced with the reflections on the water as the ferry chugs along the harborfront. The experience evokes awe in some and romance in others, especially on a balmy night with a slight breeze. The evening cruise departs at 8:00 P.M. and costs $A14 per adult.

Cruise tickets can be purchased from the Ferry Ticketing Office, located opposite Wharf 4 at Circular Quay, or you can purchase a voucher from a Countrylink Travel Centre anywhere in the city. To contact the ferry service phone 02-9207-3172.

## Classic One- and Two-Day Motor Tours from Sydney

Finding things to do is not a problem in Sydney. Considering that most North Americans rarely stay in Australia longer than ten days, the question becomes what to do that is affordable in a limited time frame. Efficiency and prioritizing are necessary. Sydney itself can be explored for weeks, but the primary focus of this book is to put people in contact with nature and the joys and thrills it provides. First, there are the two closest substantial national parks, Ku-ring-gai Chase and Royal National Parks, which can be reached by car from anywhere in Sydney within an hour. Blue Mountains National Park is also a big draw. All of these parks are frequented by tour companies and are suitable destinations in rental cars.

But what about something off the beaten track that has a nice balance of fulfilling creature comforts while allowing you to interact with nature? Something that can be called your own adventure? Here are some fairly easy-to-accomplish outings of the self-drive kind that can be experienced in a day or two. Generally, accommodations in the towns you'll be visiting will not be difficult to procure.

### Illwarara and the South Coast

Head south on Highway 1, swinging through Royal National Park, following the coastline and possibly taking one of the short walks mentioned in the coverage of Royal National Park later in this sec-

*Australian pelican.* PHOTO BY ERIC HOFFMAN.

tion. As you head south you'll come to Stanwell Park, where hang gliders soar over the cliffs on the constant onshore breeze. The road will bring you to the sizable city of Wollongong. Find Kiama on your road map. If the ocean has kicked up and the waves are big, the Blowhole in Kiama is spectacular as the spray jets skyward from pounding waves. Consider stopping to stretch your legs at Seven Mile Beach or the Minnamurra Rain Forest Centre, which has an elevated boardwalk that allows you a bird's-eye view of the upper part of the forest.

Farther to the south you'll come to Berry, the "Town of Trees," which is also known for its antiques and artisan crafts shops and cafés. From here it's a short trip into Kangaroo Valley, with its spacious farms and beautiful rivers. Stay the night somewhere along the way or head back to Sydney.

### The Southern Highlands

Located southwest of Sydney around the town of Berrima, this region is more often frequented by Sydneysiders wanting a little time away than by the big tour-bus companies. The southern highlands are generally cooler than Sydney. Berrima is an example of a 1830s Australian town. Other little towns are laid-back places known for antiques and crafts. Towns like Mittagong, Moss Vale, Bundanoon, and Roberston are fun places to browse and lunch. Morton National Park, with spectacular waterfalls, remnant rain forest, and a wide assortment of birds, is a short drive from Roberston. This is a great picnic place and suitable for a few self-guided walks. Near Bundanoon is the Wombeyan Cave complex, which is cool and fun to explore. There is also kayaking on the rivers.

## Standard and Nonstandard Guided Tours and Experiences in, over, Under, and Around Sydney

Besides the Voyages of Discovery tours outlined on page 65, Sydney has numerous tour-related businesses that offer a wide range of opportunities. From huge companies like AAT King's and Australian Pacific to small personalized adventure operators, they have all tailored their offerings to survive in a competitive market. You'll find everything from mammoth touring buses that insulate their passengers from the outdoors and offer a visual and passive sketch of the world to scuba-diving and sky-diving experiences that guarantee an adrenaline rush. Here is some of what's out there and how to hook up with something that looks appealing.

## Blue Mountains

The WonderBus may be the most novel approach to visiting the Blue Mountains. The value in the WonderBus's form of tourism is that they offer a more interactive package than many of the larger companies, and the guide-drivers are often authentic real-life "bushy" characters. The brochure advertises "The WonderBus day tour to the Blue Mountains takes in all the famous tourist attractions the others do, plus we add some off-the-beaten-track locations. Learn about the most significant Aboriginal site on the east coast of Australia that dates back 22,000 years. Up to 3 hours of bushwalking for the adventurous, options for easy walks, or just ride the bus. Finish the day with wild kangaroos." They deliver on their claim to do a little more and try a little harder. They also allow you to leave the bus you're traveling on and pick up another one later in the day, should you want to stay awhile somewhere along the line. The WonderBus also travels to Jenolan Caves, which are spectacular limestone caves in a beautiful setting rich in wildlife. One-day outings run about $A65; a three-day trip costs $A215. The WonderBus stops at nearly 20 places in and around the Blue Mountains. Phone 02-9555-2700.

Aussie Bush Discoveries also offers a one-day Blue Mountains Wildlife Discovery trip. You'll visit the dramatic geological formation known as the Three Sisters in the Blue Mountains, be given instruction in boomerang throwing, get the opportunity to cuddle a koala at Featherdale Wildlife Park, and ride the fast catamaran *Rivercat,* which runs from Parramatta to Sydney in about 45 minutes. The groups never exceed 12 passengers and the driver doubles as the guide. Tour participants usually see wild kangaroos, kookaburras, bower birds, and cockatoos and get a look at large sections of Sydney's waterfront and plush homes, all in one day. Tour price runs around $A100. Phone 02-9555-2700; the company also offers other types of trips to the Blue Mountains.

## Wineries

Many tour companies will show up at your hotel and take you to the Hunter Valley. (See the section on the Hunter Valley, p. 129.) There are one- and two-day tours. The good tours include some of the historic parts of the Hunter, which today is home to 50 wineries. There

are small tour companies and the big boys, like AAT King's, to consider. Phone the Australian Travel Specialists at 02-9555-2700 to get
the full picture and determine what best fits your interests.

## Canberra

AAT King's offers trips to Canberra, the nation's modernistic capital.
The trip stops at Mittagong for a tea break and at historic Berrima,
which boasts Australia's longest-licensed hotel and a historic courthouse. Once in Canberra you become part of guided tours that take
in the National Gallery, the Old Parliament House, embassies, the
War Memorial and Museum, and a short hike to Ainslie Lookout for
a vista of the city. About $A80 per adult; phone 02-9555-2700.

## Jervis Bay: Whales and Dolphins

Australian Pacific offers a South Coast and Highlands outing that
travels the spectacular southern coastline to Jervis Bay, stopping at the
Blowhole near Kiama. Jervis Bay is a beautiful place. Hyams Beach is
said to have the whitest sand in the world. (I'd say Whitehaven Beach
in the Whitsundays is as white.) In spring, humpback whales migrate
southward, often coming close to shore so that the calves can rest during their long journey to Antarctica. At the town of Eden, local boat
operators offer trips to view the humpbacks. The whales usually
appear during September, October, and November. Australian
Pacific's *Dolphin Watch* makes a three-hour cruise of the bay. If the
whales are out of season the boat usually gets close to resident dolphins. The trip motors on to 80-meter-high Fitzroy Falls in the interior and to the town of Bowral, which is renowned for its Tulip
Festival every October. All this for $A95; phone 02-9555-2700.

## Horseback Riding

Australians have had a long love affair with horses. They love to bet
on racehorses, and they still respond to the romantic mystique of the
mountain horseman that was captured in the *Man from Snowy River*
films. In New South Wales, the area around Armidale and Cooma
are the prime trail-riding areas covered in this book. Near Sydney
there are numerous stables. Glenworth Valley Horse Riding is one of
the closest long-standing stables with a diversity of offerings. Glenworth is about an hour from Sydney, near the Hawkesbury River.
You are picked up at your hotel and bused to the stables, where you
are given a short introduction to riding in Australia over tea and bis-

cuits; the guide then attempts to select the right horse for each rider's ability level. Riders can choose either a free or a guided ride. The trail system has ups and downs, creek crossings, and varied vegetation ranging from remnant rain forest to dryland bush. There is a good chance of seeing wildlife. This is a half-day event with an optional barbecue. Rides last about 2 hours and cost about $A85; phone 02-9555-2700. Yarrandane Lodge, about 1.5 hours from Sydney, has also been operating for years. The stable offers escorted bush rides two to three hours in length with a trail system that winds through heavily wooded Watagan State Forest. Rides cost about $A85; phone 02-9555-2700.

## Hawkesbury River

A favorite of mine is Melvy's Wharf Homestead on the Hawkesbury River. This isn't a blow-your-socks-off tour but a relaxed outing that slows down to the pace of the barely detectable current of the Hawkesbury River. The tour consists of a visit to an isolated homestead run by two delightful people, Paul and Wendy Pigneguy. The trip can be undertaken by attaching yourself to a tour group in Sydney or arranging to meet a group at the Kangaroo Point Cruise Terminal in Brooklyn. Brooklyn can be reached on the city trains; by car it takes about 40 minutes. At Kangaroo Point you board the *Marra Marra* for the 30-minute crossing up the Hawkesbury, past Muogama and Brisbane Waters National Parks, to the homestead, where the Pigneguys offer morning tea, a home bush-garden tour, barbecue lunch, and live music. This is a popular tour with retired travelers who want to get out and experience something new without going home exhausted at the end of the day. Melvy's Wharf Homestead delivers on the ambiance and food; phone 02-9555-2700 or 02-9985-9255.

## Scuba Diving

Sydney is far to the south of the Great Barrier Reef, but there is still good scuba diving in the area. Pro Dive offers one-day dives in the Sydney area; they will also book dives and diving courses in Cairns, Townsville, and the Whitsundays, which are Great Barrier Reef destinations. A one-day dive costs about $A100; phone 02-9555-2700. If you aren't going to the Great Barrier Reef to dive but have enough time to access other parts of New South Wales, there is excellent diving on Lord Howe Island, in the Jervis Bay area south of Sydney, and in Coff's Harbour to the north of Sydney. See coverage of these areas for details.

## Northern Beaches and Ku-ring-gai Chase National Park

Ku-ring-gai Chase National Park is a wonderful park (see detailed coverage) and easy to visit by car and city bus. However, if you want the security of a guided tour that starts at your hotel, that's possible too. Both Australian Eco Adventures, Australian Habitat Tours, and Boomerang Bus Tours all offer outings ranging from a half day and up to Ku-ring-gai and the northern beaches. The offerings include bushwalks, visits to impressive Aboriginal rock engravings, ferry rides, and chances to see wild wallabies, goannas, and a myriad of Australian birds and beautiful flowering plants. Some tour companies include a beach swim on one of the northern beaches, along with a picnic lunch. Some of the northern beaches are clothing optional. Phone the Australian Travel Specialists at 02-9555-2700 to discuss the merits of each company's itinerary.

## Featherdale Wildlife Park Tour

This is a good place to interact with most forms of Australian wildlife. Everything from a fairly big saltwater crocodile to koalas, wallabies, and Tasmanian devils live here. An effort has been made to allow people to interact with animals that can cope with interaction while also providing a natural setting for the captive inhabitants. With some species this is a delicate balancing act. Featherdale has its own fleet of buses and will pick you up at your hotel. Tours last about half a day and cost about $A40 per person.

## Aerial Tours of Sydney

*Floatplane.* If you want to get a look at Sydney from the air, that can be arranged in an assortment of ways. Sydney Harbour Seaplanes offers a harbor and outlying areas flight in a six-passenger de Haviland Beaver floatplane that takes off from Rushcutters Bay and lands for a bite to eat at a restaurant on the Hawkesbury River. Departure times can be flexible to suit a group. The minimum commitment is a 30-minute flight with four guests at $A30 per head; restaurant flights cost $A100 per head. Phone 02-9555-2700.

*Vintage DC-3s.* For the antique aviation approach, try Dakota National Air at Building 483, Airport Avenue, Bankstown Airport.

Founded in 1992 by Peter Starr, Dakota operates a fleet of six immaculately kept 28-seat DC-3 airplanes. Starr offers both scenic flights and special charters; he likes to play Glenn Miller on his flights, and the cabin crew wears uniforms from the 1940s. Starr thinks that flying should be a multisensory experience and likes to say, "Flying low is back in style." To find out how much, if, and when, phone 02-9791-9900.

*Helicopter.* Heli-Aus offers scenic flights over Sydney at night. Flights run $A230 per person. The flight hovers around the Sydney Harbour Bridge and Opera House with the Rocks and the financial district as a glittering backdrop; a barbecue dinner awaits you at the flight's end. Heli-Aus also does a longer Blue Mountains flight that buzzes along a dramatic sandstone escarpment, lands in a remote valley for a barbecue, and then returns. The Blue Mountains flight runs around $A300; to book a seat phone 02-9555-2700.

*Ballooning and Skydiving.* Cloud 9 offers hot-air-balloon rides near enough to Sydney to let you see the entire harbor, the Opera House, and other prominent structures. The one-hour flights leave from Parramatta. The price is $A200 per adult; phone 02-9555-2700. The Sydney Skydiving Centre offers group jumps at 12,000 feet, seven days a week, from Picton, a city suburb. Tandem jumps starts at around $A300; phone 02-9555-2700.

## On the Water

*Ferry Tours.* There is no shortage of large ferries plying the waters of Sydney's harbor, ready to take you on a cruise where you can drink and eat yourself into contentment. Maltida's Cruises is one of the busiest; phone 02-9264-7377. There is also the *John Cadman* and the low-cost Voyages of Discovery sightseeing tours offered through the Sydney Transit Authority, outlined on page 65. The daily ferry schedule lists ferries stopping at 50 wharfs in the waters of the harbor many times daily. Described below are some less well known, novel ways to experience Sydney's harbor and the nearby waters.

*Boat Charters.* Eastsail is the largest yacht charter operation in Sydney. They have 25 vessels, both sail and motor driven, ranging in size from 5 to 15 meters. Their sail charters are often Beneteaus. They also organize small ferry charters and fishing trips. To see what they have, drop by d'Albora Marinas, New Beach Road, Rushcutters Bay, NSW 2111; phone (02) 9327 1166. For further information about boat charters, also try the Australian Travel Specialists; phone 02-9555-2777.

*Sailing Schooner.* The *Solway Lass* is a 125-foot Dutch-built schooner that has traveled the world since 1902. After she made her way to Australia, it took four years to authentically restore and outfit her abovedeck and add a dining saloon belowdeck. She sails three times a day from the Aquarium Wharf, Darling Harbour. The midday and afternoon sails are two-hour excursions with lunch on board. Fares run about $A50 per adult. The Dine Under Canvas Sail includes a seafood dinner and offers a long wine list. This evening sail along the waterfront takes about three hours and costs about $A75 per adult; phone 02-9264-7377.

*Kayaking.* Most kayaking takes place north and south of Sydney, but the offerings and bookings are handled by the Australian Travel Specialists in Sydney. They represent kayak outfits that ply the calm waters around Myall Lakes (birding and kayaking), the generally mild rapids of the southern highlands around Robinson and Berrima, plus the Olympic white-water site in Penrith. Phone 02-9555-2700; about $A100 a day is standard.

*Photography and Special-Interest Tours.* Frontier Photographic Safaris, 36 Darlington, NSW 2008, specializes in 4WD adventure with photography in mind. They like working with small groups and will adjust their itinerary to meet your desires; phone 02-9319-3458. Other special-interest tours include city tours on chauffeur-driven Harley-Davidson motorcycles, parasailing tours, and Walkabout Tours that are personalized half-day walks in Ku-ring-gai Chase National Park focusing specifically on Aboriginal rock art. For information about these and other specialty tours, call Australian Travel Specialists: 02-9555-2700.

## The Olympic Games and Sydney

The summer Olympic Games in Sydney are slated to start on September 15 and end on October 1, 2000. More than 200 countries are expected to be represented.

Any city that hosts the Olympic Games goes a little crazy, and it's no different with Sydney. Since being awarded the XXVII Olympiad, Sydney has undergone a building frenzy, and public debate has chronicled the coming of the Games. The Games' planners have more than met their deadlines: construction of all major sites was completed long before the torch will be lit. Some newly constructed venues were in use a year before the Games. The Olympic events will be spread throughout the Sydney area, helping to disperse the anticipated surge in visitors.

Most of the more popular venues, however, will be in the Olympic Park and the harbor area. Located about 21 kilometers (or 30 minutes) from the downtown at Homebush Bay, the Olympic Park was created in three years. The 100,000-seat Stadium Australia will be the primary venue for the track-and-field events and the soccer contests. The Athletes' Village, which will house an anticipated 10,000 competitors, is also here. The Sydney Showground and International Centre will showcase baseball, basketball, some gymnastics, and lesser-known team sports. The International Aquatic Centre will handle swimming and water polo. Kayaking and rowing will be farther afield at Penrith Lakes, which is 44 kilometers from the center of Sydney. Equestrian events will be held at the Olympic Equestrian Centre at Homebush Bay. If you're staying in the Circular Quay area, take the ferry (avoid the bus) to Homebush Bay. It's a relaxing way to go anywhere.

Sydney's harbor (including Darling Harbour) will host boxing, weight lifting, and wrestling. Yachting is slated for Rushcutters Bay in Sydney's harbor. Bondi is the site for beach volleyball. Traditional volleyball will be at the Showgrounds.

## Tickets to the Games

Nearly six million tickets will be made available, and most of these will be sold in Australia. For details contact the Sydney Organizing Committee for the Olympic Games, 207 Kent Street, Sydney 2000; phone 02-9931-2000. The most efficient way to get answers is to visit the committee's Web site at www.sydney.olympic.org.

In the United States, Cartan Tours, 1334 Parkview Avenue, Suite 210, Manhattan Beach, CA 90266, is handling ticket sales; phone 800-818-1998 or 310-546-9662; E-mail: sales@cartan.com.

### Accommodations Alert!

As of October 15, 1999, Australian Travel Specialists, who handle much of the booking activity in Sydney, announced that most of the hotel space in Sydney was already booked for the period covering the Olympics. Finding a place to stay may require some novel approaches, including staying in an area outside Sydney. How far from Olympic activities people end up will undoubtedly be determined on a first come, first served basis.

### Expect Price and Fares Increases

At the time of this writing no drastic changes in airfares, accommodations, tour prices, or other costs had occurred, according to Australian Travel Specialists. The agency does, however, predict that there will be price increases associated with the Games. How big a change is anybody's guess, as is how long the new prices will last after the Games are over.

## Transportation Contacts for Leaving New South Wales

*Airlines—International.* Air New Zealand, phone 13-2476 for bookings; Air Niugini, phone 02-232-3100; Canadian, phone 1300-655-737; Japan Airlines, phone 02-9272-1100; my favorite for accent and track record, Qantas, phone 13-1313 domestic or 13-1211 international; Singapore Airlines, phone 13-1011; and United Airlines, phone 13-1777.

*Airlines—National and Regional.* Ansett, phone 13-1300; Qantas, phone 13-1313.

*Coach Service.* McGafferty's, phone 13-1499; Greyhound Pioneer Australia, phone 13-2030. Ask about "bus passes."

*Rail Service—Interstate.* For Rail Australia, phone 13-2232. You can book the *Alice* to Alice Springs and the *Indian Pacific* to Perth from this number. The trains are clean. I strongly recommend a sleeper car for long hauls. The *Indian Pacific* was a bit boring for me; the *Ghan* (also to Alice Springs) was more enjoyable.

# Things to Do on Your Own

## Art Galleries and Museums

*Art Gallery of New South Wales.* The Art Gallery of New South Wales, on Art Gallery Road in the Domain, phone 02-9225-1744, has visiting exhibits as well as a permanent collection of many of Australia's best-known artists.

*Australian Museum.* The Australian Museum, on the corner of College and William Streets, phone 02-9320-6000, is well worth a visit. This somewhat underfunded, old-style museum has a talented staff of top-flight research scientists. The Aboriginal, mineral, and orthniological exhibits are well done. Look for the 100-million-year-old fossilized platypus jaw discovered in 1984. The discovery was made by the museum's scientists and has had far-reaching effects in the understanding of Australian fauna. The museum's shop has excellent buys in high-quality publications, posters, cards, and jewelry. Two of my favorite hardbacks are sold here: the *Reader's Digest Complete Book of Australian Birds* (approximately $A70) and the *Complete Book of Australian Mammals* (also about $A70). Both are expertly written and photographically exciting. These reference or coffee-table books would be hard to surpass. *A Field Guide to the Birds of Australia,* by Grahame Prizzey ($A30), is an excellent paperback guide covering more than 730 Australian birds. For other specific interest areas in the realm of natural history, look at current and back issues of the museum's magazine, *Australian Natural History. Australian Geographic,* a private publication, sold here and at newsstands throughout Australia, is also an excellent publication for gaining insights into Australian flora and fauna. The museum's shop also sells good-quality Aboriginal carvings, paintings, and traditional tools.

## Darling Harbour

This 130-acre site underwent an immense face-lift. Once a commercial dock area, it is now the hub of much of the social activity in the city, with its many restaurants (see "Restaurants" and "Accommodations") and shops, the National Maritime Museum, the Sydney Aquarium, the Chinese Gardens, the nearby Harris Street Motor Museum, and the immense Imax Theatre, with an seven-story-high screen. Darling Harbour was opened in 1988.

*Sydney Aquarium.* Partly submerged in Darling Harbour, the Sydney Aquarium is a state-of-the-art aquarium featuring big clear acrylic walk-through tubes, so that visitors can literally stroll among the fish, which swim around them. There are more than 5,000 fish on display, representing 350 species, all of them from waters in and around Australia. Thematically, the aquarium is well thought out, with exhibits organized according to ecosystems. Exhibits show native fish that live in Australia's Murray-Darling River System, which is the biggest river system in the country. Murray cod, the largest freshwater fish in Australia and the subject of Aboriginal legend, are displayed here, as are other native freshwater fish that are under increasing pressure from irrigation dams and aggressive introduced nonnative fish. The marine exhibits show reef systems and big predatory fish. A large tank is dedicated to the fish that live in the waters around Sydney, and another immense tank showcases marine mammals. In the Fish from the Far North exhibit there are barramundi, a much sought after game fish, and the Queensland lungfish, which hasn't changed in 100 million years. Barramundi are normally only seen filleted, while lungfish are rarely seen by anyone. For the children and many of the adults, the earnest fascination seems to be in watching the large sharks swagger around their tanks. $A8 per adult; phone 02-9262-2300.

*The National Maritime Museum.* This is also located in Darling Harbour and is a popular destination. Australia's history is linked to the sea, and the museum does a good job of capturing the historic significance of the linkage. It even has the anchor from the *Sirius,* the British prisoner transport ship that was wrecked on Norfolk Island in 1788 while trying to procure sea turtles for meat to feed the starving prison colony in Sydney's harbour. Exhibits are organized by nautical themes: commercial, pleasure, and experimental. For the sailing buff there is an Americas Cup representative and a boat from the Flying Squadron. Outside there is a replica of Captain Cook's *Endeavor,* a rebuilt lighthouse, a World War II destroyer, and much more. $A10 per adult; phone 02-9552-7777.

*Chinese Gardens.* This is reputedly the largest Chinese garden outside of China. It was planned by master garden builders from China who designed the garden in accordance with ancient principals. To the average tourist the garden provides a tranquil and beautiful place to munch on a box lunch or just retreat from the hustle of the city for a while. $A3 per adult; phone 02-9281-8663.

*Imax Theatre.* The theater is located at the southern end of Darling Harbour. Most of the films run about an hour. The size of the screen (seven stories high) works as an illusion; I watched a film about helicopter flight here and found myself leaning into the turns and pulling back as the helicopter approached a cliff. $A10 per adult; phone 02-9281-3300.

*Harris Street Motor Museum.* Located across from the Darling Harbour complex, this museum is a chronological celebration of the automobile in Australia, featuring cars built both in Australia and abroad. On display are cars that carted around famous personages and novel attempts, such as steam-powered cars. $A7 per adult; phone 02-9552-3375.

*Powerhouse Museum.* This is an amazing place and a favorite of children, because there are over 70 interactive exhibits that teach participants about science and technology. The institution's name comes from the fact that the building was once a power station. The museum is so thematically diverse that every exhibit comes as a surprise. You'll see Soviet satellites, the Boulton and Watt steam engine that was the powerhouse to a brewery in the 1870s, modernistic paintings, and flying machines that didn't quite catch on. If there is a unifying theme here, it is the celebration of human endeavor. Rube Goldberg would have loved this place. The museum is located within walking distance of Darling Harbour at 500 Harris Street. $A9 per adult; phone 02-9217-0111.

*Sydney's Mint Museum.* Located on Macquarie Street next to the Hyde Street Barracks, the Mint Museum is housed in an impressive colonial building. The museum features valuables of all kinds: jewelry, ornaments, and ornate creations often in themes of Australian flora and fauna. Nominal fee; phone 02-9217-0311.

*State Library of New South Wales.* The state library occupies two buildings connected by a glass pedestrian tube on Elizabeth Street. The Mitchell Library building portion is a magnificent old sandstone structure with immense Ionic columns. The interior features massive vaulted ceilings. There are important historical documents here, such as the map of Australia (circa 1640) that belonged to the first European settler in the country, Dutchman Abel Tasman. The immense general reference library is open to anyone. There are also historical exhibits illustrating Australia's past. On the Macquarie Street side of the library is a statue of Matthew Flinders, who is credited with being the first man to circumnavigate Australia. Nominal fee; phone 02-9230-1414.

*Fort Denison.* In Sydney's harbor, Fort Denison is reached by special ferries that leave from Circular Quay at 2:00 P.M. daily, except for Saturdays and Sundays, when departures are also at 10:30 A.M. This place carries a little bad karma. It is also known as Pinchgut because convicts sent here for punishment in chains were put on starvation diets. Murderer Francis Morgan was hanged here in 1796 and left dangling for three years as a warning to other convicts and to prison guards, some of whom were also hanged for stealing food and like crimes. The island acquired a cannon battery later on and today is mainly a curiosity. It is an excellent vantage point from which to watch sailboat races and ferry traffic and affords a nice view of Sydney. Phone 02-9247-5033.

*Macquarie Street.* If you like elegant old architecture, this is the place to visit. Many of Sydney's historic buildings are found on and near Macquarie Street. These proud sandstone structures have impressive colonnades and nicely balanced facades; often the interiors are just as impressive. Most of the edifices were built between 1810 and 1910. Besides the Mint Museum and the State Library, which were mentioned above, there is the Parliament House, with its cast-iron facade, Sydney Hospital, the Land Titles Office, Saint James Church, and Hyde Street Barracks. The Hyde Street Barracks were designed by Francis Greenway, a prisoner of the British shipped to Australia to serve his time. For more details, phone 02-9223-8922.

*The Great Synagogue, Churches, and Cathedrals.* Sydney has some wonderful old churches. My favorite as an architectural study is Saint James at 179 King Street, with its modest four-column colonnade and oversized copper spire. This beautifully proportioned structure came from the drawing of colonial prisoner Francis Greenway. Australia's dominant religion is Christianity, but there is a long Jewish history in Australia as well. The Great Synagogue, at 166 Castlereagh, is the mother congregation of Australian Jewry. The Great Synagogue was built in the finest Byzantine architectural style and has a glorious "wheel window." If you like grand cathedral architecture, visit Saint Mary's Catholic Cathedral on College Street opposite Hyde Park. This is an impressive example of revival Gothic architecture, and the stained-glass windows are stunning.

## The Beaches

The Sydney area has more than 40 beaches spread over 250 kilometers of shoreline. These strips of sand fall into two categories: ocean beaches and harbor beaches. Most of them are readily accessible. Only a few attract body-to-body crowds the way popular urban beach areas in the United States do. Sydney's harbor beaches are typified by calm water and are good for swimming and sunning, but not surfing. They're often convenient to reach. The ocean beaches are more apt to be surfing and windsurfing beaches, and they usually require more effort to visit.

People often think of sharks when Australia's beaches are mentioned. But the last death in Sydney from a shark attack was before 1940, which means that many more Californians have been sampled by sharks than Sydneysiders in recent years. Many of the harbor beaches have entirely enclosed shark-proof swimming areas. Many of the ocean beaches are netted too, but not as completely as you might think—or hope. The nets run perpendicular from the beach out into the surf and end past the surf line. Usually, swimming is allowed between the two nets. The ocean beaches are patrolled by Australia's famous surf clubs during the summer months. The clubs usually set up flags that define the area you're supposed to swim in. Anyone swimming outside of these flags is considered an idiot or worse, since it lessens the surf club's ability to do the best possible job of keeping the area safe for swimmers.

Many of the beaches around Sydney have distinct personalities and their own die-hard fans. There are windsurfing, surfing, family, lunch-hour, body-beautiful, and neighborhood beaches, as well as a few official nude beaches and a number of unofficial ones. Topless bathing for women is common on most of the beaches. In general, Australians have a more European than U.S. attitude about their bodies. Bare breasts are rarely frowned upon or ogled at. However, when in doubt about what not to wear, take your cues from those around you. The beaches are used year-round by a cross section of Australians. November through March is the warmest part of the year.

*"North Shore" Beaches.* The beaches between Manly (see below) and Palm Beach, commonly called the north shore beaches, are highly rated by Sydney beach aficionados. Most of these beaches are long sweeps of sand backed by varying degrees of greenery or suburbs. Generally, the farther north you go the prettier, more private, and less crowded the beaches. Manly, Curl Curl, Dee Why, and Long Reef (at Long Point) are good surfing beaches. Narrabeen Lagoon is an excellent windsurfing spot because the lagoon rarely develops choppy conditions despite a constant onshore breeze. You can rent a windsurfer here. Narrabeen Beach is the longest of the north shore beaches and usually the most sparsely populated. However, my favorites are Newport, Bilgola, Whale, and Palm Beaches, which are at the northern end of Highway 14, which runs up the north shore to Palm Beach. The northern end of Palm Beach is a long-standing unofficial nude beach. Barrenjoey Heads has a spectacular view. Palm Beach has a number of top restaurants, as well as ferry service to Ku-ring-gai Chase National Park. Nearby Church Point has a ferry that goes to Scotland Island and the secluded bays in and around Ku-ring-gai Chase National Park. The ferry runs every hour during daylight.

*Harbor Beaches.* Balmoral Beach on the north shore (reached from the Quay via the Mosman ferry) is my favorite harbor beach. It's a good swimming beach with a large shark-netted area and a small offshore island. The beach has a changing area, toilets, a grassy picnic area with shade trees, a French restaurant, and a surrounding neighborhood of nicely landscaped homes. Its civilized atmosphere attracts families, singles, and pensioners. There's a variety of small boats for rent. On the south shore, Nielson Park, just south of Vaucluse, has an attractive tree-lined beach. There are also several nude beaches. Probably the best known are at Lady Bay on the south shore and Reef Beach (near Manly) on the north shore. Lady Bay is a mostly gay beach.

*"South Shore" Beaches.* The south shore beaches extend from the harbor's inner South Head to Cape Banks. Much of this area is an urban sprawl. Bondi, probably the most famous beach in Australia,

is in this stretch. The scene is a sociological study of Australians at the beach. Probably everyone in Sydney has passed through Bondi at some time. There's also a heavy sprinkling of young New Zealanders who have gravitated to Bondi because of the low rents and because it's a meeting place for young people. The area is a bit run down, but there are a number of good eating places along the beachfront. Tamarama Beach, just south of Bondi, is a "body-beautiful" beach frequented by the carrot-juice and weight-lifting set. Perfection of physique is well represented by both sexes. Coogee, with beachside restaurants, is a popular family beach three kilometers south of Bondi. See the Bondi Bay Explorer coverage, p. 64.

My own favorite Sydney-area beaches are on hiking trails in Royal National Park (see "Parks Serving Sydney").

*Manly.* Manly is a resort town you reach by the Manly ferry. It has both calm, shark-netted, tree-lined harbor beaches and surf beaches outside the harbor. It also has arcades, water slides, restaurants, shark exhibits, and other activities that are popular with the teen and twenties crowds. The beaches are generally clean, considering their level of use, but they can become crowded. There is a large rock swimming pool west of the main beach for children and the less adventuresome. As an alternative to visiting the harbor beaches, you can hop on a bus that takes you to the famous north shore beaches of Narrabeen, Curl Curl, Palm Beach, and others. Or you can simply walk two blocks down the Corso and spend the day at Manly's ocean beach. Via Durley Road you can go to nearby Sydney Harbour National Park, which encompasses the harbor's North Head. This is an interesting vantage point from which to view Sydney.

*The Manly to Split Bridge Walk.* This is a walk worth mentioning. The walk starts at the Manly Ocean World and winds westward past beachside condominiums and mowed lawns that literally stop at the harbor's waters. Eventually you pass by yacht and rowing clubs and sailboats at anchor and enter a diverse bushlands. The day I took this hike was rich in bird life. Rainbow lorikeets were constantly chattering and moving along the trail. The trail opens up to some entirely secluded beaches and eventually comes to the Split Bridge, where you can catch a bus back to Manly. For most of the hike it was hard to believe that millions of people lived in the area. The walk takes about three hours. Bring plenty of liquid with you.

## The Domain

Located on Art Gallery Road, the Domain is the place where crowds gather on weekends to listen to soapbox oratory and debate—by anyone who feels the need for verbal self-expression. You'll hear everything from the possible ramifications of the prime minister's beer drinking or lack of it during his university days to the pros and cons of Aboriginal land rights. The mood ranges from comical to angry, but it's always lively.

## Fine Arts, Film, Theater, Comedy Clubs, and Gay Bars

Australia is a country with a deep appreciation for artistic expression. Art and fashion permeate Australian society. In the realm of nature and art there is an interesting movement under way. For much of Australia's existence, since the coming of Europeans, nature was viewed as belonging to somewhere else. Schoolchildren in the 1950s read books that showed bears, deer, and wolves as wildlife—none of which live in Australia. Little attempt was made to instill a sense of the native Australian bush and its creatures into the national consciousness. This has changed.

*Fine Arts.* Today in Australia many of the most celebrated artists paint Australian nature and wildlife. Aboriginal artists are painting at a volume never imagined even ten years ago. All of this adds up to a fresh attitude by Australians toward Australia that is now hitting full stride.

Alasdair McGregor is an artist who understands this change. He was trained as an architect but instead followed his passion for painting nature. His hyperrealistic landscapes celebrate Australia's ancient human and geological past. When he started painting in the early 1980s, he struggled to be noticed. Thirty exhibitions laters, with government and corporate commissions under his belt both at home and abroad, he is now basking in the collective change in consciousness that he and others helped create. His art is even on a postage stamp. Alasdair smiles about the appreciation for his kind of art in Australia. "Australians are appreciating this beautiful land," he says modestly. Today some of his best pieces sell for $A20,000.

The Art Gallery of New South Wales, the Museum of Contemporary Art, the Museum of Sydney, the Sydney Jewish Museum, and public and private galleries throughout the city display the work of the rich continuum of native artists of both Aboriginal and European descent. Some of the better-known retail galleries and commission artists are: Geo. Styles Gallery, 50 Hunter Street, phone 02-9233-2628; Ken Duncan Gallery, the Rocks, phone 02-9241-3460; Alasdair McGregor, Neutral Bay, fax 02-9266-5544. Aboriginal art receives comprehensive coverage on pages 94 through 96.

*Film.* Australian filmmakers are known worldwide for developing their own distinctive style, whether with *The Adventures of Priscilla, Queen of the Desert, Muriel's Wedding, Breaker Morant, Strictly Ballroom,* the *Mad Max* films, *The Man from Snowy River,* or *Babe.* These films were created by Australians and attest to the creative thinking and quirky perspective that has tumbled out of Australia in recent years. If Australian film interests you, visit the Museum of Contemporary Art, Circular Quay, phone 02-9252-4033. The museum created Cinémathèque Australia, which presents screenings and fosters the study of contemporary film, television, and news media throughout Australia and overseas. The Movie Making Museum at the Blacktown Bicentennial Museum in Rivertone (not far from Sydney) traces the technology and growing sophistication of film. Visits are by appointment only; phone 02-9627-3493. There is no shortage of traditional movie theaters in Sydney. Try the Hayden Orpheum Picture Palace (380 Military Road, Cremorne; phone 02-9908-4344), which has six screens working at once. If this is too much trouble because it requires getting across town, try the Greater Union (phone 02-9267-8666) or the Village (phone 02-9264-6701). These theaters are practically next door to each other and located near Town Hall, which is easy to access by city train, bus, or taxi. And there is always the Imax, with its seven-story screen, in Darling Harbour.

*Opera, Theater, and Dance.* Theater and dance are well supported in Sydney. The Sydney Opera House, with its Opera Theatre, the Concert Hall, the Drama Theatre, and the Playhouse, has something cooking just about every night. The Australian Opera is active from January to March and June to November. The Sydney Dance Company's season is May through August, and the Sydney Symphony Orchestra runs from March through November. The Australian Ballet's season is March and April and November and December. Book a ticket by phoning 02-9250-7777.

Other theater companies in the central city are: Capitol, 13 Campbell Street, phone 02-9320-9122; Her Majesty's Theatre, 107 Quay
Street, phone 02-9212-3411; Theatre Royal, MLC Centre, Harbour
Street, Haymarket, phone 02-9224-8444; and the Stables, 10 Nim-
rod Street, Kings Cross, phone 02-9361-3817.

*Getting Cheap Tickets.* Halftix sells marked-down tickets on the day
of a performance from noon until 5:30 P.M. They're located on Martin
Place and accept only cash. Phone 02-9055-2665. Other ticket brokers
are Firstcall, phone 02-9320-9000; Ticketek, phone 02-9266-4800;
and Showtix 02-9363-2500.

*Comedy.* Fringe Bar, 106 Oxford Street, Paddington, phone 02-9360-
3554; Comedy Store, corner of Parramatta Road and Crystal Street,
Petersham, phone 02-9564-3900; and the Old Manly Boatshed, 40
Corso, Manly, phone 02-9977-4443.

*Dinner Theaters.* There are half a dozen well-known theater-
restaurants in Sydney. The Argyle Tavern and Jolly Swagman near
the Quay have something in the works nightly. Both of these establishments cater to foreigners and go through a litany of Australiana
that can include music from didgeridoos and saw violins and ballads
such as "Waltzing Maltida"; phone 02-9555-2700.

*Jazz and Blues.* This is another Australian passion. The Basement, 29
Reiby Place, usually lands top entertainers; phone 02-9251-2797.
Soup Plus, 383 George Street, has been in business a long time and
has a loyal clientele; phone 02-9299-7728. Round Midnight, Rosyln
Street, Kings Cross, also has been at it for years; phone 02-9356-
4045. Always phone first to ask about cover charges, mandatory
drinks during performance, etc. Some clubs have a habit of force-
feeding and sousing you as part of the price of being there.

*Gay Scene and Bars.* On a scale of 1 to 10, homophobia in Sydney
is down around 2. Being gay is accepted in Sydney as much as it is
in San Francisco and other liberally minded enclaves around the
world. Unlike Tasmania, where gay people will be arrested if it is
believed they had sex with each other, in New South Wales there
are no laws prohibiting relations between consenting same-sex
partners, and the heterosexual community in Sydney is generally

supportive or passive toward gays. The city endorses the annual Sydney Gay and Lesbian Mardi Gras, which is held either the last weekend in February or the first weekend in March. I once happened to get off an airplane and attempt to make it across Sydney when this parade was running at full throttle: forget going anywhere. The performances and floats, however, were outrageous and creative. For more about this annual event, contact the Sydney Gay and Lesbian Mardi Gras, 22 Erskineville Road, Erskineville, NSW 2043; phone 02-9557-4332.

The gay community is most evident on Oxford Street between Darlinghurst and scenic Paddington. There are dozens of gay bars and clubs, including Albury Hotel, 6 Oxford Street, Paddington; Burdekin Hotel, 2 Oxford Street; Exchange Hotel, 34 Oxford Street; Flinders Hotel, 63 Flinders Street, Darlinghurst; Top Gun, 100 King Street, Newtown; and Zippers, 40-42 Flinders Street, Darlinghurst.

## Traditional Sports in Sydney

*Footie.* Rugby League Football is known as "footie" and followed avidly by Australian men and less so by women, much like their counterparts glued in front of their "tellies" every Sunday in North America. Only with footie there are no pads, and the game is faster-paced. The ball must be carried and not thrown forward. The backward lateral just as the ball carrier is being nailed has been perfected to a blink of an eye. Footie season starts in April and ends in September. Matches have been held in Paddington at Moore Park (phone 02-9360-6601), but it is likely they will also be played in stadiums built for the 2000 Olympics.

If you like men banging into one another without pads, there's also Rugby Union. Sydney's team, the Wallabies, has been a top team for a decade. This game is basically rugby. Contests are held at the Waratah Rugby Oval in Concord.

There is, of course, more to sport than "Aussie Rules." The best sport is one you participate in and enjoy. If you'd like to get involved, here are some ways.

*Windsurfing.* Many of the smaller bays around Sydney are ideal for windsurfing. If you are in the mood to learn, enroll in Rose Bay Windsurfer School, 1 Vickery Avenue, Rose Bay, phone 02-9371-7036. If you already have mastered windsurfing, don't enroll; just rent a windsurfer and go sailing.

*Surfing.* Surfing schools must obtain a license in order to teach surfing. Maybe this kind of serious attitude accounts for the number of Australians who are among the world's top surfers. For serious instruction phone Surfing New South Wales, 02-9518-9410.

*Tennis.* Many of the top tennis players in the world are from Australia. Cooper Park Tennis Courts (off Suttie Road in Double Bay; phone 02-9389-9259) is in a beautiful natural setting and about five kilometers from Circular Quay. Also try Jensens Tennis Centre in Prince Albert Park next to Central Station; phone 02-9698-9451. Courts in both places have synthetic surfaces.

*Cricket.* This game takes time to understand and appreciate. The annual big event is the Ashes, a five-day match against the mother country, England. Moore Park in Paddington has been the traditional Sydney Cricket Grounds, but the Olympic venues will probably be used in the future.

*Horse Racing.* Canterbury, Rosehill, Warwick Farm, and Randwick are the main racing venues. Randwick carries the most weight in horse-racing circles. It is also the nearest to downtown.

*Mountain Biking.* There are numerous places to ride in New South Wales, but near Sydney the Blue Mountains and Budawangs are probably the two best spots. In the Blue Mountains there are endless trails. The terrain is steep and can be treacherous. Rent a bike in the Blue Mountains or in Sydney. If you get the bike in Sydney, you can take it on a train to the Blue Mountains. The Budawangs are inside Morton National Park near Milton. This is rugged riding in remote gorges. The scenery is unforgettable: waterfalls, remnant rain forest, and colorful birds.

*Golf.* More than 35 golf courses within 30 kilometers of downtown welcome visiting golfers. For 18 holes expect to pay about $A20, if you have clubs. If you aren't into walking, most courses rent golf carts. Check out your phone book to fulfill your golf quest.

*Other Sporting Events (Not Counting the Olympics).* Check with one of the ticket brokers for details for ticketing for these events. January has the NSW Open Tennis Match, which is seen as a litmus test

for the Australian Open. In March the Australian Motorcycle Grand
Prix comes to town. Slower and quieter, but more graceful and nicer
to touch are the participants in the Golden Slipper Festival, which is
the richest purse for two-year-old horses in the country. In August
the City Surf Run, a 14K event from Town Hall to Bondi, where you
can cool off in the surf, attracts 30,000 runners. In September the
Rugby League Grand Final is the climaxing event for the season.
November brings in the 1,160-kilometer Pacific Power Road Cycle
Classic event and some of the top cyclists in the world. An Ironman
contest is held in Bondi in November. December is the month for the
Sydney-to-Hobart Yacht Race, one of the world's premier yachting
events. The idea is to book a seat on a ferry so you can chug out
among the racing yachts and watch them tack their way out Sydney
Heads and into the open ocean. For jogging, head for the Royal
Botanic Gardens. I used to jog here early in the morning and was
always surprised by how few joggers I saw. The setting is stupen-
dous.

## Historic Sites

On Macquarie Street, visit the Parliament House, the Old Mint, the
Hyde Park Barracks, and the other colonial structures. Nearby are
Saint James Church and Saint Mary's Cathedral, both striking architectural feats. Many of these historic structures are made of locally
quarried sandstone. Some were designed by Francis Greenway, the
now-renowned convict architect.

Be sure to visit the Rocks, where the First Fleet's hapless convicts
began breaking sod and rocks for His Majesty in 1788. The area is
rich in old buildings, compliments of the convict labor. Now the
buildings house pubs catering to tourists and restaurant-theaters
such as the Argyle Tavern (see Dinner Theaters, above). Walking
tours of the Rocks, which cover several blocks and cost $A11, start
at the Sailors' Home, 106 George Street, phone 02-9255-1788, and
run hourly from 10:30 A.M. to 2:30 P.M. The State Archives are
located at 2 Globe Street. You can visit the reading room during
working hours and peruse convict records, excerpts from explorers'
documents, and shipping records of early Sydney. The people running the place have located the juiciest stuff. Also be sure to visit the
historic Observatory, on X Street. You'll find Cadman's Cottage, the
oldest surviving home in Sydney, also the information outlet for the
park service. The house is an historic site managed by the National

Parks and Wildlife Service that books ferry tickets to the harbor islands. There are a number of restaurants and pubs in the area (see Restaurants).

The Village Green, or lower Fort Street, is known for its historic pubs and churches and the National Trust Centre and Art Gallery. The National Trust Centre was a military hospital from 1815 to 1845 and after that a girls school. It's open from 11:00 A.M. to 5:00 P.M.; the bookshop is open from 9:00 A.M. to 5:00 P.M. The Lord Nelson pub claims to have the oldest pub license in Sydney. The Hero of Waterloo and the Harbour View (under the Harbour Bridge) also date back to the early 1800s. All have a full selection of Aussie beers and ales.

For spectacular residences, there's the Elizabeth Bay House, at 7 Onslow Avenue. It's a Regency mansion that was built in 1832. You can step back in time and grandeur by visiting the Vaucluse House, on Wentworth Road in fashionable Vaucluse. There's also historic Parramatta, the second-oldest city in Australia, which is now a Sydney suburb. And you can stroll through restored and trendy Paddington with its beautiful iron-lace terraces.

## The Royal Botanic Gardens

This is a 30-hectare manicured park that includes harbor views, exotic and native plants, the state library, and the Conservatorium of Music. Erected in 1821, the conservatorium is a historic sandstone structure. (On Wednesdays there are free lunchtime concerts when the conservatorium is in session.) Among the gardens' collections are 90 species of palms, a pyramid-shaped greenhouse with tropical plants, and a large collection of rain forest plants and trees from tropical Australia. Free guided walks start at the Visitors Centre (phone 02-9231-8111) at 10:30 A.M. daily. Be sure to pick up the free handouts—they'll aid your understanding of the gardens. The Gardens Restaurant (with adjoining kiosk) is a convenient and scenic eating place in the gardens. The Botanic Gardens is an excellent jogging area, and it's practically empty at dawn. While jogging or walking along the shore of Farm Cove, you'll think you're far from a city of three million people.

## The Sydney Opera House

The Sydney Opera House is Australia's most famous structure. The tile-coated "billowy sail" motif is a technical marvel as well as a stroke of genius for a city whose inhabitants clamber aboard hundreds of sailboats every weekend and perform myriad maneuvers under the shadows of these static sails. The Opera House is really a performing-arts complex that contains two rehearsal halls, numerous studios, five performance halls, an exhibition hall, two restaurants, a reception hall, a souvenir shop, a library, and associated offices. The concert hall is the biggest and most impressive of the performance halls. It seats 2,700. Guided tours (only $A3 and well worth it) leave the exhibition hall foyer at regular intervals every day but Sunday, from 9:00 A.M. to 8:00 P.M. You'll learn why its architect, Joern Utzon, refused to view the completed structure, and you'll also learn about the building's amazing acoustical qualities. Try the Harbour Restaurant for a quick, cafeteria-type lunch. It's on the water and includes outdoor tables. The more formal Bennelong Restaurant also has an unforgettable view. At night, the city and the Harbour Bridge come aglow with lights, and dimly lit ferries glide past the Opera House to and from nearby Circular Quay. To book tickets for avant-garde plays, symphony orchestras, operas, and/or ballets, phone 02-9250-7777. For tours phone 02-9250-7111. There are performances nightly.

### The Taronga Zoo

The Taronga Zoo (take the Taronga Zoo ferry, see "Ferry Tours," to get there) is a world-class zoo occupying prime harbor real estate. The zoo has animals from throughout the world, but the native species there are rarely exhibited overseas. The platypus exhibit is a must. You'll also see wombats, native cats, tree-climbing kangaroos, cuscuses, echidnas, Tasmanian devils, quolls, koalas, and other marsupials. Since most of these animals are active at night, the dimly lit Nocturnal House allows you to watch their activities, plus those of such rarities as bilbies and bandicoots. The colorful native parrots and other birds are astounding to visitors from the more temperate parts of the world. A new aquarium has been completed. There is a kiosk and an excellent bookstore. Opportunistic kookaburras are plentiful on the grounds. With luck you'll hear one of these feathery comedians laugh. $A9 per adult; phone 02-9251-5988 for zoo hours.

## Shopping

Those who like to "shop till they drop" can satisfy their addiction in Sydney. When I shop in a foriegn country, I look for items unique to

*Sydney Opera House, New South Wales.* PHOTO BY ERIC HOFFMAN.

that country. Aboriginal art, opal jewelry, unique leather goods, and contemporary art come to mind for Australia. For children and children-at-heart there is great shopping in the fluffy-stuffed-native-animal genre. You can find everything from life-sized wombats to down-filled platypus replicas.

If you're a seriously addicted, unashamed shopper, the Shopping Spree Tour will bus you around the city in a bright-pink bus for around $A50. The Shopping Spree bus stops at ten shopping areas and attempts to put shoppers in touch with the best deals for the best prices. A large lunch is included in the tour. The bus takes shoppers to fashion boutiques and places offering fashionable handbags, shoes, jewelry, cosmetics, chocolates, leather goods, lingerie, toys, children's wear, and opals. The bus runs Monday through Saturday; pickup is at 8:30 and the day ends at 4:30. To book a seat phone 02-9555-2700.

Here's a rundown of the major shopping areas. The Queen Victoria Building is the one building I always visit just one more time, as much for the ambience as for finding anything from good-quality Aboriginal art to children's toys in the form of native wildlife in the 200 shops and restaurants housed there. The Queen Victoria is built in the finest Romanesque tradition and was made by highly skilled craftsmen during the last century. The building is a multilevel structure with an open interior and natural lighting from a huge glass ceiling. On one of my visits here, dancers suspended from the ceiling by steel cables entertained the customers, who mostly stared in awe and disbelief, considering the long drop to the floor below. The building also has an immense copper dome that can be seen from blocks away.

Just off the Pitt Street Mall are five multilevel shopping arcades. Even if you aren't a high-end shopper you'll find it impressive to walk through the Mid-City Centre, Cosmopolitan Centerpoint, and the futuristic high-fashion Skygarden.

David Jones on Market and Castlereagh Streets is an immense emporium with a marble interior. A pianist plays daily, surrounded by a huge wreath of flowers. High fashion, gourmet foods, and housewares are the specialties. The interior and flower arrangements are amazing.

Oxford Street between Darlinghurst and Paddington is overloaded with bookshops, cafés, and new fashions. For colonial antiques visit Woollahra, at the eastern end of Paddington. Surry Hills is also known for antiques. Mosman, across the harbor from

Circular Quay, is known for its refined shops featuring antiques, gourmet foods, and stylish cafés.

To help focus your "search," here are some shops and businesses in the areas mentioned above: Country Road is known for classic Aussie country wear and home furnishings. You can find their shops in Darling Harbour, Queen Victoria Building, Skygarden, and at the corner of Pitt and King Streets; phone 02-9261-2079. R. M. Williams, 389 George Street, is an excellent source for Akubra hats, mole-skin trousers, and Aussie footware; phone 02-9262-2228. Susan Nurmealu, Elizabeth Street, is one of the most fashionable new designers, known for her beautiful colors and flowing garments. ABC Shops has the best books and music produced in Australia. There are shops throughout the city. Try the one at Queen Victoria Building; phone 02-9333-1635. For opals and opal jewelry, visit Percy Marks, 60-70 Elizabeth Street; phone 02-9233-1355. For good-quality art from New Guinea, visit New Guinea Art, 428 George Street, eighth floor; phone 02-9232-4737. For contemporary landscape and nature art by some of Australia's leading artists contact Geo. Styles Gallery, 50 Hunter Street; phone 02-9233-2628. For high-end paintings by Alasdair McGregor, one of Australia's foremost nature and wild-areas painters, contact Alasdair McGregor; fax 02-9904-4142. Folkways Music, 282 Oxford Street, has everything from Aboriginal music to Joan Baez; phone 02-9361-3980. Ariel Bookshop, 42 Oxford Street, has everything from new art books to serious history and avant-garde literature; phone 02-9332-4581. For gourmet foods visit David Jones Food Hall, in the basement, via the Market Street entrance, of the David Jones emporium on Castlereagh; phone 02-9266-5544. For cheeses, visit the Cheese Shop, 797 Military Road, Mosman; phone 02-9969-4469.

## Learning About Aboriginal Culture and Purchasing Aboriginal Art

If you feel too inexperienced to know what you're buying, rely on your own personal taste and visit museums displaying Aboriginal art to get your bearings. In the list of places to view and purchase Aboriginal art and learn about this ancient culture are several galleries that house nothing but original work. Several establishments listed below have valuation services for serious buyers of art.

There has been an explosion of Aboriginal art is Sydney in recent years, with much of the profit rightfully going directly to Aboriginal artists, but the sheer volume being produced has resulted in varying quality, which should be reflected in pricing. Aboriginal art is well represented in Sydney. Art usually has much greater significance when there is a greater understanding of the culture that produced it. In the following listing you'll read about opportunities to not only purchase art but attend talks, see dancing, and listen to Aboriginal music. Assume there is a nominal entrance fee to most of the entities listed below.

Cooee Aboriginal Art Galleries, 98 Oxford Street, Paddington, represents 30 different Aboriginal communities throughout Australia. The upstairs gallery includes central desert art, traditional bark paintings, sculptures, and an extensive collection of prints from contemporary and traditional Aboriginal artists. The gallery also offers an evaluation and consulting service for serious buyers. Downstairs you can purchase T-shirts, New Guinea artifacts, hand-printed fabrics, didgeridoos, boomerangs, and music; phone 02-9332-1544.

Dreamtime Gallery, Shop 35, The Rocks Centre, Playfair Street, claims to possess Australia's largest collection of Aboriginal art, including didgeridoos, boomerangs, sand and bark paintings, carvings, emu-egg carvings, burial poles, carrying dishes, T-shirts with art designs, spears, books, and music. It's probably more accurate to say they have the largest number of pieces for sale at any one time; phone 02-9247-1380.

The Gavala Aboriginal Art and Cultural Centre, Shop 377, Harbourside, Darling Harbour, is wheelchair accessible and one of Sydney's newer centers for Aboriginal art. The center possesses authentic paintings and works by the well-known "Utopian" artists of the Northern Territory, as well as exhibits about Aboriginal life, including displays of tools, medicine, and weapons. The craft shop sells handmade bush jewelry, boomerangs, music sticks, didgeridoos, hand-carved emu eggs, and spiritual rocks. The center also runs Nerundama Theatre ("Friendship Theater"), which presents cultural talks and demonstrations of didgeridoo playing, traditional storytelling, and contemporary Aboriginal life; phone 02-9212-7232.

Hogarth Galleries Aboriginal Art Centre, 7 Walker Lane, Paddington, established in 1973, is Australia's oldest Aboriginal art gallery. It is well known for its landmark exhibits featuring entire communities from the remotest parts of the Northern Territory. The works from Oenpelli, Yuendumu, and Maningrida are known for their rich color and intricate designs. The center changes the exhibits every four weeks and features both contemporary and traditional artists; a large informative map of Australia shows tribal groupings at the time of European settlement. The center sells posters, boomerangs, books, and postcards. Lectures by appointment can be arranged for a price; phone 02-9360-6839.

## Restaurants

There are an estimated 2,400 restaurants in and around Sydney. They fall into two categories: licensed and BYO. Licensed means they can serve alcohol; BYO means you buy a bottle of spirits elsewhere to accompany your meal. In recent years immigration to Sydney has been from all over the world. As a result you'll find excellent Arabian, Balinese, Chinese, French, German, Greek, Italian, Korean, and Vietnamese restaurants, as well as variations on the straightforward three-course standard Australian cuisine—including "meat pies." However, heed my warning about Vegemite, the popular Aussie bread spread made from beer scum (for lack of a more concise definition) that's applied like peanut butter. I've decided that liking Vegemite comes only with indoctrination started in babyhood. To put this unflattering appraisal in perspective, keep in mind that millions of fair dinkum Australians would judge my comments unfair or worse. Most Aussies love Vegemite. For Australians visiting me in the United States, I keep a jar of it at the ready to give them their fix, which immediately renders them at ease far from home.

*Sydney Cheap Eats* is a worthwhile publication that covers the eating scene in Sydney. Purchase it in bookstores and at News Agencies throughout the city.

For seafood there is Doyles; the confusing part is that there are three of them. The original is Doyles on the Beach in Watsons Bay. This is the first place I had lunch in Sydney, in 1986, and I'll never forget the balmy outdoor setting on the water. I think I ate something called "bugs," which are giant shrimp. The price of a lunch here rarely exceeds $A20; phone 02-9337-2007. The second Doyles is Doyles Fisherman's Wharf on the nearby ferry jetty. This was a takeout place that now also offers casual seating. About $A12 for a meal; phone 02-9337-1572. The Doyles most tourists frequent is Doyles at the Quay, near the passenger terminal and Bilson's in Circular Quay. The menu lists different types of fish in a basic fish-and-chips format.

The location, on top of the ferry traffic, with the Opera House as a backdrop, and the relatively low price for the setting ensure that Doyles will enjoy continued popularity. About $A20 an order; phone 02-9252-3400.

Bennelong Restaurant is in the Sydney Opera House and a must place to eat for experiencing the atmosphere that is uniquely Sydney. The menu is varied but heavy on good-quality seafood dishes. The view is spectacular. You see all the icons of Sydney as you dine: the Opera House, the Sydney Harbour Bridge, and the constant flow of ferries in and out of Circular Quay. Considering all things, meals are reasonable at about $A45 a head; phone 02-9250-7548. Try to eat here if you're attending a performance in the Opera House.

The Royal Botanic Gardens Restaurant is a personal favorite. Again, the setting does it. Situated in the middle of the Botanic Gardens and the Domain in a greenhouse decor that is surrounded on all sides by greenery and tranquillity, the setting masks the fact you are in the heart of Sydney, where millions of people live. The food is Mediterranean. Eat lunch here and try for a balcony table. Meals can run $A40 a plate; phone 02-9241-2419.

Darling Harbour has numerous top-flight, moderately priced restaurants, mostly loaded with seafood dishes and offering both outside and inside dining. If you're not squeamish, the Golden Century, 393 Sussex, allows you to select a live creature (fish, lobster, etc.) and orchestrate its preparation into a meal. A full meal costs about $A15; phone 02-9212-3901. Nearby you can dine at the Silver Spring, which serves Chinese cuisine; phone 02-9211-2232. There are numerous restaurants in and around Darling Harbour; walk the harbor and you'll find them.

Dining in the Rocks and Circular Quay area has been touched on with mentions of Doyles and Bennelong; there are many more places to eat. Restaurants are varied and tend to be a little pricey, but most of them offer a memorable view; if you can, you should try to eat at least one meal in the Rocks to experience this side of Sydney. Here are some of your choices: the Bel Mondo, Argyle Department Store, third floor, has striking views of the Opera House. The cuisine is fancy Italian and the meal ticket per plate is around $A80; phone 02-9241-3700. Probably the best meal and atmosphere for the price is Rockpool, 109 George Street, where the menu is varied but never too expensive. The decor is modernistic, with the cooks clearly visible while you are eating. Meals run around $A25 a plate; phone

02-9252-1888. Bilson's, on the upper level of the passenger-liner terminal, has exquisite seafoods served in an assortment of creative ways. The view is one of the best in the harbor. A full meal runs around $A50; phone 02-9251-5600.

In the center of Sydney you'll find the Level Two Revolving Restaurant in the Centerpoint Tower. You can't miss it. The tower is either the biggest eyesore in the city or a futuristic structure for the next millennium. It solicits comment. The Centerpoint is nearly 300 meters high and towers over the surrounding buildings. Affording an unforgettable view, the restaurant rotates all the way around in about an hour. The menu is broad, with an assortment of red-meat main courses and Asian food making up most of it. There is an all-you-can-eat buffet. There is also a Level One restaurant right below that is more tourist oriented, with higher prices. For Level Two phone 02-9233-3722.

If you're looking for good-quality vegetarian food, try Govinda's at 112 Darlinghurst Road in Kings Cross. You'll get a movie and a meal at the same time. Govinda's has an all-you-can-eat veggie buffet and a kicked-back atmosphere with big soft chairs. Meals, including a movie, run about $A14 a head; phone 02-9360-7853 to find out what's playing. Another top vegetarian stop is the Metro Cafe, 26 Burton Street, in Darlinghurst. Meals run about $A7 per plate; phone 02-9361-5356.

Pizza is popular in Sydney. One pizzeria that makes a little extra effort is Perry's Wood Fire Gourmet Pizza, 381 Glebe Street; phone 02-9660-8440. A large runs about $A11.

Sydney has many other places with top ratings and unique efforts. At the Bayswater Brasserie, 32 Bayswater Road, Kings Cross, the crowd is young and Sydney-casual, and the chefs make great pasta, beef, and fish dishes. Expect to pay $A16 a meal; phone 02-9357-2177. Choy Jin Jiang, is located on the second floor of the Queen Victoria Building, at the corner of Market and George Streets. Inventing an excuse to hang out in the beautiful Queen Victoria Building, with its refined multilevel interior and stylish shops, is the power shopper's dream. Well, here's your excuse for a long lunch at a decent price. Accompany your Chinese dishes with a selection from the lengthy wine list—to help the shopping; $A20; phone 02-9261-3388. Brooklyn Thai, on the corner of Grosvenor and George Streets, is perhaps the top Thai restaurant in Sydney. It occupies a revamped Victorian pub, symbolic of the culture changes of the past two decades. Expect to pay about $A25 per plate; phone 02-9247-6744. If you should be in Manly around sundown, try Le Kiosk at 1 Marine Parade. This is a find amid the beachgoers coated in suntan lotion, the T-shirt shops, and the fast-food stands. The restaurant is in an old sandstone building with beautiful gardens. Le Kiosk has a great wine list; the menu offers mostly fish and shellfish. $A20.

## Accommodations

Hotel, motel, and hostel reservations are sometimes difficult to get during peak periods—the end of April, July, early October, late December, and early January. Unless otherwise noted, all accommodations are located within walking distance of city buses and only a few minutes away from central Sydney.

*Economy.* The Sydney Central Youth Hostel Authority at the corner of Pitt Street and Rawson Place may be the mother of all hostels, reputedly the world's largest, with 530 beds. Rooms go for $A8 a night with a 14-night limit. Since it's located near Central Station, getting to it by train and bus is easy. This is the headquarters for youth hostels in New South Wales, and due to its mammoth size it's an impersonal place. If you use it as a starting place, however, you will learn about other hostels in the areas you are headed; phone 02-9281-9111. The YWCA, 5-11 Wentworth Avenue, Darlinghurst, has low-cost shared rooms with four beds for $A24 a night. For your own room you'll pay $A60; phone 02-9264-2451. Hostel-type accommodations are well represented in Kings Cross. If it's economy accommodation you're after, when in doubt head to Kings Cross. "The Cross" can also be a rough part of town by Aussie standards, but not comparable to the inner cities in the United States. Still, leaving valuables unattended may result in their disappearance. Try the Jolly Swagman, 27 Orwell Street; phone 02-9358-6400. The hostel has a beach shuttle and a cheap meal counter. The staff posts civic and social events for the guests. A dorm bed in a room for four goes for $A18, a double for $A44. Potts Point House, 59 Victoria St., 02-9368-0733 (in the district adjacent to Kings Cross), is a funky-looking place that actually has spacious, clean rooms, each with a television. Dorms cost $A16, doubles $A40 per night. Eva's Backpackers, 6-8 Orwell, offers four- to ten-bed dorms for $A18, doubles for $A42. There is a nightly security patrol; phone 02-9358-2185. In

Bondi try Nomads on the Beach, 2-8 Campbell Street; phone 02-9130-4900. Dorms are $A15, doubles $A38. In Manly there are several hostel-type accommodations. Try Manly Backpackers Seaside, 28 Raglan Street; phone 02-9977-3411. Dorms go for $A18, doubles for $A40. The place is tidy and the staff friendly. If these selections don't do it for you, try the *Sydney Morning Herald*'s classified ads. You can often find weekly deals at rates paid by youthful Sydneysiders, not tourists. If you can find something on the north shore, all the better. You can ride the ferry to the city each morning and cruise back across the harbor in the evening, when the city's lights are dazzling.

Campgrounds and caravan parks don't exist in the city, but there are a few in outlying areas. To get a full look at the nearest campgrounds and caravan parks in the direction you are headed, visit with the National Royal Motorist Association (NRMA), 151 Clarence Street; phone 13-1122. The association has detailed maps on all aspects of travel in New South Wales. Probably the nearest camping to the city that is reachable by city bus is the Lakeside Van Park in Narrabeen (north across the Sydney Harbour Bridge and past Mosman on the coast). There are electrical outlets and hot showers. The campground is right on the coast, so the onshore wind is fairly constant. A powered site costs $A20, which is more expensive than renting a bed in most youth hostels.

The city has quite a few budget hotels, though they are becoming more scarce. The Wattle House, 114 Hereford Street, is both a hostel and a bed-and-breakfast. The place feels like a home rather than a hostel or a B & B. Dorms go for $A20, private rooms for $A40; phone 02-9552-4997. The Bread and Breakfast Inn, 108 Oxford Street, Darlinghurst, is a vintage turn-of-the-century house. It's $A88 for a double. Clean, small rooms, and centrally located; phone 02-9332-4118. The Russell, 143 George Street, is a find. Located near Circular Quay, this is a homey place with a garden on the roof. Rooms go for about $A125; phone 02-9241-3543. Better yet is the Lord Nelson Brewery Hotel, 19 Kent Street; phone 02-9251-4044. This is a 152-year-old building right in the Quay. The pub on the first floor is a renowned city watering hole. The rooms are small and Spartan and cost around $A90.

*Moderate.* The following hotels have wheelchair access and accommodations, unless otherwise noted. All Seasons Premier Menzies, 14

Carrington Street, is a sport enthusiast's hotel, complete with a bar scene where sporting events and their progress are constantly relayed to those attending. The rooms are clean and nicely decorated. Rooms go for around $A125; phone 02-9299-1000. The Waldorf Apartment Hotel, 57 Liverpool, Darling Harbour, has roomy one- and two-bedroom rentals that are suitable for a small group or a family. It is centrally located and near dozens of restaurants; phone 02-9261-5355. Wentworth is practically a Sydney institution, as well as a hotel. The rooms are beautifully decorated and brightly painted; phone 02-9230-0700. Carlton Crest, 179 Thomas Street, Darling Harbour, is a converted hospital with big rooms in a good location. Rooms start at around $A130; phone 02-9281-6888. Dorchester Inn, 38 Macleay Street, Potts Point; phone 02-9358-2400. This is a converted mansion offering multiroom apartmentlike accommodations. Rooms start at around $A100. Down the street you'll find the Chateau Sydney Hotel; phone 02-9358-2500. This is a homey place, with nice tidy rooms trimmed in varnished wood. The refrigerator is well-stocked. The rooms are a little small, but most of them have an open view to the water that makes them feel bigger than they are. All in all, this is a quiet and comfortable place to stay. Rooms start at $A180.

*Upmarket.* There are a lot of places for high rollers. The Sheraton on the Park is one of them. Located at 161 Elizabeth Street near Town Hall, this is reputedly one of Sydney's most elegant hotels. Most of the rooms have a city view. Each room has a fax. The bathrooms are marble, and the rooms spacious and richly decorated. No wonder a double goes for around $A380; phone 02-9286-6000. The Ritz-Carlton, 33 Cross Street, Double Bay, is where visiting movie stars and heads of state stay. The hotel is quiet and away from city noises, in one of the most upscale waterside neighborhoods. Marble and antique are the dominant theme. Rooms start at about $A350; phone 02-9362-4455. For other luxury hotels try Star City Hotel (phone 02-9777-9000) and Hotel Nikko (phone 02-9299-1231) in the Darling Harbour Area.

## Tourism for Children

More and more children are traveling with their parents. Tourism New South Wales took the time to list the attractions in Sydney that were most liked by children. I've relayed their recommendations and added two possibilities of my own. Luckily, you'll notice that some top kid choices are at the top of the heap for adults as well. Here's "Children's Choice—the Top Ten," as published by Tourism New South Wales.

*The Australian Maritime Museum.* The story of Australia and the sea, told in brass, canvas, and well-polished woodwork. Antique racing yachts, a World War II destroyer, figureheads, and model ships. Rates high for imagination. Darling Harbour.

*Australia's Wonderland.* The biggest amusement park in the Southern Hemisphere. Action ranges from the ferris wheel to ultimate roller coaster to the Australian Wildlife Park. Wallgrove, Eastern Creek.

*Luna Park.* Just fun! Sydney's favorite amusement park. Big dipper, old-fashioned fun. Coney Island five minutes from Circular Quay.

*Featherdale Wildlife Park.* A roll call of Australia's extraordinary fauna that even most Australians won't see in a lifetime. 217 Kildare, Doonside. Featherdale will pick you up at your hotel.

*The Australian Museum.* Skeletons of elephants, whales, and dinosaurs, as well as creepy crawlies. 6-8 College Street, Sydney.

*Manly Ocean World.* Manly's famous aquarium. Watch the sharks being fed, applaud the performing seals. Manly.

*The Powerhouse Museum.* Fascinating, hands-on assembly of technical, scientific, industrial, and decorative wizardry. 500 Harris Street, Sydney.

*Sydney Aquarium.* The sea world as you've never seen it before. Highlights include crocodiles and giant sea turtles. Darling Harbour.

*Taronga Zoo.* Feathers, fur, fins, and fangs in carefully designed habitats. Mosman.

*Koala Park Sanctuary.* Koalas to cuddle, and emus, dingoes, kangaroos, and more. Castle Hill Road, West Pennant Hills.

*The Monorail.* This above-street connection between the central city and Darling Harbour is a 12-minute futuristic and exhilarating ride.

*Mosman Ferry.* Why Mosman? It goes to the zoo, and the zoo has one of the best views of the harbor.

# National Parks

New South Wales has more than 100 national parks, many undeveloped. The range of habitats and activities is unending. Bordering Sydney are Ku-ring-gai Chase and Royal National Parks, both worthy of day visits. Directly west of Sydney is the Blue Mountains National Park, with sharp gorges and meandering watercourses. South of Sydney near the border with Victoria is immense Mount Kosciuszko National Park, which is popular year-round. Mount Kosciuszko National Park has the most extensive alpine area in mainland Australia. North of Sydney are a dozen parks, each with something different: Barrington Tops, Dorrigo, Gilbraltar Ranges, Myall Lakes, New England, Oxley Wild Rivers, Warrumbungles, and Washpool National Parks are scattered through habitats that include semitropical rain forests, coastal wetlands, lush green open woodlands, steep and heavily forested mountains, striking rock formations, and deep plunging gorges with spectacular waterfalls. A number are World Heritage rain forest parks. A wide range of wildlife and flora is protected in these parks. Along the north coast there are idyllic and unpopulated beach parks and reserves. Inland along the western border of New South Wales are a series of outstanding desert parks, starting with Mungo National Park, which rates a World Heritage listing. And then there are Kinchega, Mootwingee, and Sturt National Parks, which probably contain the densest population of red and gray kangaroos and assorted other forms of wildlife in Australia. Getting to these desert parks from Broken Hill can constitute an adventure in itself. To top off the variety of parks around New South Wales there's Lord Howe Island, a sharply jutting, isolated, green-mantled volcanic refuge for rare plants and animals located about 700 kilometers off the New South Wales coast. This unique island is also a World Heritage listing. Just how rich the parks of New South Wales are nobody really knows. Many of them haven't been quantified yet. Of the 100-odd parks in New South Wales, I visited about half and have highlighted those I found most promising, most convenient, or most representative of a group of parks in a given area. You could easily spend a year touring the parks of New South Wales in a camper-van.

## Parks Serving Sydney

Ku-ring-gai Chase National Park (21 kilometers north of Sydney) and Royal National Park (37 kilometers south of Sydney) are 14,000-hectare parks that are both worthwhile and convenient to visit in a day or a multiday visit. Neither park is on a par with the top parks in Australia, but both are representative of the Sydney sandstone environment and the plant habitats that Sydney and its sprawling suburbs now occupy. Royal National Park is particularly rich in bird life, with more than 200 species commonly represented. It is also well known for its secluded ocean beaches that can be reached by walking tracks. Ku-ring-gai Chase National Park is heavily vegetated, semitropical, and built around protected fjords and headlands. I found Ku-ring-gai richer in swamp wallabies, echidnas, goannas, and other forms of terrestrial wildlife. Both parks can be reached by public transportation from Sydney and accommodate a wide range of activities, including boating, walking, bird-watching, picnicking, swimming, and sunbathing.

### Ku-ring-gai Chase National Park

The park's main feature, Lambert Peninsula, juts out into Broken Bay and Pittwater. The peninsula is pitted with saltwater fjords called creeks because they are fed by intermittent creeks. Most of the walks are short and steep and terminate at a beach or overlook. Ku-ring-gai Chase is well suited for a full-day visit with a half-day walk. I particularly liked the America Bay Track and the Flint and Steel Track that start on West End Road on the Lambert Peninsula. The Flint and Steel Track descends sharply to a nice swimming area. I saw several swamp wallabies in the scrub behind the beach and shared the beach with a couple of sunbathers and a goanna. I enjoyed the Mackerel Track, but found it hot and exposed and most suitable for cool days or early-morning walking. It's the track of necessity if you arrive by ferry from Palm Beach. The view from West Head Lookout is spectacular.

The Kalkari Visitors Centre (phone 02-9457-9853) is the best place to get your bearings in the park. Staffed by volunteers, the center is on Ku-ring-gai Chase Road about 3 kilometers east of the Pacific Highway. It's open from 9:00 A.M. to 5:00 P.M. daily. There are audiovisual presentations, a wide range of maps and books to purchase, and a 30-minute nature walk. The Bobbin Head Information Centre (phone 02-9457-1049) is the official information center for the park. Rangers at either center will help direct you to areas of greatest interest. There are several West Head walks to sections of tessellated pavements with large rock engravings left behind by the Guringai, the Aborigines who occupied the area before European settlement. The carvings can be photographed. The most recognizable figures are fish and goannas. The best lighting is at dawn and dusk.

More than 800 species of plants occur in the park, most well adapted to the poor-quality soil that accompanies the Hawkesbury sandstone. Winter and spring bring out the greatest variety of flowers, typically banksias, hakeas, grevilleas, guinea flowers, boronias, and grass trees. There are 30 kinds of gums (eucalyptuses), most of them unfamiliar to North Americans.

Of the 180 species of birds in the park, the lyrebird is the most talked about in the park literature. There are also a great number of parrots. Look for rainbow lorikeets, rosellas, cockatoos, honey-eaters, and kookaburras, among other species.

Lace monitors (a kind of goanna) reaching two meters in length sometimes frequent picnic areas looking for handouts. They're harmless as long as they aren't harassed or fed by hand: they don't always distinguish between fingers and what you're offering them. You may see pythons, geckos, and dragon lizards, too. There are poisonous snakes, but they're rarely seen.

Boating is a primary activity in the park. The fjordlike bays and twisting, protected shoreline provide an escape from urban rigors only an hour's drive from the city's center. You'll see plenty of luxurious yachts moored at various places around the park. You can rent a vintage cabin cruiser at Bobbin Head and smaller boats at Cottage Point. At Bobbin Head, contact Halverson Boats, P.O. Box 21, Turramurra, NSW 2074; phone 02-9457-9011. Also try Clipper's Anchorage at Akuna Bay. Write to P.O. Box 63, Tewrrey Hills, NSW

2084; phone 02-9450-1888. Either of the above may be able to help you rent a small boat, or try the Cottage Point kiosk.

On a hot day you'll be tempted to take a plunge in the cool waters of the park. There are shark nets at Apple Tree Bay and the Basin. In some of the more protected waters, pollutants are a concern. Ask the ranger at Kalkari about the water quality of areas where you want to swim.

*Accommodations.* Camping ($A6 a night; phone 02-9451-8124) is allowed in the park at the Basin, which is reached by the ferry from Palm Beach. You must make reservations. Phone 02-9918-2747 between 9:30 and 10:30 A.M. There is also a youth hostel ($A20) at the Basin.

*Access.* Located less than 30 kilometers north of Sydney, Ku-ring-gai Chase National Park is commonly reached by driving north on the Pacific Highway. Turn east at Mona Vale, Bobbin Head, or Ku-ring-gai Chase Road. The drive takes about an hour. You can reach the park by taking a train to Turramurra, then a bus to Bobbin Head. By train and bus it's about a two-hour trip each way (fares around $A5). You can also reach the park by bus from Mosman and ferry from Palm Beach to the Basin, which is a coastal area in the park. Tour buses also visit Ku-ring-gai Chase. You can hike to most of the walking tracks from the Basin. For details on the ferry, phone 02-9918-2747 or 02-9974-5235. During the week it generally runs on the hour from Palm Beach.

## Royal National Park

Declared a park in 1879, Royal National Park is the oldest national park in Australia. A variety of plant communities occur in the park. Rain forests occur along protected creeks in the less exposed areas. In these areas you'll see vines, trees with buttressed roots, and varieties of figs 20 meters tall. The exposed open areas are often low heathlands. The Hacking River flows through the park, and there are numerous creeks that intersect most of the walking tracks that generally make their way from Lady Carrington Drive to the coast.

The park's peak wildflower season is May to October. You'll see banksias, hakeas, waratahs, and many other flowering plants.

Throughout the year in the cooler areas you'll see lyrebirds, crimson rosellas, kookaburas, wonga pigeons, bowerbirds, and a great number of other birds. Lady Carrington Drive, which travels through the rain forest, is an excellent area to see birds. Bonnie Vale is also highly recommended for bird life.

Animal life is nocturnal and not very plentiful—except for a non-indigenous herd of Javan rusa deer near North and South Era. If you're lucky you may see echidnas (small egg-laying anteaters), swamp wallabies, and possums.

The walking tracks vary in length from 1 to 10 kilometers each way. There is also a multiday 26-kilometer coastal walking track that starts at Bonnie Vale (near the campground) in the north and ends at Otford Lookout in the south. This track travels along sun-parched cliff tops, through gullies of trees and ferns, along and through creeks, and along secluded beaches.

If you're looking for a secluded beach, try Burning Palms, accessible from the Garie and Garrawarra walking tracks. Burning Palms is a covelike beach surrounded by thick semitropical vegetation. Usually surf lifeguards are on duty. Wattamolla is another safe saltwater swimming and snorkeling spot. At the park's southern border, the Werrong Track leads to the only officially condoned nude swimming beach. The beach is also popular with surfers. Rely on local knowledge about the safety of saltwater swimming areas. The park has a multitude of freshwater swimming areas. Flat Rock–Crystal Pools comprises a series of secluded swimming holes on South West Arm Creek located six kilometers south of Audley. Blue Pools is another favorite swimming hole. Audley, located on the Hacking River, offers canoe and rowboat rentals as well as excellent picnic facilities. Whatever you decide to do, bring a hat because the sun can be intense.

For details on camping and the walking tracks, stop at the Audley Visitors Centre (phone 02-4542-0648) on Farnell Avenue just past the park entrance. There is a nominal charge for entering the park.

*Accommodations.* For details on booking campsites, phone 02-9542-0648 between 8:30 A.M. and 4:30 P.M. Campsites include laundry facilities and hot showers. There is a nominal nightly charge and free sites. Sites are often booked far in advance. There is also a youth hostel (phone 02-9261-1111).

*Access.* By car from Sydney, the drive takes 30 to 45 minutes. Take the Princess Highway south. Turn left onto Farnell Avenue south of

Loftus. Trains originating in Sydney on the Illawarra-Cronulla line run regularly to points along the park's western boundary at Loftus, Engadine, Waterfall, and Otford. These are also the starting points of several popular walking tracks. A less frequent but regularly scheduled train runs to the Royal National Park Station at Audley, which is the hub of boating, swimming, and walking activities.

## Blue Mountains National Park

This is a beautiful park about 100 kilometers west of Sydney on the Great Western Highway. At 215,955 hectares it is among the largest parks in New South Wales. Although it has been continually upgraded with marked walking tracks and tourist facilities since its inception in 1959, much of it is still an untouched wilderness (as is the immense, 480,000-hectare Wollemi National Park, which occupies the northern flank of Blue Mountains National Park).

The scenery includes immense plunging sandstone gorges, striking rock formations, meandering creeks, and towering blue gum forests. The forests sometimes create a blue haze from refracted light passing through the oil emitted by the trees. A great number of wildflowers bloom here in the spring, including the beautiful red waratah.

Most tourists visiting the park visit the town of Katoomba, with its scenic aerial tram and railroad advertised as the steepest in the world. The nearby Jenolan Caves is probably the most visited limestone cave system in Australia. The park itself is divided into three sections: Grose Valley, Glenbrook, and the Warramgamba Catchment Area.

The Grose Valley section (sometimes called the Northern Section) is reached by taking the Great Western Highway to Blackheath. The Blue Mountains Heritage Centre has a display and many national parks products on sale, including attractive posters and postcards. The center is on Govetts Leap Road, and the park's headquarters is located just beyond the shopping center in Blackheath. Barring holidays, the headquarters is open Monday through Friday, phone 02-4787-8877. There are campgrounds, walking tracks, and spectacular views and waterfalls throughout the Grose Valley section of the park. To best explore the area, use the walking track guides with details on flora and fauna. The walks and vistas around Govetts Leap and Perry's Lookdown are particularly striking. There's a good 3- to 6-hour round-trip walk to the blue gum forest and to the valley-

*Red Rocks Morning, Northern Blue Mountains.* PAINTING BY ALASDAIR MCGREGOR.

floor Perry's Lookdown. The forest is perhaps the purest stand of blue gums in Australia. There are also some nice day walks to swimming holes. The eight-kilometer Red Hands Cave trail meanders through sections of rain forest. It starts and ends at the Visitors Cen-

tre. Any walks off the rim should be undertaken only by the physi-
cally fit. It's often hot and always steep on the return leg. Evans
Lookout has a 4-kilometer walk along the rim for the less adventuresome.

Glenbrook (sometimes called the Southern Section) is in the lower
mountains on the east side. The Glenbrook area is popular in the
summer during heat spells because of its rock swimming holes and
creekside walks. There are a variety of short walks in the vicinity of
the Glenbrook Visitors Centre, which is located on Bruce Road south
of Glenbrook; phone 02-4739-6266. You can get a bush-camping
permit there and information about walks and camping.

Other popular walks near Glenbrook include the Wentworth Falls
walk, which takes in a series of photographic waterfalls, one over
300 meters high. The trailhead is about 5 kilometers from Woodford. The National Park Conservation Hut, which is reached via a
three-hour walk from Falls Road, is a great place to sip tea and sort
through trail-map information that is handed out here; phone
02-4757-3827. If you want to exert yourself and see the Wentworth
Falls from a different perspective, locate the nearby National Pass
Circuit trail. This is a spectacular 6-kilometer trail that takes in magnificent mature blue gum forests as it passes over steep terrain, with
the trail cut into rock ledges in places. I saw two rare gang-gang
cockatoos on this walk. There are some steep places that are sweat-
inducing. If you're in poor physical condition you might prefer a
walk that is a little less strenuous, like the Valley of the Waters Walk,
which is part of the same trail system but shorter and less challenging. It takes in some beautiful waterfalls.

In Katoomba the big natural draw is the Three Sisters, a dramatic three-spire sandstone formation that is back-lit at night. The
most popular longer walk is the Giant Stairway, which drops
quickly to the valley below. The trail continues to Orphan Rock,
where you can either climb out of the valley on Furber Steps or hop
on the Scenic Railroad, which is reputedly the steepest railroad in
the world; phone 02-4782-2699. The other mechanical draw that
everyone on the big Sydney tour buses does is the Scenic Skyway.
This is a gondola ride with a lot of air under you that leaves the
Scenic Railway station and visits spectacular waterfalls, all for
$A4.50. On the west side of Katoomba there are another half
dozen hiking trails. The Ruined Castle is reputedly a dramatic walk
that takes in a steep escarpment.

Around Blackheath additional trails have been added in recent years. Just 300 meters from the Blue Mountains Heritage Centre is Fairfax Heritage Walk, which is a broad, flat trail with good views that is suitable for wheelchairs and people with health risks. From popular Govetts Leap you can walk five kilometers to Pulpit Rock in one direction and Bridal Veil Falls in the other direction.

The Warragamba Catchment Area is relatively pristine except for the area around Katoomba, which features an aerial tram, a scenic train ride, and a lively little mountain town. Narrow Neck to Mount Solitary is the most popular walk in the area. It's for the reasonably fit. Take drinking water. Inquire at Paddy Pallin's in Katoomba for details about any hikes in the area.

*Horseback riding.* Horseback riding is well established. Werriberri Trail Rides offers rides of less than an hour and up to three hours; phone 02-4787-9171. Megalong Australian Heritage Centre also offers rides in the same area; phone 02-4787-8188.

*Cautions.* The Blue Mountains are an immense maze of interlocking vertical-walled gorges. I hiked cross-country here with a couple of seasoned Australian bushwalkers and concluded I would never have found my way out without them. It's an easy place to get lost and stay lost. Keep in mind that the first several attempts to cross these mountains ended in failure because of the seemingly endless vertical-walled sandstone gorges. Stay on the trails. Also, carry water. The stream water is not drinkable.

*Information and Guide Services.* The park runs a discovery program with ranger-guides walks, talks, and tours. For maps, guide services, eateries, and accommodations, visit the Blue Mountains Tourist Authority on Echo Point Road, Katoomba; phone 02-4739-6266. For trail maps and details on flora and fauna visit the Blue Mountains Heritage Centre on Govetts Leap Road in Blackheath; phone 02-4787-8877. If you're a rock climber, visit Paddy Pallin on Katoomba Street in Katoomba and inquire about the Australian School of Mountaineering; phone 02-4782-2014. The school has experienced instructors who will take thrill seekers out rappelling for about $A80. In Glenbrook the national parks office is on Bruce Road just outside of the park entrance.

Numerous operators based in Sydney, Katoomba, Blackheath,

and Glenbrook offer guide services ranging from big bus tours to small nature walks with naturalists who know the area intimately. The big bus tours are easy to find at any information kiosk in Sydney or at your hotel's front desk. In Sydney AAT King's in Circular Quay is always at the ready with a nice new shiny bus, big soft seats, and a professional motoring tour with a few stops along the way; phone 02-9252-2788. Wonderbus may offer the best service from Sydney in a tour with stops at many of the trailheads and scenic spots. If you decide to stay awhile you can catch a later bus back; phone 02-9555-9800. For knowing the place intimately, try Blue Mountain Adventure Company in Katoomba; phone 02-4782-1271. For equipment, rock climbing, and anything outdoor-related visit Paddy Pallin on Katoomba Road, Katoomba, phone 02-4782-2014.

*Accommodations.* There is free camping in national parks in designated camping areas. Perry's Lookdown near Blackheath is a nice spot. Near Woodford there is a campground near Murphy's Glen, and inside the Bruce Road entrance a few kilometers is the Euroka Clearing Campground. These campgrounds have "short drop" outhouses and no running water, but they're free. For a cheap place to stay try Gardner's Inn at 255 Western Highway; phone 02-4787-8347. There's also the youth hostel on Waratah Road in Katoomba; phone 02-4782-6203. Dorms cost about $A15 a bed, doubles $A60. For something more upmarket with a great view, try Lilianfells Blue Mountains, Lilianfells Avenue, Echo Point, Katoomba; phone 02-4780-1200. This is a romantic place with big, fluffy, king-sized beds and Victorian furniture. They even offer billiards and lawn bowling to help pass the time. Doubles start at around $A300; phone 02-4780-1200.

*Access.* Most of the tour companies in Sydney offer a one- or two-day trip to the Blue Mountains. Most of them include Katoomba, Jenolan Caves, and the cable car. Shop for what you want. The Cityrail extends to Katoomba and Blackheath. Fare is around $A13 one way. Non-tour buses also service the area. Greyhound buses from Sydney stop in Katoomba; phone 13-20-30. The Blue Explorer Bus makes hourly runs from Sydney and stops at nearly 20 places in the Blue Mountains; phone 02-4782-1866. Fare is around $A20.

Once you're in the Blue Mountains there is Mountainlink, a mountain bus service that runs between the small towns; phone 02-4782-3333.

# Kosciuszko National Park

Kosciuszko National Park is the premier alpine park in Australia and contains 2,228-meter-high Mount Kosciuszko, Australia's tallest mountain, and ten other peaks close to that height. Kosciuszko National Park covers an immense 629,708 hectares, and in the winter the park and outlying areas make up snowfields of more than 100,000 hectares.

The Great Dividing Range runs through the park, separating the Murray and Snowy River drainages. Much of the water runoff from the park is used in the Snowy Mountain Hydroelectric Scheme that provides power for much of New South Wales. Talbing and Tantangara reservoirs and immense Lake Eucumbene are part of the scheme. Aside from the highly promoted snowfields, the park has hundreds of kilometers of hiking trails, thermal pools, extensive limestone caves at Yarrangobilly, a historic gold-mining town at Kiandra, and stunning wilderness areas like Mount Jagunal, Bogong, and the Pilot.

If you're someone who plans ahead, get a copy of "Good Stuff to Know About Snowy/Canberra," which is published by the New South Wales Tourism Commission. You can get a copy at the Sydney Visitors Centre, 106 George Street, Sydney, NSW 2000; phone 02-9255-1788. You can also contact the Cooma Visitors Centre, 119 Sharp Street, Cooma, NSW 2630, for information about the area; phone 02-6450-1742. For the park itself, contact Snowy Region Visitors Centre, Jindabyne Road, Jindabyne, NSW 2627; phone 02-6450-5600.

## Ski Areas

The snowfields are Kosciuszko's main draw—primarily because they are the most convenient snowfields for most Australians. Snow chains must be carried in all vehicles that enter the park's alpine areas from June 1 to October 10. Strictly speaking, the often-printed claim that Kosciuszko has more snowfields than Switzerland is accurate. However, the snow quality is not as consistent or as long lasting as that in the Alps. Nevertheless, there are good alpine skiing facilities at Thredbo, Charlotte Pass, Perisher Valley, Smiggin Holes, Guthega, and Mount Sewleyn. For alpine skiing, the snowfields around Thredbo and Charlotte Pass have the most to offer. The alpine skiing is not on a par with the best in North America or Europe, but the cross-country skiing is.

The cross-country skiing is equal to that anywhere, especially when you consider that the environment you'll glide through is entirely foreign looking. This is a land of gnarled and twisted snow gums. There is an extensive hut system throughout the park; huts are available for emergency stopovers and should not be thought of as accommodation facilities. For excellent day outings in top scenery, try the Cabramurra area, located in the northern part of the park. There is an excellent view of Mount Jungungal and extensive wilderness. There are more than 30 kilometers of marked trails, all starting at a day hut. The tracks wind through snow gum forests and open areas. The area between Mount Kosciuszko and Charlotte Pass is also popular. It's a mostly open area, and the ridgeline affords spectacular views of the Victorian Alps. In heavy snows the resort at Charlotte Pass can be reached only by snow cat. The area is subject to severe weather conditions, as is most of the park. You can rent gear in Cooma or Jindabyne. Try Paddy Pallin's Adventure Equipment, Kosciuszko Road and Alpine Way, Jindabyne, phone 02-6456-2922.

*Top Ski Runs.* An article in the August-September 1998 issue of *Expanse* rated ski runs throughout New South Wales and Victoria. The magazine attempted to pick runs that were outstanding for various ability levels. Four of the top ten places were in New South Wales:

1. Supertrail at Thredbo is "wide, fast and superbly groomed, nothing to get in the way except some rollers and long corners." The best time is early morning, when the snow is crisp and the crowds are still sniffing coffee. Everybody but beginners can handle it.

2. Hidden Valley at Perisher is "intermediate plus excellent tree-dodging skills . . . beautiful glade skiing through magnificent towering snowgums—a uniquely Australian experience." Because the trees protect it, this is a good place to head when a blizzard engulfs the mountain.

3. Carruthers Peak at Kosciuszko National Park is "intermediate on 40 degree terrain. Back country skills required . . . straight, cliff-lined gullies drop at consistent and breathtaking angles toward Club Lake."

4. The Elevator Shaft at Kosciuszko National Park is "advanced on 50 degree terrain. Back country skills mandatory. A steep,

narrow dog-legged gully drops from the cirque above Blue Lake."

## Walks

Only one-thousandth of 1 percent of Australia's land surface is alpine. The Summit and the Blue Lake walks are the most purely alpine walks in the park. The walks can be combined into an 18-kilometer loop that is easy to complete in a day, provided you get an early start. If you decide to combine these walks, start in the direction of Blue Lake, which has been set aside as unique wetland habitat and hence receives greater protection than the park in general. The trail starts at the car park (at the end of the road) directly above the Charlotte Pass resort area. The walk will take you through rolling alpine meadows decorated in a wide range of colorful wildflowers, cirques, and patches of snow that in some years persist into late summer. The entire area was formed by glacial action 20,000 years ago. You'll cross the headwaters of the Snowy River and climb gradually to Blue Lake, which is about a half mile off the loop. Blue Lake sits in the only ice-made basin on mainland Australia. If you continue to Mount Kosciuszko, the trail climbs to a ridge and works below a series of windswept mountains. You'll pass by Mount Carruthers and see Mount Townsend. You'll also see smallish Club Lake, surrounded by alpine meadows. On the other side of the trail are the endless ridges and plunging valleys of the Victorian Alps. You'll pass Lake Albina, which sits in a saddle between the trail and Mount Townsend. Eventually you'll come to the summit of Mount Kosciuszko—a fairly unclimactic event unless you do it in a hail and ice storm as I did. From Mount Kosciuszko take the "old road" back to Charlotte Pass. (Don't go to Thredbo.)

The Kosciuszko Walk is another popular walk to the summit. It starts at the top of the Crackenback chairlift, which is part of Thredbo Village. From here it's a steady climb covering 7 kilometers to Mount Kosciuszko along a marked track that traverses picturesque open alpine country. The vertical rise is only about 260 meters.

The Goldseeker's Track, near Three Mile Dam on the road to Cabramurra, is a numbered nature walk that introduces many of the unique plants of the alpine areas. The 1-kilometer loop has 11 numbered stops that identify snow gums, sphagnum moss, trigger plants, mining operations, frost hollows that have a microclimate and forms of vegetation all their own, and wildflowers ranging from snow daisies to bachelor buttons. The area was heavily mined for gold until 1930. Before the miners, Aborigines came to the highlands to fatten up on bogong moths during the summer months.

Kosciuszko National Park has vast subalpine and alpine areas that are rarely visited. The Cascade Trail is highly recommended; it starts about 10 kilometers above Thredbo. The area is strikingly beautiful with frost hollows, stands of alpine ash 56 meters tall, and the Cascade hut, which was restored in the 1980s for walkers. Discuss your plans for any off-trail walks with a ranger before you go.

## Yarrangobilly Caves

The Castle Track (Yarrangobilly Caves), located on the Snowy Mountains Highway between Yarrangobilly and Kiandra, passes a number of cave entrances. Only Glory Hole Cave and North Glory Cave are open to the public. Aside from Glory Hole Cave, you are forbidden by law to enter any cave without a guide. Tickets are available at the nearby visitors center for guided tours. You can also get a special permit from the park service to investigate caves yourself, provided you're properly equipped and qualified. You should correspond by mail prior to visiting the park if you want to get a permit.

Most of the caves have stalagmites, stalactites, columns, shawls, helictites, and a number of other interesting formations. Glory Hole Cave is the only self-guided cave walk allowed in the Yarrangobilly Caves. Push the button on the viewing platform to turn on the lighting system. The cave is 330 meters long with numerous inclines. It's not difficult, but a sick or weak person is encouraged to visit a less demanding cave. The cave's temperature is about 40°F, so dress appropriately. Near the caves you can also soak in the thermal pool, a cemented pool that captures thermally produced 80°F water. The Glory Farm Walk, a short walk through the remnants of a pioneer homestead, is the third walk in the Yarrangobilly Caves area.

## Horseback Riding

Reynella, a superbly managed riding stable, operates just outside the park boundaries relatively near Adaminaby. John and Rosalyn Rudd have operated their stable for a dozen years and used the highlands for grazing before the park was expanded to its present form. Reynella is not a day-ride stable. Their guided and fully catered trips last between three days ($A500) and five days ($A950) and commonly travel along the meandering Murrumbidgee River. The stable is among the busiest and best run in New South Wales and will tailor trips for U.S. individuals and groups who contact them three months ahead of time. There are many horses to pick from, and they will find one for your ability. John Rudd says, "We're in an alpine climate, so you should bring riding clothes for all weather conditions. We prefer that you've had some riding experience but we can take beginners as long as you're game and fairly fit." John says the best time for wild-flowers and weather is January, February, and March. "We provide a bushwalk on horseback," says Rosalyn Rudd. "The pace is relatively slow. Most of our customers enjoy the outdoors and enjoy sharing it with like-minded people." Contact Reynella, Adaminaby, NSW 2630, Australia; phone 02-6454-2386.

## Other Adventure Activities

The winter activities revolve around snow sports. The summer, fall, and spring activities diversify into mountain biking, abseiling (rappeling), river rafting, hiking, bird-watching, and just enjoying the outdoors. Paddy Pallin's, on the main drag in Jindabyne, rents mountain bikes, leads abseiling groups, organizes and directs canoe outings, and rents and sells skiing equipment. They also have maps for activities ranging from hiking to cross-country skiing; phone 02-6456-2922. For river rafting contact Upper Murray White Water rafting; phone 02-6457-2922.

## Gateway Town of Cooma

*Cooma.* Cooma is the gateway city to the Snowy Mountains and Kosciuszko National Park. The town is about six blocks long and two wide. A dozen buildings are protected by the National Trust. It's also heavily endowed with motels and mountaineering and ski-equipment rental shops. Cooma is 415 kilometers south of Sydney, 114 from Canberra, and 218 from Goulbourn. The Cooma Visitors Centre (phone 02-6450-1740), located on Sharp Street next to Centennial Park, is an excellent place to get directions for everything from equipment rentals to accommodations.

For accommodations, ask at the visitors center.

# Outback Parks, Broken Hill, and Assorted Two-Pub Towns

Perhaps the most pleasant surprise during my 60,000-kilometer perusal of Australia was the western portion of New South Wales. Located in the arid interior along New South Wales's border roughly 1,100 kilometers from Sydney, the western sector of the state is true Outback and the parks in it provide a dramatic contrast to the temperate coast. The area is typified by solitude, abundance of wildlife (especially red kangaroos and bird life), and, after a rain, an overabundance of flowers—the entire growth cycle of many plants in the region commences and ends in a week. There are lunettes to contemplate, ancient traces of Aboriginal culture, giant woolsheds, sheep operations preserved from the period when sheep dominated the entire region, and dusty little Outback outposts like Milparinka, Menindee, and Tibooburra. The only sizable city in the area, and the starting place for most visitors, is silver-rich Broken Hill—the unofficial capital of the Outback rich in classic Australian architecture. This region is the Australia you've heard and read about, where the intensity of perpetual drought is omnipresent. Six million sheep have lived here in wet years—and a million have died of thirst in dry years. Harsh conditions have been the area's hallmark for most of this century. It's also a beautiful place where drought-resistant life-forms explode in vast abundance and perish just as fast upon the whims of climate. There is no compromise in this area. Avoid the scorching summer temperatures, if at all possible. Because the western part of the state is so far from Sydney, it makes sense to take a train, bus, or airplane to either Mildura (only if Lake Mungo appeals to you) or

Broken Hill and from there go on in a rental car or on a tour bus. Heed motoring cautions—your survival may depend on it.

## Mungo National Park, a World Heritage Area

Mungo National Park is part of the ancient Willandra Lakes system that dried up at the cessation of the last ice age about 20,000 years ago. The area is listed by the World Heritage Foundation because of its archaeological and paleontological significance. Aboriginal culture has been dated back 40,000 years in the area, which rivals other areas in having the earliest proven human presence in Australia. These Aborigines used ochre for artistic and ceremonial purposes and had a tool technology and a broad-based diet. The area has also yielded skeletal remains of wombats the size of horses.

Today the area is a saltbush desert featuring semihard sand formations known as lunettes. The best known of these is called the Walls of China, an excellent subject to photograph because of its soft pastel colors and stark appearance—a moonscape on earth. At one end of Lake Mungo, the park's most prominent ancient lake basin, is a sheep station with a large shearing barn that has been restored by the park service. The park's interpretive center explains the significance of the area and has replicas of the prehistoric creatures that once roamed the area.

The actual lake basin is home to large numbers of gray and red kangaroos and emus. Major Mitchell cockatoos are also fairly common in the area. From the woolshed and interpretive area a tenkilometer dirt road cuts through the dry lakebed to the Walls of China and other sand formations. I found quite a few emus behind the dunes. Look for tracks and follow them. If you sit down and remain still, these curious birds will often approach within a few meters.

*Accommodations.* There are no accommodations in the area. There is a campground with pit toilets near the park entrance, but you must bring your own water. In emergencies you can get water from the ranger's quarters near the woolshed. The nearest large town is Mildura, 110 kilometers to the south. You should enter the area prepared to travel 250 kilometers without seeing a petrol pump. There are spartan accommodations at Pooncarie and some of the other small communities in the area. The dirt roads in the area are impassable after a substantial rain. For details on road conditions and the park, call the ranger at 08-8091-5155.

*Access.* The route that makes the most sense is to travel north from Mildura (possibly starting in Adelaide) to Mungo National Park, then to Kinchega National Park, to Broken Hill, and on to Mootwingee and Sturt National Parks. This way you can see all of the western desert parks without doubling back. Most of these roads are dirt, but they're passable in rental cars during dry weather. If you plan to visit Lake Mungo only, start at Mildura (980 kilometers from Sydney) and take a charter bus.

## Kinchega National Park

Kinchega National Park is the next park north from Lake Mungo. Kinchega is located 1,020 kilometers west of Sydney, 110 kilometers southeast of Broken Hill, and 3 kilometers west of the small Outback community of Menindee. Kinchega is an oasis park with several created shallow lakes that attract and support arid-lands wildlife as well as birds not commonly found in the desert. The place is literally hopping with both red and gray kangaroos. A day after visiting Kinchega, I ate dinner in Broken Hill with Bill King, Australia's foremost Outback tour developer. He was looking over the area for its tourism potential and said, "I reckon Kinchega and other nearby parks have more 'roos bobbing around than anywhere else in Australia." Part of the reason for this is that few dingoes live in the area because of the "dog fence" that runs along New South Wales's northwest border. The fence keeps all but the wiliest dingoes out. In Kinchega the proliferation of wildlife is largely due to the Darling River (a major tributary of the Murray) and the permanent lakes that flank the park.

I found the area between Lake Emu and Lake Eurobilli particularly full of emus and large kangaroos. If you fancy yourself a wildlife photographer, try this area in the cool of the morning, especially the woodlands surrounding the wetlands near the dirt track that passes by the picnic tables. The emus seem particularly eager to pose for photographs, providing that you remain motionless during their cautious approach. Lake Cawndilla and Lake Menindee are homes to darters (anhingas), pelicans, ospreys, shags (cormorants), swans, eagles, and ducks. There's also a liberal sprinkling of desert parrots. Drive slowly in the park: you may find emus, kangaroos, and foxes trotting into your path.

There is a complete station complex including a woolshed, pens, and early-twentieth-century farm equipment near the ranger's office 16 kilometers from the park entrance. Pick up the self-guiding brochure on the sheep operation and you'll go away understanding the toil involved in "living off the sheep's back."

There are a great number of ephemeral plants in the area that germinate, mature, and bloom within a week or two of a rainfall. For more details on the plant life and the area in general, purchase a copy of *Western Parks of New South Wales,* by Barbara Mullins and Margaret Martin, in any regional National Parks and Wildlife Service office; the National Parks and Wildlife Service also publishes and updates material on western New South Wales's national parks.

*Accommodations.* There is a budget pub-hotel in Menindee that I passed on because I arrived on a rather loud and rowdy Saturday night. Opting for a good night's sleep, I bedded down in the park (two kilometers from the town) in the camping places provided along the Darling River. The campsites have no amenities, but they are peaceful and enjoy a view of the river under the shade of large, billowy trees. There is no charge for camping. There is a caravan park near Menindee, which I didn't visit. The next day I found the Albemarle Hotel in Menindee, which was a step ahead of its rowdier competitor. Rooms are around $A20 a night.

*Access.* The park is 110 kilometers southeast of Broken Hill. Both Broken Hill and Menindee are on the Indian-Pacific railroad line that spans the continent. The train is the way many people reach the area. Coaches from Adelaide (508 kilometers) and Sydney (1,100 kilometers) also run regularly to Broken Hill. Three airlines connect Broken Hill to Adelaide and Sydney. (See "Broken Hill," below.) By car, it's important to realize that the only paved road in the district is the 95-kilometer stretch between Menindee and Broken Hill. If you are coming on the Pooncarie Road via Lake Mungo, the road is dirt. All of the roads in the park are dirt.

*Driving Caution.* In wet weather the dirt roads around Kinchega and Mungo National Parks often become impassable. Particularly treacherous are patches of blue clay, which become as slick as ice and so sticky your tires suddenly grow to twice their size, until the wheel wells are entirely encased in a gooey mess, making your vehicle inoperative.

## Broken Hill: The City of the Wild West

Broken Hill is an isolated and picturesque town with giant old pub-hotels. Today's population is 23,000. The town's main drag is dominated by turn-of-the-century architecture. The city is laid out on a checkerboard grid pattern that's easy for a first-time visitor to figure out. The town's financial past and future has banked heavily on pastoralism and silver mined from beneath the town and nearby hills. The place appears to be in love with minerals. The streets have names like Bromide, Cobalt, Talc, Mercury, and Crystal. It's a comfortable town with good eateries, museums, and a wide range of hotels. While Broken Hill is in New South Wales, it's more closely tied to Adelaide and South Australia than to Sydney and New South Wales. It even sets its clocks on Adelaide time—central standard time.

Broken Hill is known throughout Australia for its "Brushmen of the Bush," Outback artists who usually work in oils. Commercial galleries throughout Broken Hill carry their work. Clifton Pugh, Pro Hart, Hugh Schulz, and Eric Minchen are some of the better-known artists.

The Tourist and Travellers Centre is one of the best organized and friendliest such organizations in New South Wales. It's located at the corner of Blende and Bromide Streets, which also houses the bus station and a rent-a-car outlet. The center is open from 8:30 A.M. to 5:00 P.M. Monday through Friday. On Saturdays and Sundays it's open from 9:00 A.M. to 12:00 P.M., and on public holidays it's open from 2:00 to 5:00 P.M. You can contact the center by mail at P.O. Box 286, Broken Hill, NSW 2880, and by phone at 08-8088-5209. It has dozens of handouts on activities and contacts in the area.

*Things to Do.* The National Parks and Wildlife Service office is located at 183 Argent Street; phone 08-8088-5933. It has handouts and pamphlets on Sturt, Mootwingee, Kinchega, and Mungo National Parks. Get a copy of the local newspaper, the *Barrier Daily Truth,* to find out what's going on in town. There are mine tours that can be booked at the Tourist and Travellers Centre. Delprat's Daydream Mine Tour (phone 08-8088-1604) is the best. You are outfitted in miner's gear before plunging deep into the earth in a crude elevator. The Railway, Mineral, and Train Museum (phone 08-8088-4660) is also popular. The Royal Flying Doctor Service (phone 08-8088-0777), located seven kilometers from town, is open to the public in the afternoon on weekdays and for a limited time in the morning on Saturdays. You can also watch the School of the Air, which beams school lessons to children on remote stations from a radio studio (not on holidays or weekends). You must book a seat the previous day at the tourist center and show up on time at 8:40 A.M. to see an hour-long lesson being taught. There are 13 art galleries in Broken Hill, 12 of them commercial outlets. Broken Hill City Art Gallery is the second-oldest public gallery in Australia. It has high-quality exhibits. It's located in the Civic Centre on Chloride Street, phone 08-8088-5491. For a list of commercial galleries, ask at the Tourist and Travellers Centre. Broken Hill also has a mosque that's open at 2:30 P.M. every Sunday. It was built by Afghan and Indian cameleers who packed materials and goods to Broken Hill during its early days. Silverton Ghost Town is 25 kilometers from Broken Hill on a paved road. This town, which has dwindled in size since its heyday, is now a mecca for the movie industry. The film companies find the isolated stone buildings and stark setting photogenic.

*Accommodations.* Broken Hill has a wide selection of accommodations and eateries. There are a great number of grand old pub-hotels left over from the boom periods in the sheep industry and mining. Of these, try the Palace Hotel. It's not luxurious but does have character, and the price can't be argued with. The artwork includes a local version of Botticelli's *Birth of Venus*—copied from a postcard according to the proprietor, a former Florentine named Mario, who painted it. Rooms range from $A40 to $A60. Or try the West Darling Motor-Hotel, Argent Street, Broken Hill, NSW 2880. This hotel is centrally located for several restaurants and shopping areas. For a decent dinner, try the Legion Club, 170 Crystal Street, or Alfresco, 397 Argent Street; phone 08-8087-5599.

*Access.* By air, Kendell Air (phone 08-8087-1969) flies to and from Sydney and has regular flights to and from Adelaide. About $A210 to Sydney and $A110 to Adelaide. By train, the Indian Pacific, which runs between Sydney and Perth, stops in Broken Hill; phone 13-22-

32. By bus, Sunraysia and Greyhound both provide regular service to Broken Hill from Sydney, Adelaide, and Melbourne. Typical bus fare from Sydney to Broken Hill is $A100. You can rent a car at Budget, 165 Argent Street; phone 13-27-27 or Thrifty, 190 Argent Street; phone 02-9380-5399. Look for rates of $A75 per day or lower.

## Mootwingee National Park

Mootwingee National Park is etched into my memory for its abundance of wildlife and its stark and remote beauty. Because of its richness in Aboriginal art, as well as its wildlife, Mootwingee is both a historic site and a national park—Mootwingee Historic Site is within the national park boundaries. The rare yellow-footed rock wallabies are found in the area. The name *Mootwingee* means grasses in the Bargundji tongue of the Wilyakali people, the original inhabitants who were pushed from the area in the 1850s.

In 24 hours at Mootwingee I was kept awake most of the night by flocks of galahs and little corellas that screeched and flapped wildly in swirling moonlit silhouettes that numbered in the thousands.

There are two self-guided walks in the park. The volume, variety, and trustful nature of the wildlife are unforgettable on both of them.

Aboriginal art sites are plentiful in Mootwingee. The primary ones were off limits during my first visit in 1987, because of vandalism. Since then only organized tours under the supervision of the park service are allowed to view the most sacred sites. Make arrangement in Broken Hill; phone 08-8088-5933. Of particular rarity is the combination of a great number of ochre paintings and detailed engravings in the same area. The permanent waterholes in rocky areas were used by Aborigines who relied on them in times of drought. The ill-fated Burke and Wills expedition stopped here in the 1860s. Jackeroo Earnest Giles, who helped in this leg of the expedition, etched his name and the date of his visits to the area at the Aboriginal art sites. You'll also find rock holes that were dammed to make them larger for stock when pastoralists lived here. Today these enlarged catchments probably support more wildlife than existed before the turn of the century. Still, even these waterholes can dry up in severe droughts, and drought is always the controlling force in the lives of the plants and animals in the region.

*Accommodations.* There's a designated camping area with pit toilets but no water. There are no other accommodations in the area.

*Access.* Mootwingee is located 134 kilometers north of Broken Hill on a detour off the Silver City Highway (dirt).

## Sturt National Park

Sturt National Park is about as remote a place as you can visit in New South Wales. Located in the northwestern corner of New South Wales, the park features vast open, rolling gibber plains and "jump up" country totaling nearly 350,000 hectares. The park was created in the 1970s when four sheep stations were purchased by the government. The western half is covered by red sandhills and plains whose combined drainage fills Lake Pinaroo during rains. The wetlands and the plethora of life that is attracted to it have been designated as "Wetlands of International Importance." The vistas in the park are endless, big-sky panoramas. The wildlife consists chiefly of red kangaroos, wedge-tailed eagles, and emus. I counted more than 150 kangaroos (some grays) in a short time in the eastern section and saw a half dozen emu family groups. Groups of emus sometimes number 50.

From Sturt, you can continue to Coopers Creek or reverse your route on the Silver City Highway to Broken Hill. Always remember to abide by motoring safety rules (see "Driving Cautions," below).

*Accommodations.* Besides the park's camping areas, there are two pub-hotels and a caravan park with a laundry in Tibooburra, the tiny town on the southern edge of the park.

*Access.* Tibooburra is located 330 kilometers north of Broken Hill on the Silver City Highway. It can also be reached from Bourke via Wanarring, which is 430 kilometers away. Both of these roads are generally passable in rental cars during dry weather. When it rains the roads can become impassable, even with a 4WD. Tibooburra is more than 1,400 kilometers from Sydney and is literally the end of the Outback in New South Wales. Charter flights of twin-engine aircraft also visit the park via a dirt landing strip just outside of Tibooburra.

*Driving Cautions.* Because there's always the chance of becoming stranded, take ample drinking water when you drive north of Broken Hill. Do not leave the main roads, as these are remote enough. If it begins to rain, stay put until the roads have dried out.

# ┌──── Canberra: Australia's Capital

Canberra is Australia's capital. It's surrounded by New South Wales but is on Australian Capital Territory, federal land not belonging to any state. More than 295,000 people make their home in Canberra and its suburbs.

There is much to see in Canberra. I strongly recommend seeing it on an organized tour. The city is spread out, and an organized tour gets you to the major points of interest faster than you would get there on your own and with more information. For tours commencing in the city, contact the Canberra Visitors Centre on Northbourne Avenue; phone 02-6205-0044. Australia Pacific and several other coach companies run two-day tours of Canberra that start and end in Sydney. Ansett Australia and Qantas run several flights a day from Sydney to Canberra. Fare is around $A120.

For me the standouts to see are the National Gallery of Australia, Parliament House, the botanic gardens, and the Australian War Memorial. The national gallery (phone 02-6240-6502) is an immense structure housing high-quality art chronicling Australia as seen by Australians since the first penal settlement. Aboriginal artists are also featured. The gallery is open from 10:00 A.M. to 5:00 P.M. daily. The Parliament House (phone 02-6277-7111) was replaced with an ultramodern structure, but what I found interest-

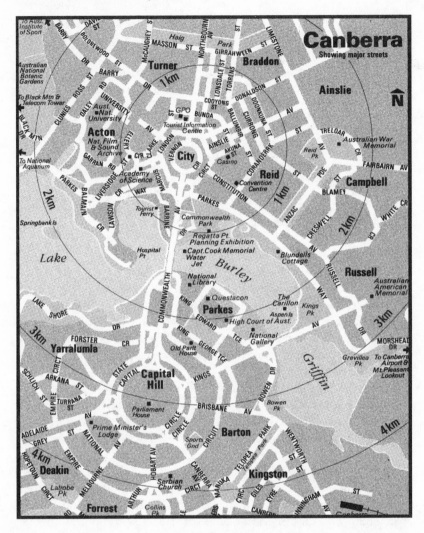

ing was watching the English form of government with wigged men (and a few women) arguing their points of view. The War Memorial, on Limestone and Fairbairn Avenues (phone 02-6243-4518) will pull at your emotions. The memorial is open from 9:00 A.M. to 4:45 P.M. daily. There are guided tours at 10:30 A.M. and 1:30 P.M. Australia has paid heavily with the blood of its young in both world wars—proportionally losing more men than the allies they sought to help. If you make it to Canberra, visit this shrine. The Australian National Botanic Gardens is on Clunies Ross Street, Black Mountain; phone 02-6250-9540. The garden is open daily from 9:00 A.M. to 5:00 P.M. There's an outstanding display of the varied and rich vegetation of Australia. The emphasis is on native plants, including a rain forest.

The rap on Canberra is that it's somewhat sterile and too spread out. I found it a difficult city to figure out by car. It's wise to study a map before entering the city. As for its sterility, you'll have to judge for yourself. I found it surprisingly peaceful and low-key for a national capital.

For information, contact the Canberra Visitors Centre, Jolimont Centre Foyer, Northbourne Avenue; phone 02-6205-0044.

*Restaurants.* There are plenty of good cheap eateries in Canberra. Timmy Kitchen in the Manuka Shopping Centre has good-quality Chinese food; phone 02-6295-6537. Little Saigon, corner of Alinga and Northbourne Avenue, serves filling meals for as little as $A5; phone 02-6230-5003. The Tryst on Bougainville Street is a relaxing place with a diverse menu of tasty meals. The cooks here add a lot of herbs and extras to most of their dishes. Meals go for around $A18 a plate; phone 02-6239-4411.

*Accommodation.* Considering that Canberra is a stylish, clean, and somewhat rural capital it is surprising that there are many places you can stay cheaply. The Macquire Hotel, 18 National Circuit, has tidy rooms and is near all the major sights and government houses. Rooms go for about $A85; phone 08-6273-2325. There are numerous bed-and-breakfast places. Two neighboring establishments that have friendly atmospheres with a friendly price of less than $A100 per night are the Chelsea Lodge on 526 Northbourne (phone 02-6248-0655) and the Blue and White Lodge, 524 Northbourne (phone 02-6248-0498). One of the better moderate-priced stays is the University House, Balmain Crescent, on the tranquil grounds of the Australian National University. Doubles go for around $A100; phone 02-6295-2244. There are plenty of high-end hotels. One of the more unique top-market places is Brindabella Station, which is outside of the city in a rural, farmlike setting with luxury rooms. Bird-watching and short hikes are part of the experience. Rooms start at $A250; phone 02-6236-2121.

*Access.* Canberra is located about 114 kilometers from Cooma and 300 kilometers south of Sydney. Bus ($A45), train ($A42), and plane ($A120) connect from Sydney daily. By car from Sydney, head south on the Hume Highway then take the Federal Highway.

# The Best of Northern New South Wales

With minor and major detours from the Pacific Highway, which runs 1,027 kilometers along the coast between Sydney and Brisbane, here are some of the more noteworthy destinations on the New South Wales side of the border, heading north from Sydney.

## The Hunter Valley

The Hunter Valley is the oldest wine-growing area in Australia, but unlike the Barossa Valley in South Australia, most of the Hunter's historic wineries have been replaced by modern ones. The heart of the Hunter is Pokolbin. Semillon, cabernet sauvignon, pinot noir, shiraz, and gewürztraminer are some of the grapes under cultivation here. The area is mostly geared for weekend wine tasting, though organized tour groups come here during the week year-round. The Hunter is also known for its expensive restaurants, such as the Chalet. There are barbecue facilities and picnic grounds as well. Hungerford Hill Wine Village at Pokolbin offers comprehensive wine tasting and wine sales as well as horseback riding and hot-air ballooning. (But you should book all balloon flights before leaving Sydney.) The Hunter Valley Wine Society, on the corner of Broke and Branxton Roads, Pokolbin (phone 02-4998-7397), has maps of the wineries in the area. The Hunter Estate on Hermitage Road (phone 02-4998-7777) houses the Golden Grape Vineyard and Historic Museum, which is open on weekends.

February is the best time to visit the Hunter Valley wineries. For contrast, try Tamburlaine, McDonalds Road, Pokolbin (phone 02-4998-7570), for a look at an award-winning small family operation and Lindemans, McDonalds Road (phone 02-4998-7684), for a volume operation.

*Access.* The Hunter Valley can be visited in one day from Sydney. It's a two- to three-hour drive each way. However, if you plan to imbibe, get on a tour bus. Remember that the Australian police operate "booze buses" that sample your alcohol level and incarcerate you, all in the same bus. Australia Pacific and other tour companies offer two-day trips to the Hunter Valley from Sydney. For a personalized guided tour from Sydney, phone 02-9555-2700 and ask about the Scenic Wine-Tasting Tour.

## Myall Lakes National Park

This coastal park has the largest freshwater-brackish lake system in New South Wales. The system consists of three medium-sized lakes, the Myall River, and other small creeks. On selected waterways there is excellent canoeing. There is a great abundance and variety of bird life throughout the park; more than 250 kinds of birds have been sighted. The park is 237 kilometers north of Sydney on the Pacific Highway, about 2.5 hours by car. The area is suitable for a two-hour or multiday visit year-round.

The park has a series of long, arcing ocean beaches with three road access points. Dark Point, with offshore Broughton Island, and Treachery Head offer excellent vistas. Both can be reached by car and a short walk. The lakes are separated from the beaches by a relatively narrow section of stabilized sand dunes.

The vegetation on the dunes and around the lakes includes large banksias, sedges, extensive stands of paperbarks and other melaleucas, and patches of rain forest and sclerophyll forests.

For a high-use coastal park in populous New South Wales, there's an amazing amount of wildlife. The terrestrial creatures are nocturnal, and most of them are only seen for an instant before they disappear into the heavy vegetation. Echidnas, bandicoots, two species of wallabies, and gliders are common. Koalas also inhabit the park, but usually stay high in the trees. The birds are a different story. In two

*Koala sprinting, north coast New South Wales.* PHOTO BY ERIC HOFFMAN.

hours I counted 37 species, including white-breasted sea eagles, darters, native hens, several kinds of ducks, pelicans, egrets, swans, rosellas, sulfur-crested cockatoos, and lorikeets and other small parrots. If you're a birder, don't leave Myall Lakes without an early-morning look around.

Canoeing and walking are two ways to enjoy this area. It's wise to avoid peak-use periods, when vacationing powerboaters also use the lake. Easter and Christmas are the worst times. But even then, by using the shallow areas and creeks, canoeists can have a fantastic experience seeing hundreds of birds on waterways they'll have entirely to themselves. The Broadwater Lake end of the park has the best canoeing. For the best sightseeing, enter the park from the south via Tea Gardens. From the Mungo Brush Road, which runs between the ocean beaches and the Myall River, there are many worthwhile short walks. The beach is about 400 meters from the road and the river is about the same distance in the opposite direction. I found the area around Piper's Creek especially interesting; there's a tremendous amount of bird activity around the waterway. The Mungo Track Nature Walk was also short and enjoyable. The ocean beaches were empty and beautiful. The park service emphasizes that swimming is dangerous because of strong riptides and the absence of lifeguards.

*Boat Rentals and Canoe Tours.* There are numerous boat rental possibilities around Myall Lakes. Bombah Point has the most centrally situated canoe rentals. From the southern entry point the ferry connecting Mungo Brush Road to Lakes Road (Legges Camp, kiosk, and canoe rentals) runs between 8:00 A.M. and 6:00 P.M. on the hour. If you want to go directly to the nearest canoe rental, drive from Buladelah down Lakes Road to Legges Camp, which is on the shore of Broadwater Lake.

*Also in the Area.* Barrington Tops (see below), Hathead, and Woko National Parks, plus the Port Macquarie koala sanctuary and Hunter Valley (see above).

*Accommodations.* Camping is allowed at designated sites throughout the park. Some campgrounds have koalas in the trees; others are in attractive lakeshore paperbark settings. Legges Camp on Bombah Point (canoe rentals) has hot and cold showers and a kiosk. Book in advance (phone 02-4997-4495). Violet Hill also has a campground and it's more difficult to reach—eliminating caravans and some of the crowd. As many as 3,000 people may camp around the Myall Lakes during holidays. During nonholidays the place is often empty.

*Access.* There are two commonly used approaches to Myall Lakes. The first route is via Tea Gardens, Hawks Nest, and along the Mungo Brush Road. This is the southern approach that allows you beach access and walks to the heavily vegetated, bird-rich Myall River. The second approach is to Legges Camp via Lakes Road from Buladelah Road. This delivers you to the heart of the lake system and canoe rentals. The roads in the park are dirt and subject to icelike slickness during rains.

## Barrington Tops National Park

Barrington Tops is a rugged tablelands park in a subalpine and temperate rain-forest setting about 320 kilometers northwest of Sydney at the northern end of the Hunter Valley. The park encompasses two plateaus: Barrington and Gloucester Tops, which are reached by different roads but linked by a walking track. The park is one of the few areas where you'll find subalpine tablelands in northern New South Wales. In May I didn't see another person during a two-day stay in the Gloucester Tops area.

The plateaus are around 1,500 meters high. From their rims the drop-offs are near-vertical faces that plunge to dense forest. The entire area receives heavy rain, and in some years there are substantial snowfalls. The rain falls mostly in the summer months. The tablelands are catchments for major river systems, which is the primary reason they have been set aside as a park. The precipitation level, different elevations, and soil types support a wide range of plant life. Snow gums, peat bogs, and grasses commonly associated with Tasmania and Mount Kosciuszko are found in the highest areas. Antarctic beeches, an ancient species linking Australia with Antarctica, are found in protected areas in the tablelands. Subtropical and temperate rain forests are found at the base of the plateaus, especially in the Williams and Gloucester River Valleys.

There's a great deal of wildlife in the park, but most of the marsupials are elusive. At dawn and dusk, pademelons and wallabies are common in the open areas along the fringes of the forests. Brush turkeys are practically tame in the Gloucester River campground. With a spotlight at night you may be able to locate gliders. In large, slow-moving pools in any of the major rivers you are apt to see platypuses paddling about at dawn and dusk. Lyrebirds and bowerbirds are common in the lower elevations.

There are several excellent walks in the Gloucester River portion of the park. Take the road from the Gloucester River campground to Gloucester Tops. The road is steep, with many spectacular views. Two short loop walks have been created for day visitors. They're reached by taking the left fork in the road onto the Tops. The walks take you through antarctic beech forests, past waterfalls, and to fantastic vistas. If you're interested in a 22-kilometer walk that connects Gloucester Tops to Barrington Tops (and other trailheads), take the right fork in the road, which climbs onto the tablelands. This walk takes in the subalpine environment and Carey's Peak, the highest point in the park. If you'd like to swim in a temperate rain forest, include Big Hole in your walk. For details on walks, contact the National Parks and Wildlife Service, 22-24 Barke Street, Raymond Terrace, NSW 2324; phone 02-4987-3108 or 02-6558-1408. The easiest way to get literature about the area may be through the park service's Sydney office; phone 02-9585-6333.

*Caution:* Be aware that snow can occur at any time, with little warning. It's often warm, but the weather can turn ugly quickly. Be prepared.

*Adventuring Opportunities.* The Barrington Outdoor Adventure Centre rents canoes and bikes and can sign you up for horse rides; phone 02-4967-3427. Bush Tours, Barrington Road, Gloucester, NSW 2422, phone 065-58-2093, offers guided treks.

*Accommodations.* In the park the Gloucester River campground is a richly green and peaceful place. There are basic amenities and no fee is charged. I was the only person in the campground. Bushcamping is allowed, provided you follow park guidelines. The Barrington Guest House (phone 02-4995-3212), provides accommodation to those entering the Williams River area. Outside the park, Gloucester, Dungog, and Scone have accommodations.

*Access.* There's no public transit to the park. The Gloucester River campground is reached via Gloucester. The Williams River (Barrington Tops) area is reached via Dungog and Salisbury.

*Driving Caution.* There are six river crossings on the road from Gloucester to the Gloucester River campground. These crossings can become impassable during and after a rain.

## Warrumbungle National Park

Located in north-central New South Wales 500 kilometers from Sydney, Warrumbungle National Park consists of gorges, irregularly shaped spires, and richly vegetated areas. The park is unique for its striking volcanic outcrops and broad representation of plant and animal species. The area was busting out in greenery when I visited in May. There are several excellent walks, picnic areas, and developed camping areas. The park is known for its mixture of ecosystems; both the wet east coast and the dry western plains environments exist in a relatively small area. For detailed coverage of all aspects of the park, purchase *A Complete Guide to Warrumbungle National Park*, by Alan Fairley, or the *Warrumbungle National Park Guide Book;*

both are available at most park service visitors centers. For general information before you go, contact Ranger-in-Charge, Warrumbungle National Park Visitors Centre; phone 02-6825-4364.

The Warrumbungle Ranges are the products of volcanic activities 13 million years ago. The results are the magnificent formations you see today. The Breadknife, a stone wall nearly 100 meters high and a uniform 1 meter thick, is perhaps the most striking geological feature. The highest peak, Mount Exmouth, is 1,200 meters. Near its summit are groves of snow gums. Lower forests have white box, white gum, ironbark, heath, and wildflowers. The drought-resistant plants of the dry west are found in the northern sector, and trees and vegetation associated with the wet eastern woodlands of New England thrive on the southern slopes.

The area is rich in the plants and wildlife of both ecosystems. Gray, euro, and red kangaroos are common in their respective habitats. Grays and euros habituated to people should not be tempted with food in the campgrounds. They will make off with goodies and even enter an unguarded tent if they smell food. Koalas, red-necked wallabies, and swamp wallabies are also common. More than 180 species of birds occur in the park, including over a third of all the cockatoo and parrot species. Crimson rosellas, sulfur-crested cockatoos, and wedge-tailed eagles were common during my visit. Red-winged parrots, a relatively rare species, are well represented, as are Major Mitchell cockatoos. Turquoise parrots and superb parrots, both considered endangered, are sighted fairly regularly.

March, April, May, October, and November are usually the best months to visit the park in terms of weather. September and October are best for flowering plants, which include more than 25 species of wattles, wild irises, grevilleas, and bottlebrush.

There are many and varied walks in the park. Talk over what's available with a ranger. Seasonal considerations are sometimes important for seeing wildlife. The six-hour walk to the Breadknife is the most popular walk. It is often done in two days, with a night at a hikers' hut along the way. The Gold Circuit is a mini version of the main event, with vistas, vegetation zones, and an overall walk similar to the Breadknife walk. It can be completed in about two hours.

Rock climbing is also popular in the park, but it's not allowed on the Breadknife because the rock is fractured and too dangerous. Bluff Mountain is popular with technical climbers. Before hiking and climbing, you must get a permit from a ranger at Camp Blackman.

*Accommodations.* There are four (Blackman, Pinchman, Wambe-long, and Burbie) campgrounds with toilets, fire pits, and water. Pinchman has the best view, and Blackman the most complete ameni-ties. Cabin and hut accommodations are at Canyon Camp. There is a nominal fee for the use of these facilities that can be paid at the park office in the nearby town of Coonabarabran or at the visitors center in the park. For details on walks or tips in locating wildlife, speak to a ranger.

Coonabarabran is the nearest town, at 37 kilometers from the western entrance. Moderately priced accommodations can be found at the Warrumbungle Motel and the Wayfare Caravan Park. Rooms range from $A16 to $A25 a night.

*Access.* Warrumbungle is off the beaten track, which is why you should consider it. The park is considerably inland and 500 kilome-ters from Sydney. (Find Dubbo on a map and then look north.) The conventional route is via the Great Western Highway to Dubbo, then the Castlereagh Highway to Gilgandra, followed by the Oxley High-way to Coonabarabran and the park. The trip normally takes about seven hours from Sydney. An alternative route would include the towns of Muswellbrook, Binnaway, and Merriwa. This is a scenic drive featuring rolling grasslands, narrow but comfortable roads, and small towns with main streets that have old storefronts and large pub-hotels that seem frozen in time.

## New England

New England is the largest wet tablelands region in New South Wales and was the focus of the logging-versus-conservation battles in the 1960s that resulted in more parks. The region has spectacular forested national parks with lush vegetation, cascading waterfalls, plentiful wildlife, the Nymboida River (a white-water rafter's favorite), plus attractive small and scenic mountain towns.

### Armidale

New England is centered around the sizable university town of Armi-dale, which is located inland, roughly midway between Sydney (550 kilometers) and Brisbane (460 kilometers).

Armidale is nestled atop the Great Dividing Range and is sur-rounded by lush cattle properties and spectacular national parks.

Pubs, such as Rumors, have been serving beer here since 1857. The mix of old architecture, the university ambiance, and beautiful surroundings make this a delightful place to visit. To get started visit the Tourist Visitors Centre on Marsh Street; phone 02-6772-4655; E-mail: armvisit@northnet.com.au. The National Parks and Wildlife Service in Armidale has maps and brochures of all parks in the area; phone 02-6773-7211. The University of New England has a great deal of influence over the town, providing live theater, light-opera companies, drama schools, and craft-type businesses in town and on campus. The Howard Hinton Art Collection, in the College of Advanced Education, is thought to be among the most valuable art collections in Australia. The Aboriginal Cultural Centre and Keeping Place is nearby. The Folk Museum displays relics from early Australian history. The town also has spectacular churches and more than 35 National Trust buildings. There are more than 20 motels and hotels, caravan parks, and about a dozen farm-holiday accommodations listed with rates in the "Armidale Visitor's Guide." There's a 20-bed youth hostel at the Pembroke Caravan Park; phone 02-6772-6470. For all transportation bookings, contact Harvey World Travel, corner of Beardy and Dangar Streets, Armidale, NSW 2350; phone 02-6772-1177.

*A Good Place to Horse Around.* Horseback riding is popular because this is an ideal area for riding. Trails wind through wild areas with huge stands of timber, over lush green pastures, and along cascading creeks. Early-morning rides have the added bonus of birdsongs, such as that of the melodic bellbird. One-day and multiday rides are possible. The Blue Canyon Gorge is a favorite overnight ride. The Armidale area and the area around Mansfield, in the state of Victoria, are arguably the best trail-riding regions in Australia. If horseback riding strikes your fancy, try Wilderness Rides (phone 02-6778-4631) or Beambolong (phone 02-6771-2019).

## Dorrigo National Park

Encompassing a mere 7,819 hectares, Dorrigo is surprisingly pristine and rich. It's also the closest New England tablelands park to the coast. This makes it relatively convenient for travelers driving the Pacific Highway between Brisbane and Sydney. The park gets about 90 inches of rainfall annually, making it one of the wettest places in

New South Wales. The resulting subtropical rain forest is so thick it's impenetrable in areas. There's no camping in the park, but the Never Never picnic area, complete with a beautifully designed roofed enclosure for inclement weather, is an idyllic spot in a lush meadow surrounded by towering subtropical rain forest. There are 15 kilometers of walks in the area. The two I enjoyed most were the Casuarina Falls (4.8 kilometers round-trip) and Cedar Falls (6.4 kilometers round-trip). Casuarina Falls is on the Blackbutt Track and affords a fantastic view. The trails are well engineered, but the terrain is fairly steep. These walks start in the Never Never picnic area. At the base of Cedar Falls there are some very big hoop pines and a stand of immense red cedar. Orchids cover the lower area of this rain forest in October. There are yellow carrabeen trees (also known as stinger trees because of their nettles) measuring 14 meters in circumference here. Wallabies are common around the Never Never picnic area, and you're sure to see a variety of birds. Ranger Neville Fenton rated the 5.6-kilometer Wonga Walk that leaves from the Glade as a top walk for seeing the rain forest and wildlife. The walk actually passes behind a waterfall. I didn't see a person during my six-hour stay in the park. The nearby small town of Dorrigo is authentic and well off the beaten path. It has a beautiful old pub-hotel.

*Accommodations.* There are caravan parks in the area and motel and hotel accommodations in Dorrigo. Prices for rooms range from $A50 to $A75.

*Access.* The park is about 2 kilometers east of Dorrigo, which is about 40 kilometers inland from Bellingen. You can pick up information on the park at the visitors center at the park's entrance. The Never Never is at the end of Dome Road. The park is about 600 kilometers from Sydney. For information, visit the park's office in Dorrigo (phone 02-6657-2309), or write to Ranger, National Parks and Wildlife Service, P.O. Box 170, Dorrigo, NSW 2453. There is no public transport to the park, though you can take a bus to Dorrigo, which is only 2 kilometers from the park entrance.

## New England National Park

This is one of the oldest parks in northern New South Wales. It has an amazingly diverse plant community and is rich in wildlife. The park is nearly 30,000 hectares and includes the New England plateau, lowlands along the Bellingen River, and dramatic plunging escarpments. Volcanic action accounts for much of the topography. The rich soil and heavy rainfall combine to make many spectacular dense forested vistas. In the high areas you'll find snow gums and antarctic beeches. In the lower rain forests, tree ferns, staghorn ferns, and orchids are found in the understory while giants such as red cedar, booyang carrabeen, and satinay gums create a towering overstory. November and December are usually best for wildflowers.

The diverse habitats attract a wide range of wildlife. Euro and gray kangaroos and red-necked wallabies are common. Platypuses are often sighted in slow-moving streams, and goannas are usually easy to find in open areas. With a spotlight at night you should be able to find gliders and possums. There are more than 90 species of birds, including lyrebirds, wonga pigeons, sulfur-crested cockatoos, brush turkeys, lorikeets, currawongs, and rosellas.

There are several marked day walks. Banksia Point and Wrights Lookout have walks that drop off the escarpment and allow you to experience different habitats. The Lyrebird Nature Walk is popular. Point Lookout gets my vote for the best view in the park. There are walks ranging from one to eight hours to complete, many of them using existing fire trails. But the trails are steep and poorly engineered in many places. The park is often shrouded in mist, and heavy rains are not uncommon. Dress accordingly.

*Accommodations.* There's no-fee camping in the park at Little Styx River and Thungutti. For bushcamping, you must check with the ranger. Ebor (25 kilometers) is the nearest town for supplies. Dorrigo, Bellingen, and Armidale have the nearest hotel and motel accommodations.

*Access.* New England National Park is 80 kilometers east of Armidale and 580 kilometers north of Sydney. Head for Dorrigo via the Dorrigo Bellingen Road. From there the turnoff is 12 kilometers past Ebor. There is no public transport to the park. For more details on both Dorrigo and New England National Parks, write Ranger, National Parks and Wildlife Service, P.O. Box 170, Dorrigo, NSW 2453.

## Washpool and Gilbraltar Ranges National Parks

Washpool National Park features a rain forest of unsurpassed beauty. The park contains the largest coachwood forest in the world.

The walk along Coombadjha Creek is one of the prettiest I've experienced anywhere. The area literally explodes in greenery of hundreds of kinds of plants—mosses, ferns, palms, vines, and giant trees. It's a natural greenhouse of the highest order. This walk starts in the Coombadjha rest area. Between the Coombadjha and Bellbird rest areas there is an assortment of short walks. Around dusk the Coombadjha rest area springs to life as forest-dwelling wallabies and ground birds appear from their hiding places. The area is also the staging area for longer walks, which require planning, skill, and notification to the park service. These longer walks are typically up mist-shrouded wild river gorges enclosed in gum forests and subtropical rain forests. For information about longer walks, contact the Ranger, National Parks and Wildlife Service, 68 Church Street, Glen Innes, NSW 2370; phone 02-6732-5133.

Sharing Washpool National Park's southern border is Gilbraltar Ranges National Park, a more developed park known for its open eucalyptus forests, striking granite formations, and abundant wildlife. Compared to nearby Washpool, it has dramatically different habitats. It also has several worthwhile walks. Visitors often set up a car camp and spend two or three days walking the trails that start at Mulligan's hut. The 20-site campground has pit toilets and cold showers. The park is particularly interesting to birders, since more than 215 species have been sighted. Tiger quolls, parma wallabies, and rufous rat wallabies, all of them rare, make their home in the park.

*Accommodations.* Camping is allowed only in Gilbraltar Ranges, not Washpool. There are hotels and motels in Glen Innes and Grafton.

*Access.* There is no public transport. These parks are off the Gwydir Highway, 80 kilometers west of Grafton and the same distance northeast from Glen Innes. The roads in both parks can become treacherous during rains.

# The North Coast via the Pacific Highway

Between Sydney and the northern border town of Tweed Heads, there are several popular resort towns, parks (including Myall Lakes National Park, 236 kilometers north of Sydney, which has already been covered), and historic sites directly off the Pacific Highway. You'll travel 900 kilometers to the Queensland border.

*Port Macquarie.* Port Macquarie Nature Reserve, 72 kilometers north of Taree and 47 kilometers north of Crowdy Bay, is a must stop. The reserve has been set aside to protect a large population of koalas that live in this coastal city. The 12-hectare reserve has two unique features: a koala hospital for animals injured by cars and dogs and the beautifully restored Roto Historic House.

The Roto Historic House was built in 1890 and is a prime example of rural Australian colonial architecture. The structure has attractive verandas, a corrugated iron roof, spacious rooms, and high-quality craftsmanship throughout. It's been painstakingly restored as a museum and serves as the Discovery Tours Centre. The grounds around the grand old structure are well maintained and suitable for a picnic. There are nearby beaches, too.

The koala hospital is a testimony to both Australia's efforts to save a favorite animal and the sad fate that awaits koalas who find their forests inundated by cars and dogs. Besides the convalescing koalas, you'll see healthy ones in the trees overhead and be educated about this undeclared ambassador for Australian wildlife. The Port Macquarie Nature Reserve is off Kennedy Drive in Port Macquarie. For more details, contact Ranger, National Parks and Wildlife Service, 152 Horton Street, Port Macquarie, NSW 2444; phone 02-6584-2203.

*Hathead National Park.* This park is 21 kilometers northeast of Kempsey and could be named Falcon Park. While falcons are commonly seen, there are more than 200 kinds of birds, including swans, spoonbills, and egrets. I enjoyed the northern end of the park most between Smokey Cape and Trial Bay Gaol. Smokey Cape Lighthouse affords an excellent coastal view of the entire park.

*Coffs Harbour.* The town of Coffs Harbour, 580 kilometers north of Sydney and an hour's drive north of Kempsey, is known as the capital of the Banana, or Holiday, Coast. The area is popular for its warm temperature, excellent beaches, restaurants, and recreational offerings such as scuba diving, horseback riding, and canoeing. Virtually every basic need can be met in Coffs Harbour, except possibly solitude. For details on all aspects of Coffs Harbour, visit the Tourist Information Centre on Woolgoola Road and Rose Street; phone 02-6652-1522. Ask for the "Coffs Harbour and Region Tourist Guide." For a good meal, try Tahurah Thai Kitchen on High Street.

*Outdoor Activities in the Area.* In the last ten years Coffs Harbour has become a favorite place for outdoor enthusiasts. A myriad of passions can be fulfilled without traveling far in any one direction. Whale watching is possible off the jetty near Muttonbird Island. Offshore, the Solitary Islands have grown in stature as a diving spot. Both cold-water and tropical fish congregate here. The islands, which have many pocket beaches, were recently declared a marine park. The water is clearest in the cool winter months. There are several dive shops for renting equipment. PADI certification or the equivalent is required. Try the Pacific Blue Dive Center, 321 High Street; phone 02-6652-2759.

The Nymboida River is about an hour west of Coffs Harbour. This is one of the most popular rafting and kayaking rivers in Australia. It offers exhilaration and plenty of drops. The rapids are class 3, 4, and 5. The river should not be taken lightly. It has real dangers that should be considered before you sign on for a rafting trip. Try Rapid Rafting; phone 02-6652-1741. It costs about $A100 a day. You can also enroll in surfing school at Coopers Surf Centre, located where High Street and the jetty meet. Two hours of instruction run about $A25; phone 02-6652-1782. There are also numerous places to rent mountain bikes or take horse rides. For horses try Valery

Trails (phone 02-6653-4301); for mountain-bike rentals contact Mud, Sweat and Gears (phone 02-6653-4577).

*Yuraygir National Park.* This park, 660 kilometers north of Sydney and 25 kilometers from Grafton and Coffs Harbour, has isolated beaches, wetlands, and semitropical vegetation. For a coastal park it also has a fair amount of terrestrial wildlife. Red-necked wallabies, swamp wallabies, and gray kangaroos are common. Reptiles are numerous, including some very poisonous snakes. Sea eagles and ospreys are often seen soaring over the wetlands and along the coast. Jabiru storks, brolgas, swans, pelicans, and emus are also common. The park is at its best in the spring and summer, when the wildflowers attract the greatest number of birds.

*Grafton.* Grafton, 686 kilometers north of Sydney and 40 kilometers north of Yuraygir, is the prettiest "large" (17,000 residents) city on the Pacific Highway. Its alias is the "Garden City" because of its flame and jacaranda trees lining the wide streets. The trees are at their best in October. The town has a number of historic buildings, with the Schaeffer House on Fitzroy Street near Alice Street probably the most notable. It now doubles as a museum. The town is on the lovely Clarence River. Susan Island in the river is covered with rich rain forest. It's an excellent spot for birding, as is nearby Lake Hiawatha. Maclean Lookout has an excellent vantage point over the Clarence Valley. The town has 11 motels and hotels and several caravan parks.

*Byron Bay.* Byron Bay is a half-hour drive south of Tweed Heads, the last town in New South Wales for travelers headed north. Tweed Heads isn't too impressive (it's the start of the "famed" Gold Coast), but the region south and east to a distance of about 60 kilometers is. Byron Bay is the best-known resort in the area because of its high-quality surfing beaches and year-round good weather. It's the most eastern point in Australia, which partly explains the consistent surf. Surfboarding is the best-known activity, but the area is also tops for windsurfing, small cat boats, scuba diving, and nude volleyball, if that should appeal to you.

Byron Bay is a tropical enclave that has no counterpart until well above Brisbane and the tropic of Capricorn in northern Queensland.

It was a top banana-growing region. Typically the area is green, be it tropical rain forest or cleared pasture. Dominating the area is Mount Warning, a volcanic crater coated in greenery that gives the area a look akin to Fiji Island. The tiny towns in the lush mountain areas around Mount Warning were the scene of counterculture happenings similar to Woodstock during the 1960s and 1970s. You can still find crafts and artists from that era.

Watego Beach is probably the best-known beach at Byron Bay. It is a family beach that's also popular with windsurfers and surfers. There are less populated beaches south of Byron Bay. These beaches are unofficially clothing optional. Seven Mile Beach and Broken Head Nature Reserve are the standouts for natural beauty. Seven Mile is a long beach fringed with palms and tropical vegetation. Broken Head Nature Reserve is a section of tropical rain forest and beaches. The reserve is signposted at a car-park area. You must walk to the beaches, which are strips of white sand in idyllic tropical coves defined at both ends by rock outcrops. The best beach in the reserve is Kings Beach, which requires a walk through a palm forest to reach it.

For details on accommodations, travel, boat and windsurfer rentals, scuba instruction, hiking on Mount Warning, and so on in the Byron Bay area, visit the Tourist Information Centre on Johnson Street; phone 02-6685-8050.

# Lord Howe Island

Alasdair McGregor, one of Australia's leading nature painters and the co-author of the excellent book *Australia's Wild Islands* (Hodge and Stoughton, 1997), told me that Lord Howe Island was among the most unique and beautiful places he had ever visited. Alasdair ought to know: he's visited many of Australia's remotest islands and traveled clear around Australia. "Lord Howe Island is a stunning environment, spectacular, dramatic, with challenging activities, unique creatures, and a commitment by the locals to preserve it, which is reassuring," explains Alasdair. When I suggested to Alasdair that I was considering Lord Howe for inclusion in my top 20 natural places for *Adventuring in Australia* he endorsed the idea. "For sure, it's a wonderful place. Much of it is accessible to people in wheelchairs, and there are plenty of opportunities for the person who wants a physical challenge. The only common thread needed is a keen appreciation for nature. The quality, uniqueness, and diversity of the experience would be hard to beat. There is only one Lord Howe Island and it should be at the top of any list."

Lord Howe Island is a World Heritage Area located 700 kilometers off the New South Wales coast about halfway to New Caledonia. If you sight it while on final approach from the air, it will look dramatic, jutting sharply out of an endless expanse of the Tasman Sea. Formed seven million ago, it is a narrow island, with beaches, cliffs, and rugged topography along its 11-kilometer length. Being isolated for such a great expanse of time has allowed Lord Howe to develop its own life-forms and remain pristine looking, despite some periods of misuse by whalers and out-of-control feral animals.

The summits of Mount Gower (875 meters) and Lidgbird (770 meters) are often shrouded in clouds, while many of the island's slopes are covered in rare palms, four of them endemic to Lord Howe. The island is coated in both tropical and subtropical greenery. According to McGregor, of the 219 species of vascular plants found on Lord Howe, 74 of them are endemic and many of the plant communities are dominated by natives. Near the summits of Mounts Gower and Lidgbird are literally tangles of mosses, ferns, and palms found nowhere else. Two of the palm species are the only living members of their entire genera. The most common plant you'll see is the howea (kentia palm). Locals capitalize on it by exporting three million seeds a year. The howea is a popular indoor palm in temperate places around the world. Scientists, particularly ornithologists, view the island as a timeless place where the underlying principles of evolution are as readily apparent as on the Galápagos—only Lord Howe is much more attractive.

The peaks and surrounding cliffs are home to hundreds of thousands of seabirds. The peaks are the only known nesting sites of the Providence petrel and the Lord Howe Island wood hen. The Lord Howe Island wood hen came within 30 birds of extinction before it was brought back from the abyss through the valiant efforts of scientists and islanders.

In addition to the land, the marine environment here is spectacular, starting with the pristine beaches and shallow reef system on one side of the island. Lord Howe possesses the most southerly coral reef in Australian waters. Because of warming currents that consistently push by the island, corals thrive here, 1,000 kilometers south of the Great Barrier Reef. Nearly 90 species of hard and soft corals have been identified, which is considerably less variety than on the reef. However, the variety in fish is astounding. Lord Howe's waters are home to both tropical and temperate-water fish species. The island sits at the confluence of two immense and different underwater worlds. The visibility under the surface is usually phenomenal, and there are no deadly box jellyfish and other coastal "nasties" to fret about. More than 500 fish species have been recorded, including ten endemics. Both diving and snorkeling are spectacular.

*Accommodations.* Accommodations must be booked before arrival. There are approximately 15 family-run overnights, ranging from modest bungalows to bed-and-breakfasts. At the top end is Capella Lodge, with a restaurant that has a view of Mounts Gower and Lidgbird; phone 02-9290-1922; E-mail: www.wine.com.au/capella.htm. Trader Nick's Hideaway is a little less costly; phone 13-0078-8708 or 13-27-47.

*Access.* Both Eastern Australia Airlines and Sunstate Airlines have scheduled flights from Brisbane and Sydney. People often visit the island on package holidays that include accommodations with two or three nights' stay plus airfare. Some of the packages, which include diving or snorkeling, are cheaper than a "straight" to-and-from ticket. Over and back is usually around $A580, but some package tours will match this price and still include lodgings. For package tours try Qantas, phone 13-13-13. The most popular transportation on the island is the bicycle. Try Wilson's Hire Service; phone 02-6563-2045. Wilson's also rents snorkeling gear and other water equipment for low prices. Several businesses cater to divers, snorkelers, and sea kayakers. For sea kayaking try Jack Shick; phone 02-6563-2218. For dive trips, contact ProDive Travel; phone 800-806-820 (toll-free in Australia) or 02-9232-5733. Birders should contact Campbell Wilson, phone/fax 02-6563-2045. He and his wife, Michelle, lead birding walks.

# PART III

# Queensland

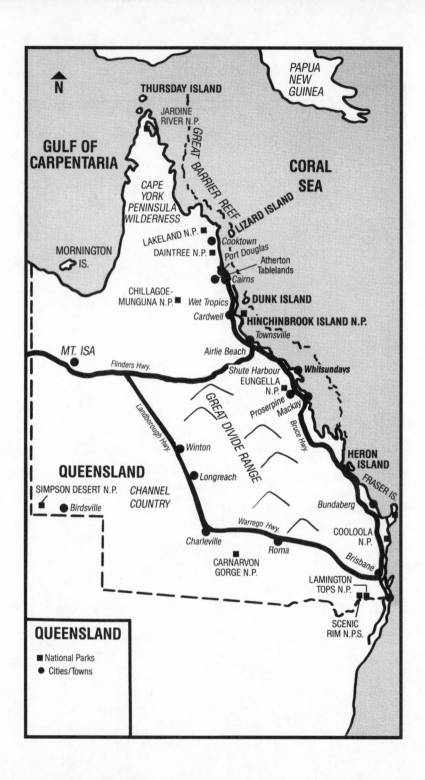

# Overview

Queensland is the most successful state in Australia in promoting tourism. It's not hard to figure out why: Queensland's twice the size of Texas, takes up nearly one-quarter of the continent, and possesses more natural treasures than any other state. The state's high-powered tourist industry is aimed at the luxury traveler, but it's also well organized for the thrifty traveler.

## Weather

Over half of Queensland is in the tropics. In the northern portion of the state, monsoons arrive in the Australian summer and autumn—usually for two months between November and April. Winter and spring, between May and December, are usually dry. The two seasons are thus called the wet and the dry. In remote areas, roads are sometimes impassable during the wet. Temperatures on the coast range from 75°F to 95°F and are usually influenced by cooling sea breezes. The highest temperatures are usually in November. In the interior, temperatures soar to 120°F during hot spells, but most of the year it is warm and comfortable.

## Natural Attractions

Queensland's natural attractions start offshore with the Great Barrier Reef, which is sometimes billed as the largest living thing on earth. It stretches for 2,000 kilometers along the Queensland coast. Dozens of emerald-green tropical islands punctuate the reef's sweep along the coast. Underwater are 1,400 kinds of tropical fish swimming amid hundreds of kinds of corals.

South of the reef's southern terminus and not far from Brisbane is Fraser Island, a cigar-shaped 120-kilometer sand island with perched lakes, crystal clear streams, stunning rain forests, and plenty of wildlife.

Midway on your journey up the coast is Shute Harbour. This is the stepping-off place to the Whitsunday Islands—which have everything from opulent resorts to idyllic uninhabited islands where you can act out your marooned-on-an-island fantasy.

Farther north lie the tropical Magnetic, Bedarra, Orpheus, Dunk, Goold, and Hinchinbrook Islands. Australians claim that Hinchinbrook Island is the largest island national park in the world. Most of it is covered with pristine rain forest.

The Great Barrier Reef and the islands are the main draw, which takes the focus away from mainland destinations that are stunning in their own right. A long day's drive from Brisbane gets you to Carnarvon Gorge, which could pass for Sir Arthur Conan Doyle's *Lost World*. The gorge has excellent walks to primitive palms, giant ferns, grottos, mazelike side gorges, naturally occurring vertical-walled amphitheaters, and mysterious Aboriginal art sites.

South of Brisbane is Lamington Tops National Park, with dozens of walking tracks in the largest area of subtropical rain forest in Queensland. Lamington is the crowning glory of the scenic rim parks that occupy the highlands.

Then there are the wet tropics, which are such a popular destination that the relatively small town of Cairns has its own international airport. Throughout the wet tropics rich mangroves and palm-lined beaches make up the coastline. Rivers cascading through this huge natural greenhouse provide excellent white-water rafting. And offshore there are always some more coral cays, emerald-green islands, and new sections of the reef to explore.

The wildlife is no less impressive. Flightless cassowaries make a trucklike rumbling noise as they scratch and strut through the rain forest. In the branches overhead you can find tree-dwelling kangaroos nibbling fruit and tender leaves. Platypuses are plentiful in many of the quieter watercourses. Ferocious saltwater crocodiles wait and watch in some of the tidal rivers. Inland, freshwater crocs bask away their days. Throughout the area there are over 250 species of birds.

The Cape York Peninsula, which is separated from New Guinea by the Torres Strait, lies above Cairns. The peninsula is a true wilderness where you can test your mettle against the harshness of a land that has kept a pristine quality because of its natural barriers to exploitation. Travel comes to a stop in the wet when the few dirt tracks turn to quagmires or rivers. Laura, in the heart of Quinkan Country, has the greatest amount of accessible postcontact Aboriginal art.

Behind the coastal strip, which is the focus of this section, lies the Great Dividing Range, which peters out in a few areas on its northern run up the backbone of Queensland. Behind the Great Dividing Range is Outback Queensland, which includes vast deserts, arid-land cattle stations, and one-pub towns. In the north lies the wild gulf savannah country.

## Information Sources

There are numerous places to collect information for travel and sights throughout Queensland. The Queensland Tourism and Travel Corporation, which heads up this effort, is well run and efficient. The bright red lettering of the tourist centers is unmistakeable in major cities throughout Queensland. In these offices you can usually find information on all aspects of travel and tourism, with special focus on regional offerings. The head office in Queensland is located at Level 36, Riverside Centre, 123 Eagle Street (G.P.O. Box 328), Brisbane, QLD 4001; phone 61-7-3406-5400 or fax 61-7-3406-5479. You can get detailed information on travel, accommodations, eateries, tours, etc. See "Regional Tourist Travel Sources" on page 153 for specific regions.

Besides throughout the state, Queensland Tourism and Travel Corporation has information-disseminating offices in seven foreign countries. Anyone living in North, Central, or South America can contact it at Avenue of the Americas, Northrop Plaza, Suite 330, 1800 Century Park East, Los Angeles, CA 90067, USA; phone 1-310-788-0997; fax 1-310-788-0128; E-mail: qttclosangeles@qttc.com.au.

There are more than 110 national parks in Queensland. Most parks can be contacted directly. However, working through the main office in Brisbane or through regional offices is the most efficient way to operate. For the main office, visit Queensland National Parks, Ground Floor, 160 Ann Street, Brisbane, Qld 4000, or write or call P.O. Box 155, Brisbane, Albert Street, Qld 4002; phone 61-7-3227-8197; fax 61-7-3227-8186; E-mail: nqic@env.qld.gov.au.

# Brisbane

Brisbane, the capital of Queensland, got its start as a penal settlement in 1824. Today it's a large modern city and the starting point for most air travelers visiting the state (Cairns and Townsville also have international airports). Situated on the Brisbane River near Moreton Bay in the southeast corner of the state, this city of 1.4 million people—half of the state's population—sprawls over low-lying hills in a subtropical setting. Much of the outlying residential area has the feeling of being in the country when it's actually a suburb. The city center is a clean-looking conglomeration of skyscrapers. The city has about 18 kilometers of river frontage and a wide range of parks, gardens, and sanctuaries in the city or on its outskirts. I've always liked driving into Brisbane from the south at night. The final leg across the Brisbane River is attractive, with floodlights shining on the river and modernistic bridges. Brisbane International Airport is about $A20 and 20 minutes away by cab from the city center. I often use city tours to get the feel of a city and note places I'll visit later. The City Sights tour stops at 20 points of interest; phone 13-12-30. For details on all aspects of Brisbane, contact Brisbane Tourism, Ground Floor, King George Square, P.O. Box 12260, Elizabeth Street, Brisbane, Qld 4002. For ferries and water travel contact the *Kookaburra Queen* (phone 07-3221-1300) or the *Stradbroke Flyer* (phone 07-3286-2666). The *Flyer* runs regularly to North Stradbroke Island.

The city is relatively tame by world standards. However, it has more than 500 restaurants, and top-flight entertainment is booked here constantly. Queen Street Mall in the center of the city and Paddington Circle are the concentrated shopping and entertainment areas that can take care of most of your needs. Queen Street is good for both souvenir and serious shopping. There are some excellent bookshops. The historic Paddington shops are housed in first-rate, classic Queensland architecture. Fortitude Valley is the stronghold for eateries. The Queensland Cultural Centre (phone 07-3840-7190) on Stanley Street is a modernistic structure that houses the Queensland Art Gallery and the Queensland Museum and Performing Arts Complex, South Bank, South Brisbane. There are guided tours; phone 3840-7303.

The Sciencentre, 110 George Street (phone 3220-0166), has more than 150 interactive exhibits designed for children and adults.

There are several restored historic homes that are worth visiting. Constructed in 1846, the Newstead House is Brisbane's oldest house. It's located on Breakfast Creek Road; phone 07-3216-1846. The hours are Monday through Friday, 10:00 A.M. to 4:00 P.M.; Sunday, 2:00 to 5:00 P.M. A more complete look at the past is Earlystreet Historical Village, located at 75 McIlwraith Avenue, Norman Park; phone 07-3398-6866. A general store, "slab hut," small pub, and an outstanding colonial home are on a two-hectare heavily vegetated site. Hours are Monday through Friday, 10:00 A.M. to 4:30 P.M.; Saturday and Sunday, 11:00 A.M. to 4:00 P.M.

## Regional Tourist Travel Sources

*General.* Regional tourist associations can be reached by phoning: Bundaberg, 61-7-4152-2333; Cairns and northern Queensland, 61-7-4051-3588; Mackay, 079-52-2677; north Queensland and Townsville, 077-71-2724; northwest Queensland and Mount Isa, 61-7-4952-2677; Outback Queensland, 61-7-4657-4255; Sunshine Coast, 071-436-6400; and Whitsunday, 61-7-4946-6673; E-mail: wvcb@130.aone.net.au.

*Bus.* Buses run regularly from Brisbane to points throughout the state; there are also daily runs to Sydney and Darwin (a really long haul). McCafferty's (phone 13-14-99) and Premier Motor Services (phone 1-300-368-100) leave several times daily for Sydney.

*Airlines.* Australian Air is at 247 Adelaide Street; phone 07-22-3333. Qantas is at 241 Adelaide Street; phone 07-234-3747.

*Automobile.* The Royal Automobile Club of Queensland (RACQ), like AAA in the United States, has road maps. It's located at 261 Queen Street, Brisbane, Qld 4000; phone 61-7-3361-2398. Ask about reciprocal membership privileges at your local auto club.

*Coach Service.* McCafferty's; phone 13-14-99. Greyhound is at 96 Victoria Street; phone 13-20-30.

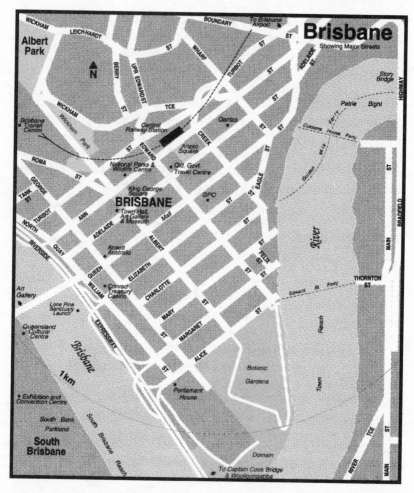

*Rail Service.* Queensland's Rail; phone 13-22-32. For details on long-distance fares and schedules to Cairns, contact the Great South Pacific Express; phone 1-800-677-777. To Sydney, try Country Link; phone 13-22-32.

## The Outer Brisbane Area

Within an hour or two's journey there is a great deal to do around Brisbane. Perhaps the most popular stop is the Lone Pine Koala Sanctuary on Jesmond Road, Fig Tree Pocket, phone 3378-1366. This is Australia's largest koala sanctuary. It's on the Brisbane River, about ten kilometers from the city's center. Access can be by road or river. Though this is a cheery place with plenty of cuddly koalas peering at you, not all is well with the koala. As koala expert Dr. Frank Carrick explains, "Australia's treatment of koalas is paradoxical. Koalas are probably the most exploited of all Australian fauna. Everybody cashes in on their good looks, but there is little serious funding to help understand the very major problems facing koalas and causing their low reproductive rate." The sanctuary is open daily 7:30 A.M. to 4:45 P.M. except Christmas day. Adults $A12.50; children $A6. The best way to get to Lone Pine is to take the Mirimar Cruise up the Brisbane River, which is $A16 round-trip for adults and $A9 for kids.

## Parks and Natural Places in and near Brisbane

In and around Brisbane are numerous smallish national parks and natural areas set aside for their unique natural or historic features. Here is what you can expect to find and how to get to them.

*D'Aguilar National Park.* D'Aguilar National Park, also known as Brisbane Forest Park, is about 30 minutes from central Brisbane. The park is in the D'Aguilar Range behind Brisbane and features rain forest, open forest, and panoramic views. There is a well-done freshwater life display at Walkabout Creek Wildlife Centre. Activities include picnicking, camping, short walks, and bird-watching. There are toilets, running water, and wheelchair access to some areas. There is a nominal fee. To get there travel along Waterworks Road to the Gap and onto the signposted visitors center.

*Glass House Mountains National Park.* Glass House is dominated by unique volcanic plugs that are frequented by experienced rock climbers. Crookneck, Tibrogargan, and Beerwah are the most challenging plugs. The park services emphasizes they should be attempted only by experienced climbers. There are also scenic picnic spots and a trail system for short hikes. There is wheelchair access to some of the trails. There is a privately operated campground on Glass House Mountains Road. To get there from Brisbane, take the Bruce Highway north; about ten kilometers past Caboolture, split off, taking Glass House Mountains Road toward Beerwah or Beerburrum.

Lamington National Park, numerous other national parks, and the Gold Coast are only an hour or two away. (They are covered in detail in separate sections.)

In the city's outskirts there are several possibilities. The Australian Woolshed, 148 Samford Road, Ferny Hills, is popular; phone 3351-5366. This is a sheepshearing and sheepdog-working demonstration set up for tourists. Sure, it's not the real thing, but these are real sheepdogs and sheep who don't know the setting isn't the Outback. There are also some koalas, kangaroos, and wallabies on display.

Venman Bushland National Park, located on the southern edge of Brisbane, is an often missed natural area worth visiting. This park is made up of open eucalypt forest and bushlands that were typical of what is now Brisbane. There are koalas in the park, and the region is considered an important koala habitat. Unfortunately, like much koala habitat, it happens to be the same habitat preferred by people. This park is a quiet place and a good spot for a picnic, bird-watching, and koala spotting. Overnight camping isn't permitted, but there are toilets, walking trails, and wheelchair access to some parts of the park. There is also running water. To get there take the Pacific Highway south until you come to the exit for West Mount Cotton Road, which will take you to the park.

## The Islands near Brisbane

Moreton Bay is downstream about 30 kilometers from Brisbane. There are many islands in this large bay. The largest ones are Moreton, Birbie, and North Stradbroke.

These islands typically have sandhills; spacious, glistening, white-sanded, still-water beaches; good snorkeling areas; wildflowers; and permanent habitations. They're heavily used by Brisbaners and have accommodations ranging from camping to caravan camping to resort stays.

## Restaurants

There is no shortage of eateries of all descriptions and cuisines. Most of them have wheelchair access, but always call in advance if this is a concern. If you're staying in Brisbane longer than a few days, get a copy of the *Brisbane News Eating Out Guide*. This free publication offers a detailed summary of Brisbane's restaurants.

For good-quality Mexican food, try Tortilla, 26 Elizabeth Arcade. Full-course meals for around $A20; phone 07-3221-4416. La Kashah, 669 Stanely Street, Woollongabba, serves Moroccan, Algerian, Tunisian, and French cuisines. Curtains divide one dining group from another. On weekends there is a belly dancer. The average meal price is $A17; phone 07-3391-7439. The Customs House Brasserie, 339 Queen Street, is in a beautiful old-heritage building with a river view. The cuisine varies, with a strong representation of Australian dishes. Full meals start at around $A30; phone 07-3365-8999. Ecco, at the corner of Adelaide and Boundary Streets, has a friendly atmosphere with vegetarian dishes and super salads. Meals start at around $A30; phone 07-3831-8344. The Rasa Sayang has over 70 Malaysian dishes to pick from, with dining in a relaxed river setting. Meals are cheap, averaging about $A13; phone 07-3870-9222. Romeo's Italian Restaurant, 216 Petrie Terrace, is nicely decorated in a Tuscan style with faded yellow plaster walls and linen tablecloths. There is both sidewalk and indoor seating. Average meals go for $A22.50; phone 07-3367-0955. Oxley's on the River, Coronation Drive, Milton, has glass walls and a terrific river view. The menu is all about seafood: octopus, prawns, "bugs," poached salmon, and fruit salads. An average meal goes for about $A22.50; phone 07-3368-1866. Emperor's Palace, 31B Duncan Street, Fortitude Valley, is a long-standing Chinese restaurant that makes the most of prawns and lobster in its menu. Meals average $A13; phone 07-3252-3368. Ridge Rooftop Restaurant, 189 Leichardt Street, Spring Hill, is a unique experience perched on the ninth floor of the Ridge Central Hotel. There is an abundance of glass, allowing sweeping views of Brisbane, nightly dancing, and live entertainment on weekends. Special dishes include barramundi and prawns. The average meal is $A19; phone 07-3831-5000.

## Accommodations

There is plenty to pick from, but for the disabled traveler Brisbane may be more challenging than other Australian cities.

*Expensive.* The Heritage, on the corner of Edward and Alice Streets, is a top-flight hotel with a great city location. Next door are the city's botanic gardens. There are stunning river views from each room, and a wonderful Japanese restaurant. Rooms start at $A350, and there are rooms for the disabled; phone 07-3221-1999. The Sheraton Brisbane Hotel and Towers, 249 Turbot Street, is another top-of-the-line establishment. There are rooms for the disabled. Rooms start at

$A250; phone 07-3835-4960. The Mercure Hotel, 85 North Street, may be the best deal for the best price. There are river views comparable to those at the Heritage, only at almost half the price. Museums and theaters are close by. No special rooms for the disabled. Rooms start at $A200; phone 07-3236-3300.

*Moderate.* The Brisbane City Travelodge, 200 Alice Street, is in the heart of the city and near good eats. Rooms start at $A150; no specially modified rooms for the disabled; phone 07-3238-2222. The Quay West Brisbane, 132 Alice Street, is a good deal for its price. It features suites rather than rooms and has views of the Brisbane River and botanical gardens. No specially designed rooms for the disabled. Rooms start at around $A150; phone 07-3853-6000.

*Inexpensive.* Hotel George Williams, 317-325 George Street, is an amazingly attractive place for the price and the fact that it is a YMCA. Originally a bank, it now has an Art Deco interior with shiny wood and ornamental lighting. It's a tasteful place that feels like someone's home. No special rooms for the disabled. Rooms start at $A85; phone 07-3308-0700. The Embassy, at the corner of Elizabeth and Edward Streets, is an ancient and attractive old structure, inexpensive, clean, and central. No special rooms for the disabled. Rooms start at around $A80; phone 07-3221-7616.

## Shopping, the Arts, and Nightlife
### Shopping

Brisbane is amazingly cosmopolitan, considering its past bouts with archaic and arcane political leaders. Most of the large shopping complexes stay open until 9:00 P.M. The Myer Centre and the Broadway on the Mall are in and around the Queen Street Mall. There are more than 250 shops and numerous restaurants. Many of the large stores have multilingual cashiers. The restored nineteenth-century Brisbane Arcade is uplifting to walk through. The building's striking interior can't help but stimulate shopping.

Shoppers who want to explore and step out of the mainstream should head for Fortitude Valley and Chinatown. You'll find a wide assortment of Asian delicacies, interesting kitchenware, and herbal medicines. On 68 Queen Street you can visit Quilpie Opals, and on Eagle Street there is Aboriginal Creations, with a wide assortment of art. On the weekends Eagle Street comes alive with artisans of all stripes and mediums. Besides opals and Aboriginal art, the other uniquely Australian products are Akubra hats, oilskin jackets, and Australian wines. For a wide selection of jewelry (in particular, opals) and the best in Australian fashion, head for Wintergarden in the Queen Street Mall. Opals are tax-free to foreign visitors.

## Arts

Queensland isn't as rich in museums as Sydney, but what it has is worth a visit and most of it is found in the same complex. The Queensland Culture Centre, located on the south side of the Victoria Bridge, is the epicenter for artistic expression. The state's art collection dates to the late 1880s, though the center has been in operation only since 1985. The art is very good quality and includes the work of top Australian artists, both white and Aboriginal. European artists are also well represented. Russell Drysdale's paintings of the harsh conditions in the Outback are moving, and Picasso's nudes are inviting. The Queensland Museum is located in the same complex. If you have a fascination with dinosaurs and megafauna, head here. The "Riversleigh dig" in northern Queensland has yielded numerous previously unknown species. You'll see replicas of the large animals that went extinct in the last 20,000 years. Just imagine: there was a time when wombats as big as a rhinoceros munched their way through the forests of coastal Queensland; phone 07-3840-7555. The Queensland Performing Arts Centre is in the complex too, as well as a concert hall and two live theaters. Depending on the night, you can see everything from large-scale musical extravaganzas to avant-garde improvisations; phone 1-800-777-699. There is a restaurant in the complex, but for peaceful and unique surroundings take a bag lunch and a fountain drink to Sculpture Courtyard.

Several museums and art displays outside of the center deserve mention. Queensland Aboriginal Creations Shop, 199 Elizabeth Street, has a wide range of Aboriginal paintings, carvings, and sculptures; phone 07-3224-5730. For a full range of small galleries, contact the Queensland Office of Arts and Cultural Development; phone 07-3224-4248. Ask where you can pick up a copy of *Brisbane's Inner-City Galleries*.

## Nightlife

Brisbane has an active nightlife endorsed by the city government. The Night Rider bus service connects outlying nightclub areas with the downtown casinos; phone 13-12-30. The opulent and gaudy Conrad International Treasury Casino, on Queen Street, always has busy gaming tables.

Australians like jazz, and Brisbane is no exception. The Bass Note and the Brisbane City Travel Lodge on Elizabeth Street are known for their great jazz musicians. International and Australian touring bands usually perform at the Boondall Entertainment Centre and the ANZ stadium.

Caxton Street has more than its share of dance clubs. Caxton Hotel is popular. If you're a latent teenybopper, you might like the neon and three floors of dancing at Jackass Ginger's. It's about being seen and crowding together—and dancing. For full-fledged adults with some gray around the temples, try Hotel L.A. The gay and lesbian scene is concentrated in Fortitude Valley; popular clubs are Cockatoo and the Tube.

# Queensland's Scenic Rim Parks

Between 100 and 150 kilometers south of Brisbane there are a number of parks that are considered to be part of a scenic rim. The series of mountain parks mostly in the McPherson Range extends from the Gold Coast westward along the New South Wales border and then arcs northwest 80 kilometers to Mount Mistake. Lamington National Park, with the Binna Burra Mountain Resort, is the jewel of these parks.

Other parks on the scenic rim include Main Range, Springbrook, Mount Barney, and, another 150 kilometers beyond the rim to the southwest, Girraween National Park, entirely unlike all the others. I was able to visit Lamington and Girraween and was impressed with both.

## Lamington National Park

Lamington National Park, in the McPherson Range, sits in the south-east corner of Queensland 100 kilometers south of Brisbane. It is a 20,000-hectare ridge-top park located 1,000 meters above sea level on a velvet green plunging escarpment. If you are reminded of a South Seas island, it's because the area was created by erosion that exposed volcanic dikes and plugs that are now covered with plant life. The park is known for its many waterfalls.

Any description of Lamington must include the Binna Burra Mountain Lodge (see "Accommodations," below), which is better known than the park itself. This is somewhat ironic, because Binna Burra is a private enterprise within the park. Founded in 1933, the lodge is owned by leading conservationists. It provides activities ranging from abseiling to guided nature walks and talks on topics that include everything from visiting glowworm caves to orchids and other wildflowers, nesting birds, rain forest trees, and the wildlife found in the area.

With 160 kilometers of well-maintained and signposted walking trails, Lamington National Park is the premier hiker's park in Queensland. The trails pass by spectacular waterfalls, meander through tropical rain forests and sclerophyll forests, pause at lookouts with expansive panoramas, and wander into an assortment of cave systems.

The forests make up the most significant rain forest in southern Queensland. Lamington and adjoining Border Ranges National Park of New South Wales together preserve 60,000 hectares of rain forest from a wetter period in Australia's prehistoric past. You'll see heavily buttressed trees like the mararie, huge Moreton Bay figs, palms, vines, and tree ferns. In other parts of the park you'll see an ancient remnant forest of the rare antarctic beech and hoop pines.

There's no shortage of wildlife at Binna Burra or around the park's kiosk and picnic area and many trails. Brush turkeys, rainbow lorikeets, Albert's lyrebirds, brush-tailed possums, and red-necked pademelons seem to be more evident here than in other parks. Koalas are also easy to find in several areas. During the warmer months you'll see goannas and carpet pythons. Both are nonvenomous and harmless, if you don't try to pick them up. And don't be surprised if you are awakened by a dingo serenade at night.

The brush turkey is a chicken-sized black bird with a yellow collar and shiny red bald head. The female lays her eggs in a nest of fermenting plant matter that incubates the eggs. When the chicks hatch and dig themselves out, they're on their own. In January or February you may see the amazing little chicks as well as the mature birds, which are plentiful year-round.

Rainbow lorikeets with orange chests, purple heads, and green backs are also common in the park and are approachable where they've been fed often by people.

Lamington National Park is one of the few places where Albert's lyrebirds are found. In winter (July) they sing their tunes of imitation for up to four hours and do a peacocklike shuffle with their fantail. Your best chance of finding these amazing birds is along the Border Track around the Joalah Lookout and Mount Hobwee.

On many of the trails that break into open areas you'll come across small macropods with reddish shoulders. These are red-necked pademelons. Like all pademelons they're a forest-dwelling macropod with an affinity for secret runs through seemingly impenetrable vegetation. If you move slowly, they'll stay put for photographs.

## Walks

Obtain the "Binna Burra Track Map" at the resort or kiosk for details on every walk in the park. Here are a few of the offerings.

The Rainforest Loop, which starts directly past the grassy area near the kiosk, is probably best for getting a feel for the place. This self-guided walk is keyed to explanatory handouts you can pick up at the kiosk or at the Binna Burra Mountain Resort. The track starts on the Border Track and is only 1.2 kilometers. Along the way you'll see pademelons and brush turkeys and get a feel for the complexities and special survival strategies of plants in this highland ecosystem.

The Gwongoorool Track, also known as the Swimming Pool Track, starts at the ranger station parking area (1.8 kilometers below Binna Burra on the only access road) and descends through rain forest and gum groves to Gwongoorool Pool on the Coomera River. Look for koalas in the trees at the start of this walk. The eels in the pool are tame, harmless, and used to people. The water is refreshing. If it's hot, expect company. The round-trip is six kilometers.

The Bellbird Lookout Circuit is the shortest walk for the greatest view. The track starts at the Lower Ballanjui Falls Trail (across from the driveway to Binna Burra Mountain Lodge) and travels through immense stands of tallowwood gums to a spectacular lookout that includes prominent and plummeting formations and the Nerang River Valley.

The Cave Track starts at the ranger station parking area. The walk cuts through a huge mixed-gum forest and along the edge of a vertical escarpment that gives you an eagle's-eye view of the forest below. The trail drops to a series of interesting white sandstone cliffs (*Talangai* in local Aboriginal dialect). Eventually the walk delivers you back to Binna Burra Mountain Resort. I enjoyed this walk a great deal.

The Border Track is 21 kilometers one way and is the chief arterial for a broad range of walks. It connects Binna Burra to O'Reilly's, a lodge in the Green Mountains. The Border Track starts on the uphill side of the grass area near the kiosk. In September and October try the fork to Dave's Creek Track for wildflowers, which include many of the park's 60-plus varieties of orchids. About two kilometers from the start of the Border Track, the Tullawallal Loop branches off to an isolated antarctic beech forest. At least a half dozen circuit walks intersect the Border Track.

The Ship's Stern Track begins opposite the Binna Burra Mountain Resort. This is a 19-kilometer circuit that drops to Nixons Creek and cuts through sclerophyll and rain forests that include red cedars and piccabeen palms. Birds along this track may include king parrots and rosellas. The Ballanjui Falls Track branches off the Ship's Stern Track and is highly recommended by Ranger Bill Flenady: "There's a drop through a series of vegetation zones to the base of 150-meter Ballanjui Falls. The base of the falls is surrounded by a cathedral of buttressed trees. It's enchanting."

*Accommodations.* Binna Burra Mountain Lodge is a class establishment: rustic, well maintained, and nestled into its environment with the minimum of notice. The cottages often have spectacular views. There is a two-night minimum, and accommodation is mostly in cabins that range from self-contained to shared. Rates are $A250 to $A335 for doubles and $A130 for additional persons per night. Longer stays and group rates are lower. Contact Binna Burra Mountain Lodge, Beechmont via Canungra, Queensland 4211, Australia; phone 1-800-074-260 in Australia or 07-5533-3622. Fax: 07-5533-3658. Ask for a list of their daily outdoor activities. Binna Burra also has a campground. Camping costs $A8 per night, and it is suggested you make reservations as far in advance as possible. For camping reservations, phone 07-5533-3536.

Also located in the McPherson Range is O'Reilly's Guest House in the Green Mountains, the sister destination to Binna Burra, and the starting place for most of the trails in Lamington National Park. O'Reilly's Guest House, which operates cabins and kiosks, can be reached by hiking the 21-kilometer Border Track or it can be reached by car via a different road system than the one to Binna Burra. O'Reilly's is an "old" getaway destination dating back to the 1930s and its custodians have made it a hub for a trail system, too. It is a wonderful place to picnic and interact with semitame colorful bird life. Short walks like the 5-kilometer Python Track are level and well maintained enough for wheelchairs and strollers. Longer walks include the Blue Pool (10 kilometers round-trip) and Albert River Circuit (21 kilometers round-trip). Wildlife is plentiful, particularly crimson rosellas and rainbow lorikeets. More than 150 species of birds have been sighted around O'Reilly's, and they are encouraged to come close to guests with offerings of food. The only drawback to visiting O'Reilly's is that booking at least 60 days in advance is recommended, and the road is a little hard on those prone to carsickness. O'Reilly's has 50 units and a setting equal to Binna Burra's. Rooms range from $A140 for singles to $A220 for doubles. You can also buy a meal package; phone 1-800-688-722 in Australia or 07-5544-0644.

For information about camping in the park and for camping permits, contact Ranger, Binna Burra via Nerang, Queensland 4211. Campsites at Lamington National Park include both bush (hike-in) and car campsites. The charge for a campsite in the national parks throughout Queensland is $A3.50 per night. There are toilets, showers, and running water. Phone 07-5544-0634 (Green Mountains) or 07-5533-3584 (Binna Burra) to make reservations; call as far in advance as is possible.

*Access.* Lamington National Park (Binna Burra) is an hour and 40 minutes by car from Brisbane via Canungra or Nerang, or one hour from the Gold Coast. From Brisbane check the bus schedule to Binna Burra at the Roma Street Transit Centre. Many visitors take a train from Brisbane to Nerang, where a shuttle bus completes the journey for less than $A20 one way for the total distance. From the Gold Coast Binna Burra runs a daily shuttle from the Surfer's Paradise Transit Centre for around $A17 one way.

The Green Mountains (O'Reilly's) are two hours from Brisbane via Canungra or Beaudesert and Duck Creek Road. The trip from the Gold Coast takes about an hour. The winding roads are not recommended for cars pulling trailers, and the "twisties" will induce car-sickness in some people. From Brisbane visit the Roma Street Transit Centre to book a seat on a regular bus to O'Reilly's. It should cost in the neighborhood of $A20 each way. From the Gold Coast try Mountain Coach Company; phone 07-5524-4249. Fare should run around $A20 one way.

## Girraween National Park

Farther west, but on the same latitude as Lamington, is Girraween National Park located on 11,400 hectares of mountainous terrain. The Pyramids, a unique escarpment of gigantic granite tors and boulders, stand nearly 200 meters high and are an awe-inspiring photographic subject. The Pyramids resulted from the erosion of an immense intrusion of molten rock that occurred about 250 million years ago.

The park's vegetation is atypical of Queensland. I was struck by how much it looked like parts of South Australia. The Wallangarra white gum and Barren Mountain mallee are two dominant arid plant forms here that aren't found in the rest of Queensland. Most visitors come to the park in September, October, and November to see the outstanding display of flowering shrubs and herbs in the understory of the gum forest. There are also creeks carving their way around boulders and a few choice swimming holes.

There are several marked trails that take from 23 minutes to 5 hours to walk. Birds and wallabies are common. Pick up maps showing the walks at the information center.

*Accommodations.* There are campgrounds with toilets, fireplaces, and showers at Bald Rock and Castle Rock. You should try to book at least two weeks in advance during September through December (peak season). Contact Ranger, Girraween National Park, via Wyberba, Queensland 4383. Outside the park, Stanthrope and Wallangarra both have hotels and caravan parks.

*Access.* There is no public transportation, though several tour companies visit the park. For the motorist, the park is 240 kilometers southwest from Brisbane. From Brisbane take the Cunningham Highway to Warwick, then head south on the New England Highway. The drive takes about three hours.

# The Gold Coast

The Gold Coast, which starts at the New South Wales–Queensland border, is Queensland's version of Las Vegas, Marine World Africa/USA, Disneyland, Miami Beach, and the canals of Lido Isle in Los Angeles. This 35-kilometer, brightly lit high-rise strip is the most intensely entrepreneurial resort area in Australia. If you think the offerings are excessive, thematically confused, artificial, ecologically questionable, generally the antithesis of how a stunningly beautiful stretch of coast ought to be developed—then we're in agreement.

The Gold Coast is made up of a series of towns that have merged into one beachside strip. Coolangatta is first up over the border from New South Wales, followed by Bilinga, Tugun, Currumbin, Palm Beach, North Palm Beach, Burleigh Heads, Miami, Mermaid Beach, Broadbeach, and Surfers Paradise, where the high rises actually shade the sand for part of each day. Past Surfers Paradise is Main Beach, and then it's on to Brisbane just an hour (or 70 kilometers) away. The Gold Coast Highway is the main drag through most of the glitter. You can bypass it all by taking the Tweed Heads Bypass around Tweed Heads and then the Coolangatta Road to the Pacific Highway, which cuts inland.

## Quasi-Natural Attractions

Fleay's Fauna Park (it may get a new name), 1.5 kilometers west of Burleigh Heads on West Burleigh Road, was founded by David Fleay, the Marlon Perkins of Australia. Fleay was a champion of Australian wildlife long before it became fashionable to be one. In 1944 he successfully bred platypuses in captivity, a feat that has been duplicated only a few times. The park abounds in native fauna, including platypuses, tree kangaroos, southern cassowaries, and greater bilbies. There are worthwhile educational and Aboriginal culture programs. The park is open daily from 9:00 A.M. to 5:00 P.M. There is an entrance fee.

The Currumbin Valley Bird Gardens in Currumbin has a well-landscaped walk-through aviary featuring exotic and native birds. The nearby 30-hectare Currumbin Sanctuary has an assortment of kangaroos, wallabies, koalas, and birds. Rainbow lorikeets will land on you in return for a handout; phone 07-5534-1266.

Sea World, north of Main Beach, offers performing dolphins, killer whales, and sea lions. For an extra charge you can swim with dolphins in a specially designed cove. There are several other theme parks, such as Dreamworld (featuring the "fastest ride in the world"), as well as businesses offering bungee jumping and indoor rock climbing. If pub crawls, gambling, dancing, drinking, "sun baking," and other social activities that attract people to this area momentarily wane in appeal, there is a natural refuge in the heart of the Gold Coast. Burleigh Heads National Park straddles Tallebudgera Creek and protects littoral rain forest, eucalypt forest, tussock grasses, and coastal heath environments. Migrating humpback whales are often sighted offshore during winter and spring. Koalas and brush turkeys are usually easy to find. There are several nice swimming areas along the creek. This park is a good place to picnic and to stretch your legs on a few short walks. To get there takes about 75 minutes from Brisbane. Many buses leave daily from the Brisbane Transit Centre, and local Gold Coast buses stop at the park.

For information about these and other attractions along the Gold Coast, contact the Gold Coast Tourism Bureau, 64 Ferny Avenue, Surfers Paradise, Qld 4217; phone 07-5592-2699.

# Carnarvon Gorge

Carnarvon Gorge has been compared to Sir Arthur Conan Doyle's *Lost World*. To me the place is a time capsule in a setting so primeval that I wouldn't be surprised if a brontosaurus suddenly lumbered out from a stand of giant-sized primitive ferns. Located in south-central Queensland, Carnarvon Gorge is worth the 10-hour drive from Brisbane, or the 2-hour flight in a small plane.

What's so special here? An airy forest of palms and ferns, towering white precipice sandstone cliffs, mysterious Aboriginal art sites, and an assortment of unique wildlife that conspires to overload your senses. A visitor can see many of the finest features in a single day—though most people set aside a week, which makes the most sense, considering the time and expense of getting here.

Tall cabbage palms, smaller primitive macrozamia palms (which are really an ancient cycad, not a palm), grass trees, towering spotted gums, flooded gums, bottlebrushes, and a ground layer of bracken ferns and grasses are what you see initially. Lofty white sandstone cliffs fold in and out on both sides of the gorge like two great curtains. Casurina-lined Carnarvon Creek gurgles its way down the main gorge.

The palm-laden environment is spellbinding enough, but the real exotica is in the side gorges, which are mostly the results of a unique kind of erosion that takes place in the narrow vertical joints between the massive sections of precipice sandstone that form the walls of the gorges. The wearing down of these narrow joints has created 60-meter-deep secondary gorges only a few meters wide. These side gorges have been polished and sculpted by water for tens of thousands of years. They feature cool microclimates, relic populations of *Angiopteris* (giant king) ferns with 4.5-meter fronds, spigotlike waterfalls, pools, tiny rivulets, and wet vertical surfaces covered with lush green lichens, mosses, hanging vines, ferns, and orchids. The very rare king fern is a 300-million-year-old species found only here, on Fraser Island, and in the Daintree rain forest north of Port Douglas. These special plants and places make Carnarvon nature's version of the Sistine Chapel. The walls of the feeder gorges extend skyward 30 meters or more, with ferns poking out of hairline cracks creating a lacelike pattern against the blue ceiling of the sky.

In the gorge itself, the most noticeable life-forms are the wedge-tailed eagles drifting on the currents along the 200-meter-high cliff tops. The gorge's subtropical climate supports a variety of flowering plants that results in a bloom of some kind year-round. Where there are flowers in Australia, there are birds, particularly honeyeaters. There are also three kinds of black cockatoos and a variety of wrens, including red-backed, variegated, and blue wrens, which are so brightly colored you'd think they'd glow in the dark. And there are always the comical and brash magpies and pied currawongs. The bustard, a tallish ground dweller with an unmistakably stately walk and a booming call during mating season, often struts along with just

*Carnarvon Gorge, Moss Gardens, Queensland*

its head visible above the tall grass. The bustard has no look- or act-alikes in North America. There are also plenty of laughing kook-aburras. A few are always sitting around the campground hoping to snatch an unguarded sandwich. The boldest ones will grab a morsel out of your hand while in flight when your head is turned.

The gorge upstream from the campground isn't particularly dense in mammalian wildlife, but you'll find "heaps" of wildlife in the 3-kilometer stretch between the park's campground (the end of the road) and Carnarvon Gorge Oasis Lodge. Eastern gray kangaroos are everywhere and quite tame. Some are so attuned to people they'll actually reach out and touch you in hopes of a handout. They're quite approachable for photographs. Like the campground birds, they'll make a meal of any unattended edibles. Don't feed them junk food. They do worse on it than people.

More challenging to photograph are brush-tailed rock wallabies, whip-tailed wallabies, and rufous and brush-tailed bettongs. The whip-tailed wallaby, also known as the pretty-faced wallaby, is unmistakable because of its strikingly attractive black-and-white face and extremely quick hopping motion. The rufous bettong is often too short for the grass. This tiny macropod is only about three decimeters (four inches) tall and weighs only half a kilogram. There's no denying its bug-eyed cuteness.

Three kinds of gliders are common in the area along the road between the lodge and the campground. Gliders are woolly tree-climbing marsupials that get their name from what they do—glide from one tree to the next just like flying squirrels. Greater gliders, yellow-bellied gliders, and my favorite, the squirrel glider, are active only at night. To find one, listen for the sharp, raspy scolding chatter that results when a gliding interloper puts down in another glider's tree. Gliders are most active during the gum bloom, in March through June.

There are platypuses in Carnarvon Creek directly across the road from the Carnarvon Gorge Oasis Lodge. If you want to photograph them, set up before dawn on the far bank overlooking any of the long pools. Look for fast-moving ripples on the surface and a low-profile head and broad bill protruding slightly above the surface.

## Walks

The best way to see Carnarvon Gorge is to walk it. (There are also helicopter rides.) The road ends at the park's interpretive center and campground at the gorge's entrance. You should check with the ranger on duty (if one is in) to get the scoop on trail conditions. If it's raining don't go. The gorge can flood; at the least, the constant creek crossings will become difficult. The well-defined main trail parallels Carnarvon Creek and is normally about as challenging as a sidewalk. This trail extends about 10 kilometers upstream, with a series of side trails branching off to the wonders of the place. The side trails range from easy to difficult but are rarely more than a kilometer detour off the main trail. The vertical walls of the gorge keep you hemmed in, making it nearly impossible to get lost.

Boolimba Bluff is the first option off the main trail. The trail split is just past the first creek crossing. This is a 3-kilometer climb with a vertical rise of about 200 meters. The view of the gorge and eastern lowlands is striking. However, the best views are still ahead on the main trail. About 2 kilometers farther along on the main trail, at the seventh creek crossing, is a left fork to Moss Garden and Hellhole Gorge. This trail forks again in a short while at another creek crossing. Though it's not clearly marked, Moss Garden is to the left and Hellhole Gorge is to the right. Both are less than 1 kilometer off the main trail. Moss Garden's rich greens of hornworts, liverworts, mosses, and ferns are enchanting. If you must skip one of these stops, make it Hellhole Gorge, which features tall trees and an up-close look at the creamy precipice sandstone.

The Amphitheatre is the next stop, about 1 kilometer farther upstream off the main trail. Again the turn is to the left. This is a spectacular spot. To gain access requires climbing a 10-meter fixed ladder while hanging onto a chain that allows you to pull yourself into a narrow crevice just wide enough to squeeze through. The next trick is working along the crevice (which doubles as a rivulet part of the year) on slippery logs to a vertical-walled amphitheater, which is really a sinkhole with a crevice leading out of it. Once over the obstacles you'll be in an oval-shaped, mossy-floored natural cathedral with smooth vertical walls and the sky for a ceiling. The acoustics are interesting, especially if the large green frogs are croaking. If they aren't, it's quiet enough to hear a pin drop.

Back on the main trail, about 0.5 kilometers farther between creek crossings nine and ten, is the right turn to Alijon Falls. This was my favorite side gorge. The climb is short but steep. It winds through tree ferns with an overstory of massive flooded gums to a spigotlike waterfall surrounded by mature tree ferns that are sometimes seven meters tall. Work your way up the right side of the falls, around the predominant rock formation, until you're above the falls. You'll find a beautifully sculpted narrow gorge featuring a relic population of king ferns that measure six meters across.

Back on the main track between creek crossings ten and eleven, about 5 kilometers from the trailhead, is the turn to the Art Gallery. Here you'll find some of the most interesting Aboriginal art in Australia: dozens of wall carvings of the human vulva and red-ochre stencils of hands (including some rare stencils of children's hands), forearms, V-shaped "killing" boomerangs, perfectly matched pairs of hunting boomerangs, and a coolaman (a carrying basket). The stenciling process is done by spitting water mixed with ochre over the object to be outlined. Look carefully and you'll find a goanna and a netlike pattern drawn freehand.

Cathedral Cave, another 4.5 kilometers up the main track, contains an equally outstanding display of stencil art. There is more variety here, but the figures are less exposed to natural light. You'll need a flash to photograph them. Note the differently shaped coolaman shields from those at the Art Gallery. Look for the freehand drawing of a humanlike figure and a broader range of stenciled tools and weapons. Anthropologists are puzzled about the significance of one pendant that is stenciled repeatedly at the Art Gallery and another that is stenciled over and over again at Cathedral Cave.

Little is known about the culture that produced these works of art because it disappeared so soon after European contact. Aboriginal presence in the region has been traced to 20,000 years ago. The art in the gorge dates to 3,600 years ago.

Big Bend, an overnight camping spot with pit toilets (no toilet paper), is the last marked destination in the gorge. It is about 1 kilometer upstream from Cathedral Cave. Not counting side gorges, you will have traveled 10 kilometers to reach Big Bend. Visitors often backpack to Big Bend and stay overnight. The next morning you can either climb Battleship Spur (the absolute end of the line) or head back down the way you came, stopping at areas you missed or would like to revisit with different lighting.

Battleship Spur is not signposted and is reached after two hours of arduous climbing from Big Bend. Discuss this climb with a ranger before attempting it.

For the nonovernighter (day walker), I recommend not going farther than the Art Gallery for a day outing. You'll find the time goes quickly while you marvel at different spots along the way.

## The Swimming Hole

Swimming is discouraged in the gorge upstream from the campground and ranger station. However, there is an excellent swimming hole two kilometers downstream from the campground on a good-quality trail. Brush-tailed rock wallabies are often perched around the waterhole at dusk and dawn.

*Accommodations.* Advance reservations are necessary for camping. The National Parks and Wildlife Service recommends you make reservations 18 weeks in advance, and even then there's no guarantee you'll get a camping place. The limit is 300 campers (at 80 sites) for overnight use; $A3.50 per night per person or $A14 per night per family. The campground has showers (cold only), toilets, running water, a pay phone, and a gas pump. The only sure way to get a spot is to write well ahead of time, receive your camping assignment, and make Carnarvon Gorge one of the places you must reach on a certain date. If this fails to work out, you can still use the park without a camping spot, and you may get one if there's a no-show. One possible option is to backpack in and stay overnight at Big Bend. To make reservations contact: Ranger, Carnarvon Gorge National Park, via Rolleston, Queensland 4702, Australia; phone 61-7-4984-4505 (overseas to Carnarvon).

Oasis Lodge is the only accommodation near the park. Staying here reminded me of the tent cabins in Yosemite National Park. The lodge does an excellent job of taking care of your basic needs while introducing you to the best aspects of the park. Guided walks and a well-stocked library are some of the offerings. Accommodation is in very clean individual cabins or safari tents that run between $A115 and $A170 per night. The lodge coordinates activities with bus tours and adventure outfitters. You can book direct by contacting Oasis Lodge, via Rolleston, Queensland 4702, Australia; phone 61-7-4984-4503, or contact the Fortland Hotels and Resort Web site at http://www.fortland.com.au. Callers within Australia can call toll-free: 1-800-644-150. To weigh transportation options as well as to book reservations, ask for the "Carnarvon Gorge Tariff Schedule," which is published annually.

*Access.* Should you drive, the route you choose from Brisbane is between 720 and 820 kilometers. Most of the trip is on good roads through boring scenery until the last stretch, which is more interesting. If you take the northern route outlined in the next paragraph, you can stop for lunch at Isle Gorge National Park, an outstanding forested gorge, just 1.4 kilometers off the Leichhardt Highway, about 525 kilometers from Brisbane.

For the northern route, take the Warrego Highway west from Brisbane to Miles (325 kilometers). Turn north onto the Leichhardt Highway. At Moura turn west onto the Dawson Highway, and at Rolleson turn south for about 90 kilometers of dirt road that ends at the park.

The southern approach calls for staying on the Warrego Highway to Roma, where you turn north toward Injune. For a tourist, getting to Carnarvon Gorge used to be an adventure attempted by only those with extra amounts of derring-do and the financial resources to rent a car for a week. The only "old way" was to procure a rental car, since there was no public ground transportation and only expensive charter flights were available from Brisbane. The routes into "the Gorge" included long stretches of "experimental road," which was apt to become an impassable quagmire after a storm. Most of the roads to "the Gorge" have now been upgraded to a sealed surface. There are only 30 kilometers of unsealed road in the last stretch. Roads are suitable for both 2WD and 4WD vehicles. But during heavy rains, the unsealed road can become impassable for all but 4WD vehicles. It is advisable to phone ahead to check on the road and weather conditions.

Transportation of all kinds has improved considerably over the last five years. Both self-drive 2WD and 4WD vehicles are available in Roma. Formerly a car had to be rented in Brisbane. The Central Queensland Travel Link operates a minibus transfer service between Emerald and Carnarvon Gorge twice a week.

Flight West Airlines can arrange for connecting flights to Ingelara Station and coach transfers to Oasis Lodge (it's approximately a half hour from the Ingelera air strip to Oasis Lodge or the Carnarvon Gorge Ranger Station). In September 1999 Skytours began offering direct flights from Brisbane to Ingelara Station (two hours). Coach tours with Australia Pacific and Australia Pacific Tours are also available. Passenger trains run regularly from Brisbane to Roma and Emerald, where a rental car can be procured. Queensland Travel Link can direct travelers to charter flights to Carnarvon Gorge from Brisbane.

# Fraser Island

Fraser Island sits at the bottom of the Great Barrier Reef, about 190 kilometers north of Brisbane. Few Americans have heard of Fraser Island, yet there are Australian naturalists who think the island's unique qualities rival the Great Barrier Reef itself. The island has been listed as a World Heritage Area since 1992.

Fraser Island is the world's largest sand island. It's 123 kilometers long and 14 to 23 kilometers wide. In the jungle interior, sand mountains top 230 meters, and the depth of the sand below sea level measures nearly 610 meters. Though it's surrounded by the ocean, the island is saturated with fresh water soaked up from centuries of rainwater. The geological energy that created the island is entirely independent of the forces that created the Great Barrier Reef. Fraser Island is a result of millions of years of river sediment washed into the sea from what is now New South Wales. Currents and tides worked to move the material north, forming the island.

With its perched lakes, tropical rain forests, Seventy Five Mile Beach, huge sand blows, plentiful dingoes and other wildlife, shipwrecks to explore, the remotest of lighthouses, Great Sandy National Park, and tropical island dune ecology, there is no other place in the world like Fraser Island. It is continually rearranging itself—burying forests, creating new lakes, changing coastlines, and forming new sand mountains.

The dingoes are among the purest strain left in Australia. A substantial horse population that was plentiful until recently accounted for sustaining the dingo population in the past. A full-grown horse could easily fend off a dingo, but colts often fell victim to dingoes hunting together. Fraser Island was dingo paradise. However, with the removal of the last horses, dingoes have found procuring a meal more of a challenge. Dingoes are smart animals and adapt quickly to their surroundings. Many have taken to begging from tourists and attempting to snatch a meal from campsites or picnic tables. The park service has issued the following warning: "DINGOES: Fraser's dingoes are wild animals but some have become threatening to people, because they have been fed or people have encouraged their attention. Enjoy their beauty, but keep your distance, supervise children at all times, *never* feed dingoes, and secure all food supplies and rubbish, preferably in a vehicle."

Offshore between Hervey Bay and the island is one of the largest concentrations of dugongs in Australia. Closely related to the manatee, this large aquatic omnivore has been pushed to extinction in many parts of Australia because of overhunting, pollutants, boat traffic, and activities affecting the health of the underwater grass beds that provide food for the animal. The protected shallow waters of Hervey Bay are ideal for dugongs. Viewing them is often difficult. The water is rather murky, but if you take a ferry from Hervey Bay to the island you will be traveling through dugong habitat and will probably see one. A dugong is much faster and more agile than a manatee, which comes as a surprise to North Americans who have seen the slow, ponderous way manatees go about their business.

There are 240 species of birds on Fraser Island, making it one of the richest bird sanctuaries in Australia. Pied oystercatchers, cockatoos, flycatchers, whistlers, honeyeaters, kingfishers, eagles, falcons, brolgas, and curlews are just some of them. There is a shooting ban on all birds.

Fruit bats, squirrel gliders, pygmy gliders, and echidnas can be found at night with the aid of a strong flashlight.

It's a true adventure to visit Fraser Island. There is only one puny seven-kilometer stretch of "improved" road, and for great stretches no roads of any kind exist. Visitors drive 4WD vehicles on the beaches, through streams, and over long-established, narrow inland (and sometimes treacherous) sand tracks to visit lakes, rain forests, creeks, and camping areas. You're on your own here and must rely on good judgment and special driving rules to return to the mainland in the rental car you started out with. Don't even consider driving a conventional vehicle. If you're a little fainthearted, there are several veteran tour companies that regularly visit the island, and the island resorts offer excursions of their own. There is also air service to two small airstrips.

Though there are petrol pumps on the island, it makes logistical and economic sense to top off in Rainbow Beach.

The ferries leave from Inskip Point. From Rainbow Beach you can either drive down the beach or take a bumpy access road until you see the *Fraser Venture, Fraser Dawn, Kingfisher II,* or other barges. These ferries, which operate like World War II landing craft, collect cars from the beach and run them 500 meters across a narrow channel to the southern tip of Fraser Island. Ferry fares, schedules, and departure points vary. For details contact the following vessel operators: *Fraser Venture,* phone 07-4125-4444; *Fraser Dawn,* phone 07-4125-4444; *Kingfisher II,* phone 07-4125-5511; *Urangan Fast Cat,* phone 07-4125-4444. The fare is around $A65 for a vehicle and driver, $A5 per extra passenger. For a motorcycle and rider the fare is $A25. Walk-on passengers are $A15 per person for adults and $A7.50 per child.

## Routes

If your landing point is at the island's southern terminus, you'll want to head for Seventy Five Mile Beach, which is about 3.5 kilometers to your right. There are two routes. You can churn across the soft sand to a pockmarked road that passes through a few kilometers of vegetated foredunes before depositing you on Seventy Five Mile Beach, or you can stay on the beach the entire way from the moment you leave the ferry. If it's high tide, I'd take the road route. The starting point for the road is neither signposted nor readily apparent from the ferry. Ask the ferry operator or a fellow traveler to point to the specific area you want to head for.

In your other option, the beach route, the problem area is near Semaphore Creek at high tide. At low tide the beach approach is usually quite safe.

Once around Hook Point, the driving on Seventy Five Mile Beach is easy as long as you stay on the hard sand near the surf. The first 23 kilometers north on the beach are usually uneventful.

At Dilli Village you have the option of attempting an inland journey that takes you past some of the island's famous perched lakes. This route is a loop that ends at Eurong Beach Resort 12 kilometers up the coast. When I tried this route, Geroweea Creek had backed up to thigh depth, so I continued on the beach and reached Eurong Beach Resort at the 34.5-kilometer mark.

The access track to the inland lakes and rain forest is always open through Eurong Beach Resort. In fact, even though starting the loop at Dilli Village is often recommended, the hub of inland activities is at Central Station, which is 6 kilometers directly east from Eurong. This means the quickest, surest access to the best of the inland areas is through Eurong, not through Dilli Village.

## Inland Points of Interest

Central Station was begun as a forestry camp in the 1920s. Today it has a small interpretive center, which is usually staffed by a single forester. The grounds around the station are open, green, well main-tained, and set up for camping and picnicking. Tour outfitters often lunch here, but even then it's rarely crowded. The setting is tranquil, amid a profusion of exotic plant life. You'll see massive satinay trees that tower 50 meters over the forest, which includes blackbutts, cab-bage palms, piccabeen palms, hoop pines, kauri pines, red blood-woods, wild passion vines, and pandani. Immense shiny-barked hoop pines will defy your concept of a pine tree. Growing out of some of these trees are staghorn, ribbon, and crow's-nest ferns, orchids, and dozens of other tropical plants. The staghorns were the biggest and healthiest I saw in Australia. The World Heritage listing, acquired in 1992, ended logging on the island.

Adding to this multilevel floral display is the constant chatter of lorikeets, honeyeaters, cockatoos, ravens, and currawongs. Around dusk large fruit bats can be seen twisting through the overstory. A dingo or two often hangs around the picnic area hoping for a handout. This is one of the best places in Australia to photograph wild dingoes.

Woongoolbuer Creek runs within a short walking distance of Central Station and through the heart of the island's rain forest. There is a splendid walking trail along this absolutely clear creek. When I first saw the creek I thought it was dry. Step onto this wet "sand," though, and you'll find yourself standing in half a meter of water. The trail climbs away from the creek into a series of habitats that include banksias and grass trees.

The most delightful walk is directly up Woongoolbuer Creek. The water is cool, the sandy bottom is comfortable on your bare feet, and you'll get a frog's-eye view at a rare pocket of rain forest that sucks much of its sustenance from your watery path. The sandy creek bottom changes from white to a velvet green as you enter the rain forest. Move slowly and count the different kinds of birds hopping through the dense vegetation. See if you can locate the ancient and giant king ferns. Also from Central Station is a 2-kilometer trail to Pile Valley and a 6-kilometer walk to Lake McKenzie, with its crystal clear water and white sandy beaches.

Fraser Island has two kinds of unique lakes: "window" lakes are the result of the water table rising above ground level and filling depressions. Water levels in window lakes fluctuate with the rise and fall of the island's amazingly high (fresh) water table. "Perched" lakes are the result of a hardpan layer of iron and sand particles that combine with decaying humus. The resulting bond makes a watertight lining. Typically, rain is the only source of water for perched lakes, and evaporation is the only way water leaves. These lakes are usually somewhat acidic, which limits the kinds of plants and animals that live in them. Swimming is thus unencumbered by water plants and visibility is often literally unbelievable. Fraser Island has the greatest concentration of perched lakes in the world. Many of them can be reached from Eurong or Dilli Village on fairly stable sand tracks.

Lake Boomanjin (also spelled Boemingen) is near Dilli Village (7 kilometers) and is the most southern of the accessible group of seven lakes I've chosen to highlight. Lake Boomanjin covers 190 hectares, making it the largest perched lake in the world. It has tea-colored water and is surrounded by gnarled melaleucas that makes for surreal photography. Camping is allowed near the lake but not on the shoreline. A new kind of sunfish has been found in the lake that has scientists pondering. Before its discovery no sunfish had been found south of Cairns, which is more than 1,000 kilometers to the north. How did the species get into an entirely enclosed ecosystem so far from its nearest living relative? Lake Boomanjin also has a small freshwater turtle that is rare but abundant here. Plus, there are freshwater shrimp and small yabbies (craw fish) that will nibble your toes if you enter the water. But, the underwater varmint to look out for is an insect called a "water boatman." It is carnivorous and will bite you. It is about as big as a fingernail with a paddle on each side. It likes to slither under bathing suits, so take your suit off and check yourself out—or don't wear a bathing suit. There are also some healthy lace goannas in the area that act as if they expect to be fed.

If you'd like a walk, there is a well-marked walking track separate from the road that winds through dune vegetation, a paperbark swamp, banksias, a forest of rusty gums, macrozamia groves, sand blows, transition forests featuring satinay gums, and a blackbutt forest before reaching Lake Boomanjin. From here it's about another 14.5 kilometers onto Central Station. On the way you'll pass by four more lakes. Remember to wear a hat and carry water.

Directly south of Central Station (about 4.5 kilometers) are tightly clustered Lakes Jennings, Birrabeen, Barga, and Benaroon. These four lakes cover about 260 hectares and can be reached by 4WD on a fairly decent one-lane track. Take special care to center your vehicle on the two log bridges.

Even though these lakes are tightly clustered, there are differences in water color and surrounding vegetation. Lake Birrabeen, the second lake south from Central Station, is the most inviting. It is crystal clear and has an attractive white sandy beach on its western shore. Besides driving, you can walk to this beach in an hour from Central Station on a clearly marked trail that passes by tiny Lake Jennings on the way. Limited car camping is allowed 100 meters from Lake Benaroon, which is a bit farther south.

Lake McKenzie is about 7 kilometers north of Central Station on a signposted two-rut, 4WD track. The track passes through Pile Valley with its mature satinay forest. These spectacular trees jut 70 meters into the sky and form the overstory to an incredibly rich and diverse pocket of rain forest. Lake McKenzie is crystal clear and surrounded by blackbutt forests. Camping is allowed near the lake.

Lake Wabby is nearer the coast and can be reached by a challenging two-rut 12-kilometer track from Central Station. There's also a 13-kilometer walking trail connecting Lake McKenzie and Lake Wabby. And you can reach it from the coast via a 2.5-kilometer walk from Seventy Five Mile Beach at the 39-kilometer mark (5.5 kilometers north of Eurong Resort). This lake is clear, and it's the deepest lake on Fraser Island. It contains seven kinds of fish and, unlike the other lakes, was formed by a sand blow damming a creek system. And, at a pace of about three meters a year, another sand blow is consuming it. You'll see trees hundreds of years old in the process of being buried. Perhaps a thousand years from now these trees will be exposed again as the fossil remains of a forest, a process that has occurred many times on constantly changing Fraser Island.

There are 40 lakes spread throughout the island. Behind Happy Valley, Lake Garawongera is supposed to be ideal for swimming in total seclusion. I believe it's true since I never reached it despite a sincere effort. I lost my nerve for fear of becoming bogged and turned around. If you're out to set records, visit Lake Boomerang. At 130 meters, it's the highest perched lake in the world. Lake Bowarrady (the turnoff from Seventy Five Mile Beach is 3.5 kilometers past Cathedral Beach Resort) is renowned for its wildlife. Turtles will eat from your hand, and the area is full of bird life. Ask at Happy Valley about the condition of the "road." Lake Bowarrady is just over the southern border of Great Sandy National Park.

But before you get to Great Sandy National Park, there's Eli Creek, the wreck of the *Maheno,* and the Cathedrals on your way up Seventy Five Mile Beach from Happy Valley. Eli Creek is a potential driving hazard and claims vehicles every year. After rains or during high tide it should be crossed with extreme care. I crossed close to the surf line, where the water had spread out to a 1.5-decimeter depth. The creek can put out 2,640 kiloliters an hour, causing its constantly changing banks to become vertical drops that sometimes must be broken down to create an incline for a vehicle.

There is a scenic picnic spot in the foredunes around Eli Creek. Pandani and banksias dominate. Walk up the creek and you'll come to pristine rain forest. The creek has a healthy and often visible population of Australian bass, a game fish.

The *Maheno* wreck is what's left of the trans-Tasman liner that ran between Tasmania and the mainland at the beginning of this century. When it was being towed to Japan for scrap during the Depression, the towline snapped, and she's been rusting away here ever since.

The Cathedrals are a multicolored coastal escarpment with supposedly 70 different colored sands on "towering" cliffs 2.5 kilometers past Cathedral Resort. I found most of the promotional descriptions of the Cathedrals exaggerated, though they are interesting timeworn formations.

Another 22 kilometers up Seventy Five Mile Beach you'll come to the only rock outcrops on the island. First is Indian Head, so named by Captain Cook, who was the first European to see it in 1770. At Indian Rock you must turn inland—which means soft-sand driving. Look for a wood ramp that allows you to climb off the beach into foredune country. You'll be traveling above the ocean through banksias and foredune vegetation on a challenging track that eventually takes you past Waddy Point to Orchid Beach Resort and the park service campground.

There's a parking area for the Aquarium or the Champagne Pools. There are several paths leading to these pools, which become separated from the ocean at low tide. I enjoyed snorkeling in them and counted 14 kinds of fish, some of them colorful reef varieties. The entire zone between Indian Head and Point Waddy (near Orchid Beach Resort) is set aside for wilderness beach camping and is officially a no-vehicle zone. This area is characterized by small beaches, rock formations, and pandani.

Orchid Beach is the farthest point north where you can get petrol. From Orchid Beach it is a tricky 15 kilometers to Sandy Cape, the island's northern tip. Without much trouble you can visit Ocean Lake, about 5 kilometers north of the resort and inland about 1 kilometer. The lake is surrounded by swamp banksia and livistona palms.

Head southwest from Sandy Cape and you'll come to the Sandy Cape Lighthouse, a well-kept and still functioning classic structure (1881) that proudly flies the Aussie flag. Dunes tower over you on this final leg, and at high tide there is very little beach left for driving. If you make it this far and are polite, the lighthouse keeper might show you around. The view from the lighthouse is spectacular. Continuing to the western side of the island from here is not recommended.

*Camping.* Camping permits cost $A3.50 per person per night, or $A14 per family. Permits are available at Marina Kiosk Boat Harbour (phone 07-4128-9800), River Heads (phone 07-4125-7133), and Hervey Bay City Council (phone 07-4123-7100). Beach camping is allowed, but don't set up camp in an area used by vehicles. There are organized campgrounds with running water at Central Station and other points on the island. There is a private campground at Cathedral Beach. Unless you are certain about a source of fresh water, plan on carrying your own.

*Accommodations.* Besides the camping mentioned above (and others on the park service's maps and brochures) there are four resorts, ranging from basic to up-market.

The premier resort is the King Fisher Bay Resort (phone 07-4120-3333), which has several rustic lodges and a nice restaurant. The resort provides good-quality guided tours of the island.

Eurong Beach Resort, 34.5 kilometers north on Seventy Five Mile Beach from the island's southern tip, is a complete facility that coordinates bookings with adventure tour outfits. The resort has cabin and motel units and a general store, bistro, pool, and restaurant in a well-kept setting. This resort is the stepping-off point to Central Station and the best of the island's interior. Contact Eurong Beach Tourist Resort, P.O. Box 100, Maryborough, Queensland 4650, Australia; phone 07-4127-9122.

Dilli Village was one of twelve camps in Queensland sponsored by the government so that educational institutions, recreation clubs, and community groups can economically enjoy the outdoors. Dilli Village caters to groups that book months in advance. A bed and meals runs around $A14 per person a day. The camp can accommodate 40 people; phone 07-4127-1930.

Cathedral Beach Resort and Camping Park is another spartan accommodation that caters primarily to fishermen. It is at the 69-kilometer mark at the island's southern tip. There are bungalows with hot showers and 27 camping sites (with more under way) with amenities. Contact Cathedral Beach Resort and Camping Park, Fraser Island, P.O. Box 1, Urangan 4658, Australia; phone 07-4127-9177.

*Access.* Most people who get to Fraser Island arrive via one of the boats offering service from the mainland; your choices were outlined earlier in this chapter. You also have the option of arriving via light aircraft to one of the island's two airstrips or making a beach landing. Air Fraser Island (Samarai Drive, Pialba) offers flights 24 hours a day; phone 07-4125-3600. To get around on the island, you can either join a tour group and become a passenger in a wide assortment of all-terrain vehicles, or you can rent a 4WD vehicle and explore on your own. Often visitors and tour groups buy packages that include all transportation and lodging on the island. Most car rentals that allow you to take a vehicle to Fraser Island offer either no insurance, or marginal insurance. If you are bound for Fraser Island from Brisbane it might make sense to contact Sunrover Rentals at 72 Newmarket Road, Windsor, Qld. 4030; phone 07-3357-9077; toll-free 1-800-077-353 (within Australia); fax 07-3357-5259. Or contact Bay 4WD hire at bay4wd@mlink.com.au for insurance and rental car prices. Otherwise consult a phone book or contact Hervey Bay City Council; phone 07-4125-0222. Hertz would not insure the vehicle I took onto Fraser Island, so be sure to ask about insurance coverage.

There are several air services that will deposit you at either of the two airstrips or on the beach. The airstrips are at Toby's Gap and Orchid Beach. Air Fraser Island (phone 07-4125-3600) operates from Brisbane and Maroochydore to both Orchid Beach and Toby's Gap (5 kilometers inland from Dilli Village).

If driving a rental vehicle seems too bothersome, sign on with a tour outfit. Contact Sunrover Expedition; phone 07-3203-4241. For whale watching contact Whale Watch Tourist Centre; phone 1-800-358-545 (toll-free inside Australia).

Seasonal considerations: In summer Fraser Island has significant rainfall, while winters are usually dry. August, September, and October tend to be the busier months, because the fishing and wildlife seasons attract a great number of the annual visitors.

# The Great Barrier Reef

The Great Barrier Reef is often called the biggest living thing in the world. It's so powerfully overwhelming that making *all* of it—an uninterrupted 3,000-kilometer stretch of Queensland coastline, offshore islands, and reefs—into a park became a reality in 1979 with scarcely a whimper of dissent throughout Australia.

It was a remarkable feat considering the parties involved. After weighing the scientific evidence, a joint statement was released by the then longtime prodevelopment Queensland premier Sir Joh Bjelke-Petersen and Prime Minister Malcolm Fraser. They agreed there would be no drilling or mining on the reef or in places near enough to adversely affect it. They also vowed that every effort would be made to conserve the reef. The two men agreed on setting aside more than 348,700 square kilometers along the continental shelf, an area twice the size of England. The Great Barrier Reef Marine Park

Authority was created to oversee the Queensland National Parks and Wildlife Service's day-to-day management of the reef. Because of this commitment, the Great Barrier Reef has escaped the kinds of exploitation and pollution that threatened it. It now enjoys the added protection of a World Heritage listing.

Today public concern about the reef centers around the degree of access visitors should get and appropriate kinds of facilities and modes of transportation.

The Great Barrier Reef isn't a solid barrier, as the name implies. It's made up of a maze of more than 2,900 reefs ranging in size from an acre to 95 square kilometers. It is the biggest reef system in the world. Most of it lies well offshore: 140 kilometers in the southern section, 65 kilometers from Townsville in the central, and only about 14 kilometers in the north near Cooktown. Often each reef has its own personality, typified by certain kinds of coral, fish, crustaceans, and so on. A reef can be separated from its neighbor by a dozen kilometers or a dozen meters. Long narrow reefs are called ribbon reefs, and broad reefs are known as platform reefs. Fringing reefs are attached to continental islands, where resorts are located. For this reason fringing reefs are the most often visited. They occur as far south as New South Wales.

Coral cays and continental islands are the two island types found in the waters of the reef. Cays occur when a reef extends above the water. These islands are made up of dead coral and are flat, usually small, and sometimes vegetated. Cays are often havens for nesting seabirds and turtles. There are more than 300 cays and 618 continental islands on the Great Barrier Reef.

The continental islands are earthen, often mountainous landforms that were separated from the mainland during the last ice age. They often have fresh water and the wildlife and vegetation found on the mainland. Generally, the continental islands are the most compatible for a prolonged stay, though some of the cays, with their surrounding reefs, offer extremely memorable experiences.

*The Coral.* Below the surface, large, irregular, delicate coral structures are the underpinnings of a plethora of life that has no parallel on land. More than 400 species of corals, 1,500 kinds of fish, plus anemones, crustaceans, and mollusks of untold numbers thrive here. Usually the picture is one of tranquillity and amazing beauty, but it's also a bubbling cauldron for the survival of the fittest.

Corals are divided into two groups: soft and hard. Most of us are familiar with hard coral. The remains of hard corals are often used as decorative items in fish aquariums and on fireplace mantles. (*Note:* Taking any of the reef home is now forbidden in much of the reef.) Soft coral does not have a hard skeleton, so its form can't be appreciated out of water. Both hard and soft corals are immensely more beautiful alive and underwater, where their tiny hydralike polyps collect whatever drifts by.

Soft or hard, each coral is a carnivorous animal that often lives in stationary colonies. Coral comes in myriad shapes, colors, and designs, but each is a tiny hydralike polyp. The polyps usually extend above their homes at night or on overcast days to collect plankton and other tiny life-forms. The feeding corals are spectacular. Interesting white forms turn iridescent colors when the polyps are out.

*The Fish.* The coral is the backdrop, food source, and hiding place of fish that are as numerous and varied as they are radiant. In a rich section of the reef the multitudes of species and their wildly different shapes and colors, hunting styles, and survival strategies would be difficult for even a roomful of the most imaginative sci-fi writers to invent.

However outrageous a fish's colors, degree of specialization, and behavior, form and function are its underpinnings. Even aesthetically striking fish only appear the way they do because their dazzling colors confuse predators and attract mates.

There are colorfully spotted coral trout (actually a cod that looks somewhat like a trout) that drift over coral colonies as if half asleep until an unsuspecting smaller fish draws too near—then it's slurp and the small fish is gone. Clown fish are coated in a protective membrane that allows them to dance like a drunken sailor in the killer tentacles of anemones. Unsuspecting fish attracted to the oddly swimming clown are killed and eaten by the anemone—which may live for 300 years! There's a kind of parrot fish that secretes a cocoon around itself every night to elude its predators. A giant sea slug spews a gummy, stringlike web out of its anus that ensnares whatever molests it. Bright yellow discus-shaped butterfly fish with pipe-stem snouts cruise about the reef, sticking their noses in tiny cracks to extract food from places other fish can't reach. Tiny sand divers flit nervously over sandy areas and burrow headfirst into the sand when a predator appears.

*Playing It Safe: Knowing the Nasties and Other Hazards. Nasties* is the Australian term for creatures that can do you harm. In an environment as rich as the reef, you would expect more dangerous critters than there are. Actually, your chance of injury from a reef creature is slim. While there are some potential dangers, there's nothing that should deter you from safely submerging your body into the reef's waters. The list below is meant to inform, not to scare. Also, keep in mind that organized outings led by competent people greatly reduce the very slight risks even more. Thousands of people dive, snorkel, and swim on the reef daily with no adverse effects.

If you get scraped or cut by the coral, thoroughly clean the wound (and make it bleed). Coral-caused lesions often become infected. If you're on a dive boat, report the slightest cuts. Quick treatment is essential. Use disinfectants that dry the wound. Always walk on coral in rubber-soled shoes (not thongs), and avoid waves that might push you against the coral. Learn to identify the fire coral, which can deliver a nasty sting.

Stingrays often burrow into the sand in shallow water near shore. If you stand on one, it will jam its stinger into your leg to encourage you to get off. When walking in shallow water, shuffle your flippers to scare rays off. If you do get stung, seek medical advice.

Some experts classify the box jellyfish (also known as the sea wasp or "stinger") as the deadliest creature on earth because it can kill a swimmer in less than 30 seconds. The box jellyfish's two-meter-long tentacles bristle with stingers called nematocysts to the tune of 500,000 per square inch. Touch a tentacle and thousands of nematocysts fire. Surviving will depend on how much of your skin was contacted. The box jellyfish is a nearly transparent grapefruit-sized creature that is blown to mainland beaches from October to May along the central and northern Great Barrier Reef north of Gladstone. Often beaches have signposted warnings, and there are spot alerts. Box jellyfish can't sting through panty hose, which is what swimmers sometimes wear for safety. A wet suit or clothing will protect you, too.

If you or someone with you is stung, minimize the victim's movements. Stings are always painful and sometimes fatal. Seek immediate medical aid. There is an antivenin.

The stonefish, a brick-sized imitator of a slimy rock, packs a lethal punch if you step on it. Unfortunately, a stonefish can't be seen, even when you're looking at one from a meter away. That's how good it is

at imitating a stone. When the fish is stepped on, the poison instan-
taneously travels up the needles in its dorsal fin. The spines have pen-
etrated rubber-soled shoes, so walk as lightly as possible on the reefs.
Deaths have occurred from stonefish on South Seas islands, but
everyone poisoned in Australia has survived. Seek medical aid immediately. Keep the victim calm and immobile. There is an antivenin.

The small blue-ringed octopus is very deadly and poses a special
threat to children. Its blue rings become brightly pronounced when
it's upset. It will make every effort to stay clear of you. All deaths
have been caused by lifting it out of the water. It's usually sighted in
shallow water and is attractive, which is why children pick it up. The
bite is barely perceptible, but paralysis and death usually aren't far
behind. Children visiting any part of coastal Australia should be
warned about the blue-ringed octopus. If someone is bitten, wrap the
wound site and apply pressure upward, away from the toes or fingers. You're trying to slow the poison's advance. Rush the victim to
a doctor.

There are many species of cones. Dozens of them are striking to
look at. However, some species can sting from anywhere near the
bottom of their shell. Fatalities have occurred. Again, there's no risk
if you look and don't touch—which is the underlying ethic on the
Great Barrier Reef. If someone is stung, apply a pressure wrap at the
wound and upward away from the hands and feet. Seek medical aid.

Marine snakes occur at different places along the reef but usually
aren't found in most prime snorkeling areas. I've talked with many
Australian scuba divers who have never seen one. Sea snakes are
rarely seen in the Whitsunday Islands, for instance. The snakes can
be inquisitive, which is sometimes mistaken for aggression. They are
slow to anger. Don't hit at one that comes near, just swim out of its
path. Sudden movements close to one can bring on a defensive strike.
Their teeth can't normally penetrate a wet suit, but fatalities have
been reported. Bites sometimes occur without poison being injected.
If pain, weakness, and paralysis don't begin within a half hour of a
bite, you probably weren't injected. If they do occur, seek medical
help. Antivenin is available.

In areas where a boat operator will take you, sharks are seldom, if
ever, a problem. In the Whitsunday Islands, for instance, there has
never been a fatality from a shark attack. The big sharks seldom
enter the raised mazelike reefs, and the sharks in the reefs are usually
smallish white-tip and black-tip reef sharks that become aggressive

only if grabbed by the tail—which has happened. If a large shark appears, it will most likely be a tiger shark, which is dangerous. Leave the water as calmly as possible.

Hypothermia seems an unlikely event in the tropics, but it can be a problem. Without a wet suit I developed a chill in about 30 minutes, which is fairly typical. If you don't have a wet suit and don't want to rent one, at least wear a T-shirt while swimming. Lastly, guard against sunburn. The sun is intense in this part of the world. Protect your skin.

## Seeing the Reef

The best way to see the reef is to don a mask and join the fishes. The usually good to excellent water visibility and the fact that most of the reef life can be found in the first ten meters under the surface make snorkeling ideal throughout the reef. The only prerequisites are the ability to swim and reasonable judgment.

Snorkeling and diving increase the quality of your reef experience a hundredfold over glass-bottomed boats and subs. The snorkeler or diver becomes part of the underwater world, and fish are less apt to go into hiding, which often happens when a glass-bottomed boat or submarine maneuvers overhead.

For the less aquatically inclined visitor, there are glass-bottomed boats, motorized floating observatories called submarines or semi-submersibles, and underwater observatories.

In the glass-bottomed boats you simply stare through the boat's bottom at whatever passes beneath you. In the submarines you climb down a hatchway and sit below the water level and peer through windows as the craft maneuvers about a reef. The name *submarine* is a misnomer because the craft doesn't entirely drop below the surface. Of these two reef-viewing vessels, subs give you a better look. But in general, underwater observatories are superior to both.

## Reaching Parts of the Reef

In the 1980s the advent of large, high-powered catamarans, known as big cats or fast cats, caused a revolution in reef travel. These aluminum-hulled, ferry-sized, double- and triple-decked catamarans can carry a hundred or more people and skim over the water at 20 knots. Their speed and carrying capacity make it possible for large numbers of day visitors to visit offshore reefs and islands that formerly were off limits because of the distance or expense.

There are still instances when helicopters, seaplanes, and/or conventional boats are the best ways to see or reach a particular area, especially when direct flights to islands surrounded by a reef are available, or when you're touring islands and reefs.

Before you take off, contact the Department of Environment, Great Barrier Reef Wonderland (P.O. Box 5391, Townsville, Queensland 4810; phone 61-7-4721-2399; fax 61-7-4771-5578), for some free printed material on the reef. The *Reader's Digest Book of the Great Barrier Reef* is a comprehensive 384-page pictorial and text look at the reef. It usually retails for around $A70. A shorter and less-expensive paperback version for the foreign traveler is in the works. Another excellent book is *100 Magic Miles of the Great Barrier Reef: The Whitsunday Islands*, by David Colfelt (about $A30).

*Island Camping.* Island resorts, throughout the Great Barrier Reef, have done a good job advertising their presence and the reasons visiting them will be a worthwhile experience. Often missing from these advertisements are the myriad of camping opportunities on many of the Great Barrier Reef's islands. Some resorts literally control all access to a particular island, while others share an island with a national park or other entities. The "Reef" is divided into several zones that have rules that govern activities such as fishing, number of visitors, and disposal of garbage and human waste. There are also rules particular to different islands, sometimes prohibiting overnight stays of any kind. Island camping (for the well-prepared and self-contained) awaits the adventure traveler all along the Great Barrier Reef.

## Southern Reef Islands and Mainland Points of Interest

Offshore from the coastal town of Bundaberg is the Capricornia section of Great Barrier Reef Marine Park. The area includes 20 reefs and 12 cays, only 2 of which are inhabited. Most of the islands are national parks, and spearfishing is prohibited or restricted in the area. For most divers and snorkelers, Lady Musgrave Island, Lady Elliot Island, and Heron Island have the most to offer.

The weather, which is usually mild year-round, is an additional plus to visiting the Capricornia group. The southeast winds that sometimes blow on the northern sections of the reef rarely occur here. The winters are usually storm-free, and the light rainy season is usually restricted to the summer months. In May (the fall) I snorkeled for 45 minutes at a time without a wet suit.

## Lady Musgrave Island

The fast cats have opened up Lady Musgrave Island to day visits, making it the most southern economy-priced quality reef experience. From Brisbane, the stepping-off point at Bundaberg is 4 hours by car or 1 by plane. From Bundaberg to the island it's 2.5 hours more on the MV *Lady Musgrave*. The island is 52 miles from the mainland.

The MV *Lady Musgrave* anchors in a large coral lagoon near Lady Musgrave Island. The day can be spent snorkeling, scuba diving (only if certified), or going ashore to watch the nesting activities of white-capped noddy terns and green and leatherneck turtles.

The lagoon surrounding Lady Musgrave Island is one of the best on the entire barrier reef for snorkeling. Coral outcrops form an immense oval with one small channel and protect the lagoon from the open ocean, which ensures water clarity and the absence of sharks. The lagoon's bottom is rarely deeper than 14 meters. Tidal fluctuations don't affect the quality of viewing. There is a rich variety of coral that has not been impacted by the crown-of-thorns starfish, though there are a few dead areas at the southern end. Staghorn, plate, brain, and gorgonia corals are prevalent, and more than 1,200 kinds of fish have been cataloged in the lagoon.

*Access.* Book your Lady Musgrave Barrier Reef cruise by phoning 07-4152-9011 or by showing up at the Port Bunaberg Tourist Jetty at 8:00 A.M. It's $A110 for adults.

*Caution.* If you are prone to seasickness, load up on Dramamine or other motion-sickness medication 1½ hours before departure.

## Bundaberg

Bundaberg sits on the Burnett River and is surrounded by lush fields of sugarcane. The town has dozens of motels, good restaurants, and a friendly atmosphere. The beaches are "stinger-free" and suitable for sunbaking and swimming. There are several significant historic points of interest and a nearby national park with a campground.

The Mon Repos Turtle Rookery (phone 07-4159-1652) is the most accessible mainland sea turtle rookery in Australia. Green and loggerhead turtles a meter in length visit the beaches from November to February to lay their eggs. Occasionally leatherback and flatback turtles come ashore, too. Hatchlings scramble for the water from January to March at night. From Bundaberg, Mon Repos is reached by driving on the road to Bargara until you see the signpost to Mon Repos. The total distance is about 15 kilometers. Walk north along the sand from the parking area. Mon Repos has been upgraded to a conservation park. Care should be taken not to disturb turtles or their eggs.

In Bundaberg, visit the Bundaberg Distillery, started in 1888. The distillery makes Bundaberg rum, known as Bundie, which is exported around the world. There are tours Monday through Friday between 10:00 A.M. and 2:30 P.M. It is located at 78 Mount Perry Road North, Bundaberg. This is one of the few places you'll find the entire process—sugar mill, refinery, and distillery—on one site.

The Hinkler House Memorial Museum (phone 07-4152-0222) is housed in the relocated home of the famous Aussie aviator Bert Hinkler. Hinkler is to Australia what Lindbergh is to the United States, only Hinkler flew to Europe from Australia, which is much farther than crossing the Atlantic. In 1932 Hinkler died in a crash in Italy at the peak of his worldwide fame. The museum is open between 10:00 A.M. and 2:30 P.M. and contains Hinkler's personal memorabilia and letters from other aviation greats, including U.S. astronauts. Phone (07) 4152 0222.

There are several excellent semirural beaches near Bundaberg. Box jellyfish don't occur there, and the beaches are patrolled by surf clubs. The beaches are about 17 kilometers from town between Woodgate and Bagara.

Other activities and points of interest near Bundaberg include: Tropical Wines (tasting wines made of tropical fruits), Dreamtime Reptile Reserve (crocodiles, pythons, and the like), and Bauer's Riding Centre. Bauer's includes swimming with a beach ride.

Woodgate National Park is about 60 kilometers south of Bundaberg. This is a 5,500-hectare coastal park with mangroves, heathland, and gum and vine forest environments. The park is renowned for its birds. Jabirus, spoonbills, ibises, and numerous ducks can usually be seen from Walkers Point Road. The park is opposite Woodgate on the southern side of the Burrum River. Camping is allowed. Contact Department of Environment, 46 Quay Street, Bundaberg, Qld 4670; phone 07-4153-8620.

*Accommodations.* I stayed at Alexandra's, a nicely restored old Queenslander that was once an original squatter's residence. Alexandra's also has a very nice restaurant. It's located at the corner of Quay and Bingera Streets. The Lady Musgrave Cruise's bus picks you up in the morning, if the hotel management has been notified.

For camping, see Woodgate National Park or consult the phone book for local caravan parks. Rates $A48–$A77. To get a camping permit, contact Woodgate National Park, c/o Post Office, Woodgate, Queensland 4660, or the Department of Environment, Lennox and Alice Streets (P.O. Box 101), Maryborough, Qld 4650; phone 61-7-4123-7100.

## Heron Island

Before the MV *Lady Musgrave* became the conduit from Bundaberg to Lady Musgrave Island, Heron Island was the undisputed most popular island in the Capricornia group. It lies about 60 kilometers north of Lady Musgrave and 72 kilometers offshore from Gladstone. The island's human inhabitants live at the Marine Biological Research Station and the island's modest resort.

Heron Island is a heavily vegetated coral cay with excellent snorkeling and diving only a few strokes from its porcelain white beaches. Nearby Wistari Reef is world renowned for its excellent scuba diving. The island itself is about 12 hectares and rises only three meters above the sea. It is known internationally as a sanctuary for a great number of seabirds, including sea eagles, noddy terns, silver gulls, mutton birds, albatrosses, and, of course, reef herons. Ninety species have been recorded visiting the island, with the greatest variety sighted in December.

Reef Week, which lasts all of November, is an annual event run by the park service and includes lectures, reef walks, and snorkeling and scuba diving excursions to nearby islands. Heron Island Resort also has a yellow submarine for people who want to see the reef without getting wet.

*Accommodations.* Camping is not allowed. For information about accommodations and your visitor's permit, contact Heron Island, P.O. Box 5287, Gladstone, Qld 4680; phone 13-2469. You can also contact the resort directly. Most units $A330 double per night.

*Access.* Heron Island can be reached by helicopter or boat from Gladstone. It takes 30 minutes by air and about three hours by sea. Sunstate Airlines flies from Brisbane and Gladstone.

# The Whitsunday Islands and the Outer Great Barrier Reef

The Whitsunday Islands were discovered by Captain Cook on June 3, 1770. What he saw pleased him. Poking out of a calm turquoise sea were heavily wooded, steep-sloped islands with rugged tops, plunging deep gorges, white sandy beaches, and countless coves and bays for safe anchorage. Cook named the route through the area Whitsunday Passage because he discovered the islands on Whitsunday — 49 days after Easter.

Today the Whitsundays are on their way to being among the top island playgrounds in the world. As they get more worldwide recognition, the challenge facing Australia will be to maintain their quality while accommodating the increasing demand for use and commercial schemes. The Whitsundays have it all: idyllic uninhabited tropical isles well suited for romantic fantasies, fringe and outlying reefs with some of the best snorkeling and scuba diving in the world, excellent yacht-rental and charter services, day sailing on everything from sailboards and small cats to former Americas Cup contenders, parasailing, opulent resorts for high rollers, casual resorts for the less flashy, seaplane flights to the Great Barrier Reef, reef-viewing subs, underwater observatories, snow-white sandy beaches, island walking tracks, and multitudes of terrestrial and aquatic life-forms.

The best way to prepare for the Whitsundays is to purchase a copy of *100 Magic Miles of the Great Barrier Reef: The Whitsunday*

*Shute Harbour, Whitsundays—dive boats on the way to outer reef.* PHOTO BY ERIC HOFF-
MAN.

*Islands,* by David Colfelt (about $A30). It's sold throughout Aus-
tralia, is well written, and contains aerial maps and descriptions of
diving areas, resorts, anchorages, services, and much more. It will
enhance your entire experience.

The Whitsundays share the same latitude as tropical Tonga and
New Caledonia and are made up of 74 continental islands. With the
cooling influence of the ocean, daytime temperatures are warm,
rarely hot. The islands are scattered between the Queensland coast
and the Great Barrier Reef, which swings around them. Because the
islands are protected on two sides, the ocean around them often is
more like a giant lagoon than a sea. The darkly vegetated mountainous islands jutting out of the azure sea are beautiful and intriguing.
Most of them are national parks, and the peninsula surrounding
Shute Harbour is 19,000-hectare Conway National Park. Of the 74
islands, 6 have resorts—West Molle, Hamilton, Hayman, Lindeman,
Long (Long has two: Palm Bay and Whitsunday 100), and South
Molle. The resorts range from opulent to inexpensive and provide
activities from parasailing to dancing, sailing, and scuba lessons.
There are also literally hundreds of places to pitch a tent on secluded

beaches on uninhabited islands and stunning safe anchorages for rented or charter yachts. There are 45 designated camping areas throughout the islands.

Airlie Beach is a resort town that caters to the Whitsundays. From Airlie Beach visitors by the hundreds rush a few kilometers down the road each morning to the tiny port of Shute Harbour to climb aboard any of dozens of watercraft. The variety is astounding: water taxis taking campers to faraway uninhabited islands; former Americas Cup contenders out for a day's sail through the islands; the ultrasleek Hamilton Island trimaran, looking like something out of a James Bond movie, gliding past everything else in the harbor; and small vintage seaplanes and modernized funky "African Queens" taking divers and snorkelers to the outer reef. The water churns and the sky buzzes with one departure after another until the lines of tourists disappear. After 9:00 A.M., the ticket takers have nothing to do until the next day. Shute Harbour will seem deserted until the flotilla for every taste returns around dusk to deposit the sun-weary passengers back on the mainland.

*Accommodations on the Mainland.* There are four main resorts and a half dozen motels in Airlie Beach. Two of the resorts make every effort to coordinate your visit with activities that may interest you. Whitsunday Terraces (phone 07-4946-6788), is a clean, well-landscaped resort on the hill overlooking Airlie Beach and the yachts anchored offshore. The staff is particularly helpful. (Rooms from $A125.) Whitsunday Wanderers Resort (phone 07-4946-6446) is richly landscaped with tropical plants and rents spacious casually decorated rooms with terrific sunsets; rooms from $A109. The Boathaven Lodge rents homey studios starting at $A55; phone 07-4946-6421. Backpackers and their associates can find a night at Whitsunday's Backpackers, which rents clean rooms with good views for as low as $A20 per night; phone 07-4946-7376.

*Entertainment and Eats at Night.* To mix with the natives over pool and bourbon try the Kentucky Bourbon Club behind the Airlie Beach Hotel. For the best view and best food try the Terraces Restaurant; phone 07-4946-6458.

For mainland resort bookings and information by mail, contact Whitsunday Information Centre, Mandalay and Shute Harbour

Roads (P.O. Box 332), Airlie Beach, Queensland 4802; phone 07-4946-7022. I stayed at Whitsunday Terraces and was impressed with how the staff hustled to place their jet-lagged customers on departing boats at Shute Harbour.

For economy accommodations aside from campgrounds, there are several low-cost overnight spots. Airlie Beach Hotel, 297 Shute Harbour Road, phone 07-4946-6233, has neat and tidy rooms. $A40 to $A75. Island Gateway Resort, about one km from town on Shute Harbour Road, has cabins ($A60) and tent sites ($A10); phone 07-4946-6228. Near Airlie Beach, the Koala, at $A12 per night, is hard to beat for the price. For dorm huts, call 07-4946-6001. There are caravan parks on the way into Airlie Beach, but they weren't highly rated by the locals I talked to. Camping is covered under "The Uninhabited Islands," below, but camping spots in mainland parks must be booked in advance.

*Access.* Most people get to the Whitsunday Islands by flying direct from Brisbane or Sydney to either Proserpine ($A200–250) on the mainland or Hamilton Island. There are numerous water taxis, boats, and small floatplanes to reach overwater destinations in the Whitsundays. Proserpine arrivals take a 40-minute shuttle bus to Airlie Beach, where they stay in motels and campgrounds or on one of the islands. Hamilton Island arrivals must be booked into the island's resort or into an island resort that connects with Hamilton Island. By car Proserpine is 126 kilometers north of Mackay and 264 kilometers south of Townsville on the Bruce Highway. By bus, Cairns to Proserpine costs about $A103 and Brisbane to Proserpine costs approximately $A45. Try Greyhound Pioneer (phone 13-20-30 from anywhere in Australia), or try McCafferty's; phone 13-14-99 from anywhere in Australia.

## The Mostly Expensive Island Resorts
### *South Molle Island Resort*

South Molle resort is located 3 kilometers from Shute Harbour and has 200 bungalow-style units partially behind palms at the end of a sandy-bottomed bay. The resort is relaxed and has a wide assortment of water toys, plus a well-managed place to park the kids. The resort also provides diving and snorkeling instruction. There is a resident band that usually plays nightly and an active nightlife. For a double expect to pay $A320 per night. Contact South Molle Island Resort, Private Mailbag 21, Mackay, Queensland 4741; phone 07-4946-9580.

## Daydream Island Resort

Think expensive and luxury, but mostly think expensive. The Daydream resort is on West Molle Island, which is about 1 kilometer directly across from South Molle and only about 2 kilometers from Shute Harbour. The resort takes up about one-third of the small island and caters to virtually all aquatic interests. It promotes itself as having a floating bar in a swimming pool that is "for the young at heart." They reputably have the best free child-care facility in Australia. How expensive? Around $A380 for an average room. Contact Daydream Island Resort, Mailbag 22, Mackay, Queensland 4741; phone 07-4948-8488. For toll-free booking from anywhere in Australia, phone 1-800-075-040.

## Lindeman Island Resort

This resort, on the island of the same name, is 17 nautical miles southeast of Shute Harbour. It's a budget- to moderate-priced family resort that has gone to considerable trouble to provide extra activities for children and child-care services while parents are enjoying themselves. Lindeman is a bit too far from Shute Harbour for day trippers, and the resort bills itself as a quiet retreat. There are dozens of excellent beaches, bushwalks, snorkeling areas, and light sailing craft to use during your stay on this 800-hectare island. Rangers at Conway National Park rate the 20-kilometer walking trails as the most varied and best of all the islands. Contact Whitsundays Visitors and Convention Bureau, Beach Plaza, Airlie Beach, Queensland 4802; phone 07-4946-6673.

## Hamilton Island

Hamilton is the crowning example of the pressures facing the Whitsundays. In 1975 Keith Williams, a self-made megabucks developer, bought the island. By 1985 the island had a yacht marina with a 300-boat capacity, its own commercial jet airstrip, 700 rooms to rent, huge swimming pools with bars, high-rises, restaurants (one with captive dolphins in an adjoining pool), a fauna park with Australian wildlife, and yacht-charter and diving businesses. Central to the island's development theme is volume—an activity for everyone that yields a profit margin. Aside from a pristine island, you name it and Hamilton Island will provide it. Parasailing, waterskiing, windsurfing, sailing small catamarans, snorkeling, scuba diving, and sunbaking are the daytime activities. There is good snorkeling on the western side of the island. At night there's good-quality live entertainment, dancing, barbecues, and a populous bar crowd.

Hamilton Island is a well-maintained state-of-the-art resort and a favorite vacation spot for thousands of Australians. However, it's also viewed with some foreboding. While I was sailing past Hamilton Island on a large sloop with about 30 people on board, a lively debate broke out among Aussies who disagreed about the intense development of Hamilton Island. One summed up his feelings by saying, "Hamilton suffers from 'Honolulu-disease,' urban blight in paradise." Rooms start at $A200 a night. Contact Hamilton Island, Whitsunday Islands, Queensland 4803; phone 07-4946-9999.

### Long Island

This island, which is about 4 kilometers southeast from Shute Harbour, has Club Crocodile, which is probably the most reasonably priced and unassuming of the major resorts. Young couples come here because of the moderate prices and the selection of water sports. It pitches its marketing to the 18- to 35-year-old crowd. Palm Bay is a low-profile tent-and-cabin facility that may be the best economy accommodation on the Whitsundays. Long Island itself is a national park with a number of marked walking tracks. Contact Club Crocodile, Private Mail Bag 26, Mackay, Queensland 4740; phone 07-4946-9400. Rooms with meals start at around $A50.

## The Uninhabited Islands

The 68 islands without resorts range from inhospitable rocky wind-blown outcrops to wooded and grass-covered mountainous islands with seductive beaches and fringing reefs suitable for camping, snorkeling, and contemplation. All but a few are national parks. However, improvements—including sources of fresh water and walking tracks—are in short supply on most of them.

Camping on islands requires a permit from Whitsunday Information Centre, Mandalay and Shute Harbour Roads (P.O. Box

332), Airlie Beach, Queensland 4802; phone 07-4946-7022; fax 07-4946-7023.

Island camping requires careful preparation because you'll be entirely without means to obtain provisions once you're "cast away" by a water taxi that will pick you up at a prearranged date. You'll also be on your own if an emergency occurs. Picking the right island is best done through consulting with a ranger. Ask for and abide by local advice. Considerations should include the cost of getting there, the availability of drinking water, the quality of the beaches (only 10 percent of the shoreline in the park system islands is considered beach) and fringing reefs, the range of possible island activities, the misery level caused by mosquitoes or sand flies, and weather conditions. Take more water, food, and sun and bug ointments than you think you'll need. There are 45 designated campgrounds containing hundreds of campsites, but individual areas have quotas ranging from 6 to 30 sites.

## Haslewood Island

Ranger Roly Howlett of Conway National Park rates Haslewood Island as best for "that idyllic castaway-on-a-tropical-beach experience." Chalkie's Beach on Haslewood Island is a combination of the turquoise water and rare white silica sand found on better-known nearby Whitehaven Beach on Whitsunday Island. There is a fringe reef near Chalkie's for snorkeling. Haslewood Island has 15 campsites. Tank water is sometimes available from January to March, and there are toilets and a picnic area.

## Hook Island

This island, 22 kilometers northeast of Shute Harbour, is worthy of strong consideration, too. If you want to mix snorkeling with camping, Hook may have the most to offer. At 5,200 hectares it's the second largest island in the Whitsundays. It has excellent fringing reefs and an underwater observatory and refreshment kiosk at its southwestern corner. There's a sandy beach just north of the observatory. Only five campsites are available at this end. At the island's north end, Butterfly Bay, which is 35 kilometers from Shute Harbour, also allows camping. Butterfly Bay is known for dozens of high-quality snorkeling and diving areas. However, there are currents throughout the area, especially on exposed promontories. Alcyonaria Point in Butterfly Bay is known for its soft corals. Manta Ray Bay is also an excellent protected dive spot that is best visited from a boat, but it can be reached from the nearby beach. Several divers told me that Manta Ray Bay has the best diving in the Whitsundays. There's more privacy and a beach in the most western of the two coves in Butterfly Bay. The Butterfly Bay area has no toilets, but tank water may be available from January through April. There's also a small resort on the island in case roughing it becomes overwhelming. Plus the resort (Hook Island Wilderness Resort) has its own campground and allows campers to use showers and other conveniences.

### North Molle Island

This island is heavily used by campers. It's only three kilometers north of South Molle Island and has year-round fresh water at Northwest Beach, where there are toilets, picnic facilities, and five campsites. On South Point there is a tank that has water most of the year. South Point also has an excellent beach and fringe reefs for snorkeling. Hannah Point at the north end is used by divers, but requires extreme care because of the currents.

### Whitsunday Island

At 11,000 hectares, Whitsunday Island is the archipelago's namesake and the biggest, most central island of the group. It is an undeveloped national park and is known for its rich bird life. Camping is allowed at four entirely separate sites. The island is often used by yachties, windsurfing safari groups, and organized adventure tour groups.

Stunning Whitehaven Beach does not have fresh water. However, it does have 15 sites with toilets and barbecue areas behind the foredune at the southeastern end of the beach. There's good snorkeling at the rocky area at this end of the beach, too. You'll also find a private pocket beach around the first rocky area. You'll never forget the snow-white color of the sand and the turquoise color of the water. About a kilometer from Whitehaven Beach are Choice and Silca Bays, two dramatic beaches with good snorkeling and usually total solitude. At the opposite side of the island, at Cid Harbour, there are three more campsites and an often used overnight anchorage for yachts. Spend enough time on Whitsunday and you'll see many of the 150 species of birds and possibly the unadorned wallabies that live there, too.

### Other Islands

Other islands with favorable ratings include Gloucester, Deloraine, Shaw, Thomas, and Goldsmith.

If island campsites are at capacity, ask about Henning Island. This tiny island, off the northwest corner of Whitsunday, is an often forgotten camping spot (it's not usually included in brochures) with a good beach and snorkeling.

*Accommodations.* To book a camping spot, contact the Marine Parks Authority at the corner of Shute Harbour and Mandalay Roads (phone 07-4946-7022; fax 4946-7023). Also, try Island Camping Connection, which specializes in transporting campers to and from islands. Book six to ten weeks in advance, if you plan on getting a camping spot during a holiday. For nonholidays, you should try to book in advance, but usually there's space on one of the islands. You can also book one of the 40 sites at Conway National Park (the peninsula park 1.6 kilometers from Shute Harbour on the road from Airlie Beach). The best mainland camping place is next to the tiny grass runway used by Air Whitsunday on the Airlie Beach–Shute Harbour Road. The campground has basic amenities and, aside from the occasional roar of takeoff or landing, it's a good spot for only $A5 a night.

*Access.* Several companies are in the interisland business. Try Fanta Sea Cruises, phone 07-4946-5111; Camping Connection, 07-4946-5255; or Seatrek, 07-4946-5255.

## Adventure Sailing

The Whitsundays are an adventure sailor's paradise. It's a particularly attractive area for bareboating. (Bareboating means you rent and skipper your own yacht.) It's hard to imagine any place better. The weather is usually warm year-round. Winds are light (10 to 15 knots) to moderate (20 to 25 knots). The windiest months are February through May. If you want less wind with a few tropical rains, try later in the year. Anchorages are everywhere and can often be combined with onshore camping and snorkeling. You could easily spend a month exploring fringe reefs and islands and feel like you just scratched the surface. Everything from schooners to small sloops, with and without a skipper, are available through bookings in the Airlie Beach area or up the coast at Bowen.

If you fancy yourself a yacht racer, the Hamilton Island Race Week, which attracts top yachts from as far away as Sydney, is held in April each year. There's also the Whitsunday Fun Race, which is made up of a flotilla that includes everything from windsurfers to schooners.

*Yacht Rentals.* Naturally, rental costs vary with the size of the yacht. Fully outfitted sloops range from $A225 to $A550 a day for 7- to 9-meter boats to $A600 to $A1,000 a day for 12- to 16-meter ones. Whitsunday Rent-a-Yacht, run by former Sydneysiders Bernie and Yvonne Kactchor, gets high marks from several yachties I talked with. Whitsunday Rent-a-Yacht is at Shute Harbour, Queensland 4741, Australia; phone 07-4946-9232. They'll also outfit you with diving equipment. There's also Australian Bareboat Charter, P.O. Box 115, Airlie Beach, Queensland 4741, Australia; phone 07-4946-9381. For sailboards (with or without instruction), contact Down Under Dive, The Esplanade, Airlie Beach, Queensland 4741. For further assistance, contact the Whitsunday Information Centre, Mandalay and Shute Harbour Roads (P.O. Box 332), Airlie Beach, Queensland 4802; phone 07-4946-7022; fax 07-4946-7023. Bowen, up the coast from Airlie Beach, also has an active yacht harbor with rental possibilities.

## Day Tripping on Maxisloops

One of the most pleasant sails I've experienced was aboard the maxi-sloop *Apollo* that leaves Shute Harbour daily for a cruise through the Whitsundays. For $A65 I was one of about 30 paying passengers. The crew encourages help. The passengers are a mix of Aussies, Europeans, Japanese, and Americans—many with sailing experience. The *Apollo* stops at Whitehaven Beach for lunch. *Gretel II*, a former Americas Cup contender, is also available for a comparable price, as are a number of other middle-sized sloops. Phone 07-4946-4444 for *Gretel II*. For *Apollo* phone 07-4946-6665. *Maxi Ragamuffin* is also a good bet; phone 07-4946-7777. For mainland windsurfing and small cats, go to Airlie Beach, not Shute Harbour. For sea kayaking, try Salty Dog Sea Kayaking (phone 07-4946-4848) or Coral Sea Boat Hire (phone 07-4946-9843).

## Day Boat Excursions

A more prolonged stay on the reef can be arranged with dozens of day and multiday boats that cater to divers, snorkelers, or just visitors. It pays to shop. Some boats will modify their trips for their customers' tastes. For example, *Summertime* will deliver campers to faraway islands and stop for a snorkel along the way; phone 07-4446-5294. The following boats offer one- and two-day cruises that might include snorkeling or diving: the *Otella* (phone 07-4946-7122); *Stargazer* (phone 07-4946-7172); and *Ambition* (phone 07-4946-6665).

## Snorkeling and Diving Services

There are dozens of diving services in the Whitsundays that rent equipment and go on one-day, two-day, and even weeklong reef outings. There are numerous opportunities to take classes and become a certified diver. Some of the regularly scheduled dives are appropriate for snorkelers. Again, shopping around in Airlie Beach and Shute Harbour is the best way to find the trip you want. Before signing on, make sure it's clear you're a snorkeler. Not all diving boats go to places suitable for snorkeling. Contact the following: Kelly Dive, phone 07-4946-6122 (this outfit will even take uncertified novices diving, which is questionable, but just the ticket for the impulsive person). There's also Reef Dive (phone 07-4946-6508), which is perhaps the longest-standing dive company in the area. If you opt for taking a course to become certified, expect to pay around $A500. Rum Runner Adventures offers PADI certification in four days for $A325; phone 07-4946-6508. Reefworld, with a boat bigger than some hotels, offers a two-night live-aboard dive charter for around $A300. Whitsunday Diver offers day trips with a cruise. For two dives it costs $A120; for snorkelers on the same journey, it is $A80. For a real immersion course try Island Divers. They offer a five-day course with at least half of the ten dives on the outer reefs; phone 07-4949-5650. They also offer a three-day trip for $A380 for certified divers and $A280 for snorkelers. Generally, all the hotels around Shute Harbour have connections with dive shops and boats catering to divers. From Shute Harbour, the *Triton* does full snorkel and reef excursions daily. For a multiday camping and snorkeling cruise, sign onto the *Checkmate*. Day costs for snorkelers run between $A35 and $A50; for multiday experiences, plan on a cost of $A90 per day or more.

*Access.* From Shute Harbour there are a host of ways to reach the Great Barrier Reef. Most reef destinations are between 35 and 45 kilometers west of Shute Harbour. The reef is visited by a fast cat from the island resorts and by conventional motor launches and small seaplanes.

# Townsville and Environs

## Townsville

Townsville is between Cairns and Proserpine on the Bruce Highway. Proserpine is 265 kilometers to the south and Cairns is 350 kilometers to the north. The stretch of road between Proserpine and Townsville is fairly drab. But from Townsville to Cairns the scenery is lush and tropical with cane fields and a jutting Tahiti-like escarpment near the highway. With 120,000 inhabitants, Townsville is the largest Australian city in the tropics and the second-largest city in Queensland.

In the 1980s Townsville went through a transition that put it on the map as a major tourist destination. The Great Barrier Reef Wonderland, with its multimillion-dollar world-class aquarium, and an attempt to attract tourism have paid off. The area's old standby natural attractions of Magnetic Island, Orpheus Island, Mount Spec National Park, and the Townsville Environment Park are worth stopping for as well.

Townsville got its start in the 1860s as a port serving the inland cattle stations. To this day it relies heavily on the primary industries of cattle and sugar for its daily bread. The city is an interesting contrast of superb examples of nineteenth-century architecture, storage depots, and structures like the glass-fronted old hotel radio station on Wickham Street that allows passersby to watch the broadcasters work. The city straddles Ross Creek, which is really a river, and almost everything is within walking distance of Flinders Mall, the award-winning, pedestrians-only main shopping area. Flinders Street East is the historic waterfront area that's undergoing revival. Castle

Hill dominates the city's skyline and affords a good vista of the city and nearby islands. Also popular for balmy evening walks is the Strand, a beachfront road through town with colorful tropical gardens and fountains. The Sheraton Breakwater Hotel/Casino is a casino-hotel complex overlooking the harbor; phone 07-4722-2333; fax 07-4772-4791. My favorite is Seagulls Resort, 74 The Esplanade, Belgian Gardens, Queensland 4810; phone 07-4721-3111. Seagulls is near the center of the city. It's surrounded by beautiful gardens, and it's moderately priced. Entirely unique to Townsville is the Home Hospitality for International Visitors Program. By contacting the Visitors Information Centre (phone 07-4721-3660), you can visit Queenslanders in their homes. This isn't a form of free accommodation, but a gesture of goodwill by people who enjoy meeting foreigners.

About five minutes out of the city on Pallarenda Road is the Townsville Environment Park (also known as Town Common), a major bird sanctuary. Go in the morning or evening. It's best at the beginning of the wet season (October through November). You'll see brolgas, jabiru storks, spoonbills, pied geese, darters, pied herons, ibises, and many other species. The brolgas perform their intricate courtship dances between October and May. The area is a rich swampland that withers in the dry season (winter), forcing the birds to go elsewhere. If you use the signposted blinds and trails, there are excellent photographic opportunities. You may also see agile wallabies, goannas, and possibly an echidna.

Billabong Sanctuary, 17 kilometers south of the city, is also worth a look. Saltwater crocodiles and cassowaries are often sighted; phone 07-4778-8344.

Great Barrier Reef Wonderland is an ambitious undertaking that showcases the Great Barrier Reef, houses the first Omnimax Theater in the Southern Hemisphere, and is the first permanent branch of the Queensland Museum outside Brisbane. Exhibits include live corals and how they reproduce, as well as venomous creatures. It also has shops and restaurants.

The complex cost more than $A20 million to build. Nothing was spared in terms of duplicating the real thing. More than 300 tons of coral sand and 700 tons of coral were used in the exhibit. Dr. Walter Adey of the Smithsonian Institution in Washington, D.C., was brought in to help establish coral colonies.

The museum portion of the facility shows the different habitats and wildlife found in northern Queensland; phone 07-4750-0800 or 4750-0891.

Admission, which includes the aquarium, Omnimax, and museum, is $A14 for adults and $A12 for students. For Omnimax phone 07-4721-1481.

*Accommodations.* In addition to the Sheraton Breakwater and the moderately priced Seagulls Resort, mentioned earlier, there are plenty of places to stay. From cheap to moderate try the following: the Reef Lodge is clean and has a roof, but there's nothing to write home about. Still, for the price of $A28 a night it's hard to complain; phone 07-4721-1112. The Student Lodge, with clean and tidy rooms, goes for $A65 a week; phone 07-4771-6875. Globetrotters takes its reservations from the Internet; E-mail: globe@ultra.net.au. Located on Palmer Street near the bus terminal, Globetrotters has connections to the main offshore attraction, Magnetic Island. Dorm rooms for $A14, rooms for $A34; phone 07-4771-3242.

## Magnetic Island

If the idea of a man-made floating island doesn't sit quite right, there's always 5,000-hectare Magnetic Island, just nine kilometers off Townsville's coast. The island got its name in 1770 when Captain Cook noted that his compass acted oddly while passing the island— something that hasn't happened to later voyagers.

Magnetic Island is one of the most popular islands on the Queensland coast. It's an inexpensive place to stay and visit, and despite its growth as a suburb of Townsville, it still has secluded beaches and walks through gum forests and tropical vegetation in the national park's 2,500 hectares.

There's a wide assortment of birds, including white-bellied sea eagles, dotterels, and ospreys on the coast, and pied currawongs, yellow-bellied sunbirds, and black ducks in the freshwater lagoons. On the steep open areas look for rock wallabies. Koalas are here, too, but harder to find. Your best chance is in the trees near the Forts. The kapok tree, with bright yellow flowers in the spring, is also common. The gullies and protected areas often have pockets of rain forest.

The walks travel through varied terrain and ecosystems. Besides gully rain forests and open forests, there are 23 pocket beaches, mangroves, and scenic lookouts. The walks in the Horseshoe Bay area on the northeast corner of the island have the most variety in terms of activities, wildlife, and scenery.

Horseshoe Bay to Arthur and Florence Bays is an easy 2-kilometer walk that starts at the high point on Horseshoe Bay Road. Look for a private road heading west. Walk through the gum forest to the bays. They have fringe reefs and good swimming and snorkeling.

Horseshoe Bay to Balding and Radical Bays involves 3 kilometers of moderately strenuous walking. At the east end of Horseshoe Bay Beach a track ascends through a gully. When the trail forks, Balding Bay is downhill to the left. Radical Bay is farther. Nude bathing is common at both bays, but especially at Balding Bay. There's good swimming at both bays (if the waters are free from box jellyfish, which sometimes appear in the summer).

Inquire about longer tracks at the ranger's office on Hurst Street (at the end of Granite Street), Picnic Bay, Magnetic Island, Queensland 4819; phone 07-4778-5378; fax 07-4778-5518.

*Swimming Caution.* Deadly box jellyfish can be present in summer months on any of the beaches. Ask if there is a risk before you enter the water.

*Recreation Contacts.* For scuba diving try Pure Pleasure Cruises; phone 07-4721-3555. This is the largest diving outfit. They visit the outer reef and accommodate snorkelers and children. Divers can also try their luck with the Magnetic Island Dive Centre (phone 07-4758-1399). They offer certification instruction, a wide range of dive experiences for divers of different confidences, and free hotel pickup. A couple of businesses offer a one-day sailing excursion around the island: try *Jazza*; phone 07-4778-5530. The 42-foot sloop takes about six hours to make the journey. This is a unique experience because the skipper is a jazz musician who plays to his captive audiences. There's also *Sun Cat*; phone 07-4758-1558. These trips cost between $A50 and $70 per head. For all kinds of water toys (inner tubes, Jet Skis, catamarans, etc.) contact Horseshoe Bay Watersports; phone 07-4758-1336. Magnetic Island Koala and Wildlife Park (phone 07-4778-5260) is worth the look. Besides koalas there's an

*The wilds of Hinchinbrook Island, northern Queensland.* PHOTO BY ERIC HOFFMAN.

assortment of kangaroos, wallabies, and other Australian fauna close at hand in natural settings suitable for excellent photography. The island also has many hikes. The most challenging and among the most popular is the all-day (round-trip) climb of Mount Cook. Sunbird Tours guides numerous hikes around the island; phone 07-4758-1213.

*Accommodations.* If you're planning to stay overnight, confirm your reservations from Townsville before leaving for the island. There's no camping in the park. Geoff's Place at Horseshoe Bay (phone 07-4778-5577) has rent-a-tent camping, airy cabins, and a restaurant in 2.5 hectares of tropical gardens. The Hideaway Hostel (phone 07-4778-5110) caters to the economy traveler. The Arcadia Hotel Resort offers a motel-style layout but the combination of lush gardens and a crescendo of birdcalls is what's unforgettable. For further assistance, contact Information Centre, Picnic Bay; phone 07-4778-5155.

*Access.* There are three main ferry services: Sunferries, 168 Flinders Street, Townsville (phone 07-4771-3855); Magnetic Island Car Ferry (phone 07-4772-5422); and Island Adventure Ferry (phone 07-4724-0555); or you can ride in a ocean racing boat owned by Island Adventure, but the fare is a little steeper. If you are on foot it's worth knowing there is a Magnetic Island Bus Service that takes you to many places on the island, plus a guided bus tour; the buses accommodate wheelchairs; phone 07-4778-5130. The island also has taxi and bicycle hires. The most intriguing rental is a Moke, an Aussie open-cockpit car that is a cross between a Volkswagen and a go-cart, at least to the untrained eye. If you want to take a spin in a Moke and see the island, give Moke Magnetic a call at 07-4778-5377. Expect a charge of around $A60 per day.

# Cardwell, Hinchinbrook Island, and Wallaman Falls National Park

## Cardwell

The coastal town of Cardwell isn't much; it would be barely worth a mention if it weren't for what's around it. Tiny Cardwell is the stepping-off point for magnificent Hinchinbrook Island, the largest island park in the world, and, on the mainland, there's the spectacular Herbert River, with its seven waterfall national parks. One of the falls is the longest year-round waterfall in Australia. Dunk, Goold, Brook, and Family Islands are also accessible from the area.

*Accommodations.* I found the Cardwell Beachfront Motel perfectly adequate for $A55 per night. They'll bring meals to your room. Contact Cardwell Beachfront Motel, Scott Street, Cardwell, Queensland 4849; phone 07-4066-8226. Economy travelers should try Kookaburra Cardwell Caravan Park; phone 07-4066-8648.

*Access.* Cardwell is in the heart of the wet tropics on the Bruce Highway, roughly midway between Townsville and Cairns.

## Hinchinbrook Island

Hinchinbrook Island looks like the island at the start of the remake of *King Kong*—shrouded in mist, reeking of adventure, and somehow ominous. The island is an immense 39,350 hectares, with lofty and massive granite fortresses jutting out of tropical forest. At 1,123 meters the tallest crag, Mount Bowen, often collects clouds that shroud the mountain and break apart into swirling forms that twist around the summit. Below the foreboding vertical-faced fortresses are steeply perched forests with myriad unfamiliar plants. The shores are either sweeping beaches broken by rocky headlands or an occasional stream, or pristine mangrove forests.

One of the most reassuring things about Hinchinbrook Island is its resort on Cape Richards on the northernmost promontory. The resort's low-key advertisements poke fun at the glitzy resorts that typify so many of the other continental island resorts: "We promise we'll never, ever, hire an entertainment director. . . . Naturally there will be some people who wouldn't dream of going to a place that doesn't have a disco. But since we only take thirty guests at a time, to be perfectly honest, we'd just as soon have those people go somewhere else. The Gold Coast perhaps." The resort's small pier is the only structure visible from the sea. You'll probably run into the resort's chef fishing for dinner here.

## Walks

Aside from the 32-kilometer Thorsborne Trail, walking tracks haven't been developed to any large extent on Hinchinbrook Island, though the cross-country possibilities are unlimited. Cape Richards and Ramsey Bay, which is about midway down the island's western shore, are the starting points for most of the established walking tracks. Most of this coast has tropical forests, wide sweeping beaches, and no people. Typically you can walk for hours and not see another human footprint.

From the resort there is a 100-meter walk to a high point on the Cape Richard promontory that affords an excellent view north to Goold, Brook, and the Family Islands.

Starting at Orchid Beach behind the resort, a little longer walk delivers you to Turtle Bay. Walk south on the beach past the tiny dam and look for a trail cutting through the bush that will take you over the headland to the next beach. This trail has a steep ascent followed by a steep descent into idyllic Turtle Bay. Past Turtle Bay lie North and South Shepherd Beaches, which are more secluded and backed with rather low tropical forest. Each beach is about one kilometer in length.

A circuit walk starts at the resort and goes 5.5 kilometers to the Macuslha Bay camping area (bushcamping) with an equal-distance return. Ask at the resort to be directed to the starting point. This is a split rain forest and beach walk. You stand a good chance of seeing a wide assortment of bird life including brahminy kites, sunbirds, sulfur-crested cockatoos, and cassowaries. You also may see feral pigs, which several locals described as usually shy and retiring. If you're up to a long haul, experienced walkers sometimes trek from Cape Richards to Ramsey Bay (where boats call via the tidal creeks), which is about 18 kilometers one way. If you spend a couple days at it, you'll experience a kind of coastal solitude that is gone from much of the world. You'll have to pack water. Discuss a walk of this duration with the rangers in Cardwell. The 32-kilometer Thorsborne Trail is one of the top five treks in Australia. See page 31 for details. It takes three to four days to complete.

Other walks require boating to your starting point. A promising area is the south end of Ramsey Bay. Boat operators from Cardwell normally include Ramsey Bay in their day tour of the island. Ramsey Beach is striking. The vegetation is thick, and looming over the white beach and bright foliage are Mount Bowen, the Thumb, and Nina Peak, each a dramatic and foreboding mass of rock. Mount Bowen is sometimes climbed by "following the creek systems up." By the look of it, getting to the summit would take rock-climbing skills, too.

A less challenging walk is south along Ramsey Beach to the next headland. I rounded this rocky headland at low tide to see a remarkably beautiful beach and behind it a crystal clear freshwater billabong sitting under the forest canopy. (A billabong is a natural swimming hole.) This beach is known as No Name Beach by boat operators. The combination of rich vegetation, wide beach, and fresh water makes this an inviting place to spend a few days. I saw azure kingfishers flitting around the billabong. Another 12 kilometers will take you to Zoe Bay, another campground, and a pickup point for small boats.

*Accommodations.* The Hinchinbrook Island Resort, Cardwell, Queensland 4849, Australia; phone 07-4066-8585; fax 07-4066-8742; E-mail: hinchinbrook@internetnorth.com.au. You end up in a clean cabin with basic amenities. Good-quality seafood meals are served in a dining room with bar.

Hinchinbrook is a camper's island. It has many places where solitude and wilderness are guaranteed. Timing your stay to low-mosquito density and outside of the hard-core rainy season (December–February) are important considerations.

You must get a camping permit by contacting the Rainforest and Reef Centre, Bruce Highway, P.O. Box 74, Cardwell, Queensland 4849; phone 07-4066-8601; fax 07-4066-8116.

*Access.* A seaplane from Townsville (30 minutes) is one way to get to the resort. More commonly, people arrive by boat. Located 8 kilometers east of Cardwell, Hinchinbrook Island can be reached by private boat or water taxi from Cardwell or Dungeness. I received good service on the *Y-not.* The boat is skippered by American George Towne; $A60 per head is normal. To find small-boat operators contact the Rainforest and Reef Centre, Bruce Highway, Cardwell, Queensland 4849; phone 07-4066-8601.

## Dunk Island

In Australia, Dunk Island may be the best-known tropical continental island chiefly because of *Beachcomber,* by E. J. Banfield. Banfield died in 1923 at the age of 26, but his natural history books about the island are still popular.

Where Hinchinbrook has a rugged, powerful, and sometimes foreboding look, much smaller Dunk has a bright green, gentle look. Despite the island's subdued profile, it receives great amounts of rain, usually between December and February.

From a boat's deck the island appears to be a green mosaic of different kinds of plants. Onshore there are 12 kilometers of marked walking tracks that pass through most of the plant communities. The main walking track to the summit of Mount Kootaloo passes through an impressive rain forest. The island has more than 110 species of birds, including Torres Strait imperial pigeons, brush turkeys, brown boobies, great frigatebirds, and sulfur-crested cockatoos. The island is also well known for the abundance of the brilliant Ulysses butterfly. There are a series of pocket beaches and good snorkeling on fringe reefs. The beaches are on the mainland side of the island and can be entirely private.

*Accommodations.* Campers staying in the park half of the island must get a camping permit at the Reef and Rainforest Centre on the Bruce Highway in Cardwell; phone 07-4066-8601. You can also obtain a permit in Cairns at the Department of Environment, 10

McLeod Street; phone 07-4052-3096. You must bring your own water.

On the nonpark half of the island, you'll stay at the Dunk Island Resort. I didn't visit it, but judging by its advertisements it caters to the luxury crowd. Contact the resort through the Great Barrier Reef Hotel, via Townsville, Queensland 4810; phone 07-4068-7099.

*Access.* Dunk Island is only 3 kilometers off the coast, 164 kilometers south of Cairns. People going to the resort often fly direct from Townsville or Cairns. By sea, Clump Point near Tully is the closest departure point.

## Wallaman Falls National Park

The Herbert River, which meets the sea at Ingham 53 kilometers south of Cardwell, is the premier jungle waterfall area in Australia. In all, there are seven parks on the Herbert River. Wallaman Falls National Park is the most accessible, though it can take a half day from Cardwell to reach it. The roads inland from Ingham are not paved and are subject to nature-caused alterations. The Herbert River is in Queensland's wet tropical region, which receives more than 2,000 millimeters (79 inches) of rain annually. The falls, the rain forest, and much of the wildlife are at their steamy tropical best during the wet season, from November to March.

Stony Creek, a tributary of the Herbert, meanders across the Lannercost Range and suddenly plummets 279 meters in a clean drop from the plateau to the bottom of a gorge. The free fall makes the longest drop of any year-round waterfall in Australia. The waterfall is often surrounded by mist and rainbows that arc across the jungle canopy. It occurs in a side gorge that is about 400 meters from the main Herbert River Gorge.

From the campground a 2-kilometer road leads to a lookout over the fall. From the lookout a 1.7-kilometer walking track climbs steeply to the base of the waterfall. There are attractive swimming holes.

*Accommodations.* The only form of accommodation is camping. The designated area has tables, toilets, and more than a dozen sites. You must get a permit in Ingham. For details, contact Ranger, Department of Environment, Herbert Street, P.O. Box 1293, Ingham, Queensland 4850.

*Access.* There is no public transportation to the park. Wallaman is 52 kilometers inland from Ingham, which is south of Cardwell on the Bruce Highway. From Ingham travel to Trebonne and turn left. Turn right past the Stone River and then take the first left. The road is steep and hazardous.

# Cairns and the Wet Tropics

## Cairns

The city of Cairns (pronounced "Cans") is the hub of tourist activity in Queensland's wet tropics. Cairns is the stepping-off point to the northern Great Barrier Reef, tropical beaches, nearby national parks, lush tablelands, and the truly wild Cape York Peninsula. For a growing number of overseas visitors, Cairns International Airport is their introduction to Australia. It's a small terminal about the size of a jumbo jet.

Cairns bills itself as the gateway to the Great Barrier Reef. In truth it's one of many gateways, though the reef is closer to the mainland here than in the southern areas. When considering the reef in conjunction with the limitless choices of terrestrial adventure opportunities in spectacular tropical rain forests, Cairns has to rate high among places to visit for any overseas traveler with the faintest appreciation for nature and adventure.

See the town aboard the Cairns Explorer, modeled after the Sydney Explorer—it's even the same color. For around $A7, you can ride the bus all day and get off and on as it makes its hourly rounds. Most visitors board the Explorer along the esplanade or in front of the Visitors Information Centre on McLeod Street.

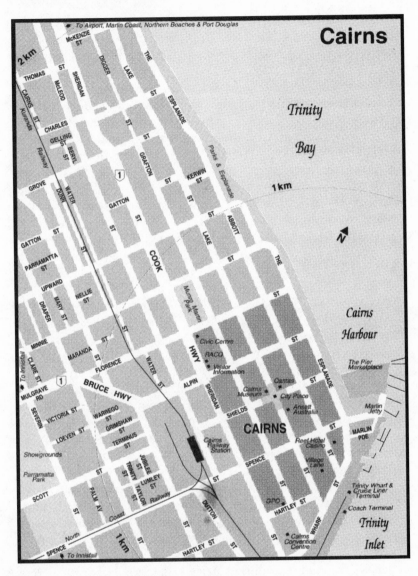

Cairns's strength is in what's around it. For starters there are more than 60 national parks, many within a day's drive, an hour's flight, or a two-hour boat trip. Typically, in the Cairns Colonial Club and other top hotels, the morning is a nonstop hustle of small tourist buses and 4WD vehicles whisking people to the parks of the

Atherton Tablelands, river rafting or caving trips, the parks and rain forests to the south, Cape York destinations, and the Cairns waterfront for boat rides to Green or Fitzroy Island and the outer reef.

It's easy enough to rent a car. The major companies have booths at the international airport. In town there is also a wide selection to choose from. Many of the companies are located on Sheridan Street. Try Jolly Frog motorbike and car rentals at 147 Sheridan Street and 140 Lake Street, Cairns 4870; phone 07-4031-2379 for a car, or 07-4031-2322 a motorbike. Standard cars rent for $A35 a day or $A285 a week. Jolly Frog also rents motor scooters, 4WDs, 8-seat buses, 12- to 22-seat buses, station wagons, camping equipment, and trailers. Also on Sheridan Street is Delta Car Rentals; phone 07-4032-2000. Other companies are: Hertz (phone 07-4051-6399 in the city, 07-4035-9033 at the airport's domestic terminal) and Thrifty, phone 07-4051-8099.

*Other Important Places in Cairns.* Most of the cruises to islands and dive and snorkel sites leave from Trinity Wharf or the nearby Marlin Jetty. To get your bearings for all activities, visit the Visitors Information Centre near the two piers; phone 07-4051-3588; fax 07-4051-0127. Cairns used to be mostly about catching up on jet lag before shoving off for the Atherton Tablelands, Port Douglas, or the numerous nearby islands, but that has changed. The overabundance of T-shirt displays still exists, but the city has come into its own with an assortment of excellent restaurants, good-quality accommodations, and places to visit right in (or near) town. One of the places worth visiting in town is the Tjapukai Aboriginal Cultural Centre. Founded by an American and French couple, Don and Judy Freeman, it is now owned by a group made up mainly of local Aborigines. The center has a film about European contact with the region and the drastic changes experienced by the surviving Aboriginal people. The show then moves on to Creation Theatre, where the Aboriginal Dreamtime legend is explained against a backdrop of New Age technology and lighting. Lastly there is a high-energy, innovative dance performance that incorporates both historic and new dances. The Magic Space Museum is also much appreciated by visitors. There is an excellent shop where you can buy high-quality Aboriginal art made by local Aborigines; for sale are cloth and clothing with Aboriginal designs, music sticks, didgeridoos, boomerangs, and other tools common to the Aboriginal culture. Set aside at least three hours for a visit. The center is located ten minutes north of Cairns on the Captain Cook Highway; $A24 for adults, $A12 for children; phone 07-4042-9999. You can buy a package deal that allows you to visit the mountain town of Kuranda via a skyrail or train.

Other places receiving high marks are: Royal Flying Doctor Visitors Centre, 1 Junction Street and Edge Hill; phone 07-4053-5687. Cairns Regional Gallery on Shields and Abbott Streets; top Australian artists display their work here. Cairns Museum at City Place (phone 07-4051-5582) has exhibits from the colonial period and is well run by volunteers. Flecker Botanical Gardens (10 kilometers from town via the Sunbus) contains a wide assortment of plants collected since 1880. Early-morning visits ensure wonderful birding opportunities; phone 07-4050-2454. A visit to the "wet tropics" would not be complete without paying homage to saltwater crocodiles, the largest and most ferocious of all crocodiles. They cause a stir when they eat someone, which happens only if the victim is foolish enough to swim in a river or swampy coastal area frequented by these monstrosities. Make sure you time your visit during a feeding, so you can truly appreciate this predator. There are two live crocodile exhibits near town: Wild World (23 kilometers north of Cairns; phone 07-4055-3669) and Hartley's Creek Crocodile Farm (40 kilometers north of Cairns; phone 07-4055-3576). Wild World has koalas, kangaroos, and other Aussie wildlife on display. Koalas can be handled. Undersea World, an immense aquarium beside the Marlin Marina, gives you a glimpse of the fish species found on the reef.

*Restaurants.* There are many eateries in Cairns. Two I liked for the quality and the price are: Hides Bar and Grill at Lake and Shields Streets; phone 07-4031-5333 (steak, chicken, seafood with superb salads, reasonable prices), and Tawny's, Marlin Parade; phone 07-4051-1722 (possibly the best seafood restaurant in Cairns, pricey). Both restaurants, like most of Cairns, have easy wheelchair access.

*Water Connections.* Port Douglas, the port of the *Quicksliver* (see p. 227) and many of the islands near Cairns offer diving, snorkeling, and other water activities. For the widest selection of offerings, contact the Great Barrier Reef Visitors Bureau before you leave for Australia; phone 61-7-4099-4644; fax 61-7-4099-4645; E-mail: visitors@GreatBarrierReef.aus.net.

Large high-speed catamarans are the boat of choice in Cairns and all along the reef. These boats carry large groups of people to choice outer-reef locations in a relatively short time. There are also sailing and conventional watercraft offering a wide range of activities and different ambiences from the large cats. Below are some of the offerings you'll find in Cairns.

*Reef Magic* is a 22-meter fast cat that offers ten different reef sites to divers and snorkelers. They'll pick you up at your hotel. They specialize in day trips, offer guided snorkel safaris, have snorkel equipment on board, and have dives for certified and introductory scuba divers. *Reef Magic* departs Marlin Jetty daily; phone 07-4031-1588; fax 07-4031-3318; E-mail: reef.magic@altnews.co.au.

*Supercat* is another large, state-of-the-art catamaran. It visits the highly rated outer Norman, Saxon, and Hastings Reefs. The *Supercat* is for day-trippers. The package includes lunch; $A70 for snorkelers and $A120 for scuba divers. There is snorkel equipment on board. The *Supercat* departs Marlin Marina at 8:30 A.M. daily.

*Green Island* is another big cat. It whizzes people out to Green Island and nearby dive and snorkel sites. They offer snorkeling, swimming, glass-bottomed-boat rides, and an Aussie barbecue lunch. You can also visit the resort on Green Island, feed fish, and visit some very large saltwater crocodiles and a nautical museum. Departs daily from the Pier Marketplace; phone 07-4051-8896. (See "Green Island" for more detail.)

Another state-of-the-art big cat is *Ocean Spirit,* which travels like the other cats with huge motors but also is equipped to cut its motors and slide through the water under sail when conditions warrant it. The *Ocean Spirit* visits remote sandy cays as well as outer-reef dive and snorkel sites. Contact Ocean Spirit Cruises, 143 Lake Street, P.O. Box 2140, Cairns, Queensland 2140; phone 07-4031-4344. And there are large sail-powered dive boats that take a dozen passengers, such as *Serica;* phone 07-4055-7670. There are also boat owners who will take you diving or snorkeling and on to the best northern rain forests in multiday outings. For this kind of experience try the *Rum Runner;* phone 1-800-686-444 (toll-free in Australia).

In the coverage of Port Douglas and the islands near Cairns there are listings of other boats catering to reef lookers.

*Accommodations.* There is no shortage of places to stay in Cairns. Anything near the Esplanade will put you within walking distance of all major interests in town and the jettys. For budget stays, try Dreamtime, 4 Terminus Street (near Sheridan Street); phone 07-4031-6753. The Irish couple who run this place work hard to connect people with excursions. Rooms have ceiling fans and refrigerators. One night for a double is $A35; $A15 for room shares. Free Spirit Travellers Accommodation, 72 Grafton Street, is also a friendly place, with all the basic amenities for a reasonable price. Dorms are $A14; rooms $A30; phone 07-4051-7620. The Cairns Girls Hostel hosts women over 30. Men can get as far as inquiring about a guest and requesting they meet somewhere else. The Girls Hostel is located at 147 Lake Street. Reserve a room by phoning 07-4051-2016; $A15 a night for a bed, but the price drops if you stay longer. Cairns has excellent accommodations in the moderate and expensive ranges. Some of them are: Coral Tree Inn, 166 Grafton Street, Cairns, Queensland 4870; phone 07-4031-3744 (five minutes from the center of the city, smallish rooms, but clean with tile floors, feels tropical, tour desk helps schedule excursions). Rooms start at $A88. This is among the best moderate-priced hotels in Cairns, considering the price and service. If money isn't a problem, try Cairns International, 17 Abbott Street, Cairns, Queensland 4087; phone 07-4031-2211; fax 07-4031-1801. This a five-star hotel near the city center. Rooms start around $A270. The interior is a wonderful tribute to tropical architecture. Moderate to expensive is the Royal Palm Villas, 184 McLeod Street, Cairns, Queensland 4870; phone 07-4052-1444; fax 07-4052-1255. There are only 16 units, each fully self-contained, with a bedroom and cooking facilities in each unit. The decor is high-grade tropical, and the staff works to help make connections with tour operators.

*Access.* Cairns is one of the gateway cities to the Great Barrier Reef and to all of Australia for international visitors. I remember my first visit here in the late 1980s. Three immense 747s from Asia and the United States disgorged hundreds of passengers to go through customs in what amounted to a glorified tin shed. Things have changed since then, but as international airports go, Cairns is simple and modest. At last check the following international carriers had regularly scheduled flights: Cathay Pacific (phone 13-17-47), Qantas (phone 1-800-177-767, toll-free in Australia), Air New Zealand (phone 1-800-061-253, toll-free in Australia), Singapore Airlines (phone 07-4031-4000), Japan Airlines (phone 07-4031-2700), and Malaysia

Airlines (phone 07-4031-0000). For readers phoning from North America, see page 10 in "Basic Travel Information and Contacts."

Qantas (domestic-flight phone, 13-13-13), Sunstate Airlines (book through Qantas), and Flight West Airlines (phone 13-23-92) are domestic carriers. Numerous small planes leave here for remote destinations in tropical Queensland. Sometimes freight and mail planes will take passengers to the remotest places on the Cape York Peninsula. You can find everything from single-engined Cherokees to DC-3s and helicopters for short hops.

It takes a long time from anywhere in North America, Europe, or most of Asia to get to Cairns. Even the distances from inside Australia are staggering. Cairns is 4.5 hours (2,700 kilometers) from Melbourne; 3 hours (2,000 kilometers) from Sydney; and 2 hours (1,400 kilometers) from Brisbane. Under most situations it will save you money to fly directly to Cairns from Hawaii or other international points rather than work your way to Cairns through domestic flights from Sydney, Melbourne, or Brisbane. Also, discounted tickets and multilanding tickets are usually much lower if booked abroad. However, Cairns has the Budget Travel Flight Centre on 24 Spence Street (phone 07-4051-9972), which claims to always undercut any ticket for a better price. This, of course, is a worthy sentiment, but it may be somewhat misleading. Domestic flights purchased in Australia are often three times higher than comparable flights in the United States and elsewhere. Undercutting an Australian purchased ticket may not be a saving at all to a ticket shopped overseas.

If you have time and patience on your side, getting to Cairns by train from Sydney is economical. The smallish Cairns Central Depot is on McLeod Street near the shopping mall. There are storage lockers; phone 13-22-32 for schedules and fares. In 1999 a one-way ticket from Sydney to Cairns was only $A200 for people holding an East Coast Discover Pass. The train ride in coach is long and arduous and passes through lengthy stretches of monotonous scenery. There are different classes of rail travel. The *Great South Pacific Express* is the luxury ride and—reputedly—so good that the scenery doesn't matter.

A local train ride is definitely worth it. The Cairns-Kuranda train (34 kilometers one way) to the Atherton Tablelands runs every day of the week. Most tickets include a one-way ride by train and the other way by Skyrail (small gondolas suspended by cable) for around $A65. A one-way rail ticket is around $A25, but there are senior and student discounts; phone 07-4031-3636. (See also "The Herberton Highlands and the Atherton Tablelands.")

By bus from any large population center is a long haul. McCafferty's (phone 13-14-99) makes runs regularly back and forth from Brisbane with stops (Proserpine, Townsville) along the way. Greyhound (phone 13-20-30) also has regularly scheduled routes to Cairns. Bus services usually offer discounts to students and youth hostel card holders. The trip from Brisbane takes around 28 hours.

Since the promotional literature on boat travel emphasizes going to the local jetty for a ride to the outer reef and back, going somewhere as a mainland destination from Cairns is a surprise. The large fast cat *Quicksilver* makes the 1.5 hour run to Port Douglas and back each day; phone 07-4099-5500.

Cairns has taxis, regularly scheduled bus runs around the city and to points north and south, plus a plethora of 4WD tours by naturalists into the hinterlands. Contact the Travellers Contact Centre, 13 Shields Street (about 150 meters from the main pier); phone 07-4051-4777; fax 07-4051-0127; E-mail: adventures@adventures.com.au.

Another excellent source for information about where to go is the Queensland National Parks and Wildlife Service office, 10 McLeod Street, Cairns, Queensland 4870; phone 07-4052-3096; fax 07-4051-7475. Ask for a copy of "Queensland Guide to Camping" and "Queensland Guide to National Parks."

## Port Douglas

Port Douglas is a budding resort area 75 kilometers north of Cairns. It was a hard-luck port for most of the 1900s and a historical landing area for gold miners in the 1850s. A cyclone nearly erased it from the map in 1911. A couple of large hotel chains built hotels here in the late 1980s, catering to eco-tourists who frequent Port Douglas as a stepping-off place to some of the best snorkeling and diving on the Great Barrier Reef and as a base of operation to the wilds of the Cape York Peninsula. The town's population is about 2,500.

## The Wet Tropics

The wet tropics is the coastal strip stretching 400 kilometers from Ingham to Cooktown, with Cairns situated roughly at the midway point. Few Americans would recognize it as belonging to Australia. Annual rainfall during the wet season (November–January) often exceeds 120 inches and in isolated pockets it exceeds 400 inches — 20 inches have fallen in a single hour! The temperature is usually around 86°F (30°C) and typically humid. This coastal band contains the largest area of continuous rain forest in Australia.

Offshore there are rich, emerald-green continental islands (Hinchinbrook and Dunk are covered in the previous section). Fitzroy, Green, and Lizard are the best-known islands visited from Cairns. Fitzroy is a classic continental island covered in lush greenery and rising steeply from the sea. Green is a coral cay. Lizard, another continental island, has some of the best diving and snorkeling on the entire reef. Of the several smaller cays, the bird-rich sanctuary at Michaelmas Cay National Park just north of Green Island is popular.

The coastline consists of mangrove communities, tidal creeks, and sweeping shell-strewn beaches with nearby fringe reefs and often crystal-clear water teeming with the thousands of life-forms of the reef community. There are more than 24 mangrove species in the wet tropics. Directly behind the mangroves and beaches is a multilevel mosaic of greenery. Deep green cane fields fill the bottomlands in many areas, but on the steep slopes the rain forest is supreme. More than 600 species of plants have been classified in the rain forests. There are massive buttressed giant figs, ferns of all sizes, and the newly discovered primitive *Idiospermum australiense,* the only member of its family and the only living link between primitive and flowering plants. There are countless palms and vines. Streams and rivers crash down the escarpment from the wet tablelands through the rain forest into the sea. Some of these waterways provide excellent whitewater rafting and kayaking.

The wildlife of the wet tropics includes saltwater crocodiles, known as "salties," which weigh up to 1.5 tons and measure 6 meters. They are fearless, and their only criteria for a meal is catching it. They've eaten enough people to cause a national debate about how to manage the species. (Queensland is removing "cheeky crocs" wherever they occur south of the Daintree River.) Smaller and not dangerous freshwater crocodiles, known as "freshies," also live throughout Australia's tropics. Freshies live farther inland, usually above the first set of rapids or falls. Cassowaries, the giant flightless birds that come equipped with crash helmets, strut and rumble through the forests throughout the wet tropics. Shiny green giant tree

*Tree kangaroo.* PHOTO BY ERIC HOFFMAN.

frogs cling to branches. Lumholtz's and Bennett's tree kangaroos, Australia's two tree-dwelling species of kangaroos, fool the casual observer into thinking they're monkeys from another continent. The rain forest is home to the green possum, perhaps the cutest of Australia's furry bug-eyed possums. The rain forest also has the world's most amazing frog—a species that gives birth in its stomach and carries its young in its mouth. The bird life is astounding—more than 210 species have been recorded at various places. In clearings you may also find agile wallabies and gray kangaroos.

## The Herberton Highlands and the Atherton Tablelands

West and southwest of Cairns are the Herberton Highlands, the Atherton Tablelands, and, farther west yet, Chillagoe and Royal Caves Arch National Park. The Atherton Tablelands contain isolated pockets of rain forest, often around small lakes, such as those found in Lake Barrine and Lake Eacham National Parks. Kuranda (see below), my favorite small town in tropical Australia, is on the tablelands. It's a must visit by train from Cairns. The caves at Chillagoe, a 200-kilometer drive from Cairns, have stalactites and stalagmites in glittery profusion and are worthy of a day's exploration.

Southwest of Cairns between the Atherton Tablelands and the coast sits the jagged razorlike granite Bellenden Ker Range, now Bellenden Ker National Park. The park has Queensland's highest mountain, Mount Bartle Frere (1,656 meters). This very rugged area contains the largest section of pristine rain forest in Australia. It's a particularly good area to find tree kangaroos and cassowaries. Bush-camping is allowed with a permit, and there are a few walks for the fit and those well versed in survival skills. Josephine Falls at the southern end is a popular picnic and swimming spot. This is also where you can get a permit to climb Mount Bartle Frere. The trail is steep and unimproved, but it's marked.

To the south of Cairns, 185 kilometers along the coast on the Bruce Highway, are Cardwell, Hinchinbrook Island, several other outstanding islands, and the waterfall national parks on the Herbert River.

The stretch of the Bruce Highway between Cairns and Cardwell is the wettest coastal band in Australia. The town of Tully, at the foot of Mount Tyson (674 meters), collects on the average 4,267 millimeters (168 inches) of rain annually. In the Tully Gorge there is a spectacular section of white water that you can experience by signing onto a raft trip in Cairns. Near Innisfail there is Palermston National Park, with luxuriant rain forests, waterfalls, and walking tracks. The North Johnstone River, which is one of Australia's supreme multiday commercially rafted white-water experiences, roars out of the highlands on its way to the Coral Sea. The coastline is often spectacular, with tropical rain forests plunging from the highland plateaus to the coastal beaches. On this stretch Etty, Bramston, Kurrimine, and Mission Beaches are popular stopping places for the around-Australia caravan camping set. Kurrimine is noted for its nearby reefs; Etty is an idyllic tropical beach with a life-saving club; and Mission, known for its resident cassowaries, has basic amenity businesses, including caravan parks. It's a stepping-off point to Dunk Island.

## Noteworthy Experiences Around Cairns

Rating experiences depends on your tastes. I had many memorable outdoor adventures around Cairns, some heightened by the personalities who shared them with me. With a little luck and a free copy of the "Travel and Tourism" guide published by the *Cairns Post,* or after a visit to the regional office of the National Parks and Wildlife Service (10 McLeod Street, Cairns, Queensland 4820; phone 07-4052-3096; fax 07-4051-7475), you may find something even more exciting.

### *The* Quicksilver

The *Quicksilver* is a big cat moored in Port Douglas, about an hour's drive north of Cairns (buses run there regularly). The *Quicksilver* takes passengers to Agincourt Reef west of Cape Tribulation in the northern Great Barrier Reef. This area is representative of the best reefs in the north. Once everyone's on board, two marine biologists bring you up to speed on reef ecology with humorous, informative, and conservation-minded lectures about the many life-forms on the reef. The crew provides snorkeling instruction. If you have snorkeled and know very little about the reef, this is probably the best education and instruction on the entire reef. The use of the snorkeling gear is gratis. Onboard diving gear can be rented upon proof of accreditation. The diving is outstanding regardless of your experience. Agincourt Reef has a rich variety of corals that haven't been affected by the crown of thorns. You're far from the mainland, so such menaces as box jellyfish, stonefish, and saltwater crocodiles aren't a worry. The reef has drop-offs that allow you to get a look at some of the middle-sized and bigger fish species, such as trout, barramundi, trevally, moorish idols, cod, puffers, and my favorite, the master of the ruse, the trumpet fish. There are shallow areas as well, where many of the colorful smaller species can be seen.

You can also stay dry and putter around in the *Quicksilver*'s semi-submersible sub, which is moored at the diving platform.

A complimentary meal featuring piles of shrimp and tropical fruit is served on board during the day. Of all my big cat rides and snorkeling experiences, the *Quicksilver* came in first.

To book, contact Quicksilver Connections Ltd., Marina Mirage, P.O. Box 171, Port Douglas, Queensland 4871; phone 07-4099-5500; fax 07-4099-5525; E-mail: quick1@internetnorth.com.au.

## Kuranda

Kuranda is a small, attractive town perched on the Atherton Table-lands 22 kilometers inland from Cairns. It's normally reached by a vintage train that chugs up the steep tropical escarpment past spec-tacular waterfalls to the town's much photographed train station. The station is a showcase for tropical plants. The tiny town's main street is lined with gargantuan tropical fig trees, and within a short walking distance is the Australian Butterfly Sanctuary, the Kuranda Wildlife Noctarium, the Jilli Binna Aboriginal Museum (owned and operated by local Aborigines), several good-quality broad-spectrum art galleries, and the Dance Theatre, which features Aboriginal chil-dren dancers. They perform at Heritage Market daily.

The Australian Butterfly Sanctuary (phone 07-4093-7575) is liter-ally a million-dollar structure and the fulfilled dream of Paul and Sue Wright. It opened in July 1987 and is billed as the top entomological enclosure in the Southern Hemisphere. Kuranda has long been known as a haven for the lion's share of Australia's 380 species of butterflies. In the sanctuary you'll be able to photograph red lacewings, blue tigers, electric-blue ulysses, and others. The entry fee is $A10; there is wheelchair access. Hours are 9:45 A.M. to 4:00 P.M. daily. Located five minutes by car from Kuranda, the Rainforestation Nature Park is popular because it introduces visitors to nature in a novel way. Visitors board a World War II amphibious vehicle that plunges into a river as the driver explains the rain forest and its crea-tures. There is also a dance performance by Aboriginal dancers and an Aboriginal-guided Dreamtime walk. You can cuddle with a koala (even though the koala is ambivalent at best) and other animals, but a picture with a koala will cost you $A8. There is wheelchair access. The cost is $A29 per adult; phone 07-4093-9033.

As soon as you walk into the Kuranda Wildlife Noctarium you'll wonder why so few zoos have thought of a noctarium to display animals that are active at night. Most of Australia's wildlife falls into this category. At each level of the three-story noctarium, you'll see such animals as flying foxes (large fruit bats), sugar gliders squabbling over territory and jump-gliding to the next tree, and echidnas (a mammalian spiny anteater whose young are hatched from eggs) scurrying and probing for insects. The noctarium is open from 10:00 A.M. to 3:00 P.M.; feedings occur on the half hour. $A8 for adults, less for children and seniors. The noctarium is at the corner of Coondoo and Therwine Streets; phone 07-4093-7334.

If you're interested in a tour in the nearby rain forest, contact Kuranda River and Rainforest Tours. The guides are nationally recognized experts on Australian fauna and are also adept at finding platypuses, which are abundant around Kuranda, and many of the tropical waterbirds, such as the blue-winged kookaburras, azure kingfishers, and the many other colorful members of the kingfishing clan.

The Kuranda River and Rainforest Tours leave from the small jetty near the railroad station at hourly intervals starting at 10:30 A.M. and ending at 2:30 P.M.; phone 07-4093-7476. This is a small folksy tour that takes 20 passengers. Besides the animals already mentioned you'll see freshwater crocodiles, turtles, fish, and the abundant plant life.

Kuranda is a tiny town with a live-and-let-live international flavor. If you stay there, browse the Kuranda Arts Co-operative at 20 Condoo. They offer opals, crafted furniture, and much more. Lunch at Frogs Restaurant. If you can't make it back to Cairns by sunrise, stay at the Kuranda Bottom Pub, which serves filling breakfasts. Rooms start at $A39; phone 07-4093-7206. There is the Kuranda Backpacker's Hostel at 6 Arara Street, where there are dozens of rainbow lorikeets. Doubles go for $A32, a bed in a dorm for $A14; phone 07-4093-7355.

*Access.* Traveling from Cairns to Kuranda is a delight. There are three methods: White Car Coaches departs from Tropical Paradise, a travel agency on Spence Street; phone 07-4091-1855. It costs about

$A14 round-trip. The other two methods are novel and unique. The Scenic Railroad (phone 07-4031-3636) departs Cairns's Freshwater Connection Station at 8:30 and 9:30 A.M. on every day except Saturday. On Saturday there is only the 8:30 train. The train climbs more than 300 meters (1,000 feet), traveling through more than a dozen tunnels and along a fern-covered steep escarpment with a vista of rain forest and coastal areas. The ride takes about 95 minutes to complete and ends at the Kuranda station, which is much photographed because of its well-kept plants. The second novel approach is the new Skyrail Rainforest Cableway that leaves from Carvonica Lakes Station ten minutes north of Cairns. Individual gondolas (like those at ski resorts) glide silently over the treetops of the World Heritage tropical rain forest of the MacAlister Range. The cable system covers 7.5 kilometers and has two stops, at Barron Falls (spectacular in the wet season) and Red Peak, where boardwalks have been constructed to allow visitors to walk above the floor of the rain forest amid ferns, palms, epiphytes, and an amazing assortment of rain forest birds.

Many visitors to Kuranda take the train one way and the Skyrail the other. The train and Skyrail don't return to the same location, so you'll need to arrange for transportation to and from your hotel. For booking a ticket of the combination that fits your taste, contact Skyrail Rainforest Cableway, Kamerunga Road at Cook Highway, P.O. Box 888, Smithfield, Queensland 4878; phone 07-4031-3636. Tickets are available that are round-trip on the Skyrail or include one way on the Skyrail and a return on the train, plus bookings that includes Kuranda Tjapukai Experience (see Cairns) and the Kuranda Rainforestation Nature Park. The split ticket, one way by rail and the other by sky, costs $A42 for adults.

## Fitzroy Island

Fitzroy Island is a popular and affordable destination for a day visit (or longer) from Cairns. The island is 24 kilometers southeast of Cairns. Starting at the Trinity Jetty, a 40-minute ride on a big cat deposits you on the 324-hectare island, which caters to everyone, including snorkelers, scuba divers (instruction on the island), windsurfers, sun worshipers, families, bird-watchers, hikers, and pub aficionados. Somehow they all fit together comfortably.

From the island's shore the stretch between Nudie Beach and the Fitzroy Island Resort has the best snorkeling. Getting to the area involves a short walk through a rain forest and a swim back. When you leave the large catamaran, turn right after leaving the jetty and you'll see signs directing you to Nudie Beach. There are often semi-tame sulfur-crested cockatoos on this walk, and there are refreshingly cool patches of rain forest.

Of the island's several walks, I enjoyed the Boulder Walk to the highest point on the island (the trail starts behind the kiosk). It took about 1.5 hours to complete. The Lighthouse Walk, which runs north of the resort to the far end of the island, is an easier walk. There's good snorkeling where the trail turns away from the shore.

Snorkeling is passable near the resort. Divers come here and make drift dives that allow them to see reef sharks, manta rays, and other large fish. The cost is $A30 but lunch and a ride in the resort's semi-submersible sub are extra. Boats go to the outer reef (Moore's Reef) for a 3-hour snorkel from an anchored platform. Contact Fitzroy Island Resort, P.O. Box 2120, Cairns, Queensland 4870; phone 07-4051-9588.

*Accommodations.* Budget units (four people to a room) are $A19.50 per person at the Fitzroy Island Resort. A double is about $A95 per night. Camping is free providing you can book a place; phone 07-4051-9588.

## Green Island

Green Island is a small coral cay 27 kilometers east of Cairns and is probably the most visited offshore destination. It's the closest and least expensive to reach. I found it a little overdeveloped, but it's still worth a visit. There's an underwater observatory that allows a better look at fish than most semisubmersibles do. There is a nice open-air restaurant. Michaelmas Cay National Park is just north of Green Island. This is a bird sanctuary and an excellent underwater viewing area. The snorkeling here is spectacular. Both coral and fish are healthy and abundant. It cost $A40 for adults.

*Accommodations.* Call the Green Island Resort (phone 07-4036-3300) for information. It's expensive: $A500 for a double.

*Access.* A big cat departs to Green Island from Cairns several times a day.

## River Rafting

Raging Thunder is a long-standing river-rafting company. They raft the Barron, Tully, and northern Johnstone Rivers. The latter two are long day or multiday trips. The Barron River is usually a half-day trip. Their prefloat instruction to customers, adherence to high safety standards, and friendly nature are much appreciated. Entirely professional, but somewhat macho, is Raging Thunder (67 Grafton Street, Cairns, Queensland 4870; phone 07-4030-7990). The company recently added a trip half of which is devoted to river rafting, half to snorkeling (off Green Island).

## The Beaches

There are no beaches in Cairns. The nearest quality beaches are north of town and extend from Machans Beach to Wangetti Beach—a distance of 50 kilometers. Ellis Beach is a nice palm-shaded beach with a kiosk. The beaches near Rocksie Point seem best for secluded camping. Most of the beaches have kiosks and organized campgrounds. Before swimming, check about the status of box jellyfish and saltwater crocodiles. Some of the beaches are netted, which allows year-round use without any fear of the "nasties."

Etty, Mission, Kerwarra, and other beaches south of Cairns have already been mentioned. All of them allow camping and have caravan parks. For economy stays in Mission Beach try the Treehouse Youth Hostel; phone 07-4068-7137. For other places to stay and for information about parks and outdoor activities, contact the Tropics Information Centre; phone 07-4068-7179. Also try Scotty's Mission Beach House (dorms $A10, doubles $A45), topless swimming at the pool is the norm for women; phone 07-4068-8767.

## National Parks

There are more than 60 national parks under the jurisdiction of the National Parks and Wildlife Service regional office in Cairns (10 McLeod Street, Cairns, Queensland 4870; phone 07-4052-3096; fax 07-4051-7475). Obtain a copy of *Queensland Guide to National Parks,* the monthly park publication that describes all the parks in Queensland.

For maps showing access routes to the national and environmental parks, contact Absell's Map Centre, adjacent to Orchid Plaza, phone 07-4041-2699.

# The Cape York Peninsula

## Overview

The Cape York Peninsula is a jagged, triangular-shaped piece of land measuring about 700 kilometers from its northern tip to Cairns in the south. Cape York, the peninsula's terminus, is the northernmost point in Australia. Across the Torres Strait from Cape York lies Papua New Guinea.

The entire peninsula falls solidly into the tropics. It's punctuated with immense cattle stations, even bigger Aboriginal reserves, meandering river drainages, billabongs, savannahs, and rain forests. For the most part, the Cape York Peninsula is a wild and exotic place. It's a refuge for Aboriginal culture and pristine tidal rivers, which are the bastions of saltwater and freshwater crocodiles. Many of the terrestrial life-forms are truly exotic and only occur here and in New Guinea.

Access to the wilds of the peninsula is difficult and at times impossible. The traveler is hampered both by the absence of real roads and by monsoon conditions that put land travel on hold until the annual deluge passes.

This difficulty has meant that Aboriginal culture on the peninsula continued unmolested long after Aborigines living farther south had succumbed to terminal European influences. Remarkable Aboriginal art sites abound, especially in Quinkan Country.

For the truly adventurous, there are eight wilderness national parks with a combined area exceeding 2.4 million hectares.

Paved roads end at the Daintree River. Once off the ferry on the northern side, there's axle-high mud and often impassable conditions during the wet season (usually December to March) and passable "bull dust" during the dry one. During the dry season, scheduled bus service goes through the spectacular and embattled Daintree rain for-

*Aboriginal dancer.* PHOTO BY ERIC HOFFMAN.

est to Cape Tribulation, and then by a different route on to Cook-town. Other destinations are usually reached in 4WD safari-type vehicles or by light aircraft from Cairns.

During the dry months, a sensible driver in a 4WD vehicle can make it as far as Coen or Weipa without much difficulty. By the end of the dry season, passenger cars often go as far as Weipa. But if you're contemplating going the whole route to Cape York on the ground, be advised that only a self-sufficient traveler with mechanical ability and above-average survival skills should continue after Coen.

Of all the rain forests I visited in Australia, Daintree was the most striking. I continually found myself stopping my car on the mud-slick road and trying to capture it on film. Only the most talented photographer can come close to capturing the moist abundance, but the beauty of it inspires everyone with a camera to try. The Daintree is simply astounding in its richness and profusion, as it tumbles and explodes in luxuriant greens of cascading ferns, palms, epiphytes, and orchids that literally hang over the ocean that laps at the shore.

Ironically, when you see this area it will be on the controversial road provided by the Queensland government that environmentalists feel endangers the forest.

## Cape Tribulation

At the end of the Daintree Road is Cape Tribulation. The cape has idyllic camping places amid many types of unique plants that are relic populations from the time when Australia was a wetter continent.

Saltwater and freshwater crocodiles are common in the tidal rivers, freshwater swamps, and upland watercourses. More than 260 species of birds have been recorded here, including golden bower-birds, cassowaries, red-tailed black cockatoos, and several species of colorful fruit doves that come in combinations of purples, bright greens, and whites. Dugongs are plentiful in the coastal waters where there are underwater grasses. Both Bennett's and Lumholtz's tree kangaroos can be found with a little help from locals. Smallish agile wallabies are probably the prevalent ground-dwelling macropod. If you see large kangaroolike creatures away from the coast, chances are they're antilopine wallaroos. Several species of flying foxes, with their meter-wide wingspans, are plentiful. They hang in the trees looking like foot-long seed pods during the day.

*Accommodations.* There's a public campground run by the National Parks and Wildlife Service that's popular in all months except the wet ones. Book a site in advance through the Cairns office: National Parks and Wildlife Service, 10 McLeod Street, P.O. Box 2066, Cairns, Queensland 4870, Australia, phone 07-4052-3096; fax 07-4052-3080.

The Jungle Village at Cape Tribulation is a budget lodge offering guided tour service to the best areas. They have their own garden and grow fresh produce. They cater to vegetarians. The range of activities is remarkable. There are guided bushwalks weekly. The walks take in the *Idiospermum australiense* (the "missing link" between flowering plants and their primitive ancestors), strangler figs, colonies of Bennett's tree kangaroos, former marijuana plantations, crocodile-free swimming holes, and the deep rain forest. For $A25 you can putt out to the reef in a launch and snorkel. If you like, you can spend the night on a deserted cay and be picked up a day later. There are idyllic beaches for sunning and swimming. For snorkelers there are the many fringe reefs. At night you can settle into the tropical pub scene or try your hand at spotlighting crocodiles (look for their ruby-red eyes) and other creatures of the night. For accommodation details, contact the Jungle Village, Cape Tribulation, Queensland 4873; phone 07-4098-0040; fax 07-4098-0006.

## Rare Animal Collections and Eco-Lodges

Eco-tourism and the concept of it have many permeations worldwide. The area around Port Douglas, Cape Tribulation, and Cooktown have seen the creation of some unique experiences. In some cases there are lodgings that combine staying and experiencing the local flora and fauna in notable ways. In other cases the habitat has been modified to attract animals, or creatures are held captive in attractive natural settings. Generally, but not always, the lodgings are expensive but well worth it if your budget permits. The following is some of what is offered.

*Habitat Wildlife Sanctuary.* Located off the intersection of Port Douglas Road and Cook Highway, this sanctuary is well worth the stop if you're interested in seeing many of the elusive rain forest animals you might get a glimpse of in a truly wild setting. The sanctuary has more than 160 species—large saltwater crocodiles, smaller freshwater crocs, endangered cassowaries, koalas, and parrot species rarely

*Aboriginal art, Laura, northern Queensland.* PHOTO BY ERIC HOFFMAN.

displayed outside of Australia. Such rarities as eclectus parrots, red-cheeked parrots, red-winged parrots, Torres Strait imperial pigeons, and bright green Wompoo fruit dove are here. Victoria's riflebird and that obsessive monster-nest builder, the orange-footed scrub fowl, are also in residence. Admission is $A16 for adults and $A8 for children; phone 07-4099-3235.

*Daintree Eco Lodge.* Nature commentator David Attenborough described a stay here as "one of the most magical experiences of my life." The lodge includes 15 cabins that sit high on stilts, affording an arboreal look at the world. It's spectacular. Care was taken in building this lodge. The lodge's bungalows are nestled in the trees. The norm in resort development of clear-cutting followed by replanting was not adhered to. Here, the emphasis was on not disturbing things. The dining area is in a large treehouse. The Daintree Eco Lodge is in good taste and has an excellent ambience. Expect to pay around $A350 per night, plus the expense of getting here; phone 07-4098-6100.

*Low-budget.* The best low-budget offering may be Crocodylus Village in Cape Tribulation. Meandering pathways connect elevated cabins that sit under a verdant green rain forest canopy. The forest is alive with bird noises, especially so while you're waking up. Three filling and tasty meals are served daily. There is a swimming pool and a free bus that goes to the beach. There are also affordable activities: horseback riding, guided nature walks, canoeing, and bird-watching. A room in a cabin is $A16, a one-room hut with a bath for two is $A55. Phone 07-4098-9166.

For more information visit the Daintree General Store, which is also an outlet for Daintree Tourist Information. You can get information on safaris into the bush, river tours, bird-watching, and nature walks, as well as a list of eateries and accommodations.

*Be Alert. Respect Crocodiles.* If you get as far as Daintree you are entering a world where wild things have a definite advantage over the foreign tourist. The habitats you travel through from Daintree north have not been sanitized for your convenience. You won't forget the scenery and wildlife, but plan your travel well and always keep in mind that ripples in the watercourses here could well be a large saltwater crocodile. You are in their stronghold and should never enter the water unless you have been advised that it is entirely safe by someone with knowledge of the area. I'll never forget my first journalism assignment in Australia, "Man Eaters" for *International Wildlife.* It was a great assignment. I got to interview crocodile scientists and people who saw friends disappear in one furious burst from a monster whose species was alive when dinosaurs walked the earth. The topic of the *International Wildlife* story speaks for itself. One of the photos I was shown during the research phase was of a full-grown dead man being extracted from a gaping hole cut in the offending crocodile's stomach. It was a graphic, nauseating photograph; amazingly, the entire man was whole except that one leg was partially missing. The point of this grisly tale is that a large saltwater crocodile is entirely willing and able to gulp you down whole, if you are unwitting enough to enter its watery world.

*Access.* Regular bus service departs from the Ansett Pioneer terminal in Cairns, providing the road through the Daintree rain forest is open. In the wet season, it sometimes becomes impassable. At the terminal try Coral Coaches; phone 07-4099-5351. They were offering the 150-kilometer trip for $A23.50.

Remember that north of Daintree River 4WDs are standard fare if you plan to drive.

# Laura and Quinkan Country

## Laura

Laura is a one-building town. The building is general store, pub, phone booth, and dance hall rolled into one. It's the only store in Quinkan Country. The dance is usually held outside on Friday and Saturday nights on selected weekends during the dry season. Those showing up are a rough-and-tumble lot, about an equal mix of Aborigines and white stockmen, and a handful of brave women from the stations.

If you'd like to catch a glimpse of today's Aboriginal culture, Laura is a good place to keep in mind. On July 4, 1987, I spent a wonderful afternoon at a corroboree (a large, ritualized gathering of Aborigines) near Laura. Dozens of traditional dances were performed in a sort of competition that included Aborigines from the remotest places on the peninsula and from islands in the Gulf of Carpentaria. Before you leave Cairns, ask at Cape York Air Services if a corroboree is in the works near Laura (usually sometime in July).

## Quinkan Country

If you're remotely interested in Aboriginal art you won't be disappointed here. This area has a number of accessible sites that rival Kakadu National Park, considered the top Aboriginal art area in Australia. The area was declared a reserve in 1977. Most of the sites are off-limits. Three that aren't are Split Rock Gallery, Gu Gu Yalangi, and Giant Horse Gallery. These galleries are just south of Laura. If you sign on with a guide service, ask to be taken to the huge horse that is one of the biggest and best postcontact pieces ever found. The horse signifies the change Aborigines in the region saw galloping their way—and, judging by the detail and sheer size of the piece, the anonymous artist did not underestimate the change that lay ahead for his culture. Whites are often depicted with their hands in their pockets—a sure way to distinguish them from Aborigines, since only Europeans had pockets. Guns, the final instruments of arbitration, also appear. There are plenty of traditional themes, like barramundi, crocodiles, kangaroos, and spirit and human figures. Photographic opportunities are excellent.

*Access.* Access to Quinkan Country is always an adventure, whether you go by a 4WD vehicle or light aircraft. My last trip here was memorable. I hopped on a small aircraft with two other paying passengers who turned out to be doctors. One was a urbane brain surgeon from Melbourne and the other was a weatherbeaten old gentleman who had spent his life providing medicine to Aboriginal communities in the Cape York area. The two had been roommates in medical school and had stayed close friends though they worked and lived worlds apart. On the return flight my companion in the back seat was an anthropologist from London and the passenger in the front seat was an Aboriginal stationhand who had hurt his leg and was seeking medical help in Cairns. You never know who you might meet in Quinkan Country. Though various air services visit the tiny dirt strip near Laura, most nonresident visitors arrive on a flight arranged by a company that takes their customers to the rich Quinkan art sites. The Ang-Gnarra Aboriginal Corporation provides a guide. Self-guided tours of Split Rock and Gu Gu Yalangi are allowed, but unescorted visitors need to contact the corporation; phone 07-4060-3214.

The Jowalbinna Bush Camp is another way to visit these impressive sites. This camp was created by Percy Tresize, who established rapport with local Aborigines and won their trust years ago. Tresize and his son have mapped many of the sites in the area. The camp is on the upper Little Laura River and about 90 minutes of slow road south of Laura. Guided tours, camping, and meals are provided. Phone the Adventure Company: 07-4051-4777.

## North of Quinkan Country

After Quinkan Country and Coen comes the McIlwraith Range and then the Pascoe River area (Iron Ranges National Park), which is a distinctly separate kind of rain forest harboring life-forms found only here and in New Guinea. One of these life-forms is the palm cockatoo of the northern Cape York Peninsula. It's sometimes called the goliath cockatoo because it's the biggest of all cockatoos, measuring half a meter from bill to tail. Its nearest relative lives in New Guinea. Another unusual creature is the spotted cuscus. It's a cat-sized tree-dwelling marsupial that is sometimes incorrectly reported as an "albino monkey." It's neither albino nor monkey. It's a slow-moving member of Australia's prodigious possum family that is more sloth-like than monkeylike, but related to neither.

There are also 25 species of butterflies only found in Cape York's northern rain forest and a wide assortment of indigenous flowering vines and orchids. This rain forest is reputed to be the most colorful in Australia. Even the reptiles are in on it. The green python, an emerald-green constrictor (harmless to humans), lives here in plentiful numbers.

## Lizard Island

Lizard Island is the premier island destination on the Cape York Peninsula. It's about an hour's flying time (200 kilometers) north of Cairns off the eastern coast of the peninsula near Cape Flattery. Lizard is a 1,012-hectare continental island surrounded by outstanding coral reefs and lagoons that have long been recognized as one of the best snorkeling and diving areas of the entire Great Barrier Reef. This is also a sportsfishermen's mecca for the rich and famous. The whole island is a national park. It got its name from Captain Cook, who climbed to its 360-meter summit in 1770 to sight a passage out of the reef system. During his stay Cook noted the plentiful large sand goannas, which are still populous over the entire island. The island has a well-publicized luxury resort and camping is allowed, though it's not advertised.

. The island's shore is typified by sparkling waters and white secluded beaches—24 at last count. The vegetation varies but is surprisingly arid compared to the nearby rain forests on the Cape York Peninsula. There is a small rain forest, but about half of the island's surface is covered by grasslands. The rest is made up of mangroves, woodlands, and swamp.

Divers are richly rewarded here. Blue Lagoon (which has delicate corals), Clam Gardens (150 feet of visibility), and Cod Hole are world-class dive sites. Cod Hole is about 20 kilometers east of the island on the outer reef. The main attraction is the huge potato cod, which can be fed by hand. Both deep-water and reef fish abound in the area.

*Accommodations.* You must be entirely self-contained and prepared for a bushcamping experience if you plan to pitch a tent on the island. You must get a permit, and it's recommended that you apply six weeks in advance. Contact the National Parks and Wildlife Service, P.O. Box 2066, Cairns, Queensland 4870, Australia; phone 07-4052-3096. There's no such thing as middle-class accommodations on the island.

## The National Parks

There are 11 national parks on the Cape York Peninsula, encompassing an incredible 2.5 million hectares.

Lakefield National Park, located adjacent to Laura, is growing in popularity and can be reached easily in the dry season via the road to Laura from Daintree. The 528,000-hectare park has rain forests, open stringy-bark forests, paperbark groves, and freshwater swamps. It also has excellent birding. Expect to see crocodiles and many of the creatures found at Cape Tribulation.

Iron Ranges National Park, in the northern rain forest above Coen, is billed as having the largest surviving (the rest have been logged) lowland rain forest in Australia. The coastline of this park consists of rain forest and sweeping white beaches without a human footprint anywhere. It also has the exotic wildlife described earlier.

Jardine River National Park is near the peninsula's northern tip. This 235,000-hectare park is built around one of the largest catchments in Queensland. Rain forest, open forest, heath, and shrubland are prevalent. The wet season here is described as spectacular in the few written accounts that exist. The river can only be crossed (everyone headed to Cape Tribulation must cross it) by a ferry that operates only from July to November. Palm cockatoos and spotted cuscuses live here.

Cedar Bay National Park contains some of Queensland's best natural coastal scenery. Tropical rain forest and beach are the dominant themes. The park is only accessible by walking or by boat. The access route passes through the rain forest to the beach and takes about an hour. Camping is allowed and drinking water is available. The park is 50 kilometers south of Cooktown.

Mungkan Kandju National Park stretches from the McIlwraith Range to the junction of the Archer and Coen Rivers. The park is a mix of seasonal melaleuca swamps and dry eucalyptus forests. This park is visited by hard-core bird-watchers because it is home to the very rare and spectacular palm cockatoo, plus the less well known but rare orange-footed scrub fowl. The park service warns visitors to swim (or dip) only in shallow rapids and to stay out of large pools because this is saltwater crocodile habitat. The park is reached on the Peninsula Development Track and is 13 hours north of Cairns by 4WD vehicle in normal conditions. The roads are impassable during the wet season.

For more information about these parks, contact the National Parks and Wildlife Service, 10 McLeod Street, P.O. Box 2066, Cairns, Queensland 4870, Australia; phone 07-4052-3096; fax 07-4052-3080. Try to apply for permits 12 weeks ahead of your planned arrival.

*Access.* If you're interested in a total wilderness camping experience, check with Cape York Air Services (phone 07-4035-9399) on the feasibility of being dropped at various parks. Also check with Wild Challenge (phone 07-4055-6504) for a tour of the whole length of the peninsula in a bush vehicle.

*Cautions.* Any do-it-yourself vacation on the Cape York Peninsula requires careful planning or sufficient funds to sign on with an adventure outfitter who will move you around safely. The park service posts the following warning throughout the peninsula: "Beware of crocodiles—Do not camp within 50 meters of any watercourse (including freshwater)." One Australian suggested the crocs were overrated as a predator. "The crocs won't eat you half as fast as the bloody mozzies [mosquitoes], mate." Prepare for bugs and be delighted if they're out of season.

## Mossman Gorge and Daintree National Park

Mossman Gorge is at the southern end of Daintree National Park and about 80 kilometers north of Cairns. The gorge is largely inaccessible; the best walking track can be found by crossing the suspension bridge at Rex Creek. The 2.7 kilometer loop is spectacular and an easy walk. Silky Oaks Lodge is located in a peaceful setting in the gorge, which is a little cooler than the surrounding tropics. Individual cabins overlook the river and a more open and penetrable area in the rain forest. Silky Oaks caters to hunters and regular travelers. The Kuku Yalanji Aboriginal Dreamtime Tours, led by a local, introduces visitors to traditional medicines; phone 07-4098-1305. The gorge is free of saltwater crocodiles, but the inviting waters need to be respected for their strong currents. For Silky Oaks, call 07-4098-1666.

*Access.* Cape York is a stunning and potentially hostile environment. For safety's sake alone, the intelligent way to visit this wilderness region is as a paid client of an experienced safari guide. Some of the companies who've been at it the longest are: Wild Track, P.O. Box

2397, Cairns, Queensland 4870; phone 07-4055-2247; fax 07-4058-1930. Wild Track takes a maximum of seven clients and visits Daintree, Cape Tribulation, Cooktown, Laura, Cape York Peninsula, and many of the parks and wild areas near these population centers. Their focus is on Aboriginal culture, bird life, wildlife, and rain forest botany. Wilderness Challenge (P.O. Box 254, Cairns, Queensland 4870) is another long-standing outfitter who offers half-day to 16-day safaris through the remotest parts of the Cape York Peninsula; phone 07-4055-6504; fax 07-4057-7226. Billy Tea Bush Safaris offers a wide range of activities combining 4WD travel with river cruises and air flights. Trips extend as far north as Thursday Island (which is as far north as you can go and still be in Australia). Contact Billy Tea Bush Safaris, P.O. Box 77N, North Cairns, Queensland 4870N; phone 07-4032-0077; fax 07-4032-0055. Contact Cape York Air Service at the domestic terminal; phone 07-4035-9399.

## Air Service and Tours

Cape York Air Services serve the Cape York Peninsula with twin- and single-engine prop planes in slightly different capacities. Cape York stops at the best-known areas and also makes mail runs to remote stations and mining communities.

Marine Air Seaplane (phone 07-4069-5915) runs small seaplanes to cays and islands between Cairns and Cooktown. It also flies to Cape Tribulation. Cape Air Transport (phone 07-4069-5007) offers adventure tourism packages to Lakefield National Park.

A typical lineup for Cape York Air Services changes each day of the week. Tickets run around $A300 for many destinations. There are also mail routes that you can pay to get on. Cape York Air Services is located at the domestic terminal in Cairns; phone 07-4035-9399.

## Torres Strait and Thursday Island

The Torres Strait is the body of water that separates Australia from Papua New Guinea. The strait is speckled with more than 17 islands, about 10 of them inhabited. Today about 15,000 people of Melanesian origins live in this area (both on the islands and on the mainland). Their ethnic origin is from New Guinea. It comes as a surprise to Europeans that Torres Strait Islanders represent an entirely different culture than the Aboriginal culture of most of Australia, but the two cultures often intermarried. The islands are the high areas of what was a land bridge between Australia and New Guinea as recently as 6,500 years ago. Such animals as echidnas (an egg-laying mammal) and numerous birds are found both in Australia and New Guinea. Quite possibly, the dingo came across this strait as recently as 6,500 years ago.

For historical footnotes the Torres Strait has been a tough place to survive. The original islanders were a fierce people who thought the first Europeans were ghosts. Generally, foreigners of any kind were treated harshly. Shipwrecked mariners and early pearlers were sometimes slaughtered and eaten. Captain Bligh, of *Bounty* fame, passed through the area on his 2,000-mile odyssey after a mutiny forced him and the loyal members of his crew into an open boat. The first Europeans saw the area and the islanders as fiercely independent and difficult to subdue. Queensland has governed the area since 1897.

That defiantly independent streak has been tempered but has not died. From Murray Island, Eddie Koiki Mabo and four friends lodged a claim with Australia's highest court, claiming inalienable tenure over traditional lands. The High Court's "Mabo Ruling" of 1992 upheld these rights and created a precedent that recognized native title in Australia. This decision has created fierce debate between native peoples and present-day landowners in many places throughout Australia and may have far-reaching impacts on land rights in much of the country. Dozens of similar claims are now lodged with the court and are slowly working their way through the legal system.

Today Thursday Island is the "capital" of the Torres Strait. This was once the center of a thriving pearl industry at the turn of the century. Many Japanese pearlers are buried in the local graveyard, testimony to the dangers and primitive technology of this occupation. Green Hill Fort (in disrepair) was built in 1891 to repel Russians.

# PART IV

# Victoria

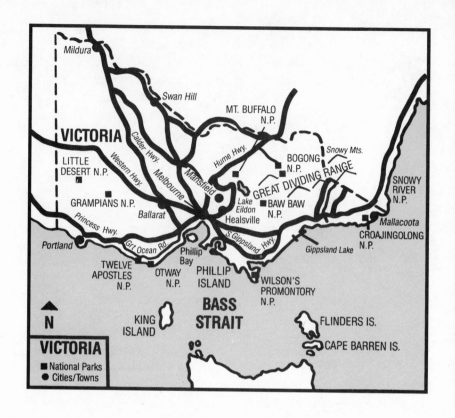

# Overview

One of the many nice things about Victoria is its reasonable size. It's Australia's smallest mainland state, measuring 227,600 square kilometers, which makes it slightly smaller than California. There are well over 150 national, state, forest, and historic parks in Victoria.

Victoria's topography is dominated to the east by the southern Great Dividing Range, much of which is informally known as the Victorian Alps. The highest peak is Mount Bogong, 1,986 meters high, surrounded by a fabulous alpine park of the same name. Moving toward the western end of the state, there's the massive sandstone uplift of the Grampians and one of Australia's most dramatic parks, with guaranteed sightings of Australia's best-known kinds of wildlife. In the shadow of the Grampians you'll find Mount Arapiles, the best rock-climbing area in Australia. Farther west, where the mountains peter out, is Little Desert National Park, home to 200 varieties of birds. The northern boundary is the Murray River. The Murray is dotted with rustic towns, each featuring historic pubs from the days when the river was a bustling conduit for goods going to the remote stations and towns in the interior. Victoria's southern boundary is the Southern Ocean and Bass Strait, which separates Victoria from Tasmania.

The state's 1,200-kilometer coastline is varied and spectacular. In the center is Torquay, Victoria's surfing capital, with its beautiful beaches. Farther west are the Otway Ranges, famous for fern gullies and desolate beaches. The Otways sometimes have 200 rainy days a year and offer a look at the ancient flora that once dominated the continent. The area around Port Campbell known as the Shipwreck Coast has the spectacular Twelve Apostles, the most photographed coastal geological formation in Victoria, if not in Australia. In the town of Portland, Victoria's first permanent settlement, nature-loving citizens have developed the 200-kilometer Great South-West Walk, perhaps the best-maintained coastal walking track in Australia. Go 85 kilometers west of Portland and you're in the state of South Australia.

Southeast of Melbourne is Phillip Island, known for its "Penguin Parade." Southeast of Melbourne is Wilsons Promontory, with its granite tors, sandy coves, and flora from both Tasmania and the mainland. Farther east are the Gippsland Lakes, the biggest inland lake system in Australia and a boater's paradise, with wildlife-rich Lakes National Park smack in the middle of it. From Gippsland Lakes you can either cut inland and pick up the Buchan-Jindabyne Road, a true motoring adventure, or continue onto New South Wales on the Princess Highway with a stop at 90-kilometer-long Croajingolong National Park. The Buchan-Jindabyne Road winds past Snowy River National Park and up the immense Snowy River Valley to Kosciuszko National Park in New South Wales.

Victoria's alpine areas are rich in tradition and natural beauty. The area is branded with the distinct character built around horsemanship and the love for steep wooded mountains captured in the *Man from Snowy River* films. This is also Australia's prime alpine recreational area. At Falls Creek, Mount Hotham, and Mount Buller there is good alpine skiing. There is cross-county skiing at numerous places, but High Plains, Mount Stoney, Mount Buffalo, and Mount Stirling may have the most dramatic scenery and trails. If you judge skiing by vertical drop on a given run as the primary criteria, you may be making a mistake in sizing up Australian skiing, and entirely overlooking the joys of cross-country. Australia's alpine areas in winter are a new kind of beauty to someone from somewhere else. I'll never forget cross-country skiing near Mount Stoney with a group of Australians. We were sliding along through twisted and gnarled snow gums when three bright red crimson rosellas suddenly dropped to the snow and began digging for food. Parrots are usually associated with the tropics, but these bright red parrots live in alpine areas. Later we came across a lone wombat brazenly walking down our cross-country trail straight into us, unconcerned about our presence and clearly self-assured about who had the right-of-way. We detoured around this determined little wombat as it padded its way through the snow.

Victoria's also the mainland state best suited for backpacking. There's the Alpine Walking Track, which cuts through the heart of the high country, and countless other tracks that add up to hundreds of kilometers of excellent walking and mountain biking in pristine and unaltered natural settings. Victoria is diverse. Besides its alpine areas, it has a varied and spectacular coastline, the wildlife-rich Grampians, wine-growing regions, desert parks with rare wildlife, historic gold-mining areas, and the backwater Murray River towns. Victoria's cultural heart is Melbourne, a cosmopolitan city that savors the arts. Its many impressive churches and grand buildings characterize the best of Victorian architecture. Arguably, the lion's share of Australia's finest restaurants are in Melbourne.

When it comes to nature, Melbourne is unique. There is no question that Melbourne is a large industrial city. But, within Melbourne's city limits and within an hour's drive of the downtown are 920 municipal, national, and state parks, plus historic sites and walking, bicycling, birding, kayaking, and sightseeing areas. Most of these recreational and scenic areas are overseen by Melbourne Parks and Waterways. Most of them are not listed in most tourist literature, even though they offer a great variety of unique experiences without requiring the traveler to marshal the major economic and logistical efforts it takes to visit such well-known areas as Wilsons Promontory and Grampians National Parks. (See "Gardens and City Parks.")

## Information Sources

Before you leave for Australia you can obtain a great deal of information from the Australian Tourist Commission in Los Angeles. For the state of Victoria call 805-755-2000 or 310-229-4892. In Melbourne the most helpful stop for visitors to make is the Victorian Visitors Information Centre, Melbourne Town Hall, at the corner of Swanson and Little Collins Streets; phone 1-800-637-763 (toll-free inside Australia) or 03-9658-9955; fax 03-9650-1212. This office has piles of detailed publications that will direct your efforts to visit national parks, historic sites, wineries, city tours, museums, botanical gardens, and any special interests you may have. Ask for "The Official Visitor's Map and Guide to Local Events." In Australia you can also phone the Victorian Information Service (13-28-42) to obtain information about Victoria. From anywhere inside Australia this number is billed as a local call. The visitors center staff can book accommodations and tours. Next door to the visitors center is the City Experience Centre, which provides information in six languages. This center offers the Melbourne Greeter Service, which allows visitors to meet Melbournians who volunteer their time to show visitors around Melbourne. For disabled travelers, the "CBD Mobility Map" gives good details about wheelchair access to many destinations throughout the city. By and large, most museums, city parks, and other places of interest in and around Melbourne have wheelchair access.

*Outdoor and National Parks Information.* Contact the Natural Resources and Environment office, 8 Nicholson Street, East Melbourne; phone 03-9412-4745. You can obtain maps and information about most of the state and national parks. If you have sufficient lead time contact Parks Victoria; phone 13-19-16. This is a mail and phone contact, but not for visiting in person. The Backpackers Travel Centre, 258 Centre Lane, is also a good source for outdoor access at the most economical rates; phone 03-9654-8477; E-mail info@backpackerstravel.net.au.

*A Must-Get Publication for Nature Lovers.* A last contact listed here, well worth pursuing for anyone spending more than a few days in Melbourne, is the book *Melbourne's Great Outdoors.* This is a meticulously written 335-page review of over 150 parks, trails, waterways, historic buildings, and natural points of interest in the Melbourne area. It is published jointly by Melbourne's highly respected newspaper *The Age* and Melbourne Parks and Waterways. The book is well illustrated, complete with maps with detailed ledger keys showing everything from public toilets to where to rent a kayak or a horse. There are also ample photographs. Most of the coverage is of points that aren't on the beaten tourist routes, like French Island National Park, where perhaps the most prolific and densely populated koala population in all of Australia can be found. It has been so successful in recent years that animals from French Island have been moved to less densely populated areas to start new koala populations.

For travelers who want to explore on their own but with detailed, accurate information, *Melbourne's Great Outdoors* is the best book. Besides a place-by-place review there is an extensive activities directory outlining kayaking and canoeing routes, biking tours, hiking trails, birding areas, horseback riding areas, and much more. Everything from the Royal Botanic Gardens to the Zoo and Royal Park, to the Braeside Park, where bird hides are set up to facilitate the viewing of black swans and Australian pelicans, to parks with small locomotives suitable for children to ride are covered in this book. When you visit the Victorian Visitors Information Centre, ask about this book.

# Melbourne: Australia's Second- Greatest City

Melbourne is a grand city with European charm. There are three million Melbournians, making Victoria's capital second only to Sydney as the most populous city in Australia. It's also second only to Sydney as the Australian city most frequently visited by foreigners.

The word *second* is often heard when talking about Melbourne and its relationship with Sydney. There's a somewhat overstated rivalry between the cities. Sydneysiders tend to paint Melbourne as a drab, humorless place. They often knock Melbourne's weather, and they allege that Melbourne has a more conservative social climate.

There's no getting around the fact Melbourne is not Sydney. There is no Sydney Opera House, Sydney harbor, or Sydney Harbour Bridge. Still, I rate Melbourne a close second to Sydney. Melbourne has polish, class, and a European atmosphere. The stretch of the city heading south from Flinders Station, over the Yarra River at Princes Bridge, and down Saint Kilda Road to Kings Domain is as elegant a stretch of urban roadway as any ever created. Arts, parks, and gardens have long been priority items on Melbourne's civic agenda. A final comparison of the two cities might best be judged by each city's leading newspaper. *The Age* is Melbourne's and Australia's finest newspaper—a truly outstanding publication. The *Sydney Morning Herald* doesn't come close.

Melbourne isn't really all that drab. In spite of a few oddly thought out urban-development schemes, Melbourne is a world-class

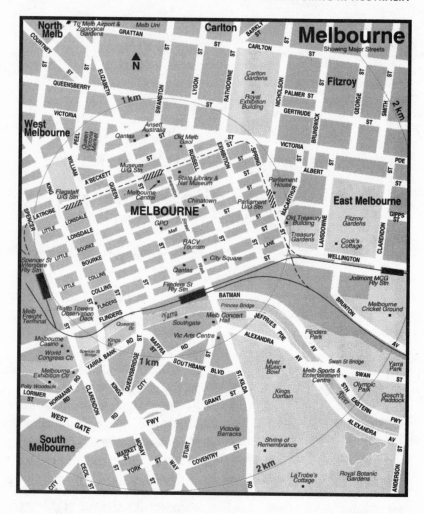

city with charming sections that seem more European than anywhere else in Australia. The "new Australians" have settled in Melbourne in great numbers since World War II and created Melbourne's high-quality and diverse cuisine.

When you first see Melbourne, you'll think it's like any other modern industrial city. Large skyscrapers define the skyline. Suburbs spread out for miles in all directions, and on a windless day smog discolors the air. But when you get into the city's center, you'll see Melbourne's special character of grand-scale Victorian-era buildings, literally hundreds of regional parks and recreation areas, and color-fully decorated tramcars rolling down the busiest boulevards. There are areas like Carlton, with its iron-lace balconies and restored neighborhoods, and there are opulent nineteenth-century hotels like the Windsor. Everywhere there are restaurants. In just about any direction you'll find botanical gardens and museums. The ultramod-ern Arts Centre is Melbourne's answer to the Sydney Opera House. The city center (north of the Yarra River) is easy to figure out for a first-time visitor because of its uninterrupted grid street pattern.

## The Weather

The weather is not appreciably different from Sydney's. Lower the thermometer by a few degrees in winter and add a week or more of rainy days and you have the difference. On the other hand, Mel-bourne's weather is more fickle than Sydney's. Even in summer be prepared for sudden blasts of inclement conditions, since Melbourne sits in an area of competing weather patterns.

## Transportation Contacts

*Airlines and Transfers.* Melbourne is second only to Sydney for com-mercial air traffic. Essendon Airport and Melbourne Tullamarine Airport both serve Melbourne. Most international travelers arrive at Tullamarine, where the first off get to the head of the sometimes long customs lines that move quickly. Australia takes customs seriously and is especially hard on visitors who "forget" to declare agricultural products. This is why they have large signs asking you to throw away fruit before you enter the final customs and passport check. Major domestic and international carriers serve Melbourne. International carriers include United, Qantas, Ansett Australia, British Airways, Air New Zealand, and others. Qantas has huge domestic service and a separate lounge area for flights serving the rest of Australia (there are hourly flights to Sydney). If you are arriving via Sydney (a com-mon routing) you will be put in a transit lounge in Sydney and go through customs in Melbourne. The flight from Sydney to Mel-bourne is about 1 hour, 20 minutes. Tullamarine isn't particularly well set up for first-time visitors, who can often be seen wandering around trying to figure out how to get to the city after clearing cus-toms. For airport transfers call 03-9335-3066 or call the Skybus (03-

9662-9275). The Skybus picks people up on the half hour from 6:30 A.M. until 11:30 P.M. daily. It cost about $A12.00 for the 35-minute ride to the center of Melbourne. You can catch a cab for about twice as much. The major car companies also have booths in the terminal immediately adjacent to where you clear customs.

*Tram.* Melbourne's electric-powered trams are extensive, cheap, and fun to ride. There is a free City Circle Tram that runs continuously through the city's center, allowing visitors easy gratis access to the entire center of the city. The complete tram system covers 250 kilometers of streets and reaches outlying areas plus all major city tourist destinations, shopping areas, and many local parks. The trams are hard to miss; they are colorfully painted and rumble down the middle of the wide streets between multiple lanes of car traffic. The trams stop at islands in the middle of the street, usually near intersections. The idea is to reach the boarding islands through crosswalks under the protection of a signal light and not to resort to sprinting across a busy thoroughfare. Melbourne's car traffic is sane but unsympathetic toward jaywalkers. Tram tickets (usually not more than a couple of dollars) can be purchased from ticket machines where you board the tram or from the conductor once on board. Routes are posted at trams stops. The system runs daily, year-round, from 5:00 A.M. until midnight, except on Sunday; then service begins at 8:00 A.M. and stops at 11:00 P.M.

*Bus.* You can visit just about anywhere in and around Melbourne by bus. The City Explorer Bus and City Wanderer Bus depart Town Hall on Swanston Street. This service stops at the city's botanical gardens, museums, zoo, government houses, shopping areas, and historic landmarks. This system runs five routes a day; phone 03-9563-9788. Within the city bus services is a discount pass known as a Getabout Travelcard that gives reduced fares to two adults and a family. For interstate travel try V-Line at the Spencer Street Station (phone 13-22-32); Greyhound at 58 Franklin Street (phone 03-9663-3299); McCafferty's at the Spencer Street Station (phone 03-9670-2533).

*Train.* For trains connecting to the suburbs go to Flinders Station, one of the most impressive buildings in Melbourne. For interstate trains go to the Spencer Street Station near the Visitors Information Centre. The Sydney-Melbourne XPT connects Australia's two largest

cities daily. Two services are offered daily from Melbourne to Adelaide, and the Canberra Link connects Melbourne to Canberra. For
reservations at a local-call rate from anywhere in Australia, phone
13-22-22; 03-9619-5000 is a toll call.

*Taxi.* There is no shortage of cabs but they are more expensive than
the tram and bus systems. To climb into a cab costs about $A3.00.
The fare is calculated at around $A1.00 per kilometer, with more
added in for late-night rides. Cab companies include: Embassy
(phone 13-17-55) and Black Cabs (phone 13-22-27).

## Things to Do

Melbourne has as much to offer in entertainment, art, architecture,
and culinary diversity as practically any large city in the world. A
good way to get your bearings is to hop onto one of the City Wanderer Buses for a quick review of the city's main attractions. Here is
some of what you may want to investigate.

*Museums.* The National Gallery of Victoria, 180 Saint Kilda Road
(phone 03-9208-0222) opened in 1861. It moved to its present location in the 1960s and possesses the largest art collection in Australia.
The building is fairly nondescript from the outside, but inside you'll
be dazzled by the immense stained-glass ceiling in the Great Hall.
The ceiling contains more than 6,500 pieces of glass and is the largest
stained-glass ceiling in the world. The museum is best known for its
collection of Old Masters and Australian contemporary art. There
are also excellent collections of Asian and Aboriginal art.

Ripponlea Museum and Historic Garden, 192 Hotham Street,
Elsternwick, is definitely worth a visit. This is a restoration of the
opulence of "old money" Victoria at the turn of the century. Located
about five miles from the city's central district, the Ripponlea house
is a fully restored example of Romanesque architecture with extensive gardens. This is both an impressive and a relaxing place to visit.
Another museum of note is the Polly Woodside Maritime Museum,
Lorimer Street East, Southbank; phone 03-9699-9760. The museum
is primarily a restored 1880s vintage sailing bark, the kind of large
sailing vessel that connected Australia to the rest of the world in the
last century. The old vessel represents a largely forgotten technology,
from the days when commercial sailpower connected the world's

continents. Visitors are treated to talks on the crew's jobs and responsibilities and living conditions, plus explanations on boat-building techniques and nautical knowledge of that era.

The Museum of Chinese Australian History, 22 Cohen Street (phone 03-9662-2888), provides a glimpse into the early years in Australia of the first large non-European and nonindigenous ethnic group. On display are exhibits and tools from the early Chinese gold miners who came in droves in the 1850s and the prejudice they had to endure. The exhibits include reenactments of the creaky, leaky ship journeys from China, the conditions in the mines, and beliefs and customs of the early Chinese, whose cultural roots in Australia now date back 150 years.

A popular and macabre tour can be experienced at the Old Melbourne Gaol, Russell Street; phone 03-9663-7228. Australia's best-known "bushranger" and folk hero, Ned Kelly, was executed here in 1880. His death mask is on display.

At the opposite end of human endeavor is the Australian Gallery of Sport and Olympic Museum, located at the Melbourne Cricket Grounds, Jolimont; phone 03-9657-8879. Melbournians love sport, and this is an impressive shrine to it. Opened in the late 1980s, the exhibits explain the histories of 20 sports popular in Australia. This includes histories of the Australian Football Clubs that represent many of Melbourne's suburbs. Known as "Australian Rules," this uniquely machismo Australian sport got its start in Melbourne. The Olympic portion of the exhibits lends a unique perspective. There is also a Cricket Hall of Fame.

Perhaps the most unique museum is the Australian Toy Museum, located at 174-180 Smith Street, Collingswood; phone 03-9419-4138. A foreign-born restaurant owner started this museum by going public with his collection of toys in the 1970s. This is a good place for both children and adults. Most of the exhibits are designed for child-sized visitors. There are a myriad of themes: religious toys (Noah's Ark), the differences between European and Australian toys, space toys, science fiction toys, mechanical toys, flying toys—and plenty of toys that are hard to categorize.

## Entertainment

Melbourne has dozens of live theaters, ballets, symphonies, operas, and rock concerts to choose from. Most of these performances are handled through Ticketmaster Bass; for information, phone 03-9654-7555 or Ticketek, phone 13-28-49. The Visitor Information Centre publishes *Events,* which chronicles upcoming live performances in detail. Get a copy of *The Age* to find out what's playing at the more than 20 active theater companies. For orchestral concerts, inquire about the Melbourne Concert Hall.

If you don't want to pay for a quality performance, the Melbourne City Council has taken care of that. During the summer season (October to April), free performances are given throughout the city at a number of locations, including the Bourke Street Mall, the Sidney Myer Music Bowl (phone 03-9281-8360), and the Treasury Garden. Known as the Melbourne Festival, it features more than 300 performances at 25 different locations. The event attracts top talent from around the world. From June to October, free entertainment is less frequent; for information, phone 03-9658-9955.

The Victorian Arts Centre, 100 Saint Kilda Road, is a multimillion-dollar modernistic complex that includes all aspects of the arts. At night its illuminated Eiffel Tower–like spire makes it an unmistakable landmark. The complex houses the State Theatre featuring dance and drama, the Concert Hall, and the Playhouse for contemporary dramatic performances. There are tours of the various venues from late morning to 6:00 P.M. For an evening that includes a tour, dinner, and performance, phone 03-9281-8000. Any performances in the impressive State Theatre in this center are well worth the money.

Melbourne has a wide range of nightclubs, theaters, and restaurants. There is everything from off-the-wall and raunchy to upscale and stuffy and just plain superb. Some of the offerings are: IMAX, Rathdowne Street, Carlton; phone 03-9663-5454. This is an eight-story screen and the biggest IMAX theater in the world. Situated in a subterranean setting large enough to accommodate the huge screen, IMAX offers a selection of short, visually overwhelming films that guarantee sensory overload. Astor Theatre, at the intersection of Dandenong and Chapel Streets, is a spectacular structure and one of the small number of grand old movie theaters still operating anywhere. It seats more than 1,000 people in multiple levels and is a favorite venue for the Saint Kilda Film Festival because of the screen size and acoustics; phone 03-9610-1414.

For live theater, La Mama, 205 Faraday, Carlton (phone 03-9347-6948) is known for Australian-produced dramatic productions and pushing the envelope with experimental productions. The Regent Theatre on Little Collins Street (phone 03-9820-0239) usually offers touring musicals and top mainstream productions. The Last Laugh, 380 Lygon Street (phone 03-9419-8600), is Melbourne's best-known comedy venue. International headliners as well as local talent are featured. For modern dance try the National Theatre; phone 03-9534-0221.

*Sports.* Any calendar of events for Melbourne will be heavily weighted to horse racing and Australian Rules football. The Aussie Rules season runs from March until September. While you're trying to figure out how a game on an oval field with four sets of goalposts actually works, you'll be "serenaded" by fans screaming their lungs out while gulping down an occasional meat pie. Then, each September, the Grand Final Day marks a period when regional loyalties throughout Melbourne go bonkers as teams from around the city beat up on each other. Most tickets are sold at the gates, or you can call 03-9643-1999.

Melbourne is also the hub of Australia's national obsession with horse racing. Every November the Melbourne Cup is held at the Flemington Race Course, Racecourse Road, Flemington. The race has become a holiday festival that brings Melbourne and the rest of Australia to a standstill as millions turn up their radios and TVs and place their bets. For information about the races, call 03-9371-7171.

Tennis is a big draw in Melbourne. The Australian Open, one of the world's four Grand Slam events, is held at the Flinders Park National Tennis Centre on Batman Avenue; phone 03-9286-1234. The Open is played during the last two weeks of January, and tickets go on sale starting in October at Ticketek; phone 61-3-9299-9079.

There are two other great spectator events in Melbourne, one old and slow and the other speedy and new. From October to March the Melbourne Cricket Ground, Brunton Avenue, Jolimont, has matches. If you're new to this sport, sign up for a one-day game, not a "Test Match," which could last for days. The popularity of this British game has plenty of supporters. The stadium seats 100,000; phone 03-9657-8879. Another Melbourne event with international focus is the Australian Formula One Grand Prix, which was originally held in Adelaide. The Grand Prix drew the ire of environmentally aware locals because Albert Park's trees were mowed down to house racing facilities. The Grand Prix takes place in March. On race day the flow of traffic and the availability of rental cars aren't what they should be. The high-pitched whine of these rocket-fast cars can be heard in most parts of the city when the race is on. For a ticket phone 03-9258-7100 or contact the Grand Prix Web site: www.grandprix.com.au.

## Gardens and City Parks

The Fitzroy Gardens, at the corner of Wellington and Lansdowne Streets, are peaceful gardens on the north side of the Yarra River within easy walking distance of the city's center. Captain Cook's cottage is here. This is the actual home of the famous explorer. It was retrieved from Britain and reconstructed stone by stone. The John F. Kennedy Memorial, honoring the assassinated U.S. president, is by the lake in the Treasury Garden.

The Royal Botanic Gardens is between Alexandra Avenue and Domain Road. There are more than 12,000 species (both natives and exotics) of plants on the 41 hectares. Melbournians claim it is one of the best botanic gardens in the world. The Tennyson Lawn portion has ancient English elms. The gardens also has fern gullies, a beautiful and ancient botanical feature of coastal Australia. The Kings Domain near the gardens contains the Shrine of Remembrance for Melbourne's World War I and II dead and LaTrobe's cottage, the colony's first government house. The gardens and the cottage with its furnishing of the 1840s are open daily.

There are a few other green and tranquil areas in the downtown or close to it. One such place is Westgate Park, located off the West Gate Freeway and Todd Road. Once the entire region was a vital wetlands consumed by city expansion. This 28-hectare park was re-created from reclaimed wetlands. Lakes were scraped out with bulldozers and native plants sown. The result is a wonderful park for birders that can be reached by city buses. A wide variety of Australia's shorebirds can be spotted here. Expect to see pied comorants, sacred ibis, Australian pelicans, black swans, and a host of other birds; phone 03-9395-1132. The park sits near the immense Westgate Bridge and a government aircraft company.

Flagstaff Gardens, between King and William Streets, is another peaceful place in the city. This park has the imprint of an English garden layout, with neat paths, rose gardens, and large deciduous trees. There is lawn bowling and a tennis court. The gardens are near the Queen Victoria Market and are a comfortable place to picnic or take a break from shopping or sightseeing.

Carlton Gardens, located between Carlton and Victoria Streets, is also a worthwhile place to visit and take a break from the city. The garden features the grand old Exhibition Building from the International Exhibition of 1880. This Florentine-style building housed the Victoria Parliament for 26 years. The garden has impressive fountains, paths, lawns, and shade trees. There is also a tennis court. City workers often lunch here, picnic style; phone 03-9658-8553.

## Historic Buildings and Impressive Architecture

In the Visitor Information Centre on Swanston Street you can pick up literature on self-guided walks to Melbourne's many grand old cathedrals, churches, lavish mansions, and public buildings. There is also a guided service led by graduate students chosen for their ability to communicate. The Melbourne Heritage Walks and Tours run throughout the day. You can either attach yourself to a regularly scheduled walk or arrange for a private tour. It's about $A35 a head to join a scheduled walking tour; phone 03-9827-1985. Any student of architectural excellence from bygone eras when artisans' skills were at their zenith won't be disappointed by spending a half or full day visiting Melbourne's finest buildings. Many of the buildings you'll see belong to the National Trust, which means the government protects them and contributes to their restoration and upkeep. Here are some of the more memorable buildings.

The Flinders Street Station, at the corner of Flinders and Swanston Streets, is a spectacular turn-of-the-century structure that is still in use as the main train station for travel within the state. More than 1,000 routes begin and end here daily, on the immense building's 14 platforms. The Parliament area on Eastern Hill (Albert and Lansdowne Streets) has a great number of grand old Renaissance- and Gothic-style buildings. This is also where you'll find Fitzroy Gardens (See "Gardens and City Parks"). Visit here and you'll learn a lot about Melbourne's history, which created these buildings. Some of what you'll see was standing in 1850. Saint Patrick's Cathedral is perhaps the most impressive of these buildings (corner of MacArthur and Cathedral Streets). The spire measures 106 meters. The interior is cavernous and finished in the finest revival Gothic architecture with a series of impressive Gothic arches and vaults. The exterior features massive buttresses. The detail is amazing, especially the mosaic floor, stained glass, and altar. The gargoyles are numerous, finely finished, and grotesque.

Nighttime adds to the cathedral's allure. Its immense spire and out-line is backlit, accentuating its gothic details. The Parliament House on Spring Street is also impressive. It was modeled after the House of Lords in London and built in 1850. It has a facade of Doric columns, but its most memorable feature is its interior. The legislative council chamber is finished in lavish red tapestry and refined woodwork. There are tours.

Across the street you'll find the equally impressive Windsor Hotel, which has a blocklong Renaissance facade. The Windsor is often cited as the best example of the grand era of hotels in Australia. It was built in 1884. If you continue southeast, on the south side of Spring Street, you'll come to the Stanford Fountain at the corner of MacArthur and Spring Streets. This fountain was made by William Stanford, a prisoner of the British sent here to serve his time. Across MacArthur Street is the Treasury Building, which is an example of Renaissance revival architecture. Today, it serves as the Museum of Melbourne. Across from the Treasury Building is Treasury Place, a well-kept city garden that is contiguous with Fitzroy Gardens, located on the other side of Lansdowne Street. (See Fitzroy Gardens in "Gardens and City Parks"). In Fitzroy Gardens you'll find quiet and manicured city greenery intersected by crisscrossing footpaths, shady glens, flower beds, and fern gullies. You'll also find Captain Cook's cottage and the Conservatory (a greenhouse with a stunning collection of blooming flowers). There are horticulture tours of the gardens. For schedules, check with the Visitor Information Centre on Swanston Street; phone 03-9658-9955.

A number of other buildings deserve mention. Many of them can be visited by boarding the free City Circle Tram. Many are on or near Swanston Street, where visitors congregate to collect literature and maps at the Victoria Visitor Information Centre. Besides Saint Patrick's Cathedral (described earlier) there are four grand old churches and cathedrals: Saint Francis Cathedral, located on the cor-ner of Elizabeth and Lonsdale Streets; Saint James Old Cathedral, on the corner of Dudley and King Streets (seven blocks from Swanston Street); Saint Paul's Cathedral, on the corner of Swanston and Flinders Streets; and Scott's Church on Collins and Russell Streets. The chapel in Saint Paul's has a superb Gothic interior. The Mel-bourne Town Hall at Collins and Swanston Streets is immense and impressive. It may be the best of the bluestone buildings and is an example of neoclassical architecture.

There are, of course, modern buildings. One worth the walk is the Rialto Towers, 525 Collins Street. These immense skyscrapers are the tallest office buildings in the Southern Hemisphere and have an observation deck that affords an expansive view of Melbourne and beyond. The elevator ride is very fast and is a thrill in itself. If a worldwide contest for opulent interiors in movie theaters was declared, it might be impossible to beat the Regent Theatre. The foyer area possesses astounding elegance (see "Entertainment"). The Shrine of Remembrance in the Royal Botanic Gardens is an impressive classic Greek structure built in memory of Australian military personnel who lost their lives in war. The Government House, in the center of the Royal Botanic Gardens and Kings Domain, is also an impressive Renaissance-style structure. The Crown Entertainment Centre, on the Yarra River near Queensbridge Street, has an immense casino and a luxury hotel. The building reputedly cost over $A1 billion to build.

Two other buildings offer examples of the "old money and turn-of-the-century elegance" that has distinguished Melbourne since its early years. Ripponlea, described in the "Things to Do" section, rates another mention here because of its extensive gardens. The other structure along the same lines is the Como House, at the corner of Williams Road and Lechlade Avenues; phone 03-9827-2500. This splendid mansion with impressive gardens was built in 1855 and owned by the same family for most of its existence, until the National Trust took it over in 1959.

## The Royal Melbourne Zoo and Royal Park

The Melbourne zoo (take the No. 55 tram from William Street or phone 03-9285-9300 for alternate routes), on Elliot Avenue in Parkville, is a world-class zoological garden with many tasteful exhibits. There are more than 400 species in residence. The staff seems proudest of the primate and big cat exhibits and the butterfly house. For me, the immense aviaries and walk-through exhibits with different species of kangaroos, emus, and other natives were well worth the trip. The butterfly house has 30 species of fluttering beauties in a tropical rain forest setting. There are exhibits of echidnas and numerous species of wallabies. Australia's colorful birds (50 species in residence) are displayed in a walk-through aviary. The zoo has worked hard to change from a Victorian menagerie to a zoo that replicates natural conditions for its residents. As a person who usually doesn't like zoos, I strongly recommend the Melbourne zoo, especially if your visit to Australia will not allow you to see native fauna in the wild. There are also beautiful gardens suitable for picnics. The zoo was the departure point for the ill-fated Burke and Wills expedition across Australia that resulted in tragedy.

## Shopping

Melbourne has the reputation of being a shopping city because of its wide selection of shopping areas. Shopping hours are normally from 9:00 A.M. to 5:00 P.M., but longer hours are becoming common. Start at the Myer, 295 Lonsdale Street, the biggest department store in Australia. It's at the corner of Bourke Street, the most concentrated shopping area in the city. The Galleria Shopping Plaza is a collection of Australian-owned stores, including Australian Geographic. Then there's the Queen Victoria Market, at the corner of Elizabeth and Victoria Streets. This 500-stall bevy of activities sells everything. It's open every day, though the hours change.

## Restaurants

Melbourne probably has the best cuisine in Australia. Among the 1,600 restaurants in the city, you'll find Chinese, French, German, Mexican, Japanese, Indian, "American," Australian, and many others. In all there are 60 national cuisines represented. Many of the hotels serve top-quality meals. The "Visitor's Guide to Melbourne" lists many eateries, but it doesn't critique them. The best publication on restaurants is the *Age Good Food Guide,* which you can find in any bookstore.

If you want to take a chance, jump on a tram for Lygon Street in Carlton. This is the unofficial restaurant capital of the city—mostly Italian, but other cuisines as well. You won't be disappointed with Casa-Dilorio (moderately priced), 139-141 Lygon Street. Just down the street is Casa Malaya (moderate) at 118 Lygon Street. This award-winning restaurant specializes in Malaysian dishes. Eating in Carlton near the University of Melbourne gives you a chance to look at a beautifully restored portion of Melbourne.

Then there's Little Bourke Street, the repository of a number of fine Chinese restaurants, from the inexpensive to the expensive. Try Mask of China, 115 Bourke Street; phone 03-9662-2116. For top-of-the-line Chinese food, try Flower Drum, 17 Market Lane; phone 03-9662-3655.

Theater restaurants are popular. Dirty Dicks, 23 Queens Road, has a bawdy act with old English tucker ($A19). The Last Laugh Theatre Restaurant, 64 Smith Street, Collingwood, gets high marks.

## Accommodations

If you aren't careful Melbourne can be an expensive place to spend a couple of nights. The prices listed here are approximate for a double bed without extras. The prices are constantly changing. The three levels below are defined as: expensive, which is in excess of $A200; moderate, which is from $A100 to $A200; and inexpensive, for $A100 or less. For more complete and up-to-date information on accommodations contact the Victoria Visitor Information Centre, corner of Swanston and Little Collins Streets, Victoria 3000; phone 03-9658-9955.

*Expensive.* Grand Hyatt, 123 Collins Street, Victoria 3000; phone 03-9629-9111; fax 03-9650-3491. Part of the Hyatt chain located within walking distance of scenic buildings and prime shopping areas. Wheelchair accommodations. The Windsor, 103 Spring Street, Victoria 3000; phone 03-9633-6000; fax 03-9633-6001. This grand old hotel is a historic landmark because of its elegance and classic facade. This is a top-of-the-line five-star hotel with charming individualistic rooms. Wheelchair accommodations. Sofitel, 25 Collins Street, Victoria 3000; phone 03-9653-0000; fax 03-9650-4261. All rooms have great views and open onto an atrium.

*Moderate.* Downtowner on Lygon, 66 Lygon Street, Victoria 3053; phone 03-9663-5555; fax 03-9662-3308. Excellent location with restaurants and city sights all around. Good-quality accommodations for the price. Wheelchair accommodations. Avoca, 98 Victoria Avenue, Victoria 3206; phone 03-9696-9090; fax 03-9696-9092. This is a bed-and-breakfast Victorian located three kilometers from the city center. No wheelchair accommodations. Victoria Vista Hotel, 215 Little Collins Street, Victoria 3000; phone 03-9653-0441. One of the city's oldest hotels, built in the 1880s, the Victoria Vista is in the heart of downtown; there is a budget block of rooms as well as upgrades. Wheelchair accommodations.

*Inexpensive.* Inexpensive accommodations are a challenge to find in Melbourne. Exford Hotel, 199 Russell Street, Victoria 3000; phone 03-9663-2697; fax 03-9663-2248. Located right at the entrance of Chinatown, this is not a bad deal but the place is a little worn. Some of the rooms have good views of Chinatown and other parts of Melbourne. The pubs in the area are sometimes fairly loud until late. Doubles for around $A45. The Friendly Backpacker, 197 King Street, Victoria 3000; phone 03-9670-1111; fax 03-9670-9911. This place fits its name. It is located near the Spencer Street Station, which makes it convenient for people arriving by bus or train. The lobby has loads of literature about Melbourne. The spartan rooms are set up for four people, and there are bunk rooms and dorms with ten or more beds. Showers and bathrooms are shared. Beds rent for about $A15 a night, and you can rent a towel for a couple bucks.

# Day Trips from Melbourne

## Healesville Sanctuary

The Healesville Sanctuary, 65 kilometers east of Melbourne, may be the best wildlife park in Australia for actually getting close to some of the rarest forms of Australian wildlife. The reserve is exclusively for Australian fauna and is also known as the Sir Colin MacKenzie Sanctuary, after the man who started it. It's now run by the Melbourne Zoological Society. This was the first place to successfully breed platypuses in captivity. There are 200 species and 1,700 creatures in residence. The grounds are not large, but the tastefully designed animal-friendly natural enclosures and parklike setting compensate nicely. The platypus display is the best one in Australia for actually getting to see the elusive platypus. The wombat exhibit is equally well thought out. You get a wombat's-eye view of the world.

Tree kangaroos from northern Queensland, lyrebirds, Tasmanian devils, and dingoes are displayed here. In fact, the dingoes are walked daily so visitors can pet them. The walk-through enclosures allow you to walk up to kangaroos (specially imported from Kangaroo Island because of their exceptional tameness), emus, Cape Barren geese, and many other species. A highlight is the Animals of the Night exhibit, where visitors can see nocturnal animals forage and interact in simulated moonlight. Be sure to bring your camera. There is an entry fee. Open 9:00 A.M. to 5:00 P.M. daily. For public transport to Healsville, phone the sanctuary at 059-62-4022.

*Other Parks in the Area.* Most foreign visitors to the Healesville Sanctuary visit via a rental car because of the 65-kilometer distance from central Melbourne. Typically they spend half a day in the sanctuary and return to Melbourne. There are, however, two small parks near Healesville that are convenient, enriching, and suitable for a half-day visit with a picnic or a short stop. The Maroondah Reservoir Park is 3 kilometers beyond Healesville on the Maroondah Highway. This 100-acre park is at the foot of a reservoir built in the 1920s to supply Melbourne with water. There are about 10 kilometers of walking trails that travel to the top of the weir through tree fern groves and mixed vegetation zones. There are several marked picnic areas with barbecue pits. The historic valvehouse is a classic-looking structure. The spillway is most apt to be full in September and October. The waterfall that spews forth is spectacular. Wombats, wallabies, lyrebirds, bronzewings, cockatoos, crimson rosellas, and brush-tailed possums are common, especially in the morning and at dusk.

Yarra Ranges National Park is also on the Maroondah Highway, but it is 11 kilometers from Healesville (8 kilometers north of Maroondah Reservoir Park). This park provides an unforgettable driving experience. The road cuts through forests of mountain ashes, which are immense eucalyptuses that rival California redwoods in height and girth. The understory consists of ancient-looking Australian tree ferns, some as tall as middle-sized palm trees. This rich green environment is startlingly beautiful to anyone from outside Australia. A picnic area on the right side (with a few large nonnative Douglas firs) is a good turnaround place and lunch spot. Several trails lead into the forest from the picnic area. For more information phone 059-62-6228 and ask for the park supervisor.

*Accommodations.* Lake Eildon, 110 kilometers north of Healesville on the direct route, is a good spot if you're camping your way around Victoria. Eildon State Park, on the far side of the lake, has an excellent campground (avoid the lake's crowded town side).

*Access.* Healesville is 65 kilometers east of Melbourne on the Maroondah Highway.

## Phillip Island and the Penguin "Parade"

Located on the Mornington Peninsula, the penguin "parade" is probably the best-known and most well attended natural bird phenomenon in Australia. Tour buses run daily from Melbourne to watch the little ("fairy") penguins waddle from the water up the beach and into their burrows. The dignified little birds are the smallest of the world's 17 species of penguins, and they are the only species that breeds on the Australian mainland. They occur along the entire southern coast and in Tasmania in areas where the coast is suitable for their burrowing and nesting activities. Phillip Island is the easiest place to see these likable birds. Tour companies are able to cash in on them because the birds are amazingly tolerant and a sure bet to show up every night at dusk. On Phillip Island they actually walk on pathways created for their convenience. There is somewhat of an unnatural feel to being part of hundreds of people watching the birds exit the water for their homes, but the birds seem used to it. Great care has been taken to safeguard them. You must stand in designated areas, cannot use a flash, and cannot wander into their colony in the area behind Summerland Beach.

*Access.* The easiest way is on an organized tour. Try Gray Line; phone 03-9663-4455. Their one-day excursion costs $US56 per adult. By car, the drive takes about 90 minutes.

## French Island State Park

There's no doubt that the big tour operators have staked out the fairy penguin phenomenon mentioned above as the must-see natural event for visitors to Victoria. Well, there's much more to the Mornington Peninsula than penguins. French Island National Park is nearby and it could easily be renamed "Koalas Galore National Park." French

Island has been supporting the most prolific koala population in Australia for quite some time. The island's population boasts a phenomenal 100 percent fertility rate while other parts of Australia's koala populations are on the decline due to disease, stress, and habitat destruction. In fact, French Island has had a peculiar problem: the koalas are so successful that 200 are removed annually to colonize historic haunts in other parts of Victoria where populations have suffered or no longer exist. This removal program also alleviates stress on the French Island population, which has come dangerously close to consuming more food than the island's eucalyptus trees can produce.

The island is a low-key place covering about 50,000 acres. It once housed a prison colony for geriatric inmates. Today it is home to about 70 farmers, who operate on the southern half of the island. The park takes up about 24,000 acres on the northern half of the island. Besides koalas the park has 200 species of birds, and Victoria's largest population of long-nosed potoroos (a cat-sized kangaroo killed off on the mainland due by feral cats and foxes). The park also has 400 species of plants, including 82 types of orchids. There are also extensive mangrove swamps and mudflats that may look drab but are actually the home to many kinds of birds and invertebrates. Sea eagles are often sighted here. In the spring the native vegetation blooms in an assortment of bright colors. A road and trail system allows easy access by vehicle, bike, or foot. For more information contact: Ranger-in-Charge, Bayview Road, French Island, 3921; phone 059-80-1294.

*Accommodations.* The island isn't set up for tourism, but there are modest bed-and-breakfasts, and nonpermit, self-contained camping is allowed. For a bed-and-breakfast stay, phone 059-80-1294. The park is managed by the Department of Conservation and Natural Resources. If the department is notified, water and firewood will be provided at the Fairhaven Campsite, as long as the request is not made during fire season.

*Access.* French Island is 70 kilometers southeast of Melbourne. By car take the ferry from Stony Point to Tankerton. You can also reach the island by taking the train to Stony Point from Melbourne. Once at Stony Point there is a passenger ferry to Tankerton. It's always best to let the ferry operator know you are coming. Book by phone: 059-55-3136.

# Wineries

Victoria has many fine wineries, so many that the Victorian Tourism Commission published "Vintage Victoria, Your Wine and Food Guide" to help guide visitors' noses to find the right cork. The guide has maps, descriptions of wines on a per winery basis, phone numbers, addresses, and tasting hours. You can get this free wine guide by contacting the Victoria Visitors Information Centre, Swanston Street; phone 03-9658-9955.

The first permanent settler in Victoria, Edward Henty, planted a vineyard in 1934, and there has been wine in Victoria ever since. There are now 23 distinct wine-growing areas. The area northeast of Melbourne boasts 22 wineries—and that's just one region. There are around a hundred wineries in all. Several tour companies include wineries in one of their day excursions. If you're on your own, read the literature from the visitors center and let your taste dictate where you'll go. The nice thing about having wineries spread over the state is that there's always one nearby.

The Yarra Valley is probably the best-known wine-growing region. Located near Healesville and at the base of the Dandenong Ranges, the area has a cool climate that is credited with contributing to the highly rated pinot noirs and chardonnays. Wineries are usually open daily, and some have restaurants. The Mornington Peninsula also has the Red Hill wineries, which are well known for their chardonnays. The part of the state around Wangaratta is also a large wine-growing region. The region is known for its great variety and specialized wineries. Some of the wineries in this region have been operating for more than 100 years.

Remember, though: Australia is tough on driving under the influence.

# The Attractions of the Dandenong Ranges

The Dandenong Ranges are a favorite weekend retreat for Melbournians. This area is an excellent day trip for motorists.

## The Dandenong Ranges National Park and the William Ricketts Sanctuary

This park encompasses a large portion of the Dandenong Ranges, which are typified by stands of huge mountain ashes, hillsides of large tree ferns, and plentiful wildlife, including such rarities as lyrebirds, quolls, and koalas. This is a surviving section of forested primeval Australia that many Australians have never seen, though to many Melbournians the Dandenongs have almost a spiritual significance. The park has 350 indigenous plant species. Sixteen of these are rare or found only in Victoria. There are 6 major vegetation communities, which provides homes to 31 mammal species, 120 kinds of birds, 21 reptile species, 6 amphibians, and 6 native fish species. The park has an extensive trail system and is used by bushwalkers, mountain bikers, birders, and picnickers. Within the park, adjoining conservation areas include Ferntree Gully, Sherbrooke Forest, Doongalla, and the William Ricketts Sanctuary. Each of these areas has its distinct character and attractions. The William Ricketts Sanctuary is most unique; 40,000 visitors a year visit this sanctuary near the top of Mount Dandenong to see the sculptures made by William Ricketts that are wedged between trees and carved in both earth and wood. Often the art is mystical in nature and involves Aboriginal figures. After living with Aborigines in central Australia, Ricketts began expressing his philosophy of the "divine essence of life," which embraced a unity between humans and wildlife. His work embodies tranquility and oneness with nature, but it also possesses a passionate fury against, as he characterized it, the rape of the earth by mankind. Ricketts was a modest hermit who did not think much of the national acclaim he achieved in his lifetime. He died in 1993 at the age of 93.

## Puffing Billy

This narrow-gauge steam locomotive has long been associated with the Dandenongs. Today this old logging locomotive chugs over trestles and along steeply wooded slopes for 13 kilometers from Belgrave to Emerald Lake. The railway carries 240,000 passengers a year and may be expanded by 11 kilometers in the future. It runs every day except Christmas. For more information phone 03-9870-8411 in Melbourne or 059-68-4667 in the Dandenongs.

## Special Gardens

The Dandenongs also have several special gardens taken over by the state because of their beauty and significance. This acquisition involved six gardens that are now managed by Melbourne Parks and Waterways. One of the gardens is William Ricketts Sanctuary, which is described above. The others include the 40-acre Olinda Rhododendron Gardens, Alfred Nicholas Memorial Gardens, George Tindale Memorial Gardens, and Pirianda Gardens. All of these gardens possess serene and striking ambiances and were developed as their previous owners' lifetime passions. The rhododendron gardens are described as spectacular and are said to rival the Royal Botanic Gardens in Melbourne during the spring bloom. Inquire at the Victoria Visitor Information Centre about garden tours in the Dandenongs.

### Ferntree Gully National Park

Ferntree Gully National Park has scenic picnic sites and many walking tracks. The three-kilometer Bush Nature Walk will give you a feel of the unmolested Dandenongs.

*More Information.* For Ferntree Gully contact the Ranger-in-Charge, Ferntree Gully Forest, Mount Dandenong Tourist Road, Ferntree Gully 3156; phone 03-9758-1342. For information about the Sherbrooke Forest portion of the park contact the same address, and for the William Ricketts Sanctuary contact William Ricketts Sanctuary, Mount Dandenong Tourist Road, Mount Dandenong 3767; phone 03-9751-1300.

*Access.* The Dandenongs are 36 kilometers east of Melbourne on the Burwood Highway. Tour companies visit the area.

## Ballarat

Ballarat plays a romantic and significant role in Australian history. Gold was discovered here in 1851, and soon there were 40,000 glinty-eyed miners in and around Ballarat trying to strike it rich. Although most of the miners, called "diggers," lived in rags and moved tons of earth without finding pay dirt, there were some big winners. A group of Cornish miners working an abandoned claim unearthed a nugget weighing 63,000 grams (about 138 pounds). They christened their find with a beer bottle, loaded it into a wheelbarrow to get it to the assay office, and soon found that they could now afford the world's most expensive champagne.

Friction developed between the colonial government and the diggers. The police harshly enforced an expensive mining license fee that most miners couldn't scrape together. Finally the miners barricaded themselves in the Eureka Stockade, flew their own flag, and prepared to fight against this "taxation without representation." When the colonial authorities moved to crush the rebellion, 25 miners and 4 soldiers lost their lives. The miners lost the battle but the incident resulted in their right to vote and a government forever more cognizant of democratic principles. The Eureka flag now hangs in the Fine Art Gallery in Ballarat, and the Eureka Stockade Park on Stalwell Street has a life-sized replica of Australia's only civil battle.

Today the town is a fully modern metropolis with 62,000 inhabitants. There are a number of historic sites and galleries in the area. The Fine Art Gallery (40 Lydiard Street North, Ballarat; nominal fee) has high-quality art from the earliest days of Australian settlement. The Gold Museum (Bradshaw Street; nominal fee) is cleverly laid out and chronicles the historic role of gold, with a specific focus on Victoria. The Montrose Cottage is the first masonry cottage in the gold fields and is now protected by the National Trust. The town hall, post office, George Hotel, railway station, and Curiosity Shop are oldies but goodies dating back to the 1860s.

Sovereign Hill (a short distance out of town) features meticulously accurate re-creations of mining equipment, a main street, and related activities capturing what it was like to live in a bustling mining town in the 1850s. Actors reenact life in this colorful period. You can try your hand at mining. The 16-hectare Botanic Gardens (Wendouree Parade) is worth a walk-through for the natural beauty and the fine European statuary supplied by men who struck it rich. The garden is known throughout Australia for its begonias. The cottage and monument of literary figure Adam Lindsay Gordon are also in this garden.

A favorite place to get the historical rundown on Ballarat is aboard the paddle cruiser *Sarah George* on Lake Wendouree. Contact Gold Centre Tourism, 202 Lydiard Street North, Ballarat, Victoria 3350; phone 03-5332-2694.

*Accommodations.* Try Sovereign Hill Lodge, Magpie Street, Ballart, Victoria 3354; phone 03-5333-3409. Also try Craig's Royal Hotel, 10 Lydiard Street, Ballarat, Victoria 3354, which also has good eats. Mark Twain slept in this grand bluestone structure. There are more than 20 hotel-motels in Ballarat and numerous caravan parks. Hotels range in price from $A50 to $A150 per night.

*Access.* From Melbourne, Ballarat can be reached in a little over an hour on the Western Freeway. Australian Pacific and Melbourne

Sightseeing run day tours along this route. Regular bus lines also travel to and from Ballarat from Melbourne daily. Contact V-Line; phone 13-22-32. It's about $A14 on V-Line one way.

# Out West in Greater Victoria

## Grampians National Park

Grampians National Park is known for its rugged mountains, spectacular wildflowers, and abundant wildlife. It is the only significant mountain park outside of the area commonly called the Victorian Alps. I rate the Grampians in the top three scenic areas in Victoria.

The park covers 167,000 hectares. It has heavily wooded valleys and ranges of massive sandstone that are tilted, fractured, and eroded, which gives the park a spectacularly irregular plunging escarpment. Wildflowers are the best-known aspect of the flora, but the park is also rich in a wide range of less colorful plants. There are 870 kinds of plants in the park, and more than 200 kinds of birds. This is a birders paradise. You'll see gang-gang cockatoos, blue wrens, rainbow lorikeets, and emus. Much of the forest has been spared from logging. The diversity and overall inspiring essence of this park are difficult to convey in words.

The Grampians rate highly in terms of wildlife. Gray kangaroos (habituated to human visitors) are willing to pose for photographs. Kookaburras are vocal and plentiful. Koalas and platypuses can be found in easily reached areas. Then there are high-quality Aboriginal art sites, with designs unlike any others I saw throughout Australia. There are secluded picnic and camping areas surrounded by great natural beauty. You could easily spend two weeks here camping, exploring, and walking.

Baroka Lookout, which can be reached by car, affords a spectacular view of much of the park and the green pasturelands that border it. The reservoirs you see supply 56 communities. The McKenzie River Walk is a short walk to a spectacular waterfall. The parking area (which is signposted on the main road from Halls Gap) has a kiosk and park literature. The Mount William Walk, which takes about 3 hours, has a superb view, though you'll share the summit with a communications tower. I was there during the winter and the chain-link fence around the relay station was a huge wall of ice. During peak-use periods, there are ranger-conducted walks and talks on a wide range of subjects. The visitors center at Halls Gap has trail maps, and nearby is the Brambuk Living Cultural Centre, which illustrates and tells the story of the Koori people, this region's inhabitants when Europeans first arrived.

For more information on the Grampians, contact the park office in Halls Gap (phone 03-5356-4381) or the regional office at Stawell, phone 03-5358-2314. *The Grampians Ranges by Road and Track* is an excellent publication on the park. It's commonly sold in tourist-oriented businesses in Halls Gap. To get literature on the park, write to the Department of Conservation, Forests, and Lands, 240 Victoria Parade, East Melbourne, Victoria 3000.

*Accommodations.* Zumstein's is a well-groomed campground with a resident population of handout-oriented kangaroos (don't feed them). Zumstein's manager has an interest in wildlife and can help you find creatures in the area, such as the resident platypuses in the creek at the far end of the campground near the bridge. There are usually a couple of fat kookaburras perched strategically to dive-bomb an unattended sandwich. Brambuk Backpackers Lodge in Halls Gap offers dorm rooms at $A16 per night.

Buandik is my favorite camping area. It's on the western border of the park. It's a beautiful low-use camping area with a nearby creek and extensive Aboriginal art sites. I remember watching male variegated wrens flit and hop about, oblivious of the beauty of their glittery violet-blue heads. On walks I saw echidnas and wallabies. The usual route into Buandik is along Lodge Road and then onto Redrock Road. It's a beautiful drive. If the Glenelg River is high, you may find the Glenisla Crossing under a foot or two of water. If the water is deeper than your midcalf, don't attempt the crossing in a rental car. Instead, continue on to Henty Highway. Head south for about 10 kilometers, turn left at Billwing Road, and you'll reach the campground. The Redrock Road area is picturesque. I saw more than 50 emus the day I drove down it. During my visit, the Burrough Campground had a half dozen koalas.

For information about guest houses, phone 03-5358-2314. There's also a well-attended flower show in Halls Gap during the last two weeks of October.

*Access.* From Melbourne the park can be reached via either Glenelg Highway or Western Highway. On either, the distance is about 250 kilometers. From South Australia, it's advisable to visit the Grampians as a diversion before reaching Melbourne. There is no public transportation to Halls Gap. There is a morning train that runs during the week from Melbourne to nearby Stawell.

## Mount Arapiles (Djurite)

Mount Arapiles—also known by its Aboriginal name, Djurite—is a rock climber's paradise. The mountain is really a flat-topped plateau defined by a maze of twisted hard-rock cliffs. There is a road to the top that provides an excellent view of the area. Jon Muir, a well-known Aussie climber who has summited Mount Everest, says there are 3,500 climbs on this mountain. This means that Arapiles has the greatest variety of climbs in Australia. According to local climber Eric Jones, Mount Arapiles is a technical rock-climber's dream. "There's something for everyone. We have easy climbs right up to the hardest climbs in the country. The rock is hard and stable. The climbs are fairly well protected from the weather, too. You can camp here free of charge and watch climbers tempt fate." *The Arapiles Guide Book* can be purchased in outdoor equipment stores in Victoria.

According to Muir in an article published in *Expanse,* the climbs range from 10- to 170-meter outings up some large faces, with great variety in difficulty. The rock is quartzite-metamorphic sandstone and is perfect for climbing. But Muir says the rock is only part of why Arapiles is often referred to as the best climbing in Australia. Arapiles, also known as "the Piles," is a Mecca of sorts that attracts climbers who share their knowledge and camaraderie. The weather is usually temperate, but when it heats up there are nearby lakes to plunge into for cooling off. Many of the routes are well protected. In Muir's *Expanse* article he listed his top climbs and their ratings. The climbs he describes are rated between 2 (easiest) and 25 (hardest) in the Australian system. Ali's is an easy grade-2 200-meter climb featuring scrambling "and [is] a great outing for the whole family"; Arachnus is an exposed grade-10 123-meter climb on exciting rock with good ledges; the Bard is an interesting grade-12 120-meter climb up a pillar that contains "jugs" and overhanging areas; Checkmate is a grade-17 120-meter route that has significant dangers, requiring that only the most skilled attempt it; Sufficiently Alarming is a grade-24 35-meter climb that Muir feels is dangerous and very challenging; in Muir's words, it's "not for the slim-hipped purse-carrying pillows I have seen slinking around Arapiles. . . . [The possibility of] serious injury or death makes this one you won't tackle—or forget—in a hurry!" No Exit is a grade-25 lasting 65 meters. Muir terms No Exit "challenging crack climbing on perfect rock." He advises going slow to appreciate each of the three pitches.

Muir recommends several books. *Rockclimbing—Getting Started,* by Glenn Tempest, is written for beginners. *Rockclimbers Guide to Arapiles/Djurite,* by Louise Sheppard, and *Arapiles: Selected Climbs,* by Glenn Tempest and Simon Metz, are written for climbers of all ability levels.

If you can't make it to Arapiles there's always the climbing gym. There are two good ones in Melbourne: the Climbing Mill (phone 03-9419-4709) and the Hardrock Climbing Company (phone 03-9894-4183).

There are professional guides in the tiny town of Natimuk, located six kilometers from the mountain.

*Accommodations.* In Natimuk there's the National Hotel. Outside of town there's the Natimuk Lake Camping Ground, which has on-site vans.

*Access.* Natimuk (and Mount Arapiles) is between Little Desert National Park and Grampians National Park, off the Wimmera Highway.

## Little Desert National Park

Little Desert National Park is mainly visited for its astounding 200 varieties of birds, including the rare mallee fowl, a workaholic among birds. It spends most of its time building a huge dirt compost heap that incubates its eggs. Besides birds, there are several interesting walks and a camping area.

Little Desert is a misnomer. Though the area is drier than most of the state, it receives suffucent rainfall to sustain mallees, banksias, and a broad range of shrubs. In appearance the park is flat and generally densely vegetated. In most of Victoria this habitat has been bulldozed to make room for agriculture, which is why this park was created—to save some of it. Without this protection birds such as the mallee fowl would not survive.

Few places can compete with the Little Desert area when it comes to birds. Five kinds of cockatoos, 4 kinds of lorikeets, an incredible 18 kinds of parrots, as well as tawny frogmouths, spoonbills, ducks, honeyeaters, emus, and eagles are just some of what you may see. To fully appreciate the park you should enter with Graham Pizzey's *A Field Guide to the Birds of Australia* in hand.

The Sanctuary Nature Walk is a numbered interpretive walk that takes about 30 minutes to complete. The walk will familiarize you with the most common plants and wildlife. It passes by a mallee fowl "incubator" mound that was worked continually from the 1880s and only recently abandoned. Other walks in the park take you to the four recognized habitats.

For information, contact the Department of Conservation, Forests, and Lands, P.O. Box 487, State Public Offices, Horsham, Victoria 3400. Be sure to ask for their bird list and trail map.

*Accommodations.* There is one campground in the park. You must bring your own water. Motel accommodations can be found in Kiata, Nhill, or the Little Desert Lodge south of Nhill.

## Whimpey Reichelt: Mr. Mallee Fowl

Whimpey Reichelt is an amazing character who has built a thriving bird-watching business near Little Desert National Park. He books birders from all over the world (including groups from the Audubon Society). Unattached individuals are also welcome, even if it's only to rent a room for a night. Whimpey's paying guests stay in his lodge and during the day they climb into specially designed 4WD vehicles that have been modified to maximize photographic opportunities. He offers half-day, full-day, and multiday trips that he'll tailor to a group's specific interests. I spent a half day with Whimpey and was impressed by his ability to locate creatures where at first nobody else could. He has several active pairs of mallee fowls on his land and has set up excellent blinds to maximize photo opportunities. These birds begin readying their mounds in autumn and by spring lay their eggs in their diligently monitored earth incubators. Whimpey also does an excellent job explaining the 650 kinds of plants that occur in the area, most of which flower during the spring. If you want to maximize your experience in this region, do it with Whimpey. For costs and other details, contact Little Desert Lodge, 26 Brougham Street, Nhill, Victoria 3418; phone 03-5391-5232 or 03-5391-1714.

## The Murray River

The Murray River is the northern boundary of Victoria. There are a number of interesting towns that offer cruises on vintage paddle wheelers. Echuca has five paddle steamers either in operation or being restored. The twin paddle P.S. *Pyap,* moored in Swan Hill, is the oldest operational boat (1.5-hour ride for a nominal fee). It was built in 1896. If you'd like an authentic riverboat cruise, these old boats are far more interesting than the huge replication paddle wheelers complete with recreation leaders that ply the lower Murray. The Murray in Victoria is steeped in Australian history, much like the Mississippi in the United States. Australians who want to be their own riverboat captain vacation here. They rent houseboats and amble up and down the slow river.

For more on the Murray, read the section in chapter 7, "South Australia." For information about the Murray in Victoria, contact Swan Hill Tourism and Development Centre, 306 Campbell Street, Swan Hill, Victoria 3585; phone 03-5032-3033. Or contact Echuca Tourist Information Centre, Customs House, 2 Heygarth Street, Echuca, Victoria 3625; phone 03-5480-7555.

# The West Coast: Melbourne to South Australia

The coastal drive on either the Princess Highway or the Great Ocean Road from Melbourne to South Australia (Adelaide) is scenic and well worth the effort. You can drive between Adelaide and Melbourne in two days, but I recommend setting aside four to five. I've outlined what I believe are the most significant points of interest along the coast on the Victoria side of the border. If you're going to Adelaide, pick up the journey in the South Australia section.

## Torquay, the Surfing Capital of Victoria

Torquay is the gateway town on the eastern edge of the Otway Ranges. It's also the top big-wave surfing area in Victoria. Many of the beaches are beautiful and have their own special qualities. Zok Zorica, a well-known Victoria surfer, feels the area is one of the world's top surfing spots. "When a storm is offshore, we get twelve-foot breaks," he says. International surfing competitions are held in Torquay every March. The Torquay Surf Lifesaving Club is the largest such club in Victoria. In a drive by the beaches, Zok pointed out windsurfing areas, rental shops, big-wave and swimming and sunning beaches. Jan Juc Beach is his favorite for the social climate, sand, and surf. Bells Beach is known for the big-wave international competition held here every Easter week. An unusual underwater rock formation enhances the size of waves at Bells. There's a clothing-optional beach west of town. There are large caravan parks throughout the area, and the beaches are amazingly clean. For dining, try Ida's and the Mexican Restaurant on the esplanade. You can rent a surfboard or a windsurfer in Torquay. Drop by the Rip Curl retail outlet and factory (phone 03-5261-0000) to chat about surfing conditions and the peculiarities of each beach. To experience the Aussie holiday pub at its clientele's suntanned best, visit the Southern Rose Garden.

Torquay is the eastern terminus of the Great Ocean Road, which is Victoria's most scenic coastal road.

## The Otway Ranges

The Otway Ranges are relatively narrow coastal mountains with high precipitation, lush steep fern gullies, tumbling creeks, desolate beaches, and heavily forested steep slopes with large stands of antarctic beech and mountain ash and in some places giant primitive king ferns with 3.5-meter fronds. Wildlife is abundant, but shy. Otway National Park encompasses 12,000 hectares, a small part of the eastern end of these ranges. Apollo Bay is a central location where you'll find accommodations and a tourist information center. Lorne, which you'll pass through before Apollo Bay, is a scenic town near Lorne State Forest Park, which is known for 40-minute to 2-hour walks to nine different waterfalls, some with swimming holes.

The Otways are off the beaten path despite their proximity to the Princess Highway and Melbourne. Car campers won't be disappointed with Blanket Beach in Otway National Park, which is about 35 minutes west of Apollo Bay on either the Great Ocean Road or Blanket Bay Road (dirt but more scenic—treacherous when wet). There is an attractive sandy beach and lush vegetation here.

The Geelong Bushwalking Club is seeking to bring more attention to the Otways. Their 145-page publication *Walking the Otways* outlines dozens of walks and many cross-country outings. Another excellent source for walks is the Otway National Park office, located on Cartwright Street in Apollo Bay; phone 03-5237-6889.

Madsens Track Nature Walk in Melba Gully State Park, located three kilometers west of Lavers Hill (roughly 240 kilometers southwest of Melbourne), typifies the lushness of the Otways. It takes about 20 minutes to complete. A park service leaflet that refers to numbered posts along the track will familiarize you with the flora. With or without the interpretive aspect, this is an enchanting walk. You'll see myrtle beeches, blackwoods, and a half dozen of the 30

*Fern trees, Otway Ranges.* PHOTO BY ERIC HOFFMAN.

species of ferns in the park. You'll also walk along the Johanna River with its many waterfalls and pools. If you walk quietly you may see a platypus in a quiet pool. In winter months rangers run guided night walks to see glowworms, which occur by the thousands for a few months each year. Camping isn't allowed. For more information, contact the Apollo Bay National Parks Office; phone 03-5237-7240.

*Accommodations.* Aside from the campground at Blanket Beach, there are campgrounds at the Aire River (turn toward the coast from Great Ocean Road at Hordern Vale) and Johanna Beach (turn from the Great Ocean Road about six kilometers south of Lavers Hill). Hotel and motel accommodations can be found in Apollo Bay and in a few of the smaller communities. I enjoyed my stay at the Greenacres Hotel, on the corner of Nelson Street and Great Ocean Road in Apollo Bay; $A60 a room. Or there's the Surfside Backpackers dorms on Gambier Street; phone 03-5237-7263.

*Access.* Otway National Park is 189 kilometers southwest (the eastern section) or 240 kilometers southwest (the western section) from Melbourne and 80 kilometers from Colac. From Melbourne, take the Princess Highway to Geelong. From Geelong take the signposted road to Torquay, the Great Ocean Road. From Melbourne there's a train to Colac. There's coach service to Apollo Bay. There is public transport past Apollo Bay, though only coach tours stop at Melba Gully. Coach from Melbourne to Apollo Bay (not Melba Gully) runs daily; $A20 one way.

## Port Campbell National Park

Port Campbell National Park is past the Otways to the west. This park is a narrow coastal strip that has been set aside in appreciation of the area's dramatically eroded cliffs. It's a sightseer's park. The Twelve Apostles, probably the most photographed coastal geological formation in Victoria, is found here, along with London Bridge and Loch Arch Gorge. (London Bridge should be renamed Fallen Arches, since this natural bridge collapsed in the early 1990s because of constant wave action.) These interesting formations were created by the surf eating away at the limestone cliffs, creating natural archs, pillar-shaped islands, and undercut cliffs. The area is also known for its dangerous seas. The *Loch Ard,* which went aground in 1878, is probably the most famous shipwreck. The graves of the luckless passengers are clearly marked in a small cemetery near where they were pulled from the surf.

*Accommodations.* Port Campbell has an information center, ranger station, eateries, and a full-amenities 113-site caravan park. Make reservations far ahead of time if you plan to be in the area during the Christmas or Easter holidays. Contact Port Campbell National Park, Treqea Street, Port Campbell, Victoria 3269, Australia; phone 03-5598-6382.

## Portland and the Great South-West Walk

Situated in the southwest corner of Victoria, Portland is a historic town and the starting place of the Great South-West Walk—an outstanding 220-kilometer walking track.

Portland was the first permanent settlement in Victoria. Today's population of 9,000 supports a town that can fulfill all your basic needs and is still uncomplicated enough to get around in. There are more than 200 buildings a hundred years old, many of them attractive bluestones from the 1850s.

### The Great South-West Walk

The Great South-West Walk is a remarkable achievement. This walking track was opened in 1983 after years of work by local high school students, teachers, and parents, plus the Crown Land Department, Forest Commission, Shire Council, and the park service. The result is a 220-kilometer walking track that starts in Heathmere. It travels along the Glenelg River to Nelson and returns along the coast to Portland. I walked sections of the Great South-West Walk and went away impressed. Generally the scenery is free of any signs of people, diverse, and often magnificent. The walk is entirely for walkers. Motorcycles and horses are forbidden. There are long stretches of virgin beaches, woodland communities, rich pasturelands, small lakes, forests, and lush rivers along the way. The walk is mostly level and usually takes ten days. However, you can opt out at many places and just walk the sections that seem most attractive. Wildlife is common. There is a great variety of bird life in the marine, river, woodland, and open grasslands environments.

## Information Contacts

For specifics on the Great South-West Walk or Portland, contact the Portland Tourist Information Centre, Portland, Victoria 3350; phone 03-5523-2671. Natural Resources and Environment has a brochure on the Great South-West Walk, complete with details on campsites, distances between them, descriptions of flora and fauna, and a map of the entire area. They also have a pamphlet entitled "Short Walks." Visit the NRE office on Julia Street.

*Accommodations.* I found the Garden Hotel at 63 Bentinck Street (phone 03-5523-1121) to be an affordable and comfortable place close to the downtown. The town has 11 hotels and motels.

*Access.* Portland is only 70 kilometers from the South Australia border and about 370 kilometers from Melbourne on the Princess Highway. Buses from Melbourne and Adelaide stop in Portland.

# Victoria's Alpine Region

## Mount Buffalo National Park

Mount Buffalo National Park is one of the oldest parks in the Victorian Alps. Consequently, it has a well-developed trail system and accommodates both downhill and cross-country skiers. I like this park because it has something for everyone in an alpine setting, which isn't the case for most of the other alpine parks. Sightseers, hikers, horseback riders, rock climbers, hang gliders, paragliders, and skiers are well served.

Most of the 31,000-hectare park sits on a granite plateau that has a great many striking outcrops. The plant life varies depending on the elevation. The road into the park climbs steeply through several zones. Snow gums and alpine ashes are common in the plateau areas. On the lower slopes there are rushing streams and waterfalls cutting through thick forests of various gums. In wet areas, sphagnum moss and other waterloving plants are found. There are short walks to some of the more scenic areas from the roadway. October through April is the best time for wildflowers, which include trigger plants and orange everlastings.

Wildlife is also abundant. More than 140 species of birds have been recorded, among them rare red-headed gang-gang cockatoos, lyrebirds, rosellas, and screeching yellow-tailed black cockatoos. I'll never forget watching a tropical-looking crimson rosella strut across the snow for handouts in midwinter. Birds are most abundant in summer. Gliders, wombats, and black-tailed wallabies are fairly common.

## Skiing

Mount Buffalo is rich in activities. Downhill and cross-country skiers are well taken care of, though the areas open to them aren't particularly extensive. The downhill area is a low-key facility best enjoyed by families, supervised groups of schoolchildren, and young couples. According to rangers, the peak times are the last two weeks in July and the first two in August. There are 1-, 4-, and 6-kilometer marked cross-country trails. The average ski season lasts about 60 days. Equipment for both kinds of skiing can be rented at the lodge. For experienced "intermediate" cross-country skiers, Ranger Adams recommends the Horn Road and Lyrebird Plain—"a relatively short distance for a fantastic view." More extensive ranger-guided nordic nature tours are usually conducted on Wednesdays, Saturdays, and Sundays. Check at the Cresta Day Visitor Centre near the winter park office or phone 03-5755-1466.

## Other Activities

Horseback riding is spectacular in the park. Rangers recommend the North Buffalo Plateau ride that takes in about 25 kilometers of alpine and subalpine country. The chalet (see below) runs the horse concession. The animals appeared well managed and trained. Horses are available from October to May by the hour or for one-day rates.

There are 140 kilometers of walking trails in the park. They vary from easy to challenging. Check at the chalet or with a ranger for maps. The stable also has maps. Rock climbing is extremely popular in this park, especially on the granite walls of the gorge. Lake Catani is the focal point of water sports in the summer and iceskating in the winter.

For further information on the park, write to Ranger, Mount Buffalo National Park, Mount Buffalo, Victoria 3745; phone 03-5755-1466.

### Also in the Area

Bogong National Park (both cross-country and downhill skiing, see below), High Country Adventure run by Graeme Stoney (see below), Wonnangatta-Moroka National Park, and the Mount Buller (see below) and Mount Sterling ski areas.

*Accommodations.* In the park, Lake Catani has a full-amenities campground that includes showers and washing machines. The camp is open from November through May. There is a nominal fee. Book ahead by calling 03-5755-1466. The Mount Buffalo Chalet (phone 03-5755-1988) is a grand old lodge that was built in 1910; Mount Buffalo Chalet, Mount Buffalo National Park, Victoria 3745. About $A80 is the daily charge per person. Dorm rooms range between $A18 and $A30. There are campgrounds, caravan parks, and motels and hotels at Porepunkah, Bright, Myrtlewood, and other nearby communities.

*Access.* Mount Buffalo National Park is about 330 kilometers northeast of Melbourne and about 100 kilometers from Wangaratta. The roads are paved and relatively fast, provided there's no snow on the pavement. Tire chains are mandatory motoring equipment from June to September. Don't chance it without them—the road from Porepunkah into the park is steep and conditions can change quickly. From Melbourne, take the Hume Highway to Wangaratta and from there take the Ovens Highway to Mount Buffalo via Porepunkah. Alternative transport is by train from Melbourne to Wangaratta and then by special coach to the Mount Buffalo Chalet. The special coach is for chalet guests who've booked in advance.

## Bluff and Beyond and the Stoney Clan

Graeme Stoney founded High Country Adventure near Mansfield (off the Hume Highway near Mount Buller). He is an authentic mountain cattleman whose ancestors have lived in the area since the 1840s. You may recognize Stoney if you saw either of the *Man from Snowy River* films. Graeme and his son Chris were two of the daredevil horsemen used in the unforgettable action sequences. Most of the other riders came from properties near Stoney's spread outside of Mansfield.

For years Graeme Stoney and his family have led nordic ski tours in winter and horse rides in summer. One of the best times I ever had was with the Stoney clan and their clients in a tin shed high in the mountains. By day we were nordic skiers exploring the alpine areas around Mount Eadley Stoney (named after Graeme's father). The scenery was fantastic—mist-shrouded peaks, plunging forested valleys, and wind-blown plateaus surrounded by half-buried gnarled snow gums. We laughed, sang, ate huge meals, and slept in a co-ed bunk room in a corrugated iron "mountain cabin." Things have changed a tad. Graeme was elected to represent his region in the state legislature. Skiing has been cut back, and Chris and Helen Stoney have been running things with an emphasis on riding. Their high-country adventure business is now called Bluff and Beyond.

If you're inclined toward horseback riding, this is the place to give it a go. Bluff and Beyond offers two-hour rides, weekend rides, cattle drives and musters, and 5- to 18-day rides. Two-hour rides run $A35 per adult; day rides $A120; and 3- to 5-day rides $A140 per day. If it's "dinky-di" (the real thing), good horses, and good company you're after, this is the place. Contact: Chris and Helen Stoney, Minto Park, Mount Buller Road, Mansfield, Victoria 3722; phone 03-5775-2212; fax 03-5775-2598; E-mail: stoneys@mansfield.net.au.

*Access.* See "Access" instructions below for Mount Buller.


## Skiing and Alpine Activities

### Mount Buller

Mount Buller is about 200 kilometers from Melbourne, making it the nearest of Victoria's three major ski areas. The road is paved, and the drive takes about three hours under normal conditions; carry chains in the winter. The Australian Institute of Winter Sport and Olympic Training is at Mount Buller. It may surprise you to learn that Australians Jacqui Cooper, a world-champion freestyle skier,

*Mountain horsemen Graeme Stoney and John Lovick, high-country neighbors on the Great Divide, near Mansfield.*

and Zali Steggall, a bronze medalist at the Nagano Olympics, both trained here.

The resort is modeled after European resorts where you can literally ski to your hotel room after a day of negotiating moguls and sliding down the slopes. The area reached by lifts exceeds 400 acres. The highest point is 1,804 meters. About 30 percent of the runs are for beginners, 40 percent for intermediate skiers, and 30 percent for experts. To learn more, contact the Mount Buller Reservation Centre; phone 1-800-398-049 (toll-free inside Australia) or phone the Mount Bueller Chalet Hotel; 03-5952-2062.

*Accommodations.* There are dozens of different kinds of accommodations at the resort. Some of the more attractive places are replicas of Swiss chalets. Contact the visitor information center at the Railway Station; phone 03-5775-1464.

*Access.* Drive north on the Hume Highway to Seymour. From Seymour take the Goulburn Valley Highway and then the Maryborough Highway to Mansfield. Mount Buller is 48 kilometers outside of Mansfield. Chains can be rented in Mansfield: they are required from Mansfield to Mount Buller. An alternative route is via Healesville and Lake Eildon (see "Day Trips from Melbourne" for details). A combination of coach services can take you from Melbourne to Mount Buller or from Mansfield to Mount Buller. Contact V-Line in Melbourne (phone 13-22-32) or the Transportation Information kiosk (phone 13-16-68).

## Bogong National Park

This 81,000-hectare park contains the ten tallest mountains in Victoria. The highest is Mount Bogong at 1,986 meters. The highlands are a favorite haunt of bushwalkers in the summer and cross-country skiers in the winter. Mount Hotham, which is outside the park but sandwiched between the park's southwestern arms, is one of Victoria's top downhill skiing areas.

The vegetation in the park includes grassy high plains, heathlands, and stands of gnarled snow gums. Below about 1,300 meters the alpine and subalpine regions give way to mountain gums, fern gullies, alpine ashes, and open forests. The spring has a glorious wildflower display. The alpine areas aren't exactly teeming with wildlife.

About 100 kinds of birds and a number of small marsupials have been recorded, mostly in areas where there is cover. Two animals deserve mention. The very rare mountain pygmy possum lives in isolated pockets in the highest areas. The stronghold of its restricted range is Mount Hotham. The animal was thought to be extinct until 1966, when a population was found. Today's estimates are that there are no more than 3,000 left. Two species of antechini live above the snowline. These are pugnacious rat-sized marsupials. Male antechini copulate so vigorously that they die from exhaustion.

## Skiing

Most winter visitors to the area come to ski. It takes about four hours to reach this area from Melbourne. Downhill skiing goes on with a vengeance at Mount Hotham Alpine Resort and Falls Creek Alpine Resort. Mount Hotham also has extensive cross-country trails and the most challenging runs and is generally recognized as appropriate for intermediate and expert skiers. It generally has lighter snow than the other resorts. Falls Creek has T-bars, poma lifts, and short runs. Equipment can be rented at both resorts. For information about the resorts, contact Falls Creek Tourist Area, Falls Creek, Victoria 3699 (phone toll-free in Australia 1-800-232-557), or Mount Hotham Alpine Resort, P.O. Box 28, Bright, Victoria 3741 (phone toll-free in Australia 1-800-354-555).

The Bogong high plains are excellent for short and extended cross-country skiing outings. The season usually runs from June to September. Joc Schmiechen, an outdoor education instructor who takes students here for a final test of their "bushcraft," says the area around Mount Feathertop is the most spectacular for both cross-country skiing and walking during their respective seasons.

Schmiechen cautions that only experienced skiers with survival training and a full complement of winter gear should attempt overnight outings. Even day skiers should be well prepared. Conditions can become brutal with sleet, snow, ice fog, and wind during winter. Surprise storms occur in summer, too. Many of the huts on the high plains are memorial huts, named for those who didn't survive. You should always review the cross-country routes with the rangers.

For information, contact Ranger in Charge, 46 Bakers Gully Road, Bright, Victoria. You can get information on cross-country skiing at the Mount Hotham and Falls Creek resorts. Cross-country skiers and hikers should state their intended travel plans in registries kept at Falls Creek Information Centre in Pretty Valley, at Watchful Creek on the Mount Nelse Track, and possibly at other places in the park.

## Top Ski Runs in Victoria

The August-September 1998 issue of *Expanse* published the top ten ski and snowboard runs in Australia. Six of them are in Victoria; the other four are in New South Wales. Below is a brief summary of the six runs in Victoria (numbers 1, 2, 5, and 6 are in Bogong National Park).

1. Valley of the Moon, Falls Creek: Intermediate with new snow, advanced when moguls are out in force. Main feature is a gradual buildup with a fantastic view of Mount Bogong before a plunge into a tree-lined gully.

2. Australia Drift, Mount Hotham: Intermediate to advanced with a walk out. Run is unobstructed and steep.

3. Bull Run Bowl, Mount Buller: Described as for "advanced only or beginners with a death wish." Steep skiing between boulders that opens into a large, fast bowl.

4. Gotcha Ridge into Gotcha Bowl: For advanced skiers. Usually ungroomed rough snow with choice of two superb fall lines that require carving around trees.

5. The Final Gully, Mount Bogong: For advanced and strong intermediate. Scenic and challenging. Starts open, then drops into steep gullies.

6. Diamantia Face, Mount Feathertop: Wide consistent slope, often referred to as Australia's best cross-country slope.

## Walks

The entire park is a favorite haunt of bushwalkers. Sandra Bardwell, author of *National Parks of Victoria*, rates Bogong National Park highly as Victoria's most extensive alpine area and says the best walking months are March through November. The 600-kilometer Alpine Walking Track passes through the park. The leg from Mount Hotham to Mount Bogong (about 35 kilometers) stretches through the heart of the park. There are huts along the route on side trails and one can exit at the midway point at Falls Creek. There are a great number of 5- to 10-kilometer loops, particularly in the Falls Creek area. The Bungalow Spur Track, which starts at the Bungalow parking area, is probably the most popular track. It is a 22-kilometer round-trip to the summit of Mount Feathertop. There is a fantastic view from the summit. If you decide to try it, start early. It takes about 10 hours to complete. Try to get a copy of the "Mount Feathertop Bungalow Spur" handout. It explains the walk in detail. Solitary Mount Feathertop is the second-highest mountain in Victoria. Ask in Bright or Harrietville about the location of the trailhead.

For details on other walks, drop by the Mount Beauty ranger station or the information centers in Bright, Omeo, or Falls Creek.

## Other Activities

Horseback riding is allowed in the park. Check with a ranger in Bright or with the resort operators for details. The park also is known for ice climbing (for qualified participants) and trout fishing (license needed).

*Accommodations.* The resorts at Mount Hotham and Falls Creek are the nearest accommodations to the park. The nearby towns of Porepunkah and Myrtleford to the northwest of the park have accommodations, as do Omeo and the coastal towns south of the park. Bushcamping is allowed in the park, providing specified guidelines are followed.

*Access.* Bogong National Park is 350 kilometers northeast of Melbourne and 120 kilometers east of Wangaratta. From Melbourne, take the Hume Highway to Wangaratta, and then take the Ovens Highway to Mount Beauty. In a bus, the ride takes about 5 hours if the roads are clear of snow. If snow is forecast, take the coastal route via the Princess Highway to Bairnsdale and then the Omeo Highway to the park or resorts. This route is also considered a scenic drive. Buses from Albury to Mount Beauty depart daily Monday through Friday.

# Victoria's East Coast

## Wilsons Promontory National Park

Wilsons Promontory National Park is really a 49,000-hectare cut of Tasmania hanging off the southernmost edge of the Australian continent. Its plant life is representative of both the mainland and Tasmania, and it was once part of the land bridge connecting Tasmania to the mainland. The "Prom" is probably the best-known park in Victoria, one of the most popular, and possibly the best managed. It's amazingly litter- and erosion-free, considering the heavy people traffic in some areas.

The chief geological feature is a huge, multifaceted granite outcrop that was the high point in the land bridge to Tasmania 14,000 years ago, before the oceans rose to their present level. Now the low points of the land bridge are under the turbulent Bass Strait, and only the granite outcrop of the promontory and Glennie and Anser Islands, plus the larger Bass Strait islands, poke above the surface. The silt-created Yanakie Isthmus, which connects the granite mass of Wilsons Promontory to the mainland, has been in existence only 4,000 or 5,000 years.

When you enter the park from the north and cross this isthmus, check the grassy areas for large numbers of gray kangaroos and emus. Your first destination should be the park headquarters at Tidal River on Normal Bay. Here you can pick up literature about the park, pay for a camping spot (if there happens to be a cancellation), or check into the tourist lodge. Your visit will be enhanced if you buy a field guide. There is also a kiosk and interpretive center at Tidal River.

The promontory is a combination of granite tors, jutting mountains, and green vegetation that ranges from rain forests to open forests. Along the coast, forests and granite tors outline striking white beaches and secluded coves with bright turquoise water. When

I first walked among the giant tree ferns and along the sandy coves, I remember thinking Wilsons Promontory was the most striking park I'd seen in Australia. There are now many contenders for that honor, but Wilsons Promontory still rates very high on my list and should be included in the top three parks in Victoria.

The promontory is home to cockatoos, small parrots, emus, wallabies, koalas, wombats, and echidnas, as well as albatrosses and other seabirds associated with the open ocean. The flat areas around Yanakie are teeming with kangaroos and emus at dawn and dusk.

Wilsons Promontory is well suited for sightseers, day and overnight hikers, car campers, and pristine-beach freaks. The park can be visited year-round, though its peninsular shape lends it to fast-changing marine weather conditions.

There are 90 kilometers of marked trails in the park. I sampled several short walks and went away wishing I had had more time. The Lilly Pilly Gully Nature Walk is a must if you're interested in enjoying this park's natural treasures. This is a 5-kilometer round-trip that is described in the park literature as taking 3 hours. I did it in less, with several stops for photographs and appreciation. The best part of this walk is at the turnaround point at the Lilly Pilly Loop. You'll find a gurgling crystal-clear creek with darting trout and a forest of tree ferns that stand nine meters high. Butterflies will dance past your head for much of the walk if you're there in spring. At the loop and along the walk you'll see an extremely wide variety of plants: meter-high grasses, redwood-sized mountain ashes, huge flowering banksias, figs, blackwoods, and a myriad of the more than 700 kinds of plants found in the park. If packing a lunch fits your schedule, do it. There are picnic tables at several places along the track. I also saw gliders and many kinds of birds. This walk could just as aptly be called the Garden of Eden Walk.

There are several summit walks that afford fantastic views. The walk to Mount Oberon (3.2 kilometers each way) is excellent. The track is steep and a little exciting at the last bit, where you must climb a ladder. From the summit you get a 360-degree view that includes faraway Tasmania and a series of offshore islands. Whiskey Beach and Squeaky Beach are scenic strips of sand that can be reached in short walks from their respective parking areas. Sealer's Cove is the most popular overnight bushwalker destination. According to Ranger Scott Campbell, however, many of the prettiest secluded coves are seldom visited.

*Cautions.* According to Ranger Scott Campbell, surf and sun are the two main hazards: "Pack water; we've had problems with people dehydrating during the hot months. Choosing a swimming area should be done after consulting with rangers." He also recommends packing a light raincoat because the promontory's weather often changes rapidly.

*Accommodations.* Inside the park, a full-amenities campground is at Tidal Creek. There is a nominal fee per person; fees fluctuate with the season. You must book a reservation—for peak season as much as six months in advance. There is also a nominal fee for entering the park. There are bushwalkers' camps that require walking before camping. Booking is suggested, but often there are openings for "on-the-spot booking." There are also a limited number of lodges and flats, ranging from $A95 to $A250 a week (contingent on the number in your party and the type of accommodation). There is also something one ranger called a "motor hut" that rents for $A14 per night. I never saw one, so you're on your own on this one. For bookings and information inside the park, contact Ranger in Charge, Wilsons Promontory National Park, Tidal River, Foster, Victoria 3960; phone 03-5680-9555.

Outside accommodations are a fair distance away. Fish Creek, the nearest sizable town, is 61 kilometers from the Tidal River campground. Foster also has hotel and motel accommodations. There are numerous "no camping" signs outside the park's northern boundary that are aimed at discouraging turned-away park visitors from setting up camp in paddocks and near townships where they aren't wanted. According to townspeople, the no-camping policy is enforced promptly.

*Access.* Wilsons Promontory is 230 kilometers southeast of Melbourne. From Melbourne the usual route is via the South Gippsland Highway to Meeniyan. From Meeniyan turn south to Fish Creek and Yanakie and into the park. The journey usually takes about 3 hours. There is no regularly scheduled public transport, but several coach-tour companies operating from Melbourne visit the park. Check with the Visitor Information Centre in Melbourne; phone 03-9658-9955. From Sydney the "Prom" is off the Princess Highway and is the most scenic park on the coastal route between Australia's two largest state capitals.

## Gippsland Lakes: The Victorian Riviera

"I take my holidays at the Gippsland Lakes, that's the beaut place in Victoria," explained the Melbournian sitting next to me on the long flight from Honolulu to Sydney. I had asked him where his favorite vacation spot was, and he'd replied, "Gippsland Lakes," a place I didn't know existed. "It's mostly fresh water but it's on the ocean, mate. It's also called the Victorian Riviera."

Gippsland Lakes encompass 400 square kilometers of coastal waterways, linked to the sea by a single narrow man-made channel. It's the largest inland lake system in Australia. The shoreline scenery includes dune systems, heavily wooded forests, swamps, lush pasturelands, tiny dockside communities, vacation homes, marinas, beaches, and islands. The lakes in the system come in all shapes and sizes. Lake Reeve is shaped like a string bean. It's 100 meters wide and 90 kilometers long. Across the narrow dune system that separates it from the sea is Ninety Mile Beach, perhaps the longest regularly used recreational ocean beach in the world. Lake Wellington is farther inland and is connected to the system by a narrow channel. It's practically round and is surrounded by mostly wetlands habitat. Other lakes are too oddly shaped to describe. The system is interconnected and fed by the Avon, Perry, Mitchell, and Tambo Rivers, which are fed by snow and runoff from the Victorian Alps. The relentless surf has effectively built its own bulwark of sand (Ninety Mile Beach) and created the system in its present form. About a million years ago the area was a giant bay.

### The Towns of Gippsland Lakes

There are several noteworthy towns around the lakes. Most of them are classic Aussie towns with wide streets and old storefronts. Sale is the informal capital of the area. The town is the access point to the western end of the lake system and the road access to Ninety Mile Beach. Bairnsdale is a larger town. It has a comprehensive regional tourism information center (phone 03-5152-3444), next to Saint Mary's Church. Bairnsdale sits on the Mitchell River and has a good-quality botanic garden. Paynesville is a popular tourist town 17 kilometers southeast of Bairnsdale. This is a boating hub and a good place to rent a boat to explore the lake system. There is a small tourist center here that can assist you in locating boat rentals and other information. Paynesville is 5 kilometers across the water from

Lakes National Park. Metung is a village on the narrow peninsula jutting into Lake King. It's a boat-hire center. It also has some naturally heated pools suitable for swimming. Lakes Entrance is the most popular tourist resort in Victoria. It is situated at the eastern end of the system where a channel joins the lakes to the sea. There are excellent vistas here, particularly Jemmy's Point. The area is advertised as the best of both worlds and appeals to surfers and boating enthusiasts. You can buy a ticket on a cruise boat and go sightseeing. Popular nearby areas are Cosstick Weir, where a colony of koalas lives, and Burnt Ridge picnic area. There are more motels and hotels here than anywhere else in the Gippsland Lakes area.

*Boat Charters.* There's no shortage of boat charter companies. If you're serious about boating, contact the Victoria Visitor Information Centre (phone 03-9658-9955) and request a current list of yacht rentals in Gippsland.

For day sailers, canoes, and windsurfers, contact South East Coast Tourism, 240 Main Street, Bairnsdale, Victoria; phone 03-5152-3444.

*Accommodations.* There are dozens of hotels, motels, and caravan parks throughout the Gippsland Lakes area. Get a copy of the "South East Region Accommodation Guide" from the Visitor Information Centre, Swanston Street, Melbourne, Victoria 3000 (phone 03-9658-9955) or at the South East Coast Tourism Centre in Bairnsdale.

*Access.* The Gippsland Lakes are clearly marked on any road map. From Melbourne the distance is 200 to 300 kilometers, depending on how you decide to reach the system. If you're contemplating reaching the park by water, head for Paynesville; if by land, head for Sale. Charter coach and bus service extends from Melbourne to the larger towns in the region.

## The Coastal Route via the Princess Highway
The Princess Highway is the primary coastal link between New South Wales and Victoria. At Lakes Entrance you must decide on either the Buchan-Jindabyne Road, with the northern terminus near Kosciuszko National Park, or the Princess Highway, which skirts the coast to Eden.

The Princess Highway from Lakes Entrance to the New South
Wales border is a good-quality two-lane road. Much of the scenery is
pastoral and wooded. I wouldn't classify it as stunning, possibly
because it reminded me of California, where I live. Croajingolong
National Park is the one noteworthy outdoor area between Lakes
Entrance (Gippsland Lakes) and the New South Wales border.

## Mallacoota

Mallacoota is a coastal town serving the eastern portion of Croajingolong National Park. The route to it is by paved road to the coast
from the Princess Highway. The extensive inlet near Mallacoota is a
drowned river valley. Betka and Bastion Point are two fine swimming
beaches close to town. Canoeing the backwaters is popular. For eats,
try Barnacles Family Seafood Bistro.

*Accommodations.* For guest house accommodations, try the Mallacoota Wilderness Lodge; phone 03-5158-0455. For more conventional accommodations, try the Flag Inn. The best car-camping spots
are at the end of the dirt roads that cut toward the coast from the
Princess Highway.

## Croajingolong National Park

This is a coastal park stretching for 90 kilometers from Sydenham
Inlet to the New South Wales border. Captain Cook's first sighting of
Australia occurred here. The park is known for its bays, inlet
beaches, wildlife, and wildflower displays in October. Half of the
park was burned by brushfires in 1983, but regeneration is nearly
complete. Heathlands and woodlands are among the more common
plant communities.

Shipwreck Creek and Wingan Inlet are two popular remote coast-
side camping areas. Shipwreck Creek is also popular for swimming
and bushwalking. Wingan is surrounded by remnant rain forest.
Shipwreck is reached by driving south along the coast from Mallacoota. However, the road is often impassable during rain. Wingan
Inlet is reached from the Princess Highway on the West Wingan
Road between Cann River (17 kilometers east) and Genoa. Wildlife
is abundant. The road is passable in a passenger car during dry conditions. The road system throughout the park is mostly gravel or dirt.
The Double Creek Nature Walk at the east end of the park (on the

Genoa-Mallacoota Road) cuts through some nice sections of temperate rain forest.

For more information, contact the Department of Conservation and Natural Resources in Cann River; phone 03-5158-6351.

For detailed maps of the area, visit the Division of National Mapping and ask for Eden, No. 8823; Mallacoota, No. 8822; and Cann, No. 8722.

*Accommodations.* As mentioned, Shipwreck Creek and Wingan Inlet are camping areas within the park. There's also a campground at Thurra River. Campgrounds have basic amenities. There is a nominal fee for using them. If you're going to camp during a holiday, it would be wise to book a spot in advance.

Cann River, Genoa, and Mallacoota (see above) have motels and caravan parks.

*Access.* Croajingolong National Park is 525 kilometers east of Melbourne and 582 kilometers south of Sydney on the Princess Highway. It is 355 kilometers southeast of Canberra, and 88 kilometers south of Eden. The journey from Melbourne on the Princess Highway takes about eight hours. From Eden the drive is a little more than an hour.

# PART V

# Tasmania

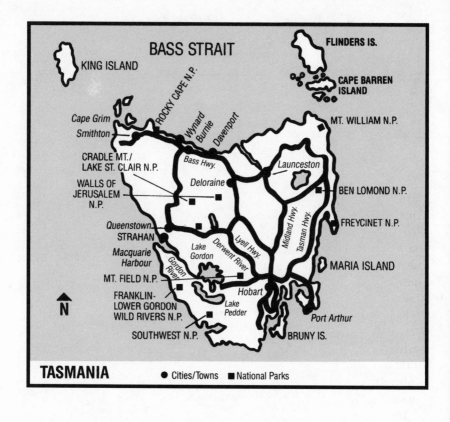

**BASS STRAIT**

KING ISLAND

FLINDERS IS.

CAPE BARREN ISLAND

ROCKY CAPE N.P.

Cape Grim

Smithton

Wynard

Burnie

Davenport

MT. WILLIAM N.P.

CRADLE MT./ LAKE ST. CLAIR N.P.

Bass Hwy.

Deloraine

Launceston

WALLS OF JERUSALEM N.P.

BEN LOMOND N.P.

Queenstown

STRAHAN

FREYCINET N.P.

Macquarie Harbour

Lake Gordon

Derwent River

Lyell Hwy.

Midland Hwy.

Tasman Hwy.

MARIA ISLAND

MT. FIELD N.P.

Gordon River

FRANKLIN- LOWER GORDON WILD RIVERS N.P.

Hobart

Lake Pedder

Port Arthur

N

SOUTHWEST N.P.

BRUNY IS.

**TASMANIA**

● Cities/Towns    ■ National Parks

# Overview

Tasmania is an island state and the coolest, most southern part of Australia. It's been separated from the mainland by the turbulent 240-kilometer-wide Bass Strait for more than 10,000 years. Tasmania has vast impenetrable rain forests, exotic wildlife not found on the mainland, stunning alpine scenery, a myriad of plants found only there, rolling pastoral lands, and everywhere the color green. There is water aplenty in Tasmania.

Roughly triangular in shape and covering 68,000 square kilometers, Tasmania is Australia's smallest state—about the size of Ireland. Perhaps its diminutive size is the underlying reason it's at the bottom of the totem pole in Australian politics and the object of jokes about "inbred prisoner stock" by mainland Australians. Still, for backpacking fanatics, Tasmania is the state to head for.

Tasmania shares the same southern latitude and ocean as New Zealand. The area is known as "the roaring 40s," which refers to the latitude known for its stormy conditions. The weather is often cool and wet, though it can be blisteringly hot. Sometimes the weather comes straight out of Antarctica, which is the next landfall to the south; at other times its origins are South America, the nearest landfall to the east. It's said that in Tasmania you can get all four seasons in a single day—a phenomenon I witnessed more than once. I've seen a temperature of 80°F, freezing snow, and hail in a five-hour period. Kent McConnell, a U.S. transplant working for the Tasmanian Parks and Wildlife Service, says, "Usually there is a three-day cycle: miserable for three days, followed by sunny for three." Anyone contemplating walking must carefully consider the weather before venturing into the wilderness.

There's nothing monotonous about Tasmania. The weather, like the scenery, can evoke a sense of utter tranquillity, inspiration, and awe.

Europeans first reached the island in 1642. Dutchman Abel Tasman named it Van Diemen's Land. Settlement under the British began in 1803. The island's legislative government officially changed the island's name to Tasmania in 1856.

During the early 1800s, Van Diemen's Land was the end of the line for criminals who transgressed after being transported from England to Sydney. Though conditions were miserable, thousands of convicts survived their stay on Tasmania. Many settled on the island after their release. The island's Aboriginal name hasn't survived, though Aborigines occupied it for 20,000 years. After just 75 years of European settlement, the Aborigines perished to the last person in what amounts to an act of systematic genocide. After most were shot on sight, the last 44 were tricked into surrendering, loaded into a boat, and first dumped on Flinders Island, then moved to the mainland, where the last man, "King Billy," died in 1869, and the last woman, Truganini, died in 1875.

Today, there are 460,000 Tasmanians, 40 percent living in the city of Hobart. More than the rest of Australia the populace is of English descent. However, ethnic homogeneity has not translated into unity of thought. The social climate is sometimes as volatile as Tasmania's weather. The island's populace is polarized on environmental issues. The environmental lobby, which successfully halted the damming of the Franklin River and is battling clear-cut logging practices, is articulate and well organized. On the other side the logging and electric power advocates are as entrenched and slow to compromise.

## Information Sources

### Tasmanian Travel and Information Centres

Tasmania competes with Queensland and Victoria for the best-run tourist industry. The government-run Tasmanian Travel and Information Centres will match your interests and pocketbook with information about transportation, tours, accommodations, campgrounds, river cruises, river rafting, maps, and the national parks. The number for general information (toll-free in Australia) is 800-806-846; they can be reached on the Web at www.tourism.tas.gov.au. There are more than 20 offices throughout Tasmania. For details on all aspects of moving about the state, get a free copy of *Travelways*. It's available in airports, from News Agencies, at ferry terminals serving Tasmania, and at Tasmanian Travel and Information Centres.

Information offices can be found in the following cities.

| City | Street Address | Phone Number |
|------|----------------|--------------|
| Burnie | Little Alexander Street | 03-6443-6111 |
| Devonport | 5 Best Street | 03-6424-4466 |
| Hobart | 20 Davey Street | 03-6230-8233 |
| Launceston | Saint Johns and Paterson Streets | 03-6336-3122 |
| Outside of Tasmania: | | |
| Adelaide | 1 King William Street | 08-8400-5533 |
| Brisbane | 239 George Street | 07-3405-4133 |
| Melbourne | 259 Collins Street | 03-9206-7933 |
| Canberra | 165 City Walk | 02-6209-2133 |
| Sydney | 60 Carrington Street | 02-9202-2033 |

# Travel
## Arrival by Airplane or Ferry

Getting to any island requires a boat or plane. If you arrive by plane, Hobart Airport is about 20 kilometers east of the city. A taxi is often in excess of $A20. The Airport Bus takes you to Hobart for $A8.50. Depending on your flight's arrival time, you may need to call to schedule a pickup; phone 0419-383-462. Both Qantas (phone 13-13-13) and Ansett (phone 13-13-00) serve Tasmania with regularly scheduled flights from Sydney and Melbourne. The flying time from Melbourne is a little shy of an hour.

Though most air travelers arrive in Hobart, you can fly to Devonport, at the other end of the island, from Melbourne on either Kendell (phone 13-13-00) or Qantas-owned South Australia (phone 13-13-13). This may make sense if you're headed toward Cradle Mountain, the most popular alpine walking area.

Devonport is also the port of call of the *Spirit of Tasmania,* the seagoing ferry that arrives from Melbourne Tuesday, Thursday, and Saturday and returns three days a week. The ferry travels at night and a fare includes meals and dormlike accommodations. For cars, the price is $A30; for passengers, prices vary between $A100 and $A130 per head, depending on the season. Booking for space as far ahead as possible is recommended; phone 13-20-10.

## Visiting the National Parks

More than 20 percent of Tasmania's land is part of a national park or reserve. There are 17 national parks. Entrance fees to parks add up quickly. To reduce this cost sharply, get either the National Parks Pass or a Backpacker Pass. The National Parks Pass, for a vehicle, can be purchased ($A30 and good for a month) at a Tasmanian Travel and Information Centre in Hobart, Launceston, or Devonport. You can also purchase it on the ferry from Melbourne. If you're traveling on foot and relying on public transportation, purchase a Backpacker Pass for $A12. It is also good for a month. For direct contact with the national parks for specific information, call the Tasmanian National Parks and Wildlife Service's information number, 03-6233-6191, or use E-mail: http//www.parks.tas.gov.au.

## Tour Operators and Buses

*Travelways,* the very complete bimonthly tourist publication put out by the Tassie tourism office, lists numerous operators in every outdoor endeavor from sea kayaking to river rafting and armchair bigbus park tours. Shop competitively, and keep an eye out for the experienced operator. Some of the bus companies and coach tour operators offer package travel deals limited in days that are supposedly for reduced rates. In some cases this may make sense, but often it is cheaper to take a public bus or rent a car for the outing you have in mind. I've preferred a rental car because it's better suited to day hikes and traveling to the next site without long waits. More than one backpacker I met complained about being stranded or being "held captive" to a bus schedule. Keep in mind that Tasmania is a relatively small area and most parts can be reached by car in an hour or two. Some of the tour outfits that have been up and running are Tasmanian Wilderness Travel (phone 03-6334-4442) and Redline Coaches (phone 03-6331-3233). These two companies issue a reduced-fare pass (Tassie Wilderness Pass) that allows a traveler to make use of the routes of either company. For more focused outings (river rafting, guided overnight hikes, etc.) Peregrine Adventures (phone 03-6231-0977), which is based in Hobart, specializes in rafting trips and hikes in the remotest and most scenic national parks. Many outdoor adventure outfits operate out of Hobart, but Launceston is also well represented by these businesses. In Launceston try Tasmanian Expeditions; phone 03-6334-3477.

## Rental Cars and Campers

If you arrive via the airport near Hobart, renting a car may make the most sense. It's the most efficient way to get around. Of the companies represented at the Hobart Airport, Thrifty was the only company with a toll-free phone number: from anywhere in Australia, call 1-800-030-730. Avis (phone 03-6248-5424) and Budget (phone 03-6248-5333) are also in the airport. The daily rate is reduced if you take a weeklong rental. For renting a camper-van try Autorent-Hertz, 122 Harrington Street, Hobart, Tasmania 7000; phone 03-6237-1111.

## Motoring

The road system in Tasmania consists of three classifications of roads: A routes, which are primary routes characterized by two-way traffic with wide shoulders; B routes, which are connecting links between the more important roads (they are narrow two-lane roads requiring vigilance while driving); and C routes, which are usually a lane to a lane and a half of pavement and require nimble driving and a willingness to get out of the way of oncoming traffic. For up-to-date touring maps, contact the Royal Automobile Club of Tasmania, Murray and Patrick Streets, Hobart, Tasmania 7005; phone 132-72-22.

## Accommodations

I split my time in Tasmania between bed-and-breakfast places and campgrounds. But there are also youth hostels, caravan parks, host farms, and colonial accommodations, as well as standard hotels and motels, usually for lower prices than in the other states. You should be able to get rooms for $A10 to $A60 per night.

Hostels throughout Tasmania are used heavily by young backpackers who have come to Tasmania to hike. Rates for hostels belonging to the Youth Hostels Association are from $A4 to $A6 per night. The annual membership is $A18. For membership, visit Youth Hostels Association of Tasmania, 28 Criterion Street, Hobart; phone 03-6234-9617.

I always prefer living with the locals to the isolation of motel living. *Travelways* dedicates pages of listings to accommodations that fall into categories of living with Tasmanians for an evening. You can stay in colonial cottages, at farms, and in bed-and-breakfasts. Keep in mind that on some of the host farms you are expected to pitch in and help with chores. Make sure you understand your commitment before you sign on. Prices vary from $A20 to $A60 per night. Book in advance through the information center offices listed above.

Tasmania has more than 50 caravan parks and campgrounds in and near the national parks. The island is the perfect size for car or camper-van touring. *Travelways* rates all campgrounds and caravan parks on a bimonthly basis. Don't travel in Tasmania without it!

# Hobart

Hobart, the capital, straddles the mouth of the Derwent River at Storm Bay and sits under the shadow of Mount Wellington. It's a convenient starting place for a trip to Tasmania and is normally reached by a 1-hour flight from Melbourne or a 1.5-hour flight from Sydney. Many visitors also arrive via the overnight ocean ferry, *Spirit of Tasmania,* which runs between Melbourne and Devonport.

Founded in 1804, Hobart is Australia's second-oldest capital. Much of the history has been preserved in its old buildings. Ninety buildings have been designated with a National Trust classification because of their historic significance. Most of these are on Davey and Macquarie Streets, including Australia's oldest theater, which dates back to 1837.

The maritime influence is strong in Hobart. Top-quality sailing yachts and fishing boats decorate the waterfront. On New Year's Eve the city celebrates the arrivals for the Sydney-to-Hobart Yachting Classic. There are numerous top-quality restaurants near the waterfront.

Battery Point is made up of grand Georgian mansions and tidy clapboard cottages on narrow streets overlooking the water. There are tucked-away neighborhood-type restaurants and pubs. Many houses offer bed-and-breakfast accommodations called colonial accommodation because the houses were built a century ago. The National Trust conducts walking tours of Battery Point on Saturday mornings. Contact the Tasmanian Travel and Information Centre, 20 Davey Street; phone 03-6230-8233.

Nearby Salamanca Place has a lineup of restaurants, pubs, and galleries housed in warehouses that date back to the 1830s. Every

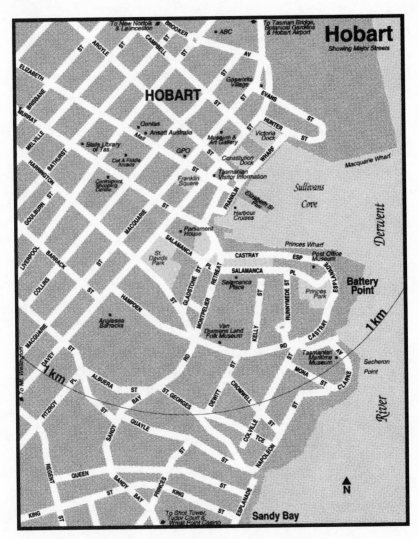

Saturday the Salamanca market is the busiest place in town. You'll see puppeteers, minstrels, and a wide range of merchandise. It's a good place to stock up on produce before traveling into the wilds of Tasmania.

There's a new Hobart, too. It's built around the port and government center and the casino hotel complexes near the waterfront. In Franklin Square you can watch a giant chess match.

A 20-minute drive to the top of Mount Wellington affords an excellent view of Hobart, the harbor, and the Tasman Peninsula, where the infamous Port Arthur convict ruins are located. Visibility from the top of 1,200-meter Mount Wellington can exceed 100 kilometers.

## Information Sources

*Hobart Tasmanian Travel and Information Centre.* Located at 20 Davey Street; phone 03-6230-8233. Basically anything you want to know about Tasmania can be answered or directed from this office, including bookings for accommodations and tours.

*Tasmanian National Parks and Wildlife.* For information, phone 03-6233-6191; E-mail: http//www.parks.tas.gov.au.

*Youth Hostels Association of Tasmania.* Located at 28 Criterion Street; phone 03-6234-9617. Good advice, especially for the low-end traveler.

*Rental Vehicles.* Aside from Thrifty, Budget, Avis, and Hertz, which are covered in the previous section, there is Rent-a-Bug (for $A25 a day) at 105 Murray Street; phone 03-6231-0300.

*Books and Maps.* The Wilderness Shop, 33 Salamanca Place, puts much of its proceeds toward conservation issues. It also has a wide assortment of Tasmanian travel and nature books, phone 03-6234-9370. The Tasmanian Map Centre, 96 Elizabeth Street, also has a good selection of nature books as well as maps; phone 03-6231-9034.

## What to Do in Hobart?

Hobart is an attractive city that feels like a town. Visitors find its waterfront and the streets lined with historic buildings especially pleasant. Out of all the major cities in Australia, Hobart is the most comfortable one for strolling, with many scenic walks along piers, where there are boats from many seas and old buildings from the colonial period.

Visit the Tasmanian Travel and Information Centre on the corner of Elizabeth and Davey Streets and inquire about city tours or self-directed walks. There will be no shortage of good literature. The National Trust offers a two-hour Natural Heritage Walk around Battery Point. There is a nominal fee; phone 03-6221-8300. The Maritime Museum of Tasmania, Secheron Road, is one of the best maritime museums I've seen. The exhibits help explain Tasmania's rich maritime past and present; phone 03-6223-5082. If you want to see how the early wealthy colonials lived, visit Naryna Van Diemen's Folk Museum, 103 Hampden Road; phone 03-6234-2791. Hobart's highly acclaimed Royal Tasmanian Botanical Gardens at Queens Domain has an interesting collection, with specimens ranging from subantarctic plants to manicured Japanese gardens. There's a good restaurant on the grounds; phone 03-6234-6299. The Tasmanian Museum and Art Gallery, 40 Macquarie Street, offers an excellent collection of paintings from early Tasmania, plus Aboriginal artifacts; phone 03-6235-0777. Criminal Courts and Penitentiary Chapel, 6 Brisbane Street, is a relic from the colonial period that captures the flavor of swift justice, redemption, and hanging in the same small complex. A visit here is chilling to the spirit but educational; phone 03-6231-0911. Theatre Royal, 29 Campbell Street, was built in 1837 and is the oldest theater in Australia. It is in original-looking decor and is still in use; phone 03-6233-2299.

The Bonorong Park Wildlife Centre, Briggs Road, Brighton, is a wonderful place to view Tasmanian wildlife. You'll see Tasmanian devils, the largest marsupial predator in the world (about the size of a Scottish terrier). You'll also see wombats, several kinds of wallabies, and koalas. A "bush tucker" meal is part of the experience. The Antarctic Adventure, at 2 Salamanca Place, is a popular new exhibit. Hobart is the last port on the way to Antarctica, and the Australian government has actively supported science and exploration of Antarctica. This exhibit attempts to capture the difficulties and discoveries—though displaying stuffed huskies seems a little weird. Having had two friends winter in Antarctica under the Australian flag, I can attest to the fact that Antarctica is a true frontier with many dangers and rewards. Two other popular tours are: the Cadbury Chocolate Factory, which is 12 kilometers out of town (phone 03-6249-0333), and the Cascade Brewery tour on Cascade Road (phone 03-6221-8300). For me, there's something unique in

Hobart's waterfront, especially around Elizabeth and Murray Piers. Here you'll find old sailing boats from bygone eras and quite possibly the *Aurora Australis,* an impressive modern-day icebreaker used in Antarctica much of the year.

Visitors bent on getting to the hinterlands as fast as possible often miss the opportunity to take a river cruise in Hobart. Cruises leave from the dock areas, where active and historic vessels are moored. Several cruise companies ply the Derwent River and the harbor, but the *Lady Nelson* does the best job at explaining the history of Tasmania; phone 03-6234-3348.

## Restaurants

Hobart is known for its seafood restaurants. Try the Fish Bar (inexpensive to moderate) at 50 King Street, Sandy Bay; phone 03-6234-5961. It has a friendly atmosphere and excellent cheap seafood. There are many neighborhood-type restaurants and pubs in this section. I also enjoyed the Drunken Admiral Restaurant (17 Hunter Street; phone 03-6234-1903), which offers seafood and chicken at moderate prices. Café Who (251 Liverpool Street; phone 03-6231-2744) is a nautical-themed café-nightclub offering an excellent broad-spectrum menu. For more eateries, see *Travelways.*

## Accommodations

Rooms in the Georgian mansions or colonial structures in Battery Point are good bets ($A60–$A120). If you want a top-of-the-line colonial accommodation, try the Tantallon Lodge, 8 Mona Street, Battery Point, Hobart, Tasmania 7001, phone 002-23-3124 or Colonial Battery Point Manor, 13 Cromwell Street, Battery Point; phone 03-6224-0888. This is a five-star Victorian guest house for a reasonable price.

# Historic Richmond and Port Arthur

## Richmond

You'll find Richmond northeast of Hobart where the Coal River meets Pitt Water. Richmond is a well-preserved historic town whose attractive stone architecture is the result of prison labor. It's not on the direct route to Port Arthur, but the 30-kilometer diversion is well worth it.

Richmond is proof that the convict overseers had the highest standards of architectural excellence—and that England's "outcast strata of society" was capable of highly skilled work. The town is remarkably free of twentieth-century eyesores. In the 1830s it was a military outpost and road station between Hobart and Port Arthur. The gaol (jail), open for inspection, held men and women on their way to Hobart to be hanged, as well as Aborigines rounded up in "black drives," and "bushrangers" (road bandits) captured in the nearby hills. It was in use five years before the prison at Port Arthur was completed, which makes it the oldest surviving jail in Australia.

The Richmond Bridge, built in 1823 by convict labor, is a graceful stone structure with a series of impressive Roman arches. Besides the jail and bridge, the town has a number of well-preserved old structures on or in very close proximity to the main drag: Bucombes General Store (1829), a museum in the oldest postal building in Australia; Bridge Inn (1833), one of the early buildings in Richmond; Luke's Church (1836), the oldest Catholic church in Australia; Prospect House (1830s), colonial accommodations, restaurant, and general store; and a half dozen other grand old stone structures. Richmond is an excellent place to stop for a meal and only 25 kilometers northeast of Hobart. There are also some novel places to stay overnight. The Emerald Cottage is a nicely converted 1830s stable; phone 03-6266-2192.

## Port Arthur

Port Arthur is situated on the tip of the Tasman Peninsula 100 kilometers southeast of Hobart. It is the most visited area in Tasmania and the best-known historic site of its kind in Australia.

About 13,000 convicts passed through Port Arthur between 1830 and 1877. About 1,700 of them lie in unmarked graves on the Isle of the Dead offshore from the main facility. The ruins of the extensive prison system are managed by the Tasmanian National Parks and Wildlife Service. More than $A9 million went into restoring the structures and improving the grounds in the 1980s. The setting is peaceful and parklike, and the message delivered by park docents is sobering. It's worth the journey.

The size of the structures at Port Arthur underlines the extent of England's deportation of "criminals." The convicts were the slave labor force that helped forge an English presence in every colonial state in Australia, with the exception of South Australia.

Among the prison population at Port Arthur were substantial numbers of prisoners who could be described as "hardened criminals" in any system of justice. However, there were plenty of prisoners who were sent to Port Arthur as a result of a brand of justice that is now seen as cruel and insensitive. In the 1800s the social fabric of Europe was wearing thin. English society was racked with unemployment and fear of the growing "underclass." More than 200 offenses were punishable by death. After the concept of transporting prisoners to work in the colonies caught on, many of those who would have been hanged were sentenced to transportation instead. Many of these hapless souls had done nothing more than snare a wild rabbit on a nobleman's estate. Prisoners were sometimes as young as twelve.

A strict prisoner-classification system was instituted that offered some rewards and plenty of punishments. Convicts were periodically reviewed and assigned to one of seven classes. Class 1 was for prisoners who had earned their freedom through good behavior. They could own land and work for wages. Less than 10 percent of the convicts achieved this status, and it could be achieved only after half the sentence was served. Class 2 was for servants assigned to colonists. This was the backbone of the economics of the prison colonies. Prisoners were clothed and fed by a colonist and in most cases performed slave labor. Women prisoners were often assigned home service, and men farm labor and other work. Nearly half of the convicts who passed through Port Arthur worked for colonists. Classes 3 and 4 were for prisoners assigned to public works, such as building roads. These two groups made up 20 percent of the convicts. Class 5 was for convicts who served their entire sentence in chains and worked at hard labor from dawn to dusk six days a week. Classes 6 and 7 were for convicts found guilty of offenses in the colonies and sentenced to "extremely" hard labor, usually in chains. Convicts judged trouble-some at Port Arthur were often sent to remote Port Macquarie, where the concept of "living hell" took on new meaning. (See "Sarah Island" later in this section.)

Punishment was severe. Floggings, sometimes severe enough to kill the convict outright, were meted out regularly by the guards for infractions. Later, solitary confinement and a code of total silence were used to break a prisoner's spirit. Suicide was not uncommon. Other prisoners, who saw the gallows as their only salvation, would procure a death sentence by deliberately killing a cellmate.

Port Arthur Historic Site is maintained with the dignity and com-mitment of a national shrine. (Many Australians can trace their ancestry to Port Arthur.) The stone masonry walls are all that is left of the once busy repository of human misery. The asylum, model prison (total silence and isolation), courthouse and library, church, hospital, medieval-looking Gothic guard tower, mammoth peniten-tiary, commandant's house, and a half dozen other structures allow you to imagine the prison society that was at one time 30,000 strong in Tasmania—with Port Arthur as its hub. There are ranger-led tours every hour during most of the year. You can also take a short boat ride to the Isle of the Dead.

*Accommodations.* There are motels, a youth hostel, and caravan parks on the Tasman Peninsula near Port Arthur. For youth hostel bookings, phone 03-6250-2311.

*Access.* Guided coach tours from Hobart can be arranged by the Tas-manian Travel and Information Centre; phone 03-6230-8233. The 100-kilometer route to Port Arthur takes about an hour and a half. In your own rental car, Port Arthur is a full-day trip from Hobart.

# Mount Field National Park

Located only 77 kilometers northwest of Hobart on paved roads, Mount Field National Park is one of the most popular parks in Tasmania. It's probably the easiest park to explore in a day and come away with a feeling for the breadth of habitats found in Tasmania.

At the park's entrance there's a kiosk, trout farm, campground, and Russell Falls Cottages, where you can stay overnight. The campground has hot showers. Firewood is provided for use in the designated fireplaces. The entrance also has day shelters and electric barbecues in the picnic area for year-round use.

I'll never forget the final leg of the road to Mount Field. It was clearly the road to possum heaven. I counted 22 road-killed possums in 15 kilometers. The local ranger said the road kills were indicative of the park's plentiful wildlife: "Bennett's wallaby, rufous wallaby [pademelon], brush-tailed possums, ring-tailed possums, and eastern quolls are common and often sighted by the observant visitor. Tasmanian devils are also here, but more often heard than seen. Platypuses are sighted in the Tyenna River, which borders the park. Wombats are often found in the higher areas." The higher lakes also have a living fossil, the mountain shrimp (*Anaspides tasmaniae*), which is identical to fossil records dating back 200 million years.

The diversity of bird life is only about 50 species, but some of them are quite colorful and entertaining. Lyrebirds, which were introduced here from Victoria in the 1930s, live in the fern gullies. The work of black cockatoos is apparent throughout the park. These big-beaked parrots tear dead trees apart in pursuit of grubs. They're so powerful that on first glance you'll think a bearlike creature must be the culprit. Green rosellas and black currawongs, found only in Tasmania, are also here.

The park itself has one road, a well-maintained dirt track that climbs from the park entrance to the foot of Mount Dobson. Mount Dobson is a popular hiking and cross-country skiing area. The road is passable for passenger vehicles in summer but requires 4WD with snow chains in winter. Along the road there are several short walks that introduce the habitats and plants peculiar to Tasmania. Keep an eye on the rearview mirror. At about the five-kilometer mark you'll get a spectacular view back down the Derwent Valley.

As the road climbs, the vegetation changes. You'll see manferns, myrtles, dogwoods, nonindigenous bracken ferns, sassafras, celery-top pines, and horizontals. Horizontals are unique trees that grow to a certain height and fall over. The branches then become new trees. A horizontal forest is impenetrable. To identify the rest of these plants, get a handout at the ranger station. About 15 kilometers away is the Lyrebird Nature Walk, which affords a short look at a section of temperate rain forest. As you enter the subalpine areas near Lake Fenton you'll see King Billy pines, pencil pines, and fagus. King Billy pines and fagus are native only to Tasmania. Next you'll come to the snow gums—the first stands are quite straight because they're protected from the wind. The snow gums in exposed areas have been sculpted by hundreds of years of violent wind and blowing snow. The road ends at a collection of small ski lodges, which are used for about three months each winter.

## Walks

The Russell Falls Track is near the park entrance. This area was declared a park in 1885, long before the park's present boundaries were defined, in 1947. In a 20-minute loop you'll walk beneath 90-meter-high swamp gums and giant manferns (a tree fern sometimes 9 meters tall with a spread of 3 meters). This enchanting walk follows a creek and comes to a series of spectacular crystal-clear waterfalls. Look for the contrasting color of the pink robin, a small bird that hops through the undergrowth. On the forest fringe, black curra-wongs are common, as are Bennett's and rufous wallabies. There are brown trout in the stream, a transplanted species found throughout inland Tasmanian waters. If you enjoy this walk, take the longer 1-hour walk to Lady Barron Falls. The walk leaves from the same parking area.

There are a number of walking tracks from the Mount Dobson car park: the Lake Dobson circuit (30 minutes), Broad River Valley

Lookout (30 minutes), cross-country ski field (1 hour), Rodway Range (2 hours), Torn Shelf (3 hours), Lake Newdegate (4 hours), Platypus Tarn, Lake Seal, and Lake Webster. On the left side of the parking area there's a short nature walk around Lake Dobson to Eagle Tarn, a small alpine lake behind the Alpine Ski Club. The Golden Stairs Track cuts sharply away and up from this track about halfway around Lake Dobson. The Golden Stairs Track is steep but relatively short, ending at Sitzmark Lodge. From the lodge you can climb Mount Field West or choose among several walking tracks for further exploration of the area. Check with the rangers at the park entrance if you'd like to attempt an overnight outing in this area. Weather conditions can shift radically in minutes.

*Accommodations.* A nominal fee is charged for staying overnight in the full-amenities campground, which even has a washing machine. Book direct by phoning 03-6288-1149.

*Access.* Mount Field National Park is reached from Hobart by driving north on Highway 1 to Granton. Turn left on Highway A10 to New Norfolk. From New Norfolk continue on B61 until you reach the park.

# Tasmania's World Heritage Parks

In 1982, as an outgrowth of lengthy and heated conservation battles aimed at halting the damming of Tasmania's rivers (in particular the Franklin), the Western Tasmania Wilderness National Park was formed as one of the world's 130 World Heritage Areas recognized by UNESCO. Three parks were brought together under the UNESCO umbrella. Cradle Mountain–Lake Saint Clair National Park, covering 132,000 hectares that include the heart of Tasmania's alpine plateau and famed Overland Track, is the most northern park. Attached to its southern border is 182,000-hectare Franklin–Lower Gordon Wild Rivers National Park, which links Cradle Mountain–Lake Saint Clair National Park with the immense and wild 442,240-hectare Southwest National Park, the southernmost park. Southwest National Park contains alpine and wet coastal temperate rain forest habitats. Combined, these parks encompass 756,240 hectares—including the largest protected temperate rain forest in the world and the largest contiguous wilderness area in Tasmania. Sightseeing is spectacular, and adventure and photographic challenges are abundant.

## Cradle Mountain–Lake Saint Clair National Park

Cradle Mountain–Lake Saint Clair National Park is the premier walking park in Tasmania, if not in Australia. The famous Overland Track, with huts strung out over the 85-kilometer alpine trail, connects the northern end of the park at Cradle Valley to the southern end at Lake Saint Clair. There are no roads through the park. Only those traveling on foot get to see the interior. *Australian Geographic* founding publisher Dick Smith described this walk as "among the very best in Australia."

If you've started your tour of Tasmania in Hobart, it makes sense to visit Lake Saint Clair first and Cradle Mountain later, when you've worked to the northern end of the state. Lake Saint Clair is 173 kilometers northeast of Hobart on the Lyell Highway. Conversely, if you've entered the state at Devonport or Launceston, start the opposite way; Cradle Mountain is only 85 kilometers south of Devonport.

### Lake Saint Clair

Lake Saint Clair is the focal point of the southern section of Cradle Mountain–Lake Saint Clair National Park. It is the starting or ending (usually ending) place of the Overland Track, but you also have a choice of day walks or multiday outings to Pine Valley and other places. The Lake Saint Clair area is not as stunningly beautiful as Cradle Mountain, but it is scenic and has outstanding walks.

At the lake there's a ranger station, kiosk, picnic area, and camping area with amenities. There's also a hut at Cynthia Bay near the kiosk. You'll be charged a nominal fee for camping. Campers and walkers must register at the ranger station near the kiosk.

The lake is 17.5 kilometers long and about 200 meters deep, making it the deepest lake in Tasmania. There's a boat that retrieves hikers from the far end of the lake.

*Walks.* The Watersmeet Nature Walk begins on the Overland Track. It's 1.7 kilometers each way and takes about 1 hour and 15 minutes to complete. It travels through six plant communities, ranging from glacial moraines to rain forests featuring Tasmanian myrtle, celery-top pines, and King Billy pines. The red waratah blooms in November. In midsummer (January) orchids and a host of other flowers bloom. Around the kiosk and starting area you should see some park-friendly Bennett's and rufous wallabies. (Don't feed them bread; it contributes to an early death.) You'll also see native hens, flightless, chicken-sized birds that run around nervously. There are also plenty of black currawongs. The tea-colored river water in the Cuvier and Hugel Creeks is caused by leached tannins from the buttongrass bogs. It's common in many rivers and creeks in Tasmania. Platypuses are plentiful in Hugel Creek. This is the turnaround point. You may want to travel back along the beach by cutting inland at Fergie's Paddock on your return.

Pine Valley is a highly recommended area that can be reached in an 8-hour walk from the ranger station at Lake Saint Clair. You can cut 5 hours off your trip by taking the boat ride ($A25) to the end of Lake Saint Clair and then walking 3 hours to Pine Valley. The boat ($A25) regularly runs to the Narcissus hut to pick up hikers who use the hut's radio to call for a boat. The boat ride takes about 30 minutes and leaves Cynthia Bay (weather permitting) at 8:30 each morning. I didn't make it to Pine Valley, but Ranger Kent McConnell claims it is the prettiest place he's ever seen. He described enchanting Cephissus Creek, with moss-covered manferns, tea trees, King Billy pines, and nearby peaks like the Acropolis. Pine Valley is a base for many visitors, who investigate the Du Cane Range with its tarns, peaks, and cirques.

For more details on the numerous day and multiday hikes in the area, purchase *Cradle Mountain National Park,* by John Siseman and John Chapman. This is a well-written 127-page hikers' guide to the entire park.

*Accommodations.* The full-amenities campground charges a nominal fee per couple per night. There is a section for camper-vans. Try to book in advance: Ranger in Charge, Lake Saint Clair, Via Derwent Bridge, Tasmania 7140; phone 03-6289-1172. For motel accommodations in Derwent Bridge, check with the Tasmanian Travel and Information Centre.

*Access*. Redline Coaches operate along the Lyell Highway, which will get you as far as the town of Derwent Bridge, 5 kilometers from the park boundary. From here you can hitch, hike, or call the only cab in Derwent Bridge.

## Cradle Mountain

The area around Cradle Mountain is one of my choices for the top five scenic areas in all of Australia. It's a fabulous place. Cradle Mountain is at the northern end of Cradle Mountain–Lake Saint Clair National Park. From Lake Saint Clair it is reached by walking the 85-kilometer Overland Track or by driving north to Cradle Mountain via Queenstown.

My trip to the Cradle Mountain Lodge ranks at the top of the most memorable wildlife experiences of my life. I was driving at night on the final stretch of the dirt road and was slowed to five kilometers per hour by the abundance of wildlife hopping, scurrying, and dive-bombing past my car. Rufous wallabies stood huddling in the center of the road, while quolls scurried across the roadway, one holding a small rodent in its mouth. Bennett's wallabies bounded every which way. The numbers were astounding. My real excitement came when a Tasmanian devil, the largest living (assuming the Tasmanian tiger is extinct) marsupial predator, ran across the road in a slow, rocking-horse gait. Minutes later two more devils, chewing on a wallaby carcass, were caught in my headlights.

I made it to the lodge around midnight and was greeted by the then owners, Simon and Anne Currant. When I explained I'd seen a Tasmanian devil and a number of other creatures, Simon grinned. "So, you like devils." We walked to the back porch and there were about five devils eating table scraps left out for them.

The next morning I woke early and followed Anne Currant up 1,545-meter Cradle Mountain, the sawtooth dolerite and quartz peak that dominates the area. The peak had been dusted by snow in the night. From its summit I could see far off across Tasmania's central plateau, with its prominent peaks, vast moorlands, cirques, and lakes. The vista was stunning and had a different look than any alpine area I'd seen. Anne, who led walks and cross-country ski adventures, pointed out a half dozen day walks in the vast valley and steep-walled terrain around us. We skidded and scrambled down through strands of King Billy pines, pandani heath, myrtles, and forms of vegetation I'd never seen before. We were back at the lodge for lunch. So ended the most inspirational 24-hour period I had during my six-month sojourn in Australia.

*Walks.* There are dozens of day walks in the Cradle Valley area that vary in difficulty and scenery. The Currants developed a guide, the "Cradle Mountain Lodge Walks, Map, and Nature Guide," which describes nearby walks and illustrates the flora and fauna in the area. You can hire a naturalist guide at an hourly charge, providing you schedule it in advance. The best map I've seen of the area is the "Cradle Mountain Day Walk Map" published by Tasmap. You can buy a copy at the lodge and at the ranger station inside the park.

There are six walks, ranging from 30 minutes to 3 hours, that start and end at the lodge. You'll pass waterfalls and rushing alpine streams while admiring King Billy, pencil, and celery-top pines. You'll also see waratahs, buttongrass, myrtles, and pandani. Several of these short walks offer excellent photographic opportunities of Cradle Mountain with these unfamiliar trees and plants as a foreground.

You must sign in and out of the register for day walks inside the park. The register is kept at the ranger station at the fork in the road that goes to either the Lake Dove or the Waldheim car park.

I strongly suggest taking one of the walks to the Kitchen hut (used only in emergencies) and to the saddle between Weindorfers Tower and Little Horn via the Face Track. There are several routes of varying difficulties to the Kitchen hut. Weindorfers Tower and Little Horn are prominent spires on a dolerite ridge that climaxes at Cradle Mountain. From anywhere on the ridge you can see far off across the highlands area of the park. At some point along the Face Track you have to cut straight up a steep brush-covered slope to reach the saddle. If you have a little extra time and energy, try for the summit of Cradle Mountain (the route is marked and is directly up from the Kitchen hut). The view is fantastic. The route is a scramble over huge dolerite boulders, but it's definitely worth it. In the course of the climb to the Kitchen hut, you'll see a great deal of the unique flora, including cushion plants, which live up to their name with a pillowlike feel underfoot. You'll also see alpine lakes and trees endemic only to Tasmania.

The outing took 5 hours. Another way down is the Rodway Track, which travels along a ridge past Twisted Lake and Lake Hanson before descending to the Lake Dove car park. The lakes are shallow and heat up enough for a hiker to take a quick dip on a hot day.

*Skiing.* The Cradle Plateau is an excellent area for cross-country skiing. Lasting snowfalls usually occur between June and October.

*Accommodations.* The Cradle Mountain Lodge is on the park border and only a few kilometers from all trailheads in the park. There are rooms in the lodge and also cabin accommodations with huge fireplaces and firewood. The dining room is open all day. The lodge's owners deliberately attract wildlife. This is one of the only places you're practically guaranteed to see a wild Tasmanian devil. Lodge accommodation with shared bathroom is $A150 for a double. Stay longer than three nights and you'll get a reduced rate. Breakfasts, lunches, and dinners are served and paid for separately. Contact Cradle Mountain Lodge, Cradle Mountain Road, Tasmania 7306; phone 03-6492-1303.

There is a tourist park with a few amenities (changes are planned) in the park a few kilometers from the Cradle Mountain Lodge; phone 03-6492-1395.

*Access.* By car the 85-kilometer drive from Devonport takes about 1 hour in daylight and three times that long at night if wildlife is as abundant as when I visited. The road twists and turns, and the last section is maintained gravel and dirt. The drive from Launceston takes about 2 hours. Maxwell's shuttle bus goes to Cradle Mountain from Devonport; phone 03-6492-1431. Tasmanian Wilderness Travel (phone 03-6334-4442) leaves from Launceston twice daily. There is a small airstrip near the lodge that can be used, if prior notice has been given.

## The Overland Track

The Overland Track is the premier walking track in Tasmania. The track's northern terminus is the ranger station in Cradle Valley, and the southern end is Cynthia Bay on Lake Saint Clair—a distance of

85 kilometers. You must sign the register at both ends of the walk. Most of the walk is through alpine moorlands punctuated with jagged solitary peaks, mirrorlike lakes, tarns, cirques, peat bogs, and twisted trees shaped by the elements. The walk is a real contrast to the arid conditions of most bushwalking on mainland Australia.

The landscape's features are both familiar and unfamiliar to a North American or European. Many of the alpine plants are oddly adapted and not found outside of Australia. Punctuating the track are large solitary ramparts, often with sheer faces that look like stony fortresses guarding the vast undulating green landscape. Most of these columnar peaks are erosion-resistant dolerite that pushed up through less erosion-resistant sedimentary layers some 165 million years ago.

The Overland Track is 85 kilometers long without side trips. You should figure on at least an extra 25 kilometers for such excursions. Subtract 18 kilometers if you take the boat ride from the Narcissus hut to the parking area at Cynthia Bay.

Most people spend 6 to 8 days on the track, though it can be done in 5 at a reasonable pace. Allowing for 6 to 8 days will permit you to explore areas of interest and sit out spells of bad weather. Ninety percent of the 3,000 to 4,000 people who use the track annually leave from Cradle Valley and finish at Lake Saint Clair. In part this is because there's more downhill this way. From November through March is usually the best time to use the track, though severe weather can occur any time of the year and without warning. Prepare for wet conditions and expect to be rained on. November and April average four days of snowfall each year. February is usually the most snow-free month. There is a nominal registration fee.

Nine huts are maintained at irregular intervals for safety and to protect the environment. However, you should not count on them, as they may be full or pulled from use. It is stipulated that visitors bring tents and otherwise be self-contained for inclement weather.

Walking conditions are generally flat and, in places, muddy, particularly on the buttongrass plains. Some sections have "floating walkways" over muddy stretches. In other places walkers trying to avoid mud have widened the track till it's all a muddy bog. To control erosion you're supposed to stay on the track. Wear gators to protect yourself against leeches, which are populous in some areas. Check for leeches after you've passed through a bog. Everything from a full-force blizzard to sweltering 80°F weather is possible at any time of the year.

From the ranger station near the Waldheim hut in Cradle Valley there are several routes up onto the central highlands. The main Horse Track is the easiest and is well marked. The alternative track past Dove Lake has a more spectacular view, but is more strenuous. There are many attractive side trips along the Overland Track. Barn Bluff, Lake Will, Mount Pelion, Mount Thetis, Mount Ossa, Mount Doris, and Mount Olympia are just some of them. Many of these peak destinations include tarns and dramatic cirques. The summits of the mountains are usually about 500 meters above the track and require rock scrambles to reach. Don't miss Kia Ora Falls. If you started at Cradle Valley, you will have been on the trail for 4 or 5 days and will need to get the grime off. There are several excellent swimming holes at these falls, which are very near the hut by the same name. Pine Valley and the many excursions from it may be the richest area to explore off the main track. The valley is relatively near the southern terminus of the Overland Track at Cynthia Bay on Lake Saint Clair and can be reached in a day from Cynthia Bay.

*Caution.* This warning is on most literature handed out to walkers contemplating the Overland Track: "Tasmania's mountain areas are prone to sudden changes in weather conditions, and the danger of death from exposure is an ever present hazard. Even greater care must be exercised when the party is large and of uneven stamina. The victim of exhaustion and exposure can pass with startling suddenness from a state of consciousness to unconsciousness and death."

For information about the Overland Track locate the "Cradle Mountain–Lake Saint Clair National Park Map and Notes" published by Tasmap. This topographical map of the entire Overland Track comes with a very complete set of notes that explains everything from "Bushwalking Ethics" to "Geology" and "Safety Essentials." *Cradle Mountain National Park,* by John Siseman and John Chapman, is a 127-page walkers' guide to the park with heavy emphasis on the Overland Track. The book can usually be purchased at Paddy Pallin's outlets or in any Tasmanian Travel and Information Centre.

*Access.* Cradle Mountain is 70 kilometers south of Devonport. Derwent Bridge (the southern terminus of the Overland Track) is 180 kilometers north of Hobart on Highway A10. Phone Redline Coaches,

Launceston (03-6331-3233); Hobart (199 Collins Street, 03-6231-3900); Devonport (9 Edward Street, 03-6424-1500). Also try Wilderness Travel, 101 George Street, Launceston; 03-6334-4447. $A36.50 to Cradle Mountain.

## Franklin–Lower Gordon Wild Rivers National Park

From Lake Saint Clair the Lyell Highway heads into the 182,000-hectare Franklin–Lower Gordon Wild Rivers National Park, which was proclaimed a park in 1981 as an outgrowth of a victory by conservationists who stopped a dam across the Franklin River. The park links Cradle Mountain–Lake Saint Clair National Park to Southwest National Park, making up the World Heritage Area and a contiguous protected area totaling 756,240 hectares. The Lyell Highway, the only road through Franklin–Lower Gordon Wild Rivers National Park, is a good-quality road. It winds and turns through lush rain forests, spectacular vistas, and plunging jagged riverine valleys.

Visitors can raft class-4 rapids in the upper Franklin River (which should be done only with a full understanding of what's involved) or take cruise-boat tours of the lower river (an easy approach to seeing the heart of the temperate rain forest). Another attraction is climbing Frenchmans Cap, a towering quartzite peak that can be reached from the Lyell Highway by experienced bushwalkers in an overnight walk. The area has two towns: Queenstown and Strahan.

There's an amazing amount of greenery in Franklin–Lower Gordon Wild Rivers National Park because of the 3.5 meters of rain the area receives annually. The park includes the Franklin, Olga, and Lower River catchments. The trees are leatherwoods, horizontals, celery-top pines, myrtles, native laurels, Huon pines, and others. After you enter the park from Derwent Bridge watch for a signpost directing you to a roadside nature walk. This short walk was created to educate visitors about the flora. Specimen trees along the short loop are labeled. There are picnic tables and a toilet. Dongaghy's Hill Wilderness Lookout is another short walk off the road. The trail climbs sharply on a meter-wide trail carpeted with wood chips and ends on a precipitous promontory with a magnificent 360-degree view that includes the plunging Collingswood and Franklin River Valleys that converge below. There are nearby quartzite peaks and Collingswood Plain and Frenchmans Cap. This short track is located near the signposting for the trailhead to Frenchmans Cap (roughly 54 kilometers east of Queenstown). If you backtrack about 75 meters from the promontory there's a trail to the Franklin River that descends 300 meters and affords the only access in the area. The descent takes about 35 minutes and at the bottom there are some delightful pools perfect for a refreshing dip.

## Rafting the Franklin River

The Franklin River is internationally known for its technical difficulty and wild beauty. Any attempt to raft or kayak it, even with a guide or as part of a group, should be undertaken seriously. Ranger Jack Buzelin says, "I'd give it a medium 4 for technical difficulty and a 10 for beauty."

The river level fluctuates wildly with the many rains in the area. River rafters travel down a twisted narrow gorge from the area of Donaghy's Hill Lookout and end their journey about 100 kilometers later at the pickup point on the Lower Gordon River. Once you enter the gorge there are no easy ways out until you appear at the far end. The narrowness of the river makes it unsuitable for large rafts. Instead, most people travel it in a single raft (called a rubber ducky) that each person paddles entirely on his or her own. About 10 percent of the annual 600 users are kayakers. Regardless of your watercraft, you're solely responsible for your vessel, which increases the risks, challenges, and thrills. Usually there are four portages, taking around 2 hours each. There are designated camping sites along the way. The river is fast. Kayakers make it in 5 days, while rafters take upward of 15.

Rafting companies generally give a training course at the put-in point. How well you learned or were instructed will become evident soon enough. If you're not comfortable with what lies ahead, *don't go*. This is not a raft trip for novices. The river plunges and churns over and around massive boulders, taking a 50-kilometer sweep around the massif of Frenchmans Cap. Rapids with names like Churn, Coruscades, Thunderush, and Cauldron must be negotiated in turn.

Several companies offer 2-day excursions from the river that include climbing Frenchmans Cap. Most stop at Kutickina Cave, which was recently found to contain archaeological evidence that people were in Tasmania 20,000 years ago, at the time of the last ice age. These sites would've been drowned had the controversial Gordon-below-Franklin dam gone ahead.

*Cautions.* Some large, established international rafting companies will not raft the Franklin because of the combination of remoteness and danger that comes with allowing each client to be entirely on her or his own through difficult rapids. Warrick Deacock, the generally acknowledged founder of the adventure-travel industry in Australia, will not carry bookings for the Franklin because, "It's too bloody dangerous for tourists who might not understand what it takes to successfully come out the other end." Kayakers must be expert and should coordinate their efforts through a Tasmanian kayak club. For details and addresses check with the most convenient Tasmanian Travel and Information Centre.

## Frenchmans Cap

Frenchmans Cap is the prominent peak (1,443 meters) in this area. Nobody knows how the peak was named. The peak is erosion-resistant granite and quartzite that was shaped by a series of glacial periods.

According to Ranger Jack Buzelin, the walk to Frenchmans Cap is only for experienced bushwalkers. The start of the walk includes a cord-wood trail across a bog and a flying fox—a boxlike contraption hanging from a cable stretched across a chasm. You climb into the box and check that the box's pulleys are squarely on top of the cable before pulling yourself across the chasm. It's an invigorating experience.

From the flying fox the walk usually takes about 6 hours to the Lake Vera hut. From there it's another 4 hours of walking to the Tahune hut and another hour to the summit. To be safe, carry your own tent and be prepared for radical weather changes that may include snow.

The walk is usually wet underfoot and travels through patches of rain forest, buttongrass, and tea trees before entering an alpine setting. The view from the summit is, in Jack Buzelin's words, "absolutely inspiring."

*Cautions.* Be prepared to cope with all kinds of weather, even blizzards. Wear gators for protection from leeches. Talk to a ranger about trail conditions and weather before starting. Phone the ranger station in Strahan: 03-6471-7122.

# Towns and Cruises in Western Tasmania

## Queenstown

Queenstown may be a precursor to the apocalypse. It's the first town west of the park. The contrast it presents is chilling. After driving through miles of dramatic and bountiful parklands you'll round a corner and see a vista for the most part void of vegetation. Copper mining has been going full tilt here since 1888, and civic pride hasn't embraced plant life in the 100 years that followed. The combination of timber needed in the mines and fuel needed for the smelters has caused a moonscape. Worse yet, the locals take pride in it and see the absence of plant life and wholesale erosion as a way to attract tourism. The King River, which runs through the area, is so polluted with heavy metals that scientists predict it would take 50 years to restore it to a healthy level. Only a sociologist would be interested in staying in Queenstown for long.

## Strahan

Located 40 kilometers west of Queenstown, Strahan is the only town on Tasmania's west coast. It's an attractive little fishing port in Macquarie Harbour and the departure point for popular river cruises of the Lower Gordon River. Macquarie Harbour is practically a saltwater lake. Its only connection to the sea is a puny shallow channel known as Hell's Gate. It's too shallow for large vessels. Strahan was the center stage in the 1980s during the fight between environmentalists and development forces who wanted to dam the Gordon. The environmentalists won. Strahan has a variety of eateries and places to stay, plus a National Parks and Wildlife Service office at the north end of town. For visitors information phone 03-6471-7622.

*Accommodations.* At the upper end, try the Franklin Manor, The Esplanade, Strahan, Tasmania 7231 (on the main drag next to the water) for around $A150 a double. This is a converted harbormaster's house with a great ambiance and greater view; phone 03-6471-7267. Gordon Gateway Chalets (Grining Street, Strahan, Tasmania 7468; phone 03-6471-7165) is a clean place with all the basics for about $A100 per double per night. At the economy end are several cabin parks on Jones Street for between $A50 and $A60 per night. You may want to compare them for the best price: try Azza's Holiday Units (phone 03-6471-7253) and Strahan Cabins (phone 03-6471-7442).

## Lower Gordon River Cruises

Cruise boats of various sizes leave Strahan daily for half-day cruises that go across Macquarie Harbour, go ashore at Sarah Island to look at the extensive prison colony ruins, and travel up the Lower Gordon River into the heart of the temperate rain forest. I enjoyed this cruise a great deal. The only dull part is the beginning. Sarah Island and the Gordon River are fascinating.

The cruise up the Gordon River affords glimpses of pristine temperate rain forest with fern-lined banks and scores of indigenous trees and plants. You'll travel on tea-colored water from the button-grass plains in the interior. You'll pass by a cascading waterfall, up the narrow Gordon Gorge, over the Big Eddy rapids, and past Warner's Landing, where protesters fought with police in what turned out to be a successful attempt to stop the Franklin River from being dammed. You'll also see solo river rafters ending their unforgettable journey down the Franklin.

*Sarah Island.* From 1822 to 1833 this tiny island was a penal settlement for the "worst" convicts from Port Arthur. The 36 ruins on the island are complete enough to give a visitor a picture of how the settlement functioned. Sarah Island can only be described as hell. Work gangs rowed out across the windswept bay daily to fell Huon pines and retrieve them for the settlement. They towed the logs back by oar power. The men often worked waist deep in the chilly water most of the day, preparing rafts of logs. They were fed meager rations at dawn and dusk, but not in the course of their 12-hour workday. They often went to bed wet and cold. Escapes and horror stories were the status quo. The settlement's surgeon reported 33,723 lashes inflicted in floggings to 167 prisoners in one year. Floggings occurred daily. Often 100 lashes were given in a single flogging. Escapes ranged from the macabre to the daring. Alexander Pearce escaped with seven men and showed up months later in the settled area of Tasmania. It was suspected that he ate some of his accomplices, and it was never determined if he did this before or after they died. He escaped again in chains with another convict and admitted to eating his companion, which resulted in his execution. Pearce was the first European to walk across southwest Tasmania.

For all the gruesome details, buy a copy of the paperback *Macquarie Harbour Penal Settlements, 1822–1833 and 1846–1847.* It's sold in the park service office and along the waterfront in Strahan.

For bookings, contact Gordon River Cruises, Box 40, Strahan, Tasmania 7648; phone 03-6471-7187. Full fares are about $A60.

## Southwest National Park

Southwest National Park is the southern extension of the three national parks that make up Tasmania's World Heritage Area. The park is a huge 442,240 hectares located in the southwest corner of Tasmania. Most of it is pristine wilderness. There are miles of rugged coastline and empty beaches. Inland are vast tracts of temperate rain forest, buttongrass plains, rugged valleys covered in vegetation, and striking alpine areas. The best-known attractions are Lake Pedder, Mount Anne, Federation Peak, and the Arthur Range. Wildlife in the park includes Bennett's and rufous wallabies, Tasmanian devils, and wombats. Huon pines and Tasmanian myrtles are found along the rivers, and various kinds of gum forests cover huge areas. The best time to visit is September, October, November, or January through April.

A chalet at Strathgordon is the stepping-off place to much of this park. Strathgordon is at the end of the road from Mount Field National Park. This is reputed to be the most spectacular section of mountain highway in Tasmania. (Unfortunately the high rainfall in the area can make seeing the scenery difficult.) Strathgordon is on the shore of Lake Pedder and a short distance from Lake Gordon, which is on the park's border. Both lakes are man-made and part of the Electric Commission's gargantuan power-development scheme. You can rent a small boat (phone 03-6288-1283) to either fish for trout or explore the shoreline. You must have a fishing license to fish.

### Walks

There are literally hundreds of trekking possibilities in Southwest National Park. The Rainforest Walk will give you a good look at the plants of the park. The walk begins on Scotts Peak Road about 2 kilometers from the Gordon River Road. At the trailhead there is an interpretive pamphlet keyed to numbered points along the track. The walk should take about 20 minutes. By the end, you'll come to know a dozen kinds of plants, many endemic only to Tasmania.

The South Coast Track, between Cockle Creek and Port Davey, may be the highlight of the park. It runs through virgin rain forest, along sweeping beaches, and up into alpine areas. It is well marked, but you will still be away from help for at least 5 days. Like most of the treks in the park, it's demanding and requires skill and planning. Itineraries for treks must be registered with the rangers at Mount Field National Park, the tiny town of Maydena, or the police.

For details about the walks in Southwest National Park, get a copy of *South West Tasmania*, by John Chapman. This is an excellent 160-page paperback walking guide to the park.

*Accommodations.* Camping facilities with amenities can be found at Edgar Dam, Scotts Peak, and the Huon River. Bushcamping is allowed throughout the park. The nearest hotel accommodation is at Strathgordon.

*Access.* The park is 170 kilometers from Hobart on the Lyell Highway and Gordon River Road. The drive takes about 3 hours. Check with the Tasmanian Travel and Information Centre in Hobart about bus service to the park (phone 03-6288-1283) for a direct link with the park. Federation Peak, which is a popular walk, is reached by an entirely different route through Huonville and Geeveston.

# Northern and Eastern Tasmania

Where Southwest and the other World Heritage parks are stunning and wild, in the north and on much of the east coast of Tasmania you'll find chiefly pastoral lands dotted with farms and small towns. You'll see many vistas of rolling grasslands descending to the ocean. This is particularly true on the northern end of Highway A10, which links Wynard on the north coast to Zeehan and Strahan.

## Woolnorth

Woolnorth is a historically significant 54,000-acre working cattle and sheep property situated on the northwest tip of Tasmania. The property encompasses Cape Grim and adjoining sections of the northern and western coastlines. Sue and Graham Gillon, Woolnorth's present owners, have only recently allowed limited tourism onto their property. Sue Gillon and her employees lead the tours, which cover Tasmania's natural and human history. You are fed a lunch and are treated to a sheepdog herding exhibition.

Woolnorth is the site of the original Van Diemen's Land Company, founded in 1825 by charter from George IV. Much of the original settlement—most of it built by convict labor—is still intact. Woolnorth is both a working property and protected enough to be considered a wildlife sanctuary.

The large lush paddocks contain thousands of Cormo sheep, Hereford cattle, cashmere goats, and the numerous horses used for stock work. As for the wildlife, I saw sea eagles, black swans, and wallabies during my short visit. Wombats, platypuses, sugar gliders, Tasmanian devils, and bandicoots are also sighted often. Woolnorth is where the last four Tasmanian tigers were captured at the turn of the century.

*Accommodations.* You can't stay at Woolnorth. I found the Bridge Hotel in Smithon to be a good lodging; $A60 per room. They also serve meals.

*Access.* To visit Woolnorth you must sign onto an organized tour that departs from Burnie a couple of times a week. The schedule is sometimes flexible, and you can be picked up in towns between Burnie and Woolnorth. You can't drive onto the property unannounced. To work out tours, phone 03-6452-1252.

## Devonport

Devonport is an industrial and tourist-based town. The vehicular ferry from Melbourne docks here, and Devonport is often the starting point for many visitors to Tasmania. The ferry ride takes 40 hours. If you're in a hurry, take a plane. Many airlines fly from Melbourne and Sydney to Devonport. The fare from Melbourne is usually around $A110–$A150 one way. Contact a Tasmanian Travel and Information Centre for the most competitive fares and schedules.

In Devonport, the information center is at 5 Best Street; phone 03-6424-4466.

## Transportation Contacts

*Air and Water Travel.* Being that Tasmania is an island, getting to and from it requires an airplane or seagoing vessel. The seagoing ferry *Spirit of Tasmania* arrives from Melbourne and departs here every other day. Usually it arrives in Melbourne on Tuesday, Thursday, and Saturday. The ferry travels at night and provides meals and dormlike sleeping. Fares run between $A100 and $A130 per head, depending on the season. Cars are an additional $A30. Book as far ahead of time as possible; phone 13-20-10.

Air travel to the mainland runs about the same price as the ferry. Contact Kendell Air (phone 03-6424-1411) or Southern Australia Airlines (phone 13-13-13).

For road maps visit the Royal Automobile Club of Australia, 5 Steele Street, Devonport, Tasmania 7310; phone 03-6421-1933.

*Camper-Van and Cars.* You can rent a car or camper-van from: Autorent-Hertz (phone 03-6424-9119); Avis Tasmanian Mobile Motels (phone 03-6427-9797); Budget Camper-vans (phone 03-6424-7088); or Rent-a-Bug (phone 03-6427-1013).

*Bus.* Contact Redline Coaches, 9 Edward Street; phone 03-6424-5100. Tasmanian Wilderness Travel (phone 03-6334-4442) provides transportation for bushwalkers to the major national parks. Most fares run around $A30. Devonport to Hobart is only $A25.

## Accommodations

There are six hotels in Devonport and numerous caravan parks. If you don't already have a copy of *Travelways,* pick up one on board the *Spirit of Tasmania,* in the ferry terminal, or at the Tasmanian Travel and Information Centre at 5 Best Street.

# Launceston

With a population of 67,000, Launceston is Tasmania's second-largest city. Even though it's a transportation hub, it has the atmosphere of a sleepy out-of-the-way town.

The Tasmanian Travel and Information Centre is at the corner of Saint John and Paterson Streets; phone 03-6331-3133.

## Transportation Contacts

You can rent a car or camper-van from: Advance (phone 03-6391-8000); Autorent-Hertz (phone 03-6335-1111); or Touring Motor Homes (phone 03-6331-1339). For car rentals: Economy; phone 03-6334-3299.

Redline Coaches (112 George Street; phone 03-6331-3233) has a multiday open ticket for travel throughout Tasmania for a reduced price. Tasmanian Wilderness Travel (phone 03-6334-4447) takes bushwalkers to Cradle Valley and other parks in Tasmania.

## Accommodations

There are 15 hotels, both modern and "modernized" historic; 11 motels; and colonial accommodations. There are also caravan parks and camping areas. Again, check *Travelways*.

# King Solomon and Marakoopa Caves

These two caves are located near Mole Creek about 85 kilometers from Launceston. Tours are conducted by the park service hourly from 10:00 A.M. to 4:00 P.M. daily. Both caves are spectacular, on a par with famous Cutta Cutta Caves in the Northern Territory. Glittery calcite-coated stalactites and stalagmites in all kinds of formations await you inside. Of the two, I enjoyed Marakoopa the most, possibly because it has running water, uniquely adapted life-forms, and glowworms. The ranger talks are excellent, and you can picnic on the grounds. For information contact the ranger at Mole Creek; phone 03-6363-1245.

# Freycinet National Park

Located on the eastern coast, Freycinet National Park is about 200 kilometers east of Hobart. It's an excellent camping and relaxing park. The park covers a 10,000-hectare peninsula and includes uninhabited Schouten Island. There are numerous coves, many of them secluded, and large outcrops of red granite. The bird life is plentiful. There are fairy penguins, yellow wattlebirds, and sea eagles. Black swans breed in Moulting Lagoon. Marsupials are also well represented.

The best time to visit the park is February through April. For more information, contact Ranger in Charge, Freycinet National Park, Coles Bay, Tasmania 7215; phone 03-6257-0107.

*Accommodations.* There is a full-amenities campground. You'll be charged a nominal fee. Coles Bay has hotels. Try the Freycinet Lodge. This lodge won awards for its ecological integrity. It sits in a beautiful beach setting; phone 03-6257-0101.

*Access.* From Hobart take the Tasman Highway to Apslawn. Turn about 8 kilometers past Apslawn to Coles Bay. The park is past Coles Bay. The drive takes about 2.5 hours.

# PART VI

# Northern Territory

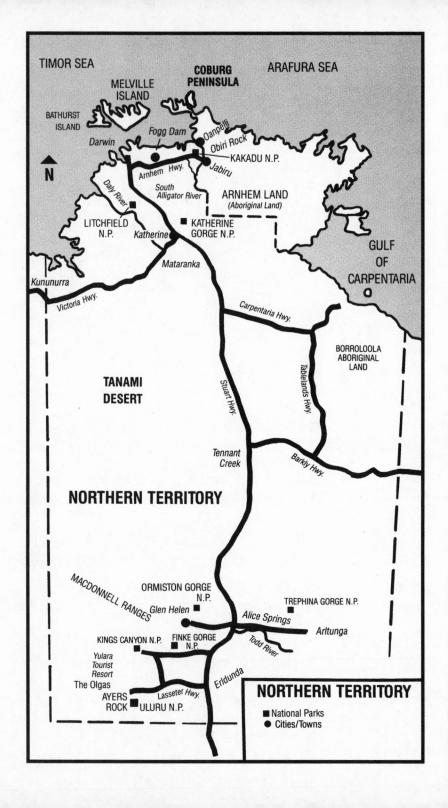

# Overview

The Northern Territory and the Outback are practically synonymous. Most of the Northern Territory is wild and remote. Only in the last decade has it been connected to the rest of Australia by the paving of the Stuart and Barkly Highways. Still, because of the great distances involved, the smartest way to visit is by air to Alice Springs or Darwin and from there by rental car or organized tour.

The Northern Territory is an immense tract of land. It covers 1,346,200 square kilometers—17 percent of Australia—making it six times the size of Great Britain and twice the size of France. The distance between the capital, Darwin, in the north and Alice Springs in the south is about the same as that between New York and Miami. Temperatures are generally high—80 percent of the Territory is in the tropics; and in the north, torrential tropical rain and high humidity are added to the high temperatures during the monsoon season, which can arrive anytime between November and April.

Though attempts had been made to establish settlements ever since the 1820s, it wasn't until 1869 that a lasting settlement at Palmerston (now a satellite community of Darwin) was finally established in the Top End. Self-government wasn't instituted in the Northern Territory until 1978. Today, 65,000 people live in and around Darwin, making it the most populous area in the Northern Territory. Darwin is a growing minimetropolis—a tough town with a shiny new face—and a stepping-off place for a great number of adventure and travel activities.

"Alice," the other population center, is 1,500 kilometers to the south of Darwin. Between the two hubs lie the Tanami Desert and a few tiny communities and pit stops along the Stuart Highway. The biggest of these roadside blurs is Tennant Creek, a mining community with a population of 5,000. The Territory's main income is mining, followed by cattle and tourism.

Aborigines have political power and considerable influence in the

Northern Territory. Uluru–Kata Tjuta National Park (formerly Ayers Rock and the Olgas) and Kakadu National Park are the federal government's two premier parks. Aborigines are part of the management of both parks. The Uluru park superintendent is hired and can be fired by the Anangu, who are the owners of the park. It is in the Northern Territory that the much talked about land-rights issue has come to have real and far-reaching meaning.

# Darwin

Flying to Darwin during the dry season is always memorable. During the descent the wild character of the Top End shows itself. Smoke from numerous wildfires forms columns of sooty vapor that rise high into the sky. The fires are a constant during the dry season and have been for thousands of years. They're set deliberately by Aborigines to flush out game. The grassy understory burns, and trees normally survive intact. As you peer down from the jet you see deep gorges with water glistening at the bottom. These are the upland watercourses. Nearer the coast ancient riverbeds filled with muddy water arch and twist across vast floodplains. About the time the plane's landing gear locks into place, you may get a glimpse of Darwin sticking out of the mangrove swamps. Darwin is a small, shiny white city with a few short skyscrapers. The city overlooks the natural harbor of Port Darwin, which opens to the Beagle Gulf and the Timor Sea.

The city is named for Charles Darwin. About the time the ill-fated Victoria Settlement (see "The Cobourg Peninsula," below) got under way in 1829, the *Beagle,* with Darwin on board, was working along the wild Top End coastline.

The city named in Darwin's honor has lived by one of the basic tenants of his theory: "survival of the fittest." From the start Darwin sweltered in the tropics surrounded by agriculturally unproductive land and extreme weather patterns that destroyed many agricultural schemes. The city was bombed unmercifully by the Japanese in World War II. When Cyclone Tracy struck on Christmas Day 1974,

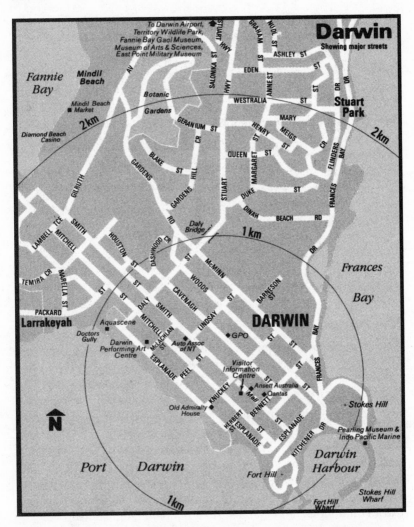

90 percent of Darwin was destroyed, with a loss of 50 lives. Yet Darwin rebounded each time because of the spunky attitude of its citizens. "The calamities are opportunities for urban renewal" is how one Darwinian explained the Cyclone Tracy disaster.

More than in any other capital in Australia, disdain toward authority is evident in Darwin. Irreverence, tattoos (before they were in vogue), pubs that feature wet T-shirt contests for women, Saturday-night brawls, and Darwin's style of rating live entertainment are some of the more conspicuous signs that "colorful characters" still abound.

I'll never forget my first visit to Darwin in the late 1980s. There was this "Gong Show" at the Nightcliff Hotel on Bagot Road, where performers "did their thing" (anything!) on a stage behind a protective net of chicken wire. When members of the audience had enough, they threw bottles of beer (always open) and anything else that wasn't tied down, which was the cue for the next performer. It was suicidal to stand up during a vote of disapproval, when the air was filled with projectiles.

Darwin now has modernistic buildings like the Diamond Beach Hotel Casino, freshly painted luxury hotels, excellent art galleries, a fine Museum of Arts and Sciences, upmarket suburbs, and civic projects. Promoters have even made clean fun out of the fact that the average Darwinian consumes 230 liters of beer annually—making Darwin a contender for the heaviest beer-drinking city in the world. One of the biggest events of the year is the Beer Can Regatta, held on August 27 in most years. All of the boats—speedboats, canoes, Viking-type ships armed with fire hoses, and boats that defy description—are made of beer cans.

## The Airport

Getting to Darwin requires a commitment of time and money. I know many Australians who have never visited Darwin because the airfares to overseas destinations make better sense to them. The two national carriers, Ansett and Qantas, fly in and out of Darwin daily. Airfare from Cairns runs about $A430 one way; from Sydney, it's about $A710; from Melbourne, $A700; from Adelaide, $A580; from Alice Springs, $A390. For flights to or from Broome, contact Skywest. Double the cost for return. To get to town, take a taxi ($A13). For those holding an Australia Pass there is a 25 percent discount on above airfares. Call the airlines for details. Singapore Airlines, Garuda Indonesia, and Qantas fly to Bali and points north.

## Arriving by Car

On the ground, you'll arrive from Alice Springs (or Adelaide) on the Stuart Highway, which runs 2,900 kilometers straight through the center of the continent from Adelaide. This highway is now paved the entire distance. From Queensland, Darwin is usually reached by the Barkly Highway through Mount Isa to Tennant Creek on the Stuart Highway. From Western Australia, entry is on the Victoria Highway via Kununurra to Katherine on the Stuart Highway.

# Information Sources

Contact the Northern Territory Tourist Commission (53 Mitchell Street, Darwin, N.T. 0800; phone 08-8999-3900; E-mail: www.nttc .com.au) for information about tours, accommodations, travel arrangements, and general information about the Northern Territory. *Top End Holiday Guide* and *Motoring Guide* are two publications keyed to the tourist. Both are handouts in the tourist office. There is a complete listing of tour operators.

The Automobile Association of the Northern Territory, MLC Building, 81 Smith Street (phone 08-8981-3837) has maps and information about driving conditions throughout the Territory.

# Transportation

## *Public Transportation*

For getting around Darwin, there's the Darwinbus. For a schedule or advice, phone 08-8924-7666. The main depot is on Harry Chan Avenue. Buses run between downtown and most tourist stops.

## *Taxis*

Darwin Radio Cabs; phone 13-10-08. It costs about $A13 for a cab from the airport to downtown.

## *Transportation Contacts*

Airlines. For local destinations try Skywest; phone 08-9334-2288. For international and domestic flights: Ansett, the Mall, phone 08-8981-6422; Singapore Airlines, the Mall, phone 08-8941-1799; and Qantas, 16 Bennett Street, phone 13-13-13

*Car Rentals.* Driving a rental car is risky around Darwin because of the combination of marginal roads, the road-walking behavior of large forms of wildlife, and hard-pressed car-rental franchises that sometimes void your insurance at the slightest pretext in order to get you to pay for any damage. My best luck for cheap 4WDs was with Territory Rent-a-Car; phone 08-8979-2552. I recommend that you pass on the Budget franchise in Darwin, though Budget seemed to be topflight in the rest of Australia. The supercheapies, like Rent a Dent, might seem like a good idea because they're so cheap and don't seem to care about dents: Don't do it. I started here. The first car's horn blasted when I turned the lights on, and the brakes worked only on the right side, so that the car veered off the road when I tried to stop. The next car (ten minutes later) caught fire a block from the business, causing only mild public interest. As I jumped out of the car, an Aussie standing in a doorway summed up my predicament: "You get what you pay for, Yank." I didn't try Avis (145 Stuart Highway; phone 08-8981-9922); Hertz (Smith Street; phone 08-8941-0944); or Thrifty (phone 08-8924-0000).

*Coach Service.* For long hauls by coach originating in Darwin, try McCafferty's (phone 08-13-14-99) and Greyhound Pioneer (phone 08-13-20-30). For local buses, visit the Darwin Bus Terminus on Harry Chan Avenue; phone 08-8924-7666. You can usually get across the Territory for about $A145. Fares vary with the seasons, and from company to company. The ride from Darwin to Alice takes 20 hours.

Note that there is no rail service in the Darwin area.

## Things to Do

Beer may be Darwin's lifeblood, but there is a lot to Darwin that has nothing to do with "the amber." In and around Darwin there are a number of sites and activities worth mention.

### Aquascene and Stokes Hill Wharf

At the end of the Esplanade in a place called Doctors Gully, fish feeding takes on a big dimension. Aquascene is a privately run business that attracts ocean fish for daily feeding. Feeding takes place at high tide, so the times vary; phone 08-8981-7837.

The Aquascene is near the Stokes Hill Wharf and Indo-Pacific Marine Aquarium (described below), which is on the wharf. The Stokes Hill Wharf also has the Australian Pearling Exhibition, which encapsulates the essentials of this once prosperous and dangerous trade. On nearby Kitchener Drive there are World War II storage areas that survived the Japanese bombings.

## The Indo-Pacific Marine Aquarium

The Indo-Pacific Marine Aquarium, on Stokes Hill Wharf, is a small-ish, homey saltwater aquarium with some noteworthy unique features. The aquarium's designers have created a self-contained ecosystem without an assortment of gadgets and filters. The aquarium bills itself as "representing one of four successful efforts in the world to isolate living reef communities from the sea." Admission is $A12 for adults; phone 08-8981-1294.

## Art Galleries and Museums

I highly recommend the Museum and Art Gallery of the Northern Territory, on Conacher Street. The museum is relatively small, but it's an entirely first-class operation, especially the Aboriginal Art Gallery. The quality of Aboriginal art is on a par with any collection in the world. There is a wide range of art from Arnhem Land, remote areas throughout the Territory, and Bathurst and Melville Islands, as well as Southeast Asian art. The stuffed carcass of "Sweetheart," a troublemaking crocodile, is a big draw. Sweetheart used to attack fishing boats.

The grounds around the museum are parklike. Fixed on the lawns, as reminders of Darwin's past maritime pearl industry and its proximity to Southeast Asia, are an old pearl "lugger" and a Vietnamese boat used by boat people who fled Southeast Asia during the 1970s.

The museum also has a coffee shop, restaurant, and gift shop. Take the No. 4 or No. 6 bus from downtown; phone 08-8999-8201.

## The Beaches

Crocodiles are removed from Darwin Harbour and the swimming beaches. *Never* swim if a beach (or other body of water) is signposted as a saltwater crocodile area. Box jellyfish (see "Playing It Safe" in the discussion of the Great Barrier Reef) also occur in these waters from January to April. Always check to see if the sea is free of these seasonal menaces. Nightcliff Beach, about a 10-minute drive from the city's center, has a jellyfish-proof net. This is the only safe swimming beach during jellyfish season. Mindil Beach, in front of the casino, is a fairly nice piece of sand with gentle or nonexistent surf and good windsurfing. The crowd is often an interesting mix of French, Malaysian, and Australian. Casuarina Beach, Darwin's sanctioned clothing-optional beach, is probably the most popular beach in Darwin. It's about 13 kilometers north of town on Dick Ward Drive and Trower Road. The beach is long and rarely seems crowded. The sun is often very intense in the Top End, so limit your exposure to avoid misery. For a little casual refreshment near the beaches, try the Beachfront Hotel, the poolside jazz at the Diamond Beach Casino, and Carlos Cool Spot at Fannie Bay Shopping Centre.

## The Darwin Botanic Gardens

Darwin's Botanic Gardens (across Gilruth Avenue, near Mindil Beach) are over 100 years old, yet about 80 percent of the trees have only been around since 1974. This contradiction was caused by Cyclone Tracy, which uprooted most of the garden's trees and destroyed the structures. The gardens have been entirely replanted. Curator David Brown's latest project is a rain forest gully with ponds and waterfalls, plus a coastal wetlands environment. In the palm garden there are more than 400 species of palms. The gardens can be reached by several roads in about 5 minutes from the city center. Garden Road cuts through the garden's center.

## City Walk and Historic Sites

Most of historic Darwin is boxed into a two- by three-block area bordered by the Esplanade, Knuckey Street, and Cavenagh Street. For a city walk start at the General Post Office on Knuckey Street. The post office is across the street from the Smith Street Mall. Walk down Knuckey Street toward the ocean to Lyons Cottage, which housed the British-Australian Telegraph Office. The stone structure is creatively ventilated to deal with the heat. Cross Knuckey Street onto the Esplanade. The Admiralty House on Knuckey Street, now an art gallery, sits on the corner. This was the official residence for the highest-ranking naval officer in the north and is one of the few remaining structures of its kind to survive Cyclone Tracy. Walk south along the Esplanade to the Hotel Darwin at 10 Herbert Street. On the harbor side where the Esplanade swings sharply to the left is the Government House, perhaps the best example of 1870 colonial architecture in Darwin. It also has beautiful gardens. Continue on the Esplanade and walk up Mitchell Street to the old post office. It now houses the Legislative Assembly. Backtrack on Mitchell Street to the Esplanade and turn left. You'll come to the police station and the old courthouse. On this block of Smith Street you'll find the "tree of knowledge" (near Harry Chan Avenue), where pensioners sit around in the shade and muse on whatever's on their minds. Also on this block is Brown's Mart, now a small theater but formerly a brothel and police station—not at the same time. Across the street is the old

town hall, which survived World War II intact but suffered greatly
from Cyclone Tracy. Continue up Smith Street to the mall. You'll
come to the Westpac Building and Commercial Bank at Bennett
Street. The bank is a handsomely restored structure with verandas
and arches. In the mall you'll find a store for every need, including
fast foods of every description and more formal restaurants. The Victoria Hotel on Smith Street is about midway along the mall. It was
built in 1894 and refurbished in 1978. It's a good watering trough,
particularly on the balcony that looks down on the mall. There is a
good bookstore near the Bennett Street end of the mall, and a wide
assortment of quick-stop eateries nearby. You're now back at the post
office, where you started. Turn right and you'll come to Raintree
Gallery, on 20 Knuckey Street; phone 08-8981-2732. This store may
have the best selection of Aboriginal art that is for sale in Darwin.

### The Fannie Bay Gaol

The spartan Fannie Bay Gaol (jail), at the corner of East Point and
Ross Smith Roads, is where hangings were conducted between 1893
and 1952. The gallows still stands, though Australia has forgone the
death penalty for over a decade. Many of Darwin's best citizens did
time in the Fannie Bay Gaol when they protested taxation without
representation during the 1920s. Much of the gaol has been restored
and now doubles as a museum, where a film of the aftermath of
Cyclone Tracy is shown and old machinery is housed.

### East Point Reserve

Just north of the depressing jail is the East Point Reserve, one of the
best places to relax and picnic in and around Darwin. The reserve is
a beautifully kept park that has wild wallabies as its primary residents. If they aren't out and about, wait until dusk and they will
appear. There is a man-made lake perfect for swimming without fear
of being eaten by the likes of "Sweetheart," the immense saltwater
crocodile stuffed in the Museum and Art Gallery of the Northern
Territory. Watch your exposure to ultraviolet radiation; it is especially intense in Australia and doubly intense in the Northern Territory. Visiting the reserve is free.

### Military History

Darwin's military history is unique. The Japanese bombed the city
relentlessly in World War II, making Darwin the only Australian city

that was bombed in that war. At the time there was great fear that a
land invasion wasn't far behind. Besides the World War II storage
areas on Kitchener Drive already mentioned in the "Aquascene and
Stokes Hill Wharf" section, more on Darwin's role in World War II
is explained at the East Point Military Museum on East Point Road.
An old film of the actual bombing is shown, and still photos of the
destroyer U.S.S. *Peary,* which went down in Darwin Harbour, killing
88 U.S. servicemen, is on display. There are also guns and photos
from that era; phone 08-8981-0702. If war technology is a theme
you like, there is the Aviatian Heritage Centre on the Stuart Highway
in the Darwin suburb of Winnellie. Here you'll find B-25 and B-52
bombers, plus other airplanes that ushered in new eras in aviation;
phone 08-8947-2145.

## Restaurants

There is great seafood and Chinese food in Darwin. Since you're
probably going to the Museum and Art Gallery of the Northern Territory, show up in the afternoon and dine at the Cornucopia Museum
Café, Conacher Street; phone 08-8981-1002. Expect to be offered
dishes of native wildlife, like barramundi and crocodile, as well as
more common dishes; a meal runs about $A25. There is also a Sun-
day brunch. Christo's on the Wharf, at Stokes Hill Wharf, has a
super view of the harbor and serves excellent seafoods. Wheelchair
access is difficult. The ambiance costs: meals run between $A35 and
$A60; phone 08-8981-8658. If you want to hang out with local
politicos and enjoy a great view of the harbor, dine at Speakers Corner Café, at the Parliament House; phone 08-8981-4833. This is
mostly a lunch spot. Meals usually run about $A20 or less. For
exquisite Chinese food try Hanuman Restaurant, 28 Mitchell Street;
phone 08-8941-3500. The shellfish soups are known throughout the
Top End. Meals run around $A35. For vegetarian dishes, visit Sim-
ply Foods on the Central Mall. Mindil Beach Market has a plethora
of food stalls specializing in everything from Thai to "American"
dishes.

## Shopping

Aboriginal culture has a strong presence throughout the Northern
Territory, and Darwin is the hub of Aboriginal art in the north.

You'll see a great deal of Aboriginal art—some of it museum-piece quality and some of it aimed at the low-end tourist trade. To get your bearings check out the art in the Museum and Art Gallery of the Northern Territory. You will see art from the Aboriginal people who live on the mainland and Tiwi Islanders from Melville and Bathurst Islands. The art of the Tiwi Islanders is different than Aboriginal art and represents a culture that is not closely tied to the mainland. Besides art from the first Australians, be they Aborigines or Tiwi Islanders, Darwin is also known for its pearls and opals. For Aboriginal art visit the Raintree Fine Art Gallery (20 Knuckey Street; phone 08-8981-2732) or the shop at the Aboriginal Fine Art Gallery (Knuckey Street; phone 08-8981-1315). For just about anything visit Mindil Beach Market. As many as 10,000 people show up here on the weekends to sample food from the 150 food stalls and spend their money on everything from fortune-telling to masseurs, jewelry, crafts, and entertainers. This is an interesting place. Besides what's for sale you get to see who lives in Darwin. For good-quality opal and pearl jewelry visit the shops on Smith Street.

## Accommodations

*Economy.* There is a YWCA at 119 Mitchell Street (phone 08-8981-8644) in Darwin. The Darwin City Youth Hostel, at 69 Mitchell Street (phone 08-8981-3995) has a swimming pool, TV, and laundry for $A18 a double. If you're dead set on pitching a tent, you'll have to go to one of the caravan parks out of town or retreat even farther to a national park. For caravan parks, try Shady Glen; phone 08-8984-3330.

*Moderate.* Try the Hotel Darwin, 10 Herbert Street; phone 08-8981-9211. This is a beautiful old colonial with a pool, surrounded by huge tropical shade trees. Mirrambeena Tourist Resort, 64 Cavanaugh Street (phone 08-8946-0111), has waterfalls and lovely gardens. It is owned by local Aborigines. Room are between $A100 and $A125. Novotel Atrium, 100 The Esplanade (phone 08-8941-0755), features a glass atrium with a creek and its own inside rain forest. The hotel complements its atmospherics with "bush" cuisine.

*Upmarket.* The MGM Grand, Gilruth Avenue (phone 08-8943-8888), is a casino hotel that offers traditional five-star service. The

Beaufort Hotel, The Esplanade (phone 08-8980-0800) is described as Darwin's best hotel by several leading Darwinians that I know. It has a tremendous view of the harbor.

# Day Trips from Darwin

## The Crocodile Farm

The Crocodile Farm is about 45 kilometers south of Darwin on the Stuart Highway. This is a multimillion-dollar privately owned farm that commercially raises saltwater crocodiles and works with the Conservation Commission of the Northern Territory in educating the public about crocodiles and crocodile conservation. The farm's lake also contains dozens of large "problem" salties that were captured and brought there. The big crocs are fed at 2:00 P.M. daily.

At the Crocodile Farm you'll see videos about salties and freshies, pools of freshies (indigenous only to Australia), and a large lake full of salties. You'll probably run through rolls of film while these prehistoric reptiles bask with mouths agape or charge into the water to cool off. There's an opportunity for closeup shots not possible in the wild. Entry fee: $A9.50; phone 08-8988-1450.

## Litchfield National Park

Litchfield National Park is so new it's not on most maps. It was declared a park in 1987. Litchfield is about 85 kilometers south of Darwin in the Tabletop Range. Access to the park is on 4WD tracks. You'll never make it in a passenger car, so don't try. The smart way to get there is on a day tour with one of the tour outfits in Darwin. The cost is usually around $A60. The park's main features are waterfalls, swimming holes, immense termite mounds, tropical woodlands, and a wide range of wildlife.

I very much enjoyed the day I spent here with a schoolteacher from Melbourne, a former kangaroo hunter and his wife, and Dave Ross, our naturalist guide. We shared our perceptions and got to know one another as we bounced and careened along on the rough tracks. Along the way we swam, climbed straight up a waterfall, and stopped to photograph dingoes, altiplano kangaroos, red-tailed black cockatoos, blue-winged kookaburras, six-meter-high termite mounds, and a wildfire (set by Aborigines) that we drove through. It was an excellent day trip. For information contact the Run Jungle Motor Lodge; phone 08-8976-0123.

## Territory Wildlife Park

I rate Territory Wildlife Park as one of the top three half- to full-day excursions from Darwin. The park is 57 kilometers south of Darwin on the paved Stuart Highway. This is a state-of-the-art animal park and zoo that features the habitats as well as the wildlife of tropical northern Australia. The park covers 400 hectares and opened in 1988. Lee Moyes, the curator, has traveled the world gleaning ideas from top zoological gardens. The layout incorporates walks, nocturnal houses, underwater viewing areas, and blinds at a typical billabong, and a mammoth walk-through bird house with four habitats and 52 species of birds. The low-intensity lighting in the nocturnal houses allows you to see such rarities as ghost bats, bilbies, bandicoots, quolls, and dunnarts. The park has rare black wallaroos, as well as water buffalo, an introduced species that now is a major part of the northern Australia fauna. The reptile collection includes frilled lizards, the rare Oenpelli python found only in the Arnhem Land region, the entirely aquatic Arafura file snake, various poisonous snakes, the recently discovered pig-nosed turtle, both fresh- and salt-water crocodiles, and two-meter-long perentie monitors. There's also a restaurant in the park and a nearby swimming and picnic area.

The Territory Wildlife Park, located 57 kilometers south of Darwin, is open 8:30 A.M.–6:00 P.M. Admission is $A12 for adults; phone 08-8988-7200.

## Edith Falls

Edith Falls is just off the Stuart Highway 44 kilometers south of Pine Creek and 46 kilometers north of Katherine. It's the northern end of

Katherine Gorge National Park. A passenger car can make it here in the dry season, but not during the wet. The park has an idyllic series of waterfalls and deep pools suitable for swimming (too far inland for salties). The falls are surrounded by pandani and other tropical vegetation. If the lower pool near the campground is crowded, there's a walk to a higher fall that offers more solitude. This is a good lunch spot, suitable for a day's rest and relaxation.

## The Town of Katherine and Nitmiluk (Katherine Gorge) National Park

I was disappointed in Katherine and Katherine Gorge National Park. This is one of the Northern Territory's most highly promoted tourist destinations, and it appears the promotion has surpassed the community's and park's ability to deal with the crowds. When I visited the area during the dry season, I couldn't find an accommodation in the town after three hours of trying. I finally talked my way into a full campground. The next day the boat tour of the gorge was more reminiscent of a ride in Disneyland than anything approximating an authentic outdoor experience. My gut impression was validated by the town's most successful tour operator, Warner Sarnay, who candidly explained, "The growth in tourism has been phenomenal since the Stuart Highway was sealed [paved] last year. We're at the point where the gorge cannot absorb more tourists during certain times." Sarnay suggests that international travelers should avoid the gorge in July and August. "April to the middle of June is the best time to visit because the weather is good and the crowds are small."

### Katherine

The town of Katherine is 330 kilometers down the Stuart Highway from Darwin. The Victoria Highway, which links the Top End with Western Australia, intersects the Stuart Highway at Katherine. The town isn't the kind of place that you'll remember for very long. Ozzie's Bistro has ample rations of standard Aussie tucker—meat, salad, and potatoes. Nitmiluk National Park Visitors Centre Bistro has passable food and an unforgettable sunset.

For accommodations in town, try the Pine Tree Motel; phone 08-8972-2533. The Low Level Katherine Nature Park and Springville Homestead are on the Victoria Highway on the western side of town.

Both are caravan parks, but tent campers can stay for a nominal fee per night. Springville Homestead has nightly activities for tourists, including an Aboriginal dance troupe. They have motel rooms for about $A75 per night; phone 08-8972-3201.

For more details on Katherine, contact Northern Territory Government Tourist Information, corner of Stuart Highway and Lindsay Avenue, Katherine, N.T. 0850; phone 08-8972-2650.

### Nitmiluk (Katherine Gorge) National Park

Katherine Gorge National Park is 39 kilometers east of town. The park's main feature is a deep gorge cut through a sandstone plateau by the Katherine River. Large, flat-bottomed launches leave several times a day to tour the gorge. During the dry season the gorge becomes a series of long deep pools. Unfortunately, there's a "cattle truck" mentality in how tourists are shuttled through the gorge. The trip amounts to being loaded into a large aluminum boat with 75 people seated 8 to 10 across. If you end up in a middle seat, it's almost impossible to see anything.

For manageable numbers of people and a chance to see wildlife, Sarnay and park service rangers suggest taking his 9-hour tour that takes 45 people to the fifth gorge. The upper gorges have more wildlife. Book your boat ride in Katherine. There are canoe rentals near the motor launch area, which would be a more solitary way to see the gorge. To book a seat on the launch, contact Nitmiluk National Park Visitors Centre; phone 08-8972-3150.

Katherine National Park also has 100 kilometers of walking tracks. Ask for details at the park's visitors center, located near the entrance.

## Cutta Cutta Caves Nature Park

Located 27 kilometers south of Katherine on the Stuart Highway, Cutta Cutta Caves is a superb limestone labyrinth with spectacular stalagmites and stalactites that look more like glistening ice cream than stone. All walks in the caves are ranger-guided. The ranger does an excellent job in explaining the geology and ecology. If you want to capture the spectacular formations on film, take a powerful flash. Your efforts will be enhanced by the floodlighting inside. Prebooked coach and group tours normally arrive hourly from 9:00 A.M. to 2:00

P.M. Public tours run at 10:30 A.M. and 1:30 P.M. Tours can be suspended or altered during the wet season, which can run for any two-month period between November and March.

# Kakadu National Park

Located about 200 kilometers southeast from Darwin, Kakadu National Park may be the premier national park in Australia. It covers an area of 13,000 square kilometers. Much of the park will seem vaguely familiar because the area served as the backdrop for the blockbuster *Crocodile Dundee* films. The park is unsurpassed in its profusion of wetlands wildlife and Aboriginal ochre rock art.

The panoramas and life-forms in Kakadu National Park are Australia's answer to the African Serengeti. The rhythm and intensity is much the same, though the creatures and environment are often unfamiliar. For example, more than 300 species of birds—one-third of all the species in Australia—live in Kakadu either permanently or on a seasonal basis. The expansive green wetlands, swamps, billabongs, and floodplains are filled with multitudes of squawking, honking, whistling, and screeching tropical birds, behemoth saltwater crocodiles, and rare macropods. There are immense tracts of undulating tropical woodlands, sandstone escarpments, and plateaus. There are more than 5,000 kinds of flowering plants in greater Arnhem Land, of which Kakadu is part. Many of the plants are still unclassified.

During the dry season, the Wildman, West, South, and East Alligator Rivers are tired, meandering watercourses occupying ancient riverbeds that have been etched into the landscape for so long they've become practically level with the sea. In the wet season, the watercourses throughout the park swell, creating thundering Twin Falls and Jim Jim Falls and spilling over their banks and spreading over the plains, replenishing isolated billabongs and freshwater swamps and transforming dry grasslands into radiant green floodplains.

Aboriginal culture in Kakadu is a shadow of what it once was, but it does survive. More than 300 Aborigines live in the park. For the out-

*Aboriginal rock art gallery, Kakadu National Park.* PHOTO BY ERIC HOFFMAN.

sider, Kakadu's rich Aboriginal art allows a deeper understanding of the ancient culture that once thrived here. Artwork is literally everywhere. Kakadu contains more than 6,000 known Aboriginal rock-art sites. Jutting out of the woodlands and wetlands is the Arnhem Land escarpment, which is the backdrop of most vistas in Kakadu and the dominant geological feature. This backdrop can also be viewed as a continuous art gallery. In cliffs along the escarpment, under overhangs, and in the caves is an endless array of Aboriginal art dating back 23,000 years—which makes it among the oldest art in the world.

Kakadu National Park was designated as Australia's first World Heritage Area in 1981 and is jointly managed by the Gagudju (Aboriginal) Association and the National Parks and Wildlife Service. The Australian government leases the park from the Aborigines, who help manage it. Former park superintendent Bruce Gall explains the park's special qualities: "The basis for Kakadu being declared a World Heritage Area is twofold. Kakadu is unequaled when it comes to rock art. We have full-time archaeologists cataloging art sites who predict we'll wind up with over 10,000 sites in all. The wetlands can be a powerful experience. It's unlikely that anyone who sees this habitat at its best, teeming with wildlife, will ever forget it."

Much of Kakadu's annual budget has gone to controlling feral water buffalo, which were introduced in the Top End in 1820 and have flourished ever since. The other management challenge is coping with the rapid increase in park visitors. In the early 1990s the park had more than 200,000 visitors annually—a 100 percent rise in just three years. During the dry season, finding a camping place or accommodation can be difficult.

## The Major Art Sites

Of the thousands of Aboriginal art sites in Kakadu, the rock art found at Ubirr (Obiri Rock) and Nourlangie are the most accessible and come closest to covering the full spectrum of the 20,000 years of Aboriginal art found in the park.

### Nourlangie Rock

The turnoff to the Nourlangie Rock art site is located between Cooinda and Jabiru on the Kakadu Highway. There are two major art sites in this area. The first is the Anbangbang Gallery, which has one of the best examples of "lightning man," called "Namarrgon" by local Aborigines. The road and walk to the gallery are signposted, and the figures are easy to identify. The large figure at the top of the site, showing male genitalia, is Namandjolg, a dangerous spirit. Namarrgon (lightning man) is the smaller figure with arcing lines that connect his limbs. (The arcs are the lightning that Namarrgon makes with his stone axes.) The female figure below Namarrgon's left leg is Barrginj, his wife. The side gallery features Nabulwinjbul- winj, a particularly evil spirit who has the nasty habit of killing women by striking them with yams and devouring them. Some of these works are so shiny they seem to be painted with enamels. Actually, they were created with ochre-based clays, possibly mixed with animal fat. The works were touched up in the 1960s by Najo- mobolmi, a local Aborigine who has since died.

The Blue Paintings are a secondary gallery within walking distance of the Anbangbang Gallery. Nobody knows for sure how the blue color was obtained, though crayons have been suggested. These are recent works, probably painted sometime within the past 50 years. They can be reached by walking about 1,000 meters from the parking area at Nawulandja Lookout. This gallery can be reached only during the dry season. There is a short trail up onto a sandstone escarpment that affords a good view, and another short trail to a nearby billabong. The Blue Paintings Gallery is near an Aboriginal burial site that caused the gallery to be closed in the past. It's now open, but visitors should keep in mind that wandering from any trail is prohibited in this area.

Nangaloar Gallery is the second major site on Nourlangie Rock. It is reached on the northern fork of the turnoff from the Kakadu Highway between Cooinda and Jabiru. I enjoyed this site a great deal because the 3.5-kilometer round-trip walk to the gallery eliminates most people. Afternoon is the best time to visit the site for photographic purposes. You should also carry drinking water. Feral buffalo and pigs are sometimes seen in the area. Allow them the right-of-way and avoid getting too close. The walk to the Nangaloar site will give you a good look at the open tropical forest that covers much of Kakadu. Look for bridal trees with yellow flowers, grevilleas, woodland pandani, turkey bushes with pink star-shaped flowers, stringybark gums, and ironwoods. You'll also pass by billabongs.

The Nangaloar Gallery offers a great variety of styles. The oldest works are dated at 20,000 years; the most recent were painted in the 1960s. You'll see hand stencils, a common motif throughout Australia. You'll also see rare drawings of hands and forearms. Many of the humanlike figures are elongated. Look for Namandi, a six-fingered spirit, carrying a dilly bag; "contact art" depicting sailing ships; and stylized barramundi, kangaroos, and turtles.

## Ubirr (Obiri Rock)

Ubirr is located on a dirt road near the East Alligator River Crossing (also known as Cahill's Crossing) into Arnhem Land. The signposted turnoff is off the Arnhem Highway a short distance west of Jabiru. The 30-kilometer dirt road is in fairly good shape. However, it is dusty.

The Ubirr art site is extremely rich and easily reached. As many as 2,000 people a week visit the site—and for good reason. It's that good. The various phases and styles of rock art span 20,000 years and are often on a single rock wall. Some paintings are superimposed over older works that can still be seen. Ubirr is in a class of its own in terms of diversity and volume. Many animals drawn in red ochre are of the oldest style. Look for the thylacine (Tasmanian tiger) high on a rock face outside the main gallery. (The thylacine became extinct in the area 5,000 years before the coming of Europeans.) To adequately photograph this rare work you'll need a telephoto lens. A flash helps in some of the darker galleries.

There are many fine examples of X-ray art. The portrayals of magpie geese and other waterbirds in this style date the style to changes in the area that occurred more than 6,000 years ago, when freshwater fowl arrived in Kakadu in great numbers. At Ubirr there's also an impressive characterization of Namandjolg, the dangerous spirit that is also found at Nourlangie Rock. The Ubirr depiction of this powerful spirit is at eye level, of excellent quality, and at a perfect distance for photographing. The main art gallery also has examples of postcontact art, mostly men with guns and metal axes. By following the marked walk up onto a sandstone outcrop you'll come to several other sites that have entirely different styles. You'll find bands of stick figures of heavily armed warriors drawn in white ochre (sometimes called mimi art) that were most likely created 15,000 to 20,000 years ago. A climb to the lookout also affords an excellent view of the nearby wetlands and sandstone escarpment—a vista you will have shared with countless Aboriginal hunters who stood on the same rock during the millenniums.

## River Cruises

There are several river tours in Kakadu National Park and on watercourses near the park. Yellow Waters is a superb short cruise and should not be missed. The tours are run on the South Alligator River near Cooinda several times daily. Shallow-draft boats that carry about 40 people travel down the South Alligator River into the heart of Kakadu's wetlands. The boat operators are well versed on the wildlife and enthusiastic about imparting their knowledge. Wildlife is so abundant that you should count on running through a few rolls of film.

When I took this trip we came across several large basking saltwater crocodiles that showed a total disregard of our presence. White-breasted sea eagles and ospreys swooped past the boat and snatched fish. Magpie and green pygmy geese and snowy white radjah shelducks paddled out of our way. Wading along in the shallows, perhaps aware of crocodiles, were plumed whistling ducks. Decorating the shallows and shoreline were human-sized red-legged jabiru storks and so many egrets that they actually dotted the floodplain. Herons, bitterns, water buffalo, a few brumbies, mobs of agile wal-

*Saltwater crocodile, Kakadu National Park.* PHOTO BY ERIC HOFFMAN.

labies, and prowling goannas were some of the more memorable creatures. Flocks of parrots and little corella cockatoos screeched by the boat on their way to their next resting place. Afternoon cruises are best because creatures are beginning to stir after sitting out the heat of the day. The cruise leaves from Yellow Water, which is 1 kilometer from Cooinda; phone 08-8979-0111. The cruise costs $A23.50 per adult.

The Gulyambi Aboriginal Culture Cruise is as much of a draw as the very popular Yellow Waters cruise. The Gulyambi cruise explores the wildlife-rich East Alligator River. The guides, who are Aborigines, explain aspects of their culture. The cruise departs from the "boat launching ramp" several times during the day, beginning at 9:00 A.M. The cost is $A25 per adult; phone 08-8979-2411.

## Walks

The extreme heat and wild nature of the area discourage most people from attempting long walks in Kakadu. If you plan on overnighting in the bush, discuss it with a ranger at the park headquarters on the Kakadu Highway or at the Bowali Visitor Centre. There are a number of short walks that will allow you to get a feel of the various habitats and special qualities of the park. The best walking time is May to December, though many of the walks can be completed year-round.

There are two superb walks relatively near Ubirr, the spectacular art site. The Wurdijileedji Walk (pronounced "wood-jill-ee-gee") is an easy 3-kilometer round-trip walk that starts in the day-use area. The walk goes through monsoon forests and broken sandstone escarpments and along the East Alligator River. Look for ochre rock art in the area near the cave. The Mangarre Forest Walk starts near the Border Store. If you can't find the trailhead, ask at the store. This 1.5-kilometer round-trip walk introduces you to a great deal of the wildlife. To maximize your experience, walk quietly without talking. There's a good chance you'll see goannas, agile wallabies, flying foxes (high in the trees), Torres Strait imperial pigeons, pittas, and red-tailed black cockatoos. In the dry season, there's an assortment of colorful flowering plants.

The name *Iligadjarr* means file snake in the local Aboriginal language. The Iligadjarr Nature Walk starts near the original park headquarters and campgrounds on the Kakadu Highway (south of the Malabanbandju campground on the road to the Baoalba campground). The walk is a 3.8-kilometer loop that travels past mangroves, paperbarks, pandani, billabongs, and buffalo wallows. The water is clear enough to see barramundi, catfish, and archer fish (the spitting fish sold in aquarium stores throughout the United States). You'll also see a variety of birds and possibly a crocodile or two.

Mamukala Nature Trail is off the Arnhem Highway about 7 kilometers east of Kakadu Holiday Village. The main feature is a large wetlands area packed with magpie geese, several species of egrets, and many other waterfowl. Blinds have been set up, which makes it likely you'll get some decent photographs. Be sure to take bug repellent. Late afternoon is the best time to visit.

The Baark Sandstone Trail Walk is one of the only marked long walks in the park. This is a 12-kilometer loop that starts at the Anbangbang Gallery and twists through and around the rugged base of Nourlangie Rock until you've circumnavigated the sandstone outcrop. *Baark* is the Aboriginal name for the rare and spectacular northern black wallaroo that lives in steep fissured-stone country like the area the walk goes through. If you're lucky, you may see one of these coal-black kangaroos. Early morning is probably the best time to attempt the walk.

## New Walkabouts

The park service has created several new walks in the last several years. In the Mary River region, the Yurmikmik Walking Tracks wander over mostly flat terrain along billabongs and wet-season waterfalls. There are four Yurmikmik trails, ranging in length from 2 to 11 kilometers. The opportunity to see spectacular bird life is guaranteed. Watch for everything from jabiru storks to magpie geese and red-tailed black cockatoos. Also watch for snakes and crocodiles. Both are harmless enough, if you don't stand on the former or enter the water and become food for the latter.

In the Nourlangie area there are several new walks. The Gubara Pools Walk is a 6-kilometer excursion through varied terrain with rock outcrops and large lily-filled pools. Much of the walk is forested. You'll have the opportunity to see the rare black wallaroo here, as well as more common macropods. Bird life is also plentiful. Walk quietly and watch the treeline. Often spectacular red-tailed black cockatoos dine very quietly, and it is possible to walk near them without noticing them. The Nanguluwur Walk is a 3.5-kilometer walk that originates from the west side of the Nourlangie rock art site in the Nanguluwur parking area. This walk takes in a half dozen galleries that cover a broad continuum of rock art from very early to postcontact.

## Interpretive Centers

The park has two interpretive centers, both well worth a visit. The Warradjan Aboriginal Cultural Centre is near the Cooinda Lodge. The center is built in the shape of a turtle (*warradjan* in the local dialect) and has excellent exhibits and a video explaining Aboriginal culture. Tools, art, live dancing, and videotaped statements by local Aborigines, describing their feelings and their forecasts for the future of the land, will leave you with a strong impression. There is a crafts shop for purchasing art and gifts; phone 08-8979-0051. The Bowali Visitor Centre at the entrance to Jabiru is an award-winning interpretive center with excellent multisensory exhibits on wildlife, Aboriginal beliefs, and the geological forces that shaped Kakadu. There is a well-stocked gift shop with locally produced art; phone 08-8938-1100.

## Jim Jim Falls

Photos of Jim Jim Falls are usually part of every travel brochure on Kakadu, for the simple reason that Jim Jim and nearby Twin Falls are spectacular. But that's only part of the story. As I found out the hard way, the road to Jim Jim Falls is a top contender for worst signposted road in Australia—and that's saying something, considering I've logged over 60,000 kilometers on Outback roads. Worse yet, I went to Jim Jim Falls during the dry season—and there was no water in the falls even though the trip was recommended by park personnel and tourism department staff!

I bounced and coughed to Jim Jim Falls in a rented Suzuki Samurai. It took me four hours to travel 60 kilometers from the paved highway to the falls. Intermixed with the washboard surface were sand traps that required finesse to negotiate even in a 4WD. Unless the challenge of such a drive is somehow appealing to you, skip these falls until the park service does something about the road. You've been warned!

*Cautions.* Water buffalo and saltwater crocodiles must be kept in mind when walking or camping in Kakadu. Water buffalos can be very dangerous if surprised at close range. "Enter the water and expect to be eaten" is the rule of thumb when large saltwater crocodiles are nearby. Driving hazards include bad roads, large animals on the roads at night, and occasional problems with car insurance contracts.

## Accommodations

Camping. There are numerous campgrounds, but if it is the wet season always inquire about flooding of roads. If it's the dry season, try to book as far in advance as possible. The park often operates at carrying capacity during the dry season. There is a nominal fee for using a campground that has running water and toilets. The Mardugal Campground is a couple kilometers off the Kakadu Highway near Cooinda and the Yellow Waters cruise. The Muriella Park Campground is 6 kilometers off the Kakadu Highway at a point 22 kilometers from the Arnhem Highway intersection. The most upscale campsite is at Frontier Kakadu Village, 39 kilometers west of Jabiru on the Kakadu Highway. It has a swimming pool and powered sites;

phone 08-8979-0166. If you plan on bushcamping, get a permit from the Bowali Visitor Centre at the entrance to Jabiru. You can also buy detailed maps there.

*Motels and Hotels.* Frontier Kakadu Village is part of the same camping complex described above. It is located 39 kilometers west of Jabiru on the Kakadu Highway. It is far from the main attractions but has attractive gardens and plenty of bird life. Rooms start at $A130; phone 08-8979-0166. The "village" and other accommodations listed here are set up for wheelchair access. The Gagudju Crocodile Hotel, Flinders Street, Jabiru, gets the prize for thematically most correct architecture. The hotel is shaped like a huge crocodile, and you enter through its mouth. Once inside the belly of the beast you'll find full amenities and good service. Rooms start at $A150; phone 08-8979-2800. The Gagudju Lodge in Cooinda, Kakadu Highway, is a fairly modest multiple-cabin setup. Not glamorous, but it has all the essentials, including air-conditioning and tiny refrigerators. There are small stores for buying gifts and provisions. The best thing about the Gagudju Lodge is its location near Yellow Waters, a small airstrip that serves to take visitors on scenic flights of Kakadu, and the Warradjan Aboriginal Cultural Centre. Phone 08-8979-0145 for accommodations and bookings for river tours and scenic flights.

*Access.* There's no public transportation to the park, but practically every travel outfit working the Top End goes to Kakadu. For a tour outfit, contact the Darwin Region Tourism Office, Mitchell and Knuckey Streets, Darwin, NT 0800; phone 08-8981-4300.

I opted for a rental car instead of a tour bus. This is risky because insurance contracts are often voided if damage occurs on dirt roads. It's a catch-22 situation, since many scenic destinations in Kakadu are on dirt roads. The roads to Kakadu are paved and amply signposted. Head south on the Stuart Highway. Turn left on the Arnhem Land Highway and you'll be in Kakadu National Park about 2.5 hours after leaving Darwin. The total distance is 138 miles. My best experience was with Cheapa; phone 089-81-8400.

# The Tiwi of Bathurst and Melville Islands

Bathurst and Melville Islands, the home of the Tiwi, lie about 70 kilometers north of Darwin. Visitors usually reach the islands by a 30-minute flight in a light aircraft. Melville is the second-largest Australian island; only Tasmania is larger. Bathurst is about one-third the size of Melville. From an airplane the islands appear to be irregularly shaped sections of flat, fuzzy green carpet afloat in an azure sea. The carpet is really low-growing tropical forest. Rising into the sky are columns of smoke that mark where the islands' indigenous Tiwi people have pursued game.

The special aspect of Bathurst and Melville Islands is the friendliness of the low-key Tiwi Islanders, who live much the way they have for centuries. Tiwis are hunter-gatherers with a rich culture that is different from mainland Aboriginal cultures. They are also world renowned for their abstract art, which is available for sale at the small commercial center at Nguiu on Bathurst Island. My time spent with the Tiwis at Putjamirra in 1988 was by far the most memorable cross-cultural experience I have had in Australia.

Visiting the Tiwi Islanders isn't something you can do on your own without going through considerable red tape to get special permits. The long-standing way to see the Tiwis is through Tiwi Tours, which offers one- and two-day excursions to the islands. The Tiwi Tours aren't as dramatic or personal as now-defunct Putjamirra safari camp, but after a lecture by a Tiwi Tours representative you'll learn a great deal about Tiwi culture and history.

Only one of the full-day tours includes both islands. The other day tour visits only Bathurst Island. If you decide on a one-day tour, take the one that includes crossing Apsley Strait and visiting Tiwi burial sites and Turacumbie Falls. Bring a bathing suit. The pool beneath

*Tiwis hunting turtles, Bathurst Island.* PHOTO BY ERIC HOFFMAN.

the falls is refreshing and enchanting. You can actually walk behind the waterfall and look into the pool beneath the falls through a sheet of water. The two-day trip includes an overnight at a lake at Moantu, where locals will encourage you to hunt for oysters and try your hand at spearfishing.

The chapel on Bathurst Island is decorated in colorful Tiwi works of art and is an excellent subject to photograph. All the tours allow browsing time in the Bima Wear Shop, Tiwi Pottery, and Tiwi Pima (carvings) shops in Nguiu. You can save up to 50 percent by purchasing works of art and clothing on Bathurst Island rather than in Darwin or other parts of Australia.

The Tiwi Design and Jilmarra clothing products are excellent buys. The fabric has highly stylized designs on everything from dresses to tablecloths and T-shirts. The colorfully painted totemlike wood carvings rate highly as works of art. Works from Tiwi wood carvers are shown in the world's best museums and galleries in Europe, North America, and Australia. The resemblance to Northwest Indian totem art is in appearance only. Tiwi art is abstract and colorful, not symbolic. Birdlike figures are popular subjects.

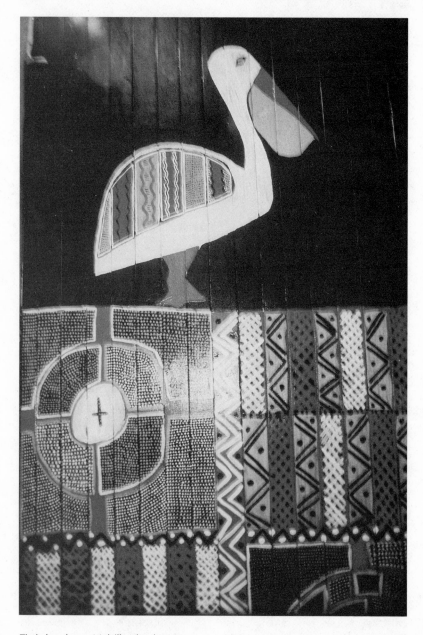

*Tiwi church art, Melville Island.* PHOTO BY ERIC HOFFMAN.

Besides lectures and shopping, there's sightseeing from a small bus, and there may be time for a refreshing dip in a large pool.

You should book your Tiwi Tour in advance. Contact Tiwi Tours, 27 Termira Cres, Darwin, N.T. 0800; phone 08-8981-1633. The full-day tours cost $A240 per adult, the two-day trip $A460. Be sure to carry extra cash or a major international credit card to make purchases.

# Arnhem Land

Arnhem Land is an immense tract of land bordering on Kakadu's eastern boundary. Named after a Dutch sailing ship that slid along the coastline in 1623, Arnhem Land has always been a rarely disturbed wild area, possessing endless floodplains, countless billabongs, tropical lowland forests, and jagged sandstone escarpments; it is home to a plethora of undisturbed wildlife in a multifaceted and healthy ecosystem. From the air Arnhem Land's tortured coastline, with its endless beaches, rocky headlands, and quiet azure bays, has many appendages: Cobourg Peninsula, Gove Peninsula, and Groote and Elcho Islands. The region is vast, steamy, an immense sponge during "the Wet," mysterious, and moody. There is an almost religious reverence toward Arnhem Land by both white and Aboriginal Australians living in the Top End. It is a stronghold of the much publicized monster predator the saltwater crocodile. Such rarities as the black wallaroo (a black kangaroo that glistens in the sunlight) also live here, and one-third of Australia's bird life either migrates through or makes permanent residence here. It is the one large tract of land that has been an uninterrupted homeland to Aboriginal people, whose ancestors were here for thousands of years and who today control who visits Arnhem Land. Arnhem Land is officially off-limits to non-Aborigines. Besides visiting the Seven Spirit Bay Wilderness Lodge on the Cobourg Peninsula, procuring a permit to Gurig National Park in the north, or walking across Cahills Crossing (the road to

Oenpelli) to say you've put a foot in Arnhem Land, it is a tough place to visit—which doesn't mean it's impossible.

Visitors to Arnhem Land in general must apply for a permit at the Northern Land Council, P.O. 42921, Casaurina, N.T. 0811, or at P.O. Box 18, Jabiru, N.T. 0886.

# The Cobourg Peninsula

For most visitors to the Northern Territory, Darwin and Kakadu National Park are the extent of their travels in the Top End. The few tourists who venture north of Darwin visit the Tiwi Islanders or the Cobourg Peninsula. The Cobourg is truly off the beaten path. It lies about 150 nautical miles northeast of Darwin. It's an irregularly shaped peninsula jutting into the Arafura Sea at the "top" of Arnhem Land. The entire peninsula and most of its offshore islands have been designated the Gurig National Park. The park is managed jointly by local Aborigines and the Northern Territory Conservation Commission. The joint management never allows more than 15 vehicles at one time in the park.

The Cobourg Peninsula is gently undulating country, with pristine sandy beaches, red cliffs, she-oaks, mangroves, and deeply indented bays that are ideal for sailing and exploring by boat. A great deal of the peninsula is an open forest of mixed gums and a wide variety of palms. The tall kentia palms are the most striking of the palms. Water buffalo, banteng (another now feral bovine transplant from Asia), wild pigs, sambar deer (they bark when alarmed), and a wide assortment of birds, large bats, and reptiles make the peninsula their home. As you walk the beaches, meter-long goannas are sometimes busily digging for turtle eggs. Porpoises, dugongs, flying fish, and several species of seagoing turtles seemed common during my visit. Behind the beaches in some areas are paperbark swamps dominated by resident saltwater crocodiles and an eerie stillness. There are also large open grasslands that are populated with both feral herbivores and agile wallabies. Port Essington, the large bay that nearly cuts the peninsula in half, is the dominant geographic feature. It also affords excellent boat access to the special qualities of the Cobourg.

The ruins of Victoria Settlement are fascinating. The ruins are on a remote promontory in Arnhem Land, about an hour's flight east of Darwin. The settlement was started in 1838 as a British outpost to keep the Dutch out of the region. It was closed in 1849, largely due to the poor location chosen and the hardships suffered by the inhabitants. Ironically, the best brickwork was done by convict masons—the cruder masonry is the work of their jailers.

*Accommodations.* When I visited the Cobourg Peninsula in 1988, for the first time, I was a passenger on the sail-charter yacht *Zachariah*. It was a once-in-a-lifetime experience, a trip to the remotest, wildest environment I'd ever visited. What a difference ten years make. Now, right where *Zachariah* dropped anchor and I explored the coastline in a small rubber boat and disturbed countless flying foxes (large bats with foxlike faces) sleeping in the mangroves sits Seven Spirit Bay Wilderness Lodge. This is luxury and wilderness. The lodge is just about as exclusive as exclusive gets. Guests are flown in by light aircraft from Darwin, which is more than an hour away. Sometimes guests arrive via Katherine and Kakadu, which requires less air time. The lodge takes care of all creature comforts and is a well managed eco-tourism destination. Guides take guests on walks to the ruins of the ill-fated British colony that perished here in 1849 and to wildlife viewing areas. There are also 4WD-vehicle excursions, short reconnaissance flights, and treks to newly discovered Aboriginal art galleries. The fishing here is as good as anywhere in the Top End for the desired fish—barramundi. The resort features 25 freestanding units that are well furnished and tastefully simple. There is also a library and dining area. It's a great place, if you can afford it. How about $A700 a night for a double in the high season and $A600 in the off-season? Air transfer from Darwin runs about $A300; phone 08-8979-0277.

# The Red Centre

Many people who have never visited Australia know something about the "Red Centre" of the country, where vast red deserts and stark landscapes make up the Outback. There is nowhere like the deserts of central Australia. This is where the great red monolith known for most of this century as Ayers Rock (now as Uluru) is found, as well the Kata-Tjuta (formerly the Olgas). These geologic images represent a timeless place baked unmercifully by the sun and mysteriously haunted. Uluru and Kata-Tjuta are the primary focus of most visitors to the region, but there are many other places worth exploring. If you can make the time, or have a special interest in birds and desert life-forms in general, you may want to spend a little extra time here.

There is a tendency to think of the Red Centre as extremely inhospitable and devoid of life, even by people who visit the region for short stays. The region can be unbearably hot when visited during the summer, but during the winter the weather is pleasant during the day and chilly at night. The spring can be spectacular when the desert plants bloom, and the fall can be pleasant too.

The region is populated with many kinds of spectacular wildlife, such as the pink Major Mitchell cockatoo, which is arguably the prettiest of all cockatoos. This is the home of the sleek perentie goanna, the largest lizard in Australia. Its markings of white circles on dark skin make it easy to identify. It measures six feet in length and glides slowly along, whipping its tongue out to pick up the scents wafting through its surroundings. There are dingoes, wild horses, and camels and a long list of colorful birds rarely seen outside of Australia. Much of the wildlife has learned to adapt to hot, dry conditions and is active only in the cooler parts of the day. The Red Centre is a pulsating place with many micro-environments and a plethora of desert vegetation, and is a place that has been inhabited by Aborigines for centuries. In fact, much of the Red Centre is owned by Aboriginal people, whose cultural and political presence will affect both subtle and overt aspects of your stay here.

## The Weather

The climate in the Red Centre is usually hot and dry. Midsummer temperatures (January) range from about 80°F to 125°F, while the winter (July) temperatures range from 36°F to 85°F. Nights can be cold.

## Information Sources

Central Australian Tourism Agency, corner of Hartley Street and Gregory Terrace, Alice Springs, N.T. 0870; phone 08-8952-5800. You'll get a lot of practical information on how to get to Uluru–Kata Tjuta National Park (Ayers Rock and the Olgas), Kings Canyon, Trephina Gorge, and other desert parks and areas of interest. You can also get information about the flora and fauna of these areas.

## Transportation

*Airlines.* The Alice Springs Airport is just off the Stuart Highway 20 kilometers south of the city. The Airport Shuttle costs about $A10 one way; there is a lower per-head rate for families. Cabs cost about $A20 one way and are generally overpriced in Alice Springs; phone 08-8952-1877. Airnorth flies throughout the Northern Territory; phone 08-8952-6666. Qantas also flies into and out of Alice. They have an office at the airport and on Todd Street; phone 08-8950-5211. Ansett has offices on Todd Street in Alice and at the airport; phone 13-13-10. Approximate ticket prices to other parts of Australia are as follows: Adelaide $A380; Sydney $A525; Perth $A500; Cairns $A450; Darwin $A350; Uluru $A160.

*Car rental.* Renting a car can be expensive. The company that I've used, which clearly tries to undercut the competition, is Territory-Thrifty, Scott Terrace; phone 08-8952-9999. Anything below $A70 a day for a mechanically sound car with air-conditioning is a good deal for a 2WD. The lowest you can expect a 4WD for is $A120 per day. Most destinations can be reached with a 2WD vehicle. Outback Rentals meets you at the airport and usually undercuts the bigger companies; phone 08-8953-5333. You can find Hertz at 76 Hartley Street; phone 08-8952-2644. Budget is on Gap Road; phone 08-8952-8899. Read your contract carefully. Often the insurance is voided if an accident occurs on a dirt road. Broken windshields are a constant problem in the Territory, most often because of a rock tossed up by an oncoming vehicle or by a passing car or truck.

*Camper-vans.* Try Budget (listed above) and Koala; phone 08-8952-9177.

*Buses.* Both McCafferty's and Greyhound operate out of Alice. For Greyhound phone 13-20-30; for McCafferty's phone 08-8952-3952. Approximate fares are as follows: Adelaide $A130; Darwin $A150. Darwin is about 20 hours away and Adelaide, 23 hours.

*Train.* One of the most pleasant trains rides I've had was on the *Ghan* (named after the Afghanis who, during the 1800s, helped open up the desert around Alice with their camels), which leaves Alice Springs for Adelaide in the afternoon two days a week. It also arrives from Adelaide two times a week. A seat costs about $A180, but most people splurge and purchase either a second-class sleeper for $A350 or a first-class sleeper for two for $A540. First-class includes meals. Phone Rail Australia: 08-8213-4429.

*Tour Coach Companies.* Numerous operators in Alice Springs offer everything from luxury coach—armchair tours that wouldn't know if you were awake or not—to smaller 4WD trips whose guides will take you anywhere and specialize their services for birders, rock hounds, or those wanting evidence of extraterrestrials. Visit the Central Australian Tourism Industry Association on Todd Street for advice and brochures.

## Alice Springs

Alice Springs was a lonely telegraph relay station practically smack dab in the middle of Australia. The town was romanticized and drew worldwide attention from the television series *A Town Called Alice.* However true to life the dramatization of Alice was, the town portrayed is not today's Alice Springs. Alice is a small, generally nondescript town of 27,000 inhabitants with supermarkets, shopping malls, a crisis hotline, a busy airport, and an overabundance of motels. Aside from the arid location, numerous Aborigines walking about town, and a few historic buildings, Alice Springs looks like a comparable-sized town anywhere in the United States. For the road traveler, Alice is a resting place midway across Australia on the Stuart Highway. For the air traveler (usually from Sydney) or rail rider (from Adelaide and Sydney), Alice is the starting point for touring Uluru (Ayers Rock) National Park and the spectacular gorge parks that lie east and west of the town.

## Things to Do

### Walkabout in Alice

While standing in the Todd Street Mall, you may wonder if any of historic Alice has survived. Here's an eleven-stop walk (two to three hours) that will introduce you to this aspect of Alice Springs. Most historic buildings open their doors to visitors at 9:00 A.M. and close them at 4:00 P.M. There is usually a nominal admissions fee.

The Museum of Central Australia in the Alice Building on Todd Street is a good place to get started. The museum houses minerals from the region, including parts of meteorites. There is also an outstanding collection of Aboriginal art and traditional tools.

Cross the street to the Flynn Memorial Church, which was constructed in memory of the Reverend John Flynn, the founder of the famed Royal Flying Doctor Service. Next door you'll find the Adelaide House. This was Alice's first hospital. Walk north and turn left at the Ansett Building. On the corner you'll find the Residency, which was the official residence for the ranking governmental officer. It's now a museum. Inside you'll find parts of meteorites from the Henbury Meteorite Craters south of Alice, a wildlife exhibit, and paintings by Albert Namatjira, Pro Hart, Sidney Nolan, and other top Australian artists. Continue walking west and you'll come to the modern courthouse and the Stuart Town Gaol (jail). The gaol is no longer used, but it is the oldest structure in Alice. Next, turn right onto Bath Street, follow it up to Wills Terrace, and cross near the Catholic Church. Look for the Lion's Walk next to the Youth Centre. This path leads to Anzac Hill, where you can look down on the city. After descending the hill, turn right onto Wills Terrace again and you'll come to the John Ross Memorial Park. Now travel south on

Railway Terrace until you come to the Coles Wall mural, a colorful depiction of Alice's history through the brushes of several local artists. Continue on Railway Terrace, turn left at Gregory Terrace, and cross Bath Street. Look for Panorama Guth, a large white structure. This is a privately owned gallery with a very rich pictorial history of the Centre. Walk south on Hartley Street, across Stott and Stuart Terraces. In the roundabout sits the John McDougall Stuart Memorial, in honor of the first explorer to cross the Centre. About 50 meters south of the memorial is the Royal Flying Doctor Service. End of walk.

### Events

Everything from national weight-lifting contests to rodeos, camel races, art shows, and wine tasting are scheduled annually on the town's hyperactive events calendar. The October Henley-on-Todd regatta featuring boat races in a dry riverbed is perhaps the best-known event. Each "boat" occupant's legs stick out of the bottom of the sometimes elaborate craft, "so they can get around in the absence of water." The event is a zany contest that features races and water fights. The Lion's Camel Cup, held in May, also rates as worthy of a look-see if you're in town. This race features some of the Centre's wildest characters in a flat-out camel race. For a schedule of events contact the Central Australian Tourism Industry Association on Gregory Terrace; phone 08-8952-5800.

## Restaurants

Oscar's Café at the Todd Street Mall offers good Italian food for a good price, about $A15 a head; phone 08-8953-0930. The Red Ochre Grill, also in the Todd Street Mall, is a unique experience. The food is varied, with vegetarian dishes offered. The atmosphere includes Aboriginal music and art; phone 08-8952-2066. Another good, low-cost restaurant is Kings Restaurant, Lasseters Casino, 93 Barret Street; phone 08-8950-7734. This is buffet style, with all you can eat at a fixed price. Bar Doppio, Todd Street Mall, has good vegetarian dishes for under $A20; phone 08-8952-6525.

## Accommodations

*Economy.* Pioneer Youth Hostel is at the intersection of Leichardt Terrace and Parsons Street, near the Todd Street Mall. Clean rooms with a swimming pool for cooling off. Six-to-a-room dorms, for $A15 per person; phone 08-8952-8855.

*Moderate.* Desert Rose Inn, 15 Railway Terrace; phone 08-8952-1411. Clean and quiet rooms near the center of the city. Wheelchair access. Rooms for about $A80. Territory Motor Inn, Leichardt Terrace; phone 08-8952-2066. Clean, helpful staff. Several rooms specially designed for the disabled. Rooms for approximately $A90.

*Upmarket.* Rydges Plaza Hotel, Barrett Drive; phone 08-8952-3822. This is supposed to be Alice's best hotel. It ought to be, with rooms that start around $A200. Wheelchair access.

*Camping and Caravan Parks.* Try the Heavitree Gap Complex; phone 08-8952-4866. This site is south of town, but it's amply outfitted to fulfill food and other daily needs. $A7 per site.

# Trips from Alice

## Day Trips

The activities in the area around Alice include bushwalking, wildlife photography, hot-air ballooning, gliding, camel rides (and treks), and motor adventuring.

## *Old Telegraph Station*

The Old Telegraph Station is about 3 kilometers north of town off the Stuart Highway. The stone buildings date back to the 1870s and are nicely restored. The settlement is complete and uncluttered. You will get a good sense of how it felt to live in the remote Centre during this era, and you'll come away with an understanding of how these people went about their daily lives. There were quite a few galahs and other parrots on the grounds the day I visited. There's a grassy picnic area with large shade trees and toilets.

The Strehlow Research Centre, at the corner of Larapinta Drive and Memorial Avenue, is a celebration of the local Aboriginal communities and Theodore Strehlow, a professor who worked among the Aborigines until his death in 1978. Strehlow was born on a government-run Aboriginal mission in the 1920s. He later returned and earned the trust of the Aranda (a local Aboriginal group) elders, who allowed him to record their vanishing customs. It is largely due to Strehlow that many of the details of initiation ceremonies are understood. But, in keeping with his agreement with the Aranda people, many of the most secret customs are still under lock and key because Aranda custom forbids public sharing of sacred knowledge. The center has one of the best collections of Aboriginal artifacts in Australia. There is a nominal entrance fee; phone 08-8951-8788.

The School of the Air, near the Old Telegraph Station on Head Street, is the world's largest classroom. This is where school lessons are broadcast to the remotest stations in the Red Centre. If school is in session you can watch the instruction. If school isn't in session, the lessons and how the school operates will be explained to you; phone 08-8951-6834.

The Frontier Camel Farm, 8 kilometers out of town on the Ross Highway, is the camel place near Alice that's the easiest to find. Dromedary (one-humped) camels arrived in Australia with their Afghani owners in the nineteenth century. Pushed by greed and the hope of finding gold and other precious mineral deposits, Afghanis, with their camels, helped open up the Centre by toting equipment and men inland into areas too inhospitable for a horse. When the automobile and train came into the region, the camel, as a commercial form of transport, was suddenly obsolete. The result was that camels were released into the wild. Camels did well on the vast brushlands of the Centre and now number in excess of 40,000 animals, making Australia's wild camel population the largest in the world. In the 1970s camels began to catch on again, this time as pack animals taking adventurers into remote areas. Several outfits operating around Alice and South Australia offer long-distance camel treks of 10 to 500 kilometers. For a lineup of offerings, check with the Central Australian Tourism Industry Association, Gregory Terrace, Alice Springs, NT 0870; phone 08-8952-5800.

I've taken several long multiday camel treks in Australia and found the ones with well-trained animals to be a top-quality experience. Despite rumors to the contrary, a well-trained camel is predictable, easy to control, and even affectionate. However, camels are large, strong animals and must be managed properly to ensure the safety of clients who may not have prior experience with large live-stock. Also, some camels have strangely spiteful attitudes. Unfortu-nately, not all camel-trek operators take reasonable precautions to ensure the safety of their customers. As a litmus test for the operator, ask him if you can "free-rein your camel." This means ride him solo, not in a string. If the operator says, "Sure mate, no problem," think twice. It's only the exceptional camel that can be reined by a stranger. Camels are herd animals that work very well tied to one another, which is how to safely ride most of them. I was on a camel once who panicked upon seeing a feral goat and bolted. At the time I was free-reining out of sight of the rest of the camels in my group. As my camel wheeled in panic I realized jumping off was out of the ques-tion. It's a long way down from a camel, especially from one who is careening over rough terrain at a full gallop and bellowing at the top of his lungs. By time things calmed down, we'd run over a mile and all my equipment was spread behind us—and I considered myself fortunate because the camel hadn't tripped and landed on top of me.

The Frontier Camel Farm is an introduction to camels. You can ride one in a safe manner, and there is a small museum explaining the roles of camels in the white settlement of Australia. There are also bits of information on feats of endurance and strength accomplished by camels; phone 08-8953-0444.

## Parks and Reserves East of Alice Springs

Six nature parks and reserves on the Ross Highway offer a variety of experiences. Camping is allowed in five of these areas.

### Emily and Jessie Gap Nature Park

At the 13-kilometer mark down the Ross Highway from Alice Springs is the Emily and Jessie Gap Nature Park. This is a place of "usually" permanent water and was once popular with Aborigines. It is distinguished by two gaps punched through the narrow Mac-Donnell Ranges. Camping isn't allowed, but it's a good picnic spot.

### Corroboree Rock Conservation Reserve

The reserve is at the 48-kilometer mark. This is also an area used his-torically by Aborigines. It's the first camping area on Ross Highway from Alice Springs. I saw a half dozen sand goannas here making the best of an unguarded lunch.

## Trephina Gorge Nature Park

This is 85 kilometers from Alice Springs. It has excellent day walks and enough wildlife (in the morning) to hold your interest. There are two deep gorges in this 1,800-hectare park. The Trephina Gorge itself and the John Hayes Rockhole are memorable natural features. The contrast of shiny white-trunked ghost gums and red cliffs is striking. I saw large flocks of galahs and budgies. The park can be reached by passenger car, and camping is allowed.

## N'Dhala Gorge Nature Park

Next, 98 kilometers from Alice Springs, is the N'Dhala Gorge Nature Park, which is primarily known for its rock engravings. Camping is allowed and there are toilets. It's located on the dirt road to Ross River Station.

## Arltunga Historical Reserve

At 111 kilometers is Arltunga, a historic gold-mining ghost town with many of its stone buildings still standing. Arltunga was a bustling town at the turn of the century. There's a police station, jail, cemetery, government works office, numerous parts of other buildings, and a number of mines. The weathered stone structures are excellent photographic subjects.

## Ruby Gorge Nature Park

If you're in a 4WD, you can reach Ruby Gorge Nature Park by heading east another 47 kilometers. Ruby Gorge is remote and reputedly teeming with wildlife. I didn't have the right vehicle to find out.

# Parks West of Alice

There are eight national parks or nature reserves directly west of Alice Springs (not counting Uluru and Kings Canyon, which are to the southwest). The farthest one is 175 kilometers from Alice. A one- to three-day excursion to the west is well worth the effort.

To get to the western parks and reserves you must find Larapinta Drive. Larapinta intersects the Stuart Highway just below the railroad station. About 5 kilometers down the track you'll come to the

Alice Springs Desert Park, which has an excellent series of exhibits featuring a great number of the Centre's rarely seen nocturnal animals. There is also a well-done film explaining the evolution and adaptation of the surprisingly prolific plant life found throughout the region. There are good opportunities to photograph rare wildlife. John Flynn's grave is about 1 kilometer farther on Larapinta Drive. (Flynn was the founder of the Royal Flying Doctor Service.) At the 16-kilometer mark is White Gums Park—not a real park, but a place to dine (except Mondays) in a wild setting that has a few nature trails and abundant bird life.

## Simpson's Gap National Park

Just down the track a few more kilometers is 30,950-hectare Simpson's Gap National Park, the second-largest park of the eight western parks and reserves. Simpson's Gap has an interpretive center and several marked short walks. There's a sizable colony of rock wallabies in the scenic gaps in the MacDonnell Range escarpment. At the 51-kilometer mark you'll come to Standley Chasm, a striking red-walled cut through the MacDonnell Ranges made by the usually dry Hugh River. The chasm's straight vertical red walls and sandy bottom are the cleanest-cut gorge through the MacDonnells. The walk through the chasm takes about 20 minutes. There are several semitame resident dingoes here who will pose for photographs if they think they'll get a handout. Keep in mind, though, that they are wild. The park has a kiosk and barbecue areas.

## Finke Gorge National Park

As you continue west on Larapinta Drive, the road forks at about the 54-kilometer mark. Larapinta Drive continues to the left and becomes dirt where it enters the Hermannsburg Aboriginal Land and eventually comes to Finke Gorge National Park, the largest and probably the most noteworthy of the parks directly west of Alice. Finke Gorge is not advisable for a passenger car. The 45,856-hectare park is a true wilderness area. It features the Finke River Gorge and Palm Valley, with its cabbage palms that offer an interesting contrast to the red-walled gorges. There's a large area of sand dunes in the southern end of the park.

Finke Gorge National Park was established to protect plants unique to central Australia. Of the 400 species in the park 30 are classified as rare. *Livistona mariae,* a rare cabbage palm, has survived for more than 10,000 years from a time when the area was much wetter. The park also has a wide assortment of wildlife. Dingoes and euro kangaroos are common and most readily sighted around dawn.

For short walks I'd recommend exploring Palm Valley and walking to Initiation Rock, where initiation ceremonies of the Aranda Aborigines were held. The park has toilets and showers that are most often used by tour company clients that visit the area in 4WD vehicles from Alice Springs.

## Glen Helen Gorge National Park

The right fork of Larapinta Drive (at the 54-kilometer mark) is Namatjira Drive, named after Australia's most famous Aboriginal painter, who lived in the area. On Namatjira Drive are a number of small reserves—Ellery Creek, Serpentine Gorge, Helen Gorge, Ormiston Gorge, Glen Helen Gorge, and Redbank Gorge. Ormiston Gorge and Glen Helen Gorge proved the most worthwhile. They're close to each other and about 132 kilometers from Alice Springs.

*Accommodations.* Glen Helen Gorge has a campground, pub, counter meals, and an outside deck that looks out across the Finke River (often with water!) to sheer red-rock walls; phone 08-8956-7489.

## Ormiston Gorge National Park

Ormiston Gorge National Park is a few kilometers north of the Glen Helen Lodge across Namatjira Drive. Encompassing 4,655 hectares in the heart of the western MacDonnell Ranges, Ormiston is the most complete park on Namatjira Drive. Its main feature is a deep fissure cut by Ormiston Creek through the quartzite escarpment. The creek flows into Ormiston Pound, where it creates a large permanent water hole surrounded by sharp ridges.

There are more than 400 kinds of plants in the park. Look for the ghost gums. If you rub your hand across their trunks, your palm will be covered by a fine white dust. The much bigger, flaky white-barked river red gums are also prominent. The native fuchsia bush is also common. It stands about two meters high and has a tubular lilac-blue flower. The drooping willowlike tree is ironwood, a kind of acacia.

The park's wildlife is wary but plentiful. Euros and rock wallabies live on the steep escarpments. Perentie and sand goannas are commonly sighted. More than 160 species of birds have been recorded. Look for ring-necked parrots, galahs, budgies, and Major Mitchell cockatoos. You may also see Bourke's parrot in the mulga trees. It's a middle-sized bird with blue shoulders and a pink chest.

There are three good walks. Probably the most popular is the 4-kilometer walk through the gorge and along Ormiston Creek to Ormiston Pound. The round-trip is 8 kilometers. Take drinking water.

# Heading South Toward Uluru–Kata Tjuta National Park

Uluru–Kata Tjuta National Park (Uluru was formerly called Ayers Rock and Kata Tjuta was known as the Olgas) is the primary destination of people visiting the Centre. However, along the Stuart and Lasseter Highways, which take you to Uluru, there are a number of worthwhile points of interest.

## *Kings Canyon National Park*

Kings Canyon National Park is 324 kilometers from Alice Springs. It's often visited on the return from Uluru by tour companies. It's a spectacular canyon bigger than any other in the Centre. There is a somewhat challenging and entirely inspiring walk from the parking area along Kings Creek, which runs at the base of a huge arcing red cliff. Eventually the walk comes to a rock pool (and waterfall, if you're lucky) where the gorge narrows and turns sharply north. You'll see cycad palms and other remnant tropical vegetation. Continue walking for about 600 meters and look for a track heading east. The trail climbs up a potentially treacherous incline, past caves, and onto the escarpment along the canyon's spectacular south wall. The trail then descends a steep incline to complete the loop. The walk takes two to three hours. You can do it in either direction. Take ample water. It's an easy walk except for the inclines, which are smooth rock surfaces. Bush camping exists in the area. There are full-amenities campsites for $A25 at Kings Canyon Resort; phone 08-8956-7442. Dorm rooms go for $A35. Kings Canyon Resort also has high-end accommodations. "High-end" in this part of the desert means a nice room that isn't a dormitory with enough privacy so that you can actually sleep with your spouse. If you've been to Yulara you know the drill for a double for a night: $A250.

# Uluru–Kata Tjuta National Park: Ayers Rock and the Olgas

Uluru–Kata Tjuta National Park is Australia's best-known park and is visited by thousands of people from throughout the world annually. It's about 480 kilometers from Alice Springs. The two outstanding geological features at Uluru–Kata Tjuta National Park are known around the world as Ayers Rock and the Olgas. Today the official name of the monolithic Ayers Rock is Uluru. The Olgas are now formally Kata Tjuta ("many heads"). These "new" official names are Aboriginal titles that were always used by the local people, who speak the Pitjantjatjara dialect common to central Australia.

The Anangu, the Pitjantjatjara-speaking people living in the park, were reestablished as legal owners of Uluru National Park in 1985 in a precedent-setting move by the Australian government. This was the first time traditional owners were given legal ownership and authentic power in running a park. Today the Anangu have the majority voting power on the management board that runs Uluru. Former superintendent Chip Morgan, a white Australian trained in park management, explains Uluru's unique method of management: "This isn't a Yellowstone or Yosemite model. We worked under the direction of the traditional owners in protecting Uluru. I listened and fulfilled their wishes. They are the moral and spiritual managers of this park and despite the prestige that may be credited to my formal education, I'm a child compared to the traditional owners. They are the world's greatest conservationists and representatives of the world's oldest surviving culture. The focus is to protect the culture and the environment."

Uluru is a powerful place that embodies the spirit and strength of an ancient culture and timeworn continent. The park covers 132,566 hectares of the arid center of Australia. It is surrounded by immense tracts of Aboriginal reserves. The huge shimmering monoliths of Uluru and Kata Tjuta jut above the flat vegetated sand plain like great alien creatures. Uluru is listed on the register of the National Estate and is on the World Heritage list. For centuries the region has been the focus of cultural activities of the western desert peoples. The Anangu (the name used by the Aborigines living near Uluru) who are active in creating park policy wish to broaden the visitors' understanding of the park to include their perceptions of their homeland. The Anangu have also moved to protect some sacred sites and their community at Mutitjulu. You will see signposted areas forbidding entrance. These are sacred areas that aren't to be visited by outsiders under any circumstances. If you'd like to learn more about Uluru, buy a copy of *Uluru: An Aboriginal History of Ayers Rock*, by Robert Layton ($A35) at the Uluru–Kata Tjuta Cultural Centre near the base of Uluru. The book is approved of by the Anangu.

Contrary to popular belief, the arid Centre around Uluru–Kata Tjuta National Park is not devoid of vegetation. Irregularly shaped mulgas, large desert oaks, and spinifex (waiting to turn you into a pin cushion) are found in the park. Plants actually flower most of the year around Uluru. In winter (June) desert thryptomene with its small pink-and-white flowers is prevalent around Yulara. Later, yellow myrtle and desert fringe-myrtle bloom. If you come across a large green flower with dark stripes you've found a parrot flower. In spring the wattles take center stage, with the yellow clusters of the murray wattle and the bright white bark and white masses of the Victorian wattle's flowers. Grevilleas and hakeas also occur in the park.

There are many other parks in Australia where you'll see more wildlife than at Uluru. The Centre is a harsh country where the shortage of water holes limits the numbers of animals. When there is water, creatures are plentiful.

The reptiles are well represented. Geckos, skinks, goannas, dragons, legless lizards, and a wide variety of snakes occur throughout the park. The spiny-tailed gecko, with a tail that makes it clear how it got its name, is the most common reptile. There are six species of goannas in the park, ranging from the pygmy goanna to the nearly two-meter perentie goanna.

More than 160 kinds of birds have been sighted in the park. I've included the Anangu name with the English name. Usually, the most plentiful species are: zebra finches (*nyiinyii*), black-faced wood swallows (*tjalputjalpu*), budgerigars (*kiilykiilykari*), Major Mitchell cockatoos (*kakalyalya*), galahs (*piyarpiyarpa*), black kites (*pninkgka*), wedge-tailed eagles (*walawuru*), and brown falcons (*kirkinpa*). When the water holes are full, birds are generally plentiful.

Three of Uluru's four large mammals are marsupials: the red and euro kangaroos and the black-footed rock wallaby. Each is found in a different habitat. The red kangaroo is usually found in open flat areas. The euro prefers steep slopes and rocky areas. Rock wallabies are always found near precipitous rocky outcrops. Dingoes, the fourth large mammal in the park, are placental mammals. They're found throughout the park—especially around the campground at Yulara and near picnic areas.

## Uluru: The Rock

Uluru is often billed as the world's "largest solitary monolith," possessing "mystical powers." I was skeptical of these claims. I'm still doubtful of the "largest monolith" claim, but I can verify that it does have a special quality. It's the kind of feeling I've had in Yosemite Valley, Death Valley, the Grand Canyon, and other places where nature's power is so pervasive that preservation and protection are given. These natural cathedrals transcend mere physical description.

In simple figures Uluru's circumference is 9 kilometers. It takes about 3 hours to walk around the base. From east to west Uluru measures 3.1 kilometers, and from north to south, 2 kilometers. The summit is 348 meters above the desert floor. Its dimensions don't seem so grand, yet foreigners flock to ogle it. They leap from their cars, leaving the doors open as they madly adjust their cameras and angle off through the scrub to locate the perfect position from which to press the shutter. Uluru's power is partly in the contrast. It's a red mass of weathered granite jutting out of an endless desert of dancing mirages. The rock, though unchanged for untold centuries, is a constant visual illusion. In a few moments at sunrise and sunset it changes from a dull brown to hues of scorching red. During the few moments of color change, cameras click furiously to capture the glow. Bring a wide-angle lens and a polarizing filter with you.

*Uluru (Ayers Rock), Uluru–Kata Tjuta National Park.* PHOTO BY ERIC HOFFMAN.

Uluru and Kata Tjuta are above all else visual experiences, and the best visual effects are at sunrise and sunset. The park opens 30 minutes before sunrise and closes 1 hour after sunset. If you're "doing Uluru in a day," visit the rock in the morning and Kata Tjuta in the evening. A ranger will make sure you don't linger long when closing time comes. There's no camping at either site.

The sunrise viewing area for Uluru is located on the northeastern side of the rock. The sunset viewing area is 5 kilometers south of the rock. Most visitors seem to hang around Uluru for sunsets and sunrises and for good reason—they're spectacular. However, I found sunset at Kata Tjuta equal in quality and absent of people.

While you rush about Uluru dutifully listening to the rangers, keep in mind what a senior Mutitjulu said about tourists: "They hear a little about this place and a little about that place and they put it all together in one bucket and shake it up. Everything gets broken and mixed up, and when they pour it out in their country they don't know what pieces go together. They should take it home in their hearts. Then they remember."

## *Walks*

Climbing the rock is the most strenuous way to get to know it. The 1.6-kilometer route to the summit is known as the "climb." It takes about 2 hours round-trip, but the park service is now currently discouraging climbing "the Rock" in accordance with policies of the Aboriginal elders who own the park. There have been more than 25 recorded deaths during the climb: most from heart attacks, and some from falls.

Ranger-guided walks unrelated to the climb are conducted daily. They start at the base of the climb and last a little more than an hour. The Liru Walk is probably the most popular guided walk. It starts at the ranger station, lasts around 2 hours, and ends at the base of the climb. It's sometimes guided by local Aborigines. The number of people allowed on this walk is limited, so book at the ranger station. There's also a 9-kilometer walk around Uluru. I found this as pleasant and as private as the pre–tour bus climb to the top of Uluru. The walk around the monolith gives you a constantly changing view of the rock that is more personal than driving the Ring Road. There are several signposted sacred sites that must not be entered under any circumstances. The walk takes about 3 hours.

## Kata Tjuta: The Olgas

Kata Tjuta is on a 30-kilometer dirt road that slows your approach. It's as powerful as Uluru and goes through the same hues of brown and red color alterations at dawn and dusk. Kata Tjuta is actually 36 rock domes, the biggest being Mount Olga, which rises 546 meters above the desert. The domes cover 35 kilometers and are a virtual maze once you walk into their narrow valleys. The best photographic opportunities are on the west side at dusk.

## *Walks*

There are three main walks in Kata Tjuta. On all of them it is important to heed the safety recommendations of the park service. The Mount Olga Gorge Walk is the most popular. The first part is relatively easy. But as the gorge narrows, the climb becomes more strenuous and requires rock scrambles over bus-sized boulders. This portion is suitable only for people with climbing experience or reasonable balance and judgment. Talk to the rangers before attempting the entire walk. I found the latter part of the walk more strenuous than scenic, and the first half the other way around.

## Punu Ngura

Some 700 Pitjantjatjara- and Yankunytjatara-speaking Aborigines contribute artwork from points throughout the Centre to the Maruku Arts and Crafts Centre. The outlet at Uluru–Kata Tjuta National Park for this artwork is Punu Ngura, which means "woodcraft place" in Pitjantjatjara. Punu Ngura is next door to the ranger station, which is practically under the shadow of the rock. There are often Anangu elders at Punu Ngura who are quite willing to converse and explain the artwork. The better your Pitjantjatjara, the more expansive the conversation. There is a wide selection of artwork to choose from, both mass-produced and one-of-a-kind pieces. The Anangu have constructed three structures at Punu Ngura: a senior men's meeting place, a senior women's meeting place, and a grandmother's shade. You may take pictures of the buildings but not of the Anangu: they consider being photographed offensive.

## Yulara (the Tourist Community near the Rock)

Uluru–Kata Tjuta is such a world-renowned destination that an entire small town–monopoly sits right outside the park boundary (20 kilometers from the Rock), where it serves the needs of tourists. You could argue pretty easily that it fleeces tourists as well as serves them. Prices are high, and since there's nowhere else to go, hotel rooms will probably stay high, unless a "tourists' rights group" makes a stand.

*Real Information and Rental Cars.* Don't stop at the Visitors Centre; it's really a glorified tourist shop that I suspect is coyly dubbed with the name Visitors Centre to lure the unsuspecting into the premises. For real information visit the Tourist Information Centre in the main square (Yulara Town Square, NT 0872); phone 08-8956-2240. Here you'll find piles of literature, maps, weather information, and rental-car companies: Territory Rent-a-Car (phone 08-8956-2030), Hertz (phone 08-8956-2244), and Avis (phone 08-8956-2266).

*Air Travel.* Many visitors arrive directly by air instead of by the traditional method of air travel to Alice Springs and a 460-kilometer bus ride to Yulara. Connellan Airport is about 10 kilometers north of Yulara. There is an airport shuttle. Airnorth, Qantas, and Ansett all regularly fly in and out of Connellan Airport (See "Airlines" in the section on the Red Centre for phone numbers.) A one-way ticket from Alice Springs is about $A165; from Sydney, $A500; from Darwin, Cairns, Melbourne, and Adelaide, also about $A500.

*Bus.* Greyhound Pioneer makes regular runs to and from Alice Springs.

*Accommodations.* The campground here has powered sites, and a one-night stay costs about $A20. There are showers, toilets, and cooking pits. Outback Pioneer Hotel is a youth hostel with large dorm rooms with about 20 beds per room. They charge for luggage storage, which isn't the norm for hostels; phone 08-8956-2737. Forget moderate accommodations: everything else goes for more than $A250 a double. Could this be a one-town monopoly? Or is this monopricing phenomenon just a coincidence that stimulates tourist lawyers and legal scholars to ponder over and inquire into the application of price-fixing laws in Australia? Regardless, think $A250 a night and then take your choice: Sails in the Desert; phone 08-8956-2200. Some of the rooms look toward Uluru. The gardens are impressive. Outback Pioneer Hotel; phone 08-8956-2170. Separate cabins large enough for a normal-sized family is the main feature. Desert Gardens Hotel; phone 08-8956. This 60-room hotel has the best capacity for large groups, and many rooms view Uluru. Addresses for all the above are Yulara Drive, NT 0872.

# PART VII

# South Australia

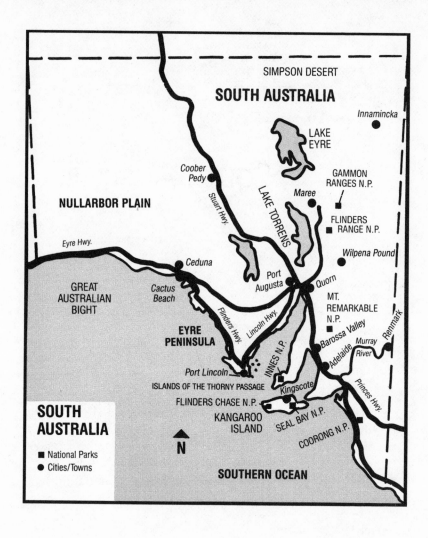

# Overview

For the adventurer, South Australia is the best-kept secret in Australia. Even Australians are more likely to visit New South Wales, Queensland, or Tasmania. But when I asked *Australian Geographic* founder Dick Smith to list the top five wild areas in Australia, Kangaroo Island and Cooper Creek were the first two he mentioned—both in South Australia. He also favorably mentioned the Flinders Ranges, Coober Pedy, the Coorong, and the vast Nullarbor Plain—all in South Australia. There's also the Murray River, Australia's biggest river system; the Barossa Valley wineries; and the remote islands off the Eyre Peninsula, ideal for adventure-sail charters. And then there's Adelaide, surrounded by parklands and nestled under Mount Lofty. It's my nominee for second-best large city in Australia.

South Australia is a gigantic 984,000 square kilometers. That's about the size of Texas, Mississippi, Louisiana, and half of Oklahoma. There are a scant 1.3 million people living in this area, mostly clustered around Adelaide.

South Australia presents an extremely inviting picture—especially for the do-it-yourself traveler. For starters there are scores of offshore islands, with Kangaroo Island having the most to offer. Most of them are rarely visited and many have unique ecosystems and unusually unafraid wildlife. Along the shorelines of these islands and on the Yorke Peninsula are some of the best temperate-zone scuba-diving areas in the world, with underwater visibility often exceeding 100 meters.

South Australia is the driest state on the driest continent. But this doesn't mean the interior is a featureless, flat surface good only for solar egg frying. Just a half day's drive from Adelaide is the heart of the Flinders Ranges, probably the most spectacular and accessible arid mountain range in Australia. For the dedicated trekker there's the ambitious Heysen Trail, which starts south of Adelaide and meanders for 1,200 kilometers through the heart of the Flinders before ending at Mount Hopeless. There are three national parks in the Flinders Ranges. And throughout the Flinders are marked trails for the day hiker or long-distance trekker.

Farther north in the Flinders is Gammon Ranges National Park. The park is run entirely by the Adnjamanthahna Aborigines. Simmering out in the flats is Lake Eyre, the largest salt expanse in the world, and similarly featureless Frome, Gregory, and Torrens Lakes. The glittery white salt surfaces, pastel-colored surroundings, and unique plant forms—plus the dancing mirages—create a strikingly different landscape for a North American. The stark beauty could just as well be on another planet.

Back on the coast, and only 45 minutes south of Adelaide, is the Coorong, a 123-kilometer undulating plant-and-dune-covered coastal sand spit. The Coorong is one of Australia's great seabird habitats, accentuated with the ghostly remains of a once-thriving Aboriginal culture. On the way to the Coorong are a series of Australia's safest surf beaches. Inland is the Riverlands, where the Murray River has arched and twisted for thousands of years, forming secondary waterways and tree-lined lagoons that are ideal for quiet-water canoeing, camping, and viewing wildlife.

On the western expanse of the state is Port Lincoln, a tuna-and-grain port and the stepping-off place for scores of offshore islands. Farther west the treeless and seemingly endless Nullarbor Plain abruptly terminates 100 meters above the Southern Ocean. The limestone cliffs that plunge from the Nullarbor to the sea outline the Great Australian Bight. Adventure-tour groups going into the area have found fossilized footprints of now-extinct giant kangaroos. On the way to the Nullarbor you pass through immense barley holdings punctuated with sentinel silos, Aboriginal reserves, conservation parks, small towns, huge sheep stations, and spectacular coastal dune systems. There's world-class surfing at remote Cactus Beach. There's no place else on earth like the Nullarbor.

The human history in South Australia was one of abundance for the Aboriginal peoples, who were decimated with the coming of the Europeans. However, for the most part, the European history in South Australia is one of higher ideals than in the other colonies. This is the only state that didn't rely on convict labor, and Adelaide has benefited by enlightened stewardship that has avoided many of the pitfalls of helter-skelter growth. Near the coast around Adelaide are many excellent wineries.

# Adelaide

Despite Adelaide's nearly one million people, it still enjoys the charm and friendliness of a prosperous large town. Adelaide doesn't have Sydney's flash or Melbourne's staid reserve. Instead, its underpinnings are "old money," a sane pace, and a freshly scrubbed wholesomeness where higher human ideals and appreciation for nature have been at the forefront of civic discussion from the start.

Adelaide got its splendid layout from its founder, Colonel William Light. In 1836, despite considerable sniping from his fellow Brits, Colonel Light laid down his vision of Adelaide. He mapped a grid of streets into a square mile along the Torrens River. This was to be the city proper. Light declared that parklands would surround the city. The city was named Adelaide by King William IV in honor of his wife, Queen Adelaide.

The skyline has changed considerably over the years—always reaching farther upward—but the wide streets and surrounding parklands, grand old brick and stone churches, and vintage buildings from the early years are still prominent features.

Getting around Adelaide is easy. The streets that box in the city's square mile (which is really a rectangle) are North Terrace, West Terrace, South Terrace, and Hutt Street. Running south and north through the center is King William Street. All other through streets intersect these, and the entire city can be crossed on foot in less than 45 minutes. It's nearly impossible to stay lost for long in Adelaide. The suburb of North Adelaide is across the Torrens River and parklands.

## Transportation

*Air Travel.* Adelaide International Airport is 6 kilometers to the west of Adelaide. A cab to the city costs about $A15. The airport bus costs about half as much; phone 08-8381-5311. Several airlines operate here: Qantas (phone 13-13-13), Airlines of South Australia (phone 08-8682-5688), Kendell Air (part of Ansett; phone 11-13-00). Emu Airlines serves Kangaroo Island; phone 1-800-182-353 (toll-free).

*Bus.* There is a well-run city bus system. In addition, the free Beeline system runs between the train station and Prince William Street in the central city. The Central Bus Station, 101 Franklin Street in the city's center, is where the long-haul buses come and go; phone 8415-5533. Both Greyhound Pioneer (phone 13-20-30) and McCafferty's (phone 13-14-99) make runs to Melbourne, Sydney, Alice Springs, and Perth. It's 800 kilometers to Melbourne for $A48 and 10 hours; 1,600 kilometers to Sydney for about $A100 and 23 hours of your time. Perth is $A190 and 34 hours; Alice Springs, $A130 and 19 hours. These prices are roughly 10 to 25 percent of what it costs to fly to the same destinations. For specific destinations inside the state, Premier Stateliner often provides the best service. Besides regular routes to Wilpena Pound, Port Lincoln, and other off-the-main-track destinations, they offer special tours of Kangaroo Island and the Barrossa Valley; phone 08-8415-5500.

There is also an "alternative" long-haul bus service. The Wayward Bus Company offers a unique service. The bus travels between Adelaide and Melbourne, and Adelaide and Alice Springs. The bus is usually on the road for four to six hours a day, and the driver doubles as the guide. The bus holds 20 people and stops at interesting places along the route. The trips takes about three days. If you like this idea, contact the Wayward Bus Company, 237 Hutt Street, Adelaide, S.A. 5000; phone 08-8232-6646. The fare is higher than that of the straight-through haulers.

For information on all forms of transportation, locate a free copy of *Metroguide,* which can be found in newsstands, transportation terminals, and restaurants.

*Rail.* Adelaide is a rail hub. The Keswick Interstate Rail Passenger Terminal is a modern, clean, and busy station located about 3 kilometers west of the city center. There are two famous services: the *Indian Pacific* from Adelaide to Perth, which takes 39 hours, and the *Ghan,* which takes 20 hours to reach Alice Springs. The *Indian Pacific* also goes to Sydney (28 hours). I can fully recommend the *Ghan* as a premier rail experience because of the international flavor,

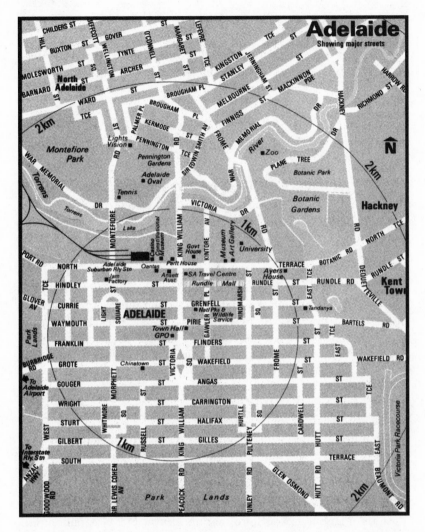

high-quality evening meal, and comfortable sleeping cars. When you awake there is a leisurely breakfast service while a changing panorama glides past; in the afternoon, the journey ends. The *Ghan* is the right length, travels through interesting country, and has people from all over the world on board who are going to or coming from Alice Springs. On the *Indian Pacific* I had the opposite experience. The endless monotony of the Nullarbor Plain, with all wildlife scared away by the train's approach, induced claustrophobia. And when I tried to chat up my fellow passengers, most of whom were geriatrics making use of travel vouchers, I couldn't get a conversation started.

There are two other trains: the *Melbourne Express* stops at Adelaide on its way between Sydney and Melbourne, and the *Overland* runs between Melbourne and Adelaide.

*Car.* There's no shortage of car-rental companies. For a cheap rental, try Rent-a-Bug; phone 08-8234-0655. For a conventional new car, there's Avis (136 North Terrace; phone 08-8410-5552) and Hertz (233 Morphett Street; phone 08-8231-2856). Try Caudell's Explorer Self-Drive for 4WDs; phone 08-8410-5552. Since 4WDs are not needed for most destinations, make sure you need one before you fork out the considerably higher rental costs. The Royal Automobile Association, 41 Hindmarsh Square, has many detailed motoring maps and advice on car insurance; phone 08-8202-4500.

*Bicycles.* If you like bikes you might consider renting one in Adelaide. The streets around the Torrens River and the Botanic Gardens are good casual riding areas, as is the coast around Glenelg. Try Freewheelin (phone 08-8232-6860) or, in Glenelg on the Anzac Highway, Holdfast Cycles (phone 08-8294-4537). Ride in the Adelaide Hills if you want friendly scenery and some steep ups and downs.

## Information Sources

The South Australia Tourism and Travel Centre, 1 King William Street, has piles of literature and maps. The friendly and professional staff members speak several languages and can make travel and accommodation reservations; phone 08-8303-2070; E-mail SthAusTour@Tourism.sa.gov.au.

At the National Parks Information Centre (77 Grenfell Street; phone 08-8204-1910) you'll find concisely written pamphlets on all of the national parks. In some cases there is a great deal of detail. Flinders Ranges and Outback South Australia Tourism, 142 Gawler Street, has copious information on the Flinders Ranges, Wilpena Pound, the Gammon Ranges, and other remote scenic areas; phone 08-8223-3995. For detailed trail maps for the Flinders Ranges and other remote areas, contact the Department of Industry and Trade, Recreation and Sport, 27 Valetta Road, Kidman Park, S.A. 5001; phone 08-8416-6677.

For a complete insider's look at Adelaide, purchase *Adelaide's Secrets,* a 165-page guide by Cristene Carey and Margaret-Ann Williams. These women have included everything from city and suburban walking trails to pastry shops, pubs, and the like. The emphasis is on places where you can take the whole family. The book is well worth it if you aren't content with just scratching the surface. Try Imprint Booksellers at 80 Hindley Street.

Adelaide—and its surrounding parks and nearby countryside—has a great number of excellent day walks. *Adelaide and Country Walks,* by James D. Crinion, describes 30 walks. Crinion also outlines walks in a dozen conservation parks within an hour's drive of Adelaide. The publication is clearly written and provides maps. It is available in local bookstores.

## Things to Do

### Adelaide Arts Festival and Festival Centre

If you happen to hit town in an even-numbered year during February and March, the big event is the Adelaide Arts Festival, which has achieved international status. The festival takes place at the Adelaide Festival Centre, located on the Torrens River on the northern edge of the city. It lasts 20 days and features about 350 live performances in drama, dance, music, and poetry. The range is remarkable: everything from cabaret to full-blown symphony orchestras, from Aboriginal dance troupes to Shakespearean drama. There are also art exhibits and lectures by top writers, sculptors, and painters from Europe, North America, and Asia.

Even on odd-numbered years the $A30 million Adelaide Festival Centre has a full venue of artistic events: drama, music (jazz, rock, and classical), ballet, modern dance, and cinema. The Festival Centre has theaters, outside amphitheaters, and auditoriums that seat between 300 and 2,000 guests nightly.

### Botanic Gardens

On North Terrace are the 690-hectare Botanic Gardens and the Adelaide Zoo. Australian flora makes up a 15-hectare portion of the gardens. The colorful water lily collection is perhaps the best of its kind in the world. The Bicentennial Conservatory houses a small tropical rain forest. The gardens can be reached by walking east past the University of Adelaide on North Terrace.

## Historic Buildings

Adelaide shed its "city of churches" image long ago, but many of the grand old stone churches and buildings from that era still decorate the city. The greatest concentration of historic buildings is on North Terrace (easy walking distance from the government travel center at 1 King William Street. On nearby North Terrace you'll find the Parliament House and Constitutional Museum, the Government House, Trinity Church, the University of Adelaide, the state library, and the South Australian Museum.

## Museums

Everyone in Adelaide seems to be proud of the South Australian Museum, on North Terrace, and for good reason. It has excellent collections of Aboriginal and South Pacific island cultures. The natural history section will give you a look at many forms of nocturnal wildlife that make up the bulk of Australia's fauna; phone 08-8207-7500.

A number of other museums and historic buildings are noteworthy. The Tandanya-Aboriginal Cultural Institute, 253 Grenfell Street, is the first exhibit hall of its kind in South Australia. Speakers explain the Aboriginal history of South Australia. The Art Gallery of South Australia, near the university on North Terrace, has a high-quality collection of oil paintings, sculptures, and watercolors from top Australian and European artists; phone 08-8207-7000. All of the museums have a nominal entrance fee of a few dollars.

## Historic Houses

One of the most memorable aspects of Adelaide is its wealth of beautiful stone houses, in the style often termed "colonial" or "classical" Australian architecture. Throughout Adelaide you will see stunning public and private historic buildings, usually made out of large sandstone or bluestone blocks with corrugated metal roofs. The best example is probably the Ayers House on 288 North Terrace. This is the former home of Sir Henry Ayers, a man who arrived a pauper but rose to become premier, a copper tycoon, and an advocate of the exploration of Australia's interior. Ayers Rock (now Uluru) carried his name. The Ayers House has the best Victorian furnishing of its era (late 1880s). The State Dining Room is true opulence, with its intricate woodwork, ornate cornices, hand-painted ceiling, and beautiful hardwood floor. The sprawling house is managed by the

National Trust. Part of it is open to the public, and there are two restaurants; phone 08-8223-1234. Carrick Hill, 46 Carrick Hill Drive, is a step back to a turn-of-the-century English country manor, complete with 70 acres of manicured gardens featuring plants from all over the world; phone 08-8379-3886.

## Nightlife

For nightlife that ranges from top-quality exotic cuisine (see "Restaurants," below) to discos, belly dancing, strip shows, and off-beat bookshops, try Hindley Street. The Third World Bookshop is open all night and is filled with a vast array of reading material, from the *Fabulous Furry Freak Brothers* comics to philosophical discourses. There are belly dancers at the Lebanese restaurants. For the gay scene, procure a copy of *Adelaide Gay Times*.

## Shopping

Rundle Street, which is closed to traffic, is perhaps the most highly concentrated and tastefully done shopping mall in Australia. The mall extends from King William Street through Pulteney Street. Virtually everything is sold here. You'll find emporiums, camera shops, good moderate-priced restaurants, counter meals, and plenty of people.

For food items of every description for the best prices, shop at Adelaide's Central Market, located adjacent to Victoria Square. You'll find stalls with pastries, fresh fish, banana-sized prawns, abalone, fruit, freshly baked bread, Chinese food, and pasta. In all there are more than 70 retail stalls in this market.

## Warrawong Wildlife Sanctuary

The Warrawong Wildlife Sanctuary is in the Adelaide Hills about 45 minutes out of Adelaide. It's a must visit for anyone interested in Australian wildlife. The $A15 entrance fee is well worth it. The sanctuary's owner, Dr. John Wamsley, has put 18 years' labor into 14 hectares "to re-create an inkling of what the Adelaide Hills were like before feral foxes and cats decimated the small marsupials and before plant life was permanently altered." Warrawong is on Stock Road in Mylor, a small town in the Adelaide Hills.

To visit the sanctuary, phone 08-8370-9422. Guided tours occur daily. To get there take the South Eastern Freeway, exit at Bunker Road, turn right on Longwood and left on Stock.

At night the place literally hops to life. Macropods of all sizes bound by as Wamsley whispers nonstop about the creatures his spotlight captures amid their foraging, mating, and squabbling activities. There are four kinds of rare bettongs (rabbit-sized kangaroos) that were the Aboriginal staple in much of Australia before predators brought from Europe asserted themselves. Other macropods include red, gray, and euro kangaroos, and tammar, Bennett's, rufous, potoroo, and red-necked wallabies. There are also tiny pygmy possums, quolls, ring-tailed and brush-tailed possums, bandicoots, and bats. There are 16 mammal species, as well. The pond system contains platypuses, native ducks, wood ducks, black ducks, and a comically hyperactive animal known in Australia as the water rat.

Warrawong staffers can arrange fairly expensive accommodations in fancy tents on the sanctuary grounds.

## Restaurants

Hindley Street is the place to go to eat. For good cheap food ($A8 for a main dish), try Mekong Thai, with its authentic Cambodian atmosphere and clientele; phone 08-8231-5160. The Flash Gelati Bar is a local institution with superlative freshly ground coffee and, of course, the best gelati in town. The place is packed after movies and theaters close. Toward the western end of the street you'll see Yugoslav, Greek, Italian, and Vietnamese restaurants. For good, inexpensive meals representing their namesakes, try Golden Triangle and Athens. Across Light Square Street is Rigoni's Bistro, at 27 Leigh Street, which has very good Italian food. Try the lasagna. Main courses run about $A10.

There's no shortage of excellent restaurants outside of action-packed Hindley Street. Most of them offer a full selection of South Australia's famous wines. You can get silver-spoon treatment at the Grange, at 233 Victoria Square. Or you can dine at a traditional Australian pie cart on the sidewalk outside Parliament House. Try a "pie floater"—a strange concoction of oily meat floating in pea-soup-colored liquid punctuated with splashes of Aussie tomato sauce (catsup) and encased in pie crust.

In between the extremes are numerous middle-range restaurants. A couple of the best are Nediz Tu and Jolleys Boathouse, which are known for a mixture of foods from different cultures. The Red Ochre Grill, on Ebenezer Place, is an authentic Aussie restaurant, serving kangaroo, emu, and other dishes; phone 08-8223-7566.

## Accommodations

There's usually no shortage of places to stay in Adelaide, from economy to upmarket.

*Economy.* The YHA youth hostel is at 290 Gilles Street. On a city map you can find Gilles next to better marked Halifax Street. The hostel is clean and near the downtown. A bed in a dorm runs $A16. East Park Lodge, at 341 Angas Street, sits amid some of Adelaide's best old colonial public buildings. Dorm accommodations are $A16; twins, $A36. This would be my first choice in the economy market.

*Moderate.* Moore's Brecknock Hotel, 401 King William, is a wonderful find, especially for the price (about $A50 per night per couple). The hotel is above an old Irish pub that was built in the 1800s. Next door is a backpackers hostel. Disabled accommodation is available; phone 08-8231-5467. North Adelaide, which is where businessmen stay, often has more for less in the moderate range.

*Upmarket.* The Adelaide Hilton, 233 Victoria Square, is a top-flight hotel with more than its share of accommodations for disabled persons. It's centrally located but expensive. Rooms start at around $A320; phone 08-8217-2000. Samford Plaza Hotel, 150 North Terrace, has impressively decorated rooms with views of the city and faraway mountains. Accommodations for the disabled are available. Rooms start at $A290; phone 08-8461-1111.

# ┌─── The Beaches Around
# Adelaide

The beaches around Adelaide are strips of fine white sand bordered by the calm waters of the Gulf of Saint Vincent. With Kangaroo Island offshore acting as a buffer, these beaches are usually spared the turbulence of the Southern Ocean. Often the water merely laps the shore with no wave action whatsoever. You'll find the Adelaide beaches sedate places, suitable for swimming, snorkeling, scuba diving, and sailboarding. Much like those in southern California, the beaches are warm in the summer (November–January) and mild in the winter (June–August). The water is temperate, not tropical. Beneath the surface, you won't find coral or tropical fish. Instead, there's usually good visibility, revealing rock formations, sandy bottoms, seaweed, and varieties of fish most people recognize on restaurant menus. There's something for everyone on the beaches around Adelaide, even if it's only a complete tan at Maslin Beach, the first legalized nude beach in Australia. In all there are 30 recognized beaches spread along 70 kilometers of coastline. All are within a 35-minute drive of Adelaide.

If you're out to visit the best of the bunch, you can skip most of the beaches north of Glenelg. The possible exceptions would be Henley Beach and West Beach. At Henley you can rent a catamaran for $A10 per hour, a paddleboard for $A8, and Jet Skis for $A24. (These are fairly standard prices at the Adelaide beaches.) West Beach has good swimming and catamarans for rent. Aside from these exceptions, the beaches generally improve in terms of cleanliness and the quality of the natural setting as you head south from Glenelg.

Glenelg is the logical point to start a beach crawl. It's a mini–Coney Island, an amusement park without much architectural charm. Glenelg is reached from Adelaide's city center by hopping on the tram at Victoria Square on King William Street. The vintage tram rolls through the suburbs before depositing you in Glenelg. The cost for this service varies with the time of day, but it's less than $A2.

South Glenelg Beach can be reached by walking from the main beach. There's an attractive kiosk with outside tables complete with umbrellas. The public toilet block and showers are usually clean.

For the rest of the beach crawl, head south from Glenelg on Brighton Road (which becomes Ocean Boulevard). Somerton Beach is a clean, flat, good swimming beach with few facilities and scant crowds. Brighton Beach and North Brighton are similar to Somerton except that Brighton has a fishing jetty. You can rent a catamaran at North Brighton. South Brighton is the least clean of the Brightons, but there are sailboards you can rent. You can skip Kingston Park Beach because the beach has all but disappeared. Marino Rocks has a rock outcrop and usually good underwater visibility. It's an attractive uncrowded section of sand used by scuba divers and fishermen. Hallett Cove is a conservation park with a short trail to a rocky beach that was an unofficial clothing-optional beach on the day I visited it. Christies Beach is a clean, good swimming beach with public toilet facilities and shops and moderate crowds. Port Noarlunga is a popular beach with seafront restaurants, public toilets, catamaran rentals, and a jetty. It's regularly patrolled by a surf club. You can reach Noarlunga by train from Adelaide (not to be confused with the tram that deposits you at Glenelg), and buses run to all the beaches along the coast.

From Noarlunga it's on to Moana and Maslin Beaches. Moana is a surfing beach.

Maslin Beach is a government-designated nude beach. Considering that the rights of the unclad usually rate low on politicians' agendas, it's ironic that nude bathers were awarded Maslin. It's by far the prettiest beach. Officially, the north end facing the beachside parking lot is for clothed bathers and the south end is for nudes. In reality it's less defined.

*Accommodations.* Try the modestly priced Ensensada Motor Inn on Colley Terrace, Glenelg, S.A. 5045; phone 08-8294-5822. If you want to stay on the beach, try Glenelg Holiday Flats, 2 South Esplanade, Glenelg, S.A. 5045, for around $A110 per night; phone 08-8295-1952. For an upmarket stay, there's Stamford Grand Hotel, Moseley Square Glenelg, S.A. 5045; phone 08-8376-1222.

*Access.* The easiest way to reach the coast is via the tram that runs throughout the day to Glenelg from Victoria Square. Once on the coast you can take buses to the rest of the beaches. If you're too shy to ask your average friendly Aussie which bus to take, look for buses headed south on Brighton Road (which turns into Ocean Boulevard). Once on board tell the driver where you're going, so he'll know where to stop. If you're going north you want a bus headed for Military Road.

# Kangaroo Island

Dick Smith told me Kangaroo Island is the best place to view wildlife in Australia. He ought to know. He founded *Australian Geographic* and flew a helicopter around Australia's 36,735-kilometer shore in search of top wildlife habitats. It took me 60,000 Outback kilometers on my own before I was sure Smith was right. Kangaroo Island is a must for anyone interested in Australian wildlife. You could devote an entire Australian holiday to Kangaroo Island and return home wanting to come back for more. Set aside at least three days to visit it.

The island is a birder's paradise. There are more than 216 species, including 12 species of raptors; subantarctic and open-ocean species (penguins, gannets, albatrosses); 8 kinds of raucous cockatoos; brightly colored lorikeets; 13 different honeyeaters; kingfishers and laughing kookaburras; more than 36 kinds of waterfowl; crimson-flecked finches; and brush turkeys. Overhead, white-breasted sea eagles, wedge-tailed eagles, ospreys, and black-shouldered kites soar on the air currents.

The biggest entirely terrestrial life-form, the Kangaroo Island kangaroo, is an impressive macropod. It differs in physical characteristics and behavior from its mainland parent species, the western gray kangaroo. The males can weigh as much as 55 kilograms. The island gray is less wary (especially in Flinders Chase National Park) than its mainland relative and is easier to photograph.

Few animals are more endearing than a tammar wallaby, which stands about 45 centimeters (18 inches) high. They are rare and restricted to Kangaroo Island and a handful of other islands and are now restricted here.

After the island's macropods, platypuses, koalas, echidnas, and Gould's sand goannas are as common as anywhere in Australia. And when it comes to pinnipeds (seals and sea lions), Kangaroo Island is the top place in Australia.

More than four dozen species of plants live only on Kangaroo Island, and the island's flora isn't completely cataloged yet. At first glance Kangaroo Island's native vegetation may look like typical Australian scrub. However, there were no human-made earth-scorching fires here for the 2,200 years prior to European occupation. And there have been no feral rabbits, which have denuded so much of the mainland.

The plant communities are rich and varied. There are sclerophyll forests, coastal heaths, mallee scrub, grass trees, subtropical gullies, and temperate freshwater swamps. There are more than 750 species of plants, among them 19 gums, 20 acacias, and more than 60 orchids identified thus far. Banksias, casuarinas, stringybarks, tea trees, and sugar, pink, and swamp gums are common. Given the variety, something is always blooming on Kangaroo Island.

## The Townships

Kangaroo Island has four small towns. Parndana, the tiniest and least visited, is located at the island's center. The other three are situated on the northeastern coast and are linked by 40 kilometers of bitumen roads. The westernmost town is Kingscote; the easternmost is Penneshaw, and American River is halfway between the two.

### Penneshaw

Penneshaw is on the Dudley Peninsula, which is connected to the rest of Kangaroo Island by a narrow isthmus. It's the starting point for most visitors coming to the island because the ferry that runs from Cape Jervis on the mainland offers the least expensive transport to Kangaroo Island. Penneshaw is a sleepy little hamlet of 250 families. A few businesses, a post office, and private homes sit behind a row of mature Norfolk Island pines. There are two general stores, a pub, and advertised as well as unadvertised accommodations. If you look presentable and ask around, it's possible to rent a centuries-old stone cottage owned by a mainlander who only uses it during the holidays.

By turning left on leaving the jetty, you'll find Muggeltons and the Penneshaw Pub, across the street from each other. These are convenient places to get your bearings. Muggletons is a restaurant, general store, souvenir shop, petrol pump, and source of good advice under a single roof. The owner is knowledgeable about road conditions and accommodations. The town also has a caravan park where you can pitch a tent and take a shower.

### American River

American River is on Pelican Lagoon, not a river as the town's name implies. Its nine motels rank it as the most tourist-oriented of the three towns. But it's basically a low-key resort catering to sport fishermen and nature lovers who use their motel rooms as a base of operation. Regularly scheduled charter-bus tours of the island originate from some of the motels. You can also rent a horse for a half day, or a small boat to poke around Pelican Lagoon for snorkeling and bird-watching. White pelicans, black swans, wading birds, and several species of ducks are abundant. Very venomous black tiger snakes live on the lagoon's five tiny islands. The lagoon is a marine sanctuary. Fishing is prohibited above the town.

### Kingscote

Kingscote is the largest and most complete town. If you fly to the island, chances are you'll land in Kingscote. Regular but less frequent air service extends to other parts of the island. Kingscote is only 112 kilometers from Adelaide and has shops and businesses to cater to any visitor's basic needs. Nearby Brownlow's Beach is a popular fishing, swimming, and yachting spot.

## Getting to and About on the Island

*Air Connection.* The island's airport is in Kingscote. Book your round-trip flight in Adelaide. Three airlines serve the island; Kendell is the busiest (phone 08-8231-9567). You can also try Emu Airlines (phone 08-8234-3711) and Albatross Airlines (phone 08-8234-3399). Fare is around $A80 for an over-the-counter transaction. With a two-week advance it's about 20 percent less.

*Ferry.* The ferry ride is usually calm and takes only 45 minutes. The car and passenger ferries leave from Cape Jervis on the mainland (68 kilometers from Adelaide) and land at Penneshaw. Kangaroo Island Sealink charges $A62 for adults round-trip and $A130 for a vehicle; phone 08-8553-1122. Book as far in advance as possible. There is a second option: a passenger-only, high-powered superfast catamaran that runs back and forth from Glenelg and Kingscote in September through May. A round-trip costs around $A50; phone 08-8295-2688.

*Rental Cars and Tour Services.* Renting a car on the island has advantages. For starters, you don't spend $A130 for the ferry crossing. And you can travel at your own pace, stopping and investigating as your curiosity dictates. Cars can be picked up in either Penneshaw or Kingscote. I prefer a car to tour groups and think anyone with an adventuresome spirit, an appreciation for the natural world, and the judgment to drive carefully on Kangaroo Island's deceptive roads will have a wonderful trip on their own—providing they hoard park-produced brochures and take turns reading aloud to their fellow travelers. It's also wise to stock up on groceries and have a light tent and sleeping bags. I like Kangaroo Island Rental Cars and have used them on two occasions. Their cars have a few years on them but are well maintained and competitively priced; phone 08-8553-2390. You can also try Boomerang Rentals (phone 08-8553-9006) and Budget (phone 08-8553-1034).

## Information

Both Penneshaw and Kingscote have good information outlets. Kingscote, with 1,800 residents, is the metropolis to Penneshaw's paltry 250. In Penneshaw visit Tourism Kangaroo Island Information Centre on Howard Drive; phone 08-8553-1185. Accommodation and road-map needs can be met here. In Kingscote visit Dauncey Street and you'll find both the National Parks and Wildlife Service and tourist information in the same building; phone 08-8553-2381. The park service has developed good-quality pamphlets that introduce the various parks and the flora and fauna you're likely to see. For about $A8 you can take a shuttle from the airport to your accommodations in Kingscote.

*Accommodations.* In Kingscote many of the tour groups put you in the overpriced Ozone and Queenscliffe Hotels. Instead try the converted youth hostel, now named Ellson's Seaview, on Drew Street; phone 08-8553-2030. This place has all the basics for around $A50 for a double. In Penneshaw there is a youth hostel on North Terrace;

phone 08-8553-1284. There are good campgrounds at the far end of the islands in and around Flinders Chase National Park.

*Camping.* If you're camping and want to shower, try Penneshaw's Caravan Parks. Generally, bushcamping is allowed on the island unless stated otherwise. In the summer months, there are strict fire restrictions that apply to bushcamping and outdoor cooking.

To camp in any of the island's 17 parks you must pay a nominal fee for a permit. Not all the parks allow camping. Of those that do, only Kelly Hill and Flinders Chase have water. Permits can be obtained at the National Parks and Wildlife Service, Dauncey Street, Kingscote, S.A. 5223; phone 08-8553-2381. On the mainland, contact National Parks and Wildlife Service, 310 Richmond Road, Netley, S.A. 5222; phone 08-8553-2531.

*Scuba Diving.* Even with the great white sharks the diving here is among the best temperate-water diving in the world. Visibility is sometimes 200 meters. You'll dive with Australian sea lions, giant blue cod, and rare forms of seahorses. Contact Adventureland Diving, Post Office, Penneshaw, S.A. 5222; phone 08-8553-1072.

*Driving Caution.* The best way to see Kangaroo Island is by car, which means the island's mildly challenging maze of roads needs to be mentioned. Besides the bitumen that connects the three towns and the stretch to Parndana, the island's roads are unpaved. The unpaved surfaces are readily negotiable but often dangerous. The rock-hard dirt surface covered with a veneer of ball-bearing-like gravel invites uncontrolled skids. Seven cars (one driven by a ranger) were wrecked during the week I visited Kangaroo Island.

## Human History on the Island

Contrary to the usual mainland scenario, Europeans did not exterminate the Kangaroo Island Aborigines. For unknown reasons they became extinct on their own about 2,200 years before the Europeans arrived.

In 1802 the *Investigator,* under the command of Matthew Flinders, dropped anchor along the island's southeastern shore. Flinders claimed the island for England and noted the absence of Aborigines and the tameness of the kangaroos. The abundance of the kangaroos impressed Flinders so much that he named the island after them. The tameness of the animals is still evident.

## Conservation Parks

There are 17 parks on Kangaroo Island. Most of the conservation parks are undeveloped and offer only road access. Many of them are outstanding for one or two featured reasons—a rare plant community or a rare animal—but for a visitor with limited time, Flinders Chase National Park should be the primary goal.

### Seal Bay Conservation Park

Seal Bay Conservation Park is a must visit. It is the home of the rare and personable Australian sea lion. The park is located on the south coast approximately 40 kilometers from Kingscote. It can be reached via the South Coast Road with a left turn at Seal Bay Road. (South Coast Road terminates at Flinders Chase National Park.)

Seal Bay Conservation Park shares the exposed southern coast with undeveloped 21,000-hectare Cape Gantheaume Conservation Park. Seal Bay Conservation Park is a series of pocket beaches with surrounding cliffs, some dune systems, and impenetrable wind-blown mallee scrub. The park is home to the second most populous colony of Australian sea lions in the world. Usually there are between 300 and 500 animals present in the park and from 30 to 70 on the beach. Australian sea lions are Australia's only endemic pinniped and the rarest sea lion in the world.

To many visitors it's love at first sight with Australian sea lions. They possess the double whammy of personality and good looks. Adult animals are commonly silver gray to tan and sometimes creamy white. The contrast between the animal's light-colored face and large brown eyes, black nose, and bristly whiskers accentuates its features and allows its facial expressions to be readily noticeable. The animals are mischievous, curious, comical, nurturing, argumentative, and fond of sunbathing. Even though their chief beach activity is snoozing, there are usually enough mischievous pups, grousing females, and young bulls testing the depth of slumber and tolerance of older bulls to keep things interesting. When I first visited here in the 1980s, there were no people, just seals. Today there are guides, planked walkways, and a $A7.50 entrance fee for adults. The park's popularity—there are 120,000 visitors a year—has caused this change to protect the seals.

*Australian sea lion pup, Kangaroo Island.* PHOTO BY ERIC HOFFMAN.

## Other Conservation Parks

On the South Coast Road (dirt) you'll pass by Cape Gantheaume, Seal Bay, Vivonne Bay, and Kelly Hill Caves Conservation Parks. Cape Gantheaume has 200 species of birds, including great densities of waterfowl at Murray Lagoon. There are a few walking tracks. Vivonne Bay has spectacular coastal scenery and a rare plant community of windswept vegetated and barren dune systems.

*Kelly Hills Caves Conservation Park.* Kelly Hills is the most popular conservation park on the island. The most visited attraction is the limestone cave system, which features stalagmites, stalactites, and helictites. Guided tours lasting 45 minutes run twice daily. The 4.5-kilometer walking track to the coast (9 kilometers and 4 to 6 hours round-trip) through banksias and mallee scrub, along the shore of a freshwater swamp, past dune systems, and onto empty beaches may be the best marked track on the island. I sighted sand goannas, echidnas, kangaroos, and spoonbills. New Zealand fur seals occupy rocky areas along the beaches where the track meets the coast. Don't use up too much time here, though. Keep in mind that the main event is Flinders Chase National Park.

*Parndana Conservation Park.* If you're taking the Playford Highway to Flinders Chase National Park, you'll pass by the small Parndana Conservation Park, which is home to the rare black glossy cockatoo and excellent stands of remnant vegetation. The park is generally unimproved but does have a walking track around its 310-hectare area. The access road to it, off the Playford, is unmarked. It's 6 kilometers northeast of the tiny settlement of Parndana. There is also an interesting aviary with many rare birds nearby, at the Open House (see "Accommodations").

The Playford Highway ends at the island's northwestern corner, at the Cape Borda lighthouse, which is a top contender for the best sunset-viewing area on the island.

# Flinders Chase National Park

Located on the west end of the island, the Flinders Chase National Park is over 74,000 hectares of wild and rugged scenery. Visitors can view hundreds of species of native plants and animals. Chances are you'll enter the park at the Rocky Rivers headquarters, where you'll find a ranger, a campground with running water, a toilet block, an interpretive center, and multitudes of wildlife. As you pull up to the center, you'll see gray kangaroos and emus acting as toll collectors. An emu staring into your face with its ruby-red eyes and wooden-looking beak may be a bit unnerving, but according to the rangers they aren't a threat.

The other wildlife found easily near the park headquarters include koalas, Cape Barren geese, brush-tailed possums, tammar wallabies, Gould's sand goannas, platypuses, and galah cockatoos. The colorful Cape Barren geese, with their chartreuse bills, gray bodies, and pink legs, are everywhere—honking, landing, taking off, and grazing. The koalas live in swamp and manna gum trees and come to the ground fairly frequently. The wallabies appear in open areas around dusk.

In the 1920s and 1940s David Fleay, the legendary Australian naturalist, transplanted platypuses from the mainland to Kangaroo Island, where they had never occurred. They've taken to their new home in a big way. In the Flinders Chase river systems they're easier to spot than on the mainland.

The most accessible platypus pools are within walking distance of the interpretive center. Head north along Shackle Road for 2 kilometers until you come to the Rocky River. Find a hiding place at the end of a pool and watch for fast-moving ripples on the surface. Platypuses are nocturnal and are most often sighted at dawn and dusk. Seeing them is often only momentary, especially if they see you first.

But if you remain motionless, a platypus will dive for crustaceans and larvae, float on the surface, chew its catch, and groom.

## Remarkable Rocks

Remarkable Rocks are a collection of spectacular 500-million-year-old granite and xenolithic outcroppings located 15 kilometers south of Rocky Rivers. To reach Remarkable Rocks take the dirt road signposted for Cape du Couedic that runs directly south from the campground. Turn left on Boxer Drive. When you reach the sea you've reached the rocks. Sitting atop this solid formation are huge oddly shaped boulders. The most spectacular is in the shape of an eagle's beak. A pair of real-life sea eagles usually nest and soar along the spectacular cliffs just east of Remarkable Rocks.

## Cape du Couedic

Cape du Couedic, the southwest corner of the island, is 5 kilometers west of Remarkable Rocks along the cliff-side portion of the Boxer Drive loop. At the cape there's a historic lighthouse and a remarkably well engineered flying fox that was the only means to retrieve provisions left by supply ships. Admiral's Arch is a spectacular limestone arch with a unique combination of stalactites on the underside of the arch and surf and seals under its massive shadow. The arch is a short walk past the lighthouse.

There's a New Zealand fur seal colony about 200 meters due west of the three keepers' houses near the lighthouse. This colony isn't signposted. Amble downhill through the low scrub and exposed limestone and you'll come to it. November and December are times of peak activity in a New Zealand fur seal colony. The females give birth, and the males fight for mating rights. Most of the males leave in January, but the females use the rookery year-round.

The vantage point over the seal colony is an excellent place to watch a sunset. However, if you're really into sunsets, the stretch along the 200-meter-high cliffs from Cape Borda to Cape Torrens is the most spectacular.

## Walks

There are a half dozen walks in Flinders Chase. There are five signposted tracks that originate off the West Bay Track at different intervals. The West Bay Track is the dirt road that meanders through the park to the northwest corner at Cape Borda. The marked tracks are generally short. The one with the greatest beauty is the Breakneck River Walking Trail (6 kilometers round-trip).

*Accommodations.* There are three campgrounds with water at the southern end of the park: Rocky River, West Bay, and Snake Lagoon on the southern half of the West Bay Track. At the northwestern end of the park, there's Harveys Return, near the intersection of the Playford Highway and the West Bay Track. There are also two cottages: Old Homestead, near the ranger station at Rocky River, rents for $A27.50 per person per night for multiple nights and sleeps six. It has modern amenities. The nearby Postman's Cottage has no running water but is even less expensive ($A15) and sleeps four. Linen and towels will run you $A10 per person per stay. Book directly with the ranger; phone 08-8559-7235.

You can also stay at the Open House in Parndana; phone 08-8559-6113. It's 25 kilometers from Seal Bay and is a friendly place with home-cooked meals. There is a wonderful aviary here, with many rare native birds.

*Access.* If you take a tour originating from Kingscote, American River, or Penneshaw, you merely sit back and enjoy the trip to Flinders Chase. If you're traveling by car, the fastest way to Flinders Chase is on the Playford Highway. The Playford is paved for 70 kilometers, runs down the middle of the island, and enters the northern end of the park. This is the safest route, but it's not as scenic as the South Coast Road, which takes you past the aforementioned conservation parks on your way to Flinders. The Playford ends at the island's northwestern corner.

If you're aiming at Flinders Chase, don't go to the end. Instead, turn left at the eastern boundary of the park (about 35 kilometers west of Parndana) at West End Highway, approximately 25 kilometers east of Cape Borda. West End Highway is a slow, dust-inhaling 23-kilometer stretch that intersects the South Coast Road at Tandanya Farm. From Tandanya it's only 3 kilometers to the park headquarters.

Round-trip to Flinders Chase from one of the east coast towns takes between two and three hours and requires that you start out with a full tank. Petrol pumps are in short supply at the west end of

*Remarkable Rocks, Kangaroo Island.* PHOTO BY ERIC HOFFMAN.

the island. To the west of Kingscote there are three pumps at Parndana (the island's midpoint) on the Playford Highway. On the South Coast Road there are pumps near Vivonne Bay and at Tandanya Farm.

# South Australia's Wineries

South Australia is one of the premier wine-growing areas in the world. Of the six wine regions in the state, the gilded cork of the bunch is the Barossa Valley. Located 50 kilometers northeast of Adelaide on the Stuart Highway, the Barossa Valley produces the lion's share of Australia's top wines. In 1987 only 12.4 percent of the exhibitors at national wine competitions were from Barossa-based wineries, yet they won more than 50 percent of the trophies. There has been some erosion of this dominance from winegrowers in other states, but the Barossa is still "king."

Even more impressive is that many of the Barossa's closest competitors come from South Australia as well. The Clare Valley lies just over the hill from Barossa and can be reached in an additional hour's drive. An extra attraction that comes with the Clare Valley is historic Bungaree, a working sheep station that dates back to the mid-1800s. McLaren Vale (also known as Southern Vale) is just an hour south of Adelaide and directly inland from Maslin Beach—offering the combined hedonistic pursuits of nude sunbathing and wine tasting in the same proximity. The Riverlands is farther to the east along the Murray River. Here you can combine riding a paddle wheeler or canoeing with wine tasting. And then there's the Adelaide Hills wineries tucked in the Mount Lofty Ranges directly north of Adelaide. They're easy to reach and scenic. The sixth region, Coonawarra, is near the Victoria border and is most conveniently visited when traveling from one state to the next. Together these vineyards produce nearly 55 percent of Australia's wine.

## The Barossa Valley

The Barossa Valley was settled in the 1840s by Silesian Lutherans escaping religious persecution in Germany. The well-built and massive sandstone, bluestone, and brick structures show that these immigrants came to stay. Attractive churches and historic cemeteries punctuate the countryside and are worth a visit even without the wineries. There are scenes so imitative of the Rhine that you'll swear you've been teleported to Germany—even the mature trees are from the old country. If you're a wine aficionado you'll love the Barossa Valley. If you aren't, it's a historical and picturesque architectural conclave worth a look-see.

For maximum merrymaking, the time to visit the Barossa is during the Vintage Festival, which is celebrated in odd-numbered years in or around Easter week. This is the Australian autumn, when the vines are in color. The festivities usually run for a week and feature traditional feasts, dancing troupes in traditional German garb, grape-stomping contests, hot-air balloon rides, and always more wine that needs tasting.

Paul Lloyd, a longtime wine critic for the *Advertiser,* one of Adelaide's leading newspapers, says, "South Australia's unique wines embrace all styles because the state is blessed with the full spectrum of climatic and soil conditions. Mostly, the product is table wines for the fashionable dinner table, red, white, and rosé, brilliant of colors, big and bold of flavor while subtle in structure."

If you're enough of a wine freak to know about grape pedigrees, you may be surprised to know that this small area grows a tremendous variety that includes shiraz, cabernet sauvignon, pinot noir, grenache, riesling, chardonnay, sauvignon blanc, semillion, and traminer.

## Towns and Wineries

The small town of Lyndoch is at the entrance of the Barossa Valley. There are numerous places here to get an inexpensive counter meal and, if you want to pay extra, there's the Posktusche Restaurant, housed in a 100-year-old former roadhouse. The Château Yaldara, which is open for tours Monday through Friday, is a model of European architectural and artistic grandeur. The château is packed full of artwork from around the world. Tours are free. You can also picnic or barbecue on the grounds.

You can stop at Redgum Cellars, Wilsford Wines, and Karlsburg Wine Cellars on your way from Lyndoch to Château Yaldara.

North of Lyndoch is Tanunda, the most German-looking town in the Barossa. The pastor of the Langmeil Church arrived here around 1840 with his entire congregation.

Just north of Tanunda is Seppeltsfield, an enormous stone winery with palm-lined roadways and palatial grounds. Seppeltsfield exports to 40 different countries and accommodates busloads of tourists daily during daylight hours. It's a busy place with the next busload never far behind. I found it a bit too busy, but nonetheless cheerful and tasteful. The owners allow picnics and barbecues on the grounds.

If you want to see a winery that can compete in volume with an oil refinery, drive up the road 6 kilometers to the town of Nuriootpa, where Penfolds corks more than 10,000 bottles an hour.

To me the smaller wineries with old charm that cater to cars rather than buses have the most to offer. Two standouts are Redgum Cellars, near Lyndoch, and Saltram, near Angaston. Both are open seven days a week. Orlando Winery on the road between Lyndoch and Tanunda is also interesting.

There are 40 wineries in the Barossa, so I'm sure you'll find your own favorite. Practically all commercial ventures in the Barossa Valley have maps showing the locations of the wineries.

*Restaurants.* Aside from the eateries mentioned in Lyndoch, there's the Angaston Hotel, 59 Murray Street, Angaston; phone 08-8564-2428. Die Weinstube Restaurant, in Nuriootpa (phone 08-8562-1416), specializes in German cuisine. The 135-year-old Stockwell Hotel, Duckponds Road, Stockwell (phone 08-8562-2008), is a top contender for the original architecture award. The Tanunda Hotel (phone 08-8563-2030) gets high marks for charm and cuisine.

*Accommodations.* Rooms start at $A150, but the Hermitage of Marananga, on Seppeltsfield Road, sits on a hill overlooking the Barossa Valley; phone 08-8562-2722. In Angaston, there's the moderately priced Vineyards Motel, on Stockwell Road; phone 08-8564-2404. Among the most complete and authentic places to stay is the Tanunda Hotel (51 Murray Street, Tanunda; phone 08-5638-2030), which has cozy, fully outfitted rooms, a public bar, counter meals, and full-course dinners. The Collingrove Homestead, Eden Valley, Angaston, is a gem of a place, built in 1856 but embellished with the best of this century, including a spa. No TVs or phones. Rooms are $A150 per night; phone 08-8564-2061.

There are caravan parks in the valley. Try the Barossa Caravan Park, Lyndoch; phone 08-8524-4262. The tiny town of Bethany also has a caravan park and a grassed picnic area.

*Access.* By car take the Stuart Highway 50 kilometers from Adelaide and look for signs to Lyndoch or Tanunda.

There are coach tours that regularly run through the Barossa and stop often for tasting bouts. Contact the South Australia Tourism and Travel Centre (1 King William Street, Adelaide; phone 08-8303-2033) for particulars on tours that leave the center daily.

## Bungaree Sheep Station

Bungaree is one of the few accessible historic and still active pastoral holdings that used to dominate Australian society. The present owners are George and Sally Hawker. George Hawker is the great-grandson of George C. Hawker, who settled in the area in 1841. Out of the many active cattle and sheep stations I visited in Australia, only Bungaree was uncluttered by unsightly prefabbed additions. It's an immense wheat and sheep operation with emphasis on the sheep. Outwardly it appears to be running much as it did a hundred years ago.

Bungaree, like many stations in the grand period of Australian pastoralism, was its own community isolated from the rest of the country by distance. Among the collection of sandstone buildings is Saint Michael's Chapel, built as a place of worship for the station's isolated inhabitants. The church is still used for special events. Its original roof was stringybark gum. The manager's office (now used by the overseer), the Gothic-windowed council chamber where the district council once met, the stable yards, the office, the store, and the blacksmith's shop are intact.

*Accommodations.* For Bungaree, phone 08-8842-2677. If you merely want to visit, phone first to see if a tour is scheduled. This is a working business, so there's no time for casual drop-ins. Self-contained shearers' quarters and quaint cottages are available for overnight stays; $A40 for adults with a 25 percent reduction for multiple nights.

Besides Bungaree in the Clare Valley, there's the Taminga Motel, Main North Road, Auburn (phone 08-8892-2808) and the Clare Motel, Main North Road, Clare (phone 08-8842-2816).

## The Riverlands Wineries

Located about two hours from Adelaide on the banks of the Murray River and among the towns of Renmark, Berri, Loxton, Barmera, and Moorook, the Riverlands wineries are largely known for producing bulk wines, fortified wines, and some of the best brandies in Australia. If you're searching for a canoe, houseboat, or paddle wheeler experience you'll be able to combine it with wine tasting in the Riverlands area.

Most of the region's 14 wineries are open during normal business hours. Among the more interesting is Lubiana Winery in Moorook. Lubiana has won a great number of awards in national competitions for the quality of its whites and reds. The Loxton Co-op Winery and Distillery features volume to the tune of processing 30,000 tons of grapes annually. The Berri co-operative winery is reputed to be the largest in the Southern Hemisphere.

# The Flinders Ranges

The Flinders Ranges rival Uluru (Ayers Rock) as Australia's number one Outback tourist attraction. Unlike Uluru, the preponderance of visitors frequenting the Flinders are Australians, not foreigners. The Flinders are an entire mountain range containing towns, sheep stations, hundreds of kilometers of hiking trails, bountiful pockets of wildlife, caves with Aboriginal artwork, ruins of failed settlements, and mountains to climb and gorges to explore. You could easily spend a year exploring the Flinders. A good place to get started is the Quorn Tourist Information Office on Seventh Street; phone 08-8648-6419.

The quartzite ridges and peaks of the Flinders rise sharply above the flat plains. This distinctly jutting escarpment is most pronounced at the huge natural amphitheater called Wilpena Pound. Wilpena is part of 78,000-hectare Flinders National Park. At the northern end of the Flinders is 128,228-hectare Gammon Ranges National Park. Mount Remarkable National Park, in the southernmost Flinders, is sometimes listed as the third national park in the Flinders, which it technically is. However, it's much smaller than the others and lacks the truly Outback characteristics of the two northern parks.

The Flinders began in the Precambrian, 750 million years ago, as sediment laid down by an ancient sea. In the aeons that followed, uplifting occurred, creating the buckled and steep-faced ranges. Fossil remains of some of the earliest marine animals (jellyfish and segmented worms) have been found in the Flinders. Fossils are easy to find in the Flinders for even the casual visitor.

Today's Flinders are a mostly arid landscape that's sprinkled with native pines, native oranges, yaccas, black oaks, wild peaches, Bullock bushes, needlewoods, 33 kinds of acacias, bluebush Sturt peas, and, after substantial rains, an assortment of wildflowers. The deep gorges that cut through the ranges are lined with magnificent white-barked river red gums with twisted trunks and branches.

Some species of wildlife are abundant in the parks, less so in the ranges between the parks where graziers often shoot native and feral wildlife that they view as harmful to their stock. In their respective haunts in the parks you'll find red, gray, and euro kangaroos and yellow-footed rock wallabies. Don't expect any of them to be as approachable as those on Kangaroo Island or in Tasmania and the desert parks of New South Wales.

The dominant birds are galahs, little corellas, wedge-tailed eagles, and emus. There are plenty of sleepy lizards creeping about. They're nonvenomous, but do have a strong bite.

To many Australians the Flinders are the classic Australian landscape—partly because of world-famous landscape painter Sir Hans Heysen. There's a good chance that Heysen's landscapes have conditioned you to think of the Flinders as what Australia should look like.

The towns tucked around the Flinders are no less stereotypic of rural Australia than the landscape. Some seem frozen in time—and haven't had their authenticity eroded by tourism promotion yet. They have dusty streets, old pubs, and hotels built of sandstone at the turn of the century.

Any mention of the Flinders Ranges is not complete without including the Adnjamanthahna people, who were the custodians of the Flinders for thousands of years before Europeans appeared. *Adnjamanthahna* means Rock Hills people. The Adnjamanthahna still live in the Flinders, but their culture has been greatly altered. There is an active effort to revitalize the culture by the South Australian government and the Adnjamanthahna themselves.

## Information Sources

To obtain maps and leaflets of the area, contact Flinders Ranges and Outback South Australia Regional Tourism Association, 56B Glen Osmond Road, Adelaide, S.A. 5000; phone 08-82-23-3991. In transit stop in Quorn at the Quorn Tourist Information Office, Seventh Street, Quorn, S.A. 5433; phone 08-8648-6419.

## Mount Remarkable National Park

Located only 260 kilometers north of Adelaide, Mount Remarkable is the easiest of the Flinders Ranges parks to reach. Mount Remark-

*Echidna, Mount Remarkable.* PHOTO BY ERIC HOFFMAN.

able is dominated by the rugged red-and-brown sandstone outcrops and deep gorges that typify much of the Flinders. The park is a meeting place for a variety of habitats. In areas of consistent rainfall there are groves of peppermint, sugar, red, and gray gums. Native pines are also prevalent, as are more than 35 kinds of orchids. The park visitors center is at Mambray Creek about 50 kilometers north of Port Pirie.

## Walks

Probably the most popular walk is the Alligator Gorge Trail, which starts in the parking lot above Alligator Creek. The 2-kilometer walk takes about 1 hour. The main feature is a descent into a colorful quartzite gorge to the steplike formation known as the Terraces, which the gorge's stream trickles over.

If you want to make a day of it, inquire about the Hidden Gorge and Battery Ridge Trail. This is a 15-kilometer loop that an average walker can do in 4 to 5 hours. The walk takes you through the remotest gorge areas of the park and you return along a ridge line that affords an excellent view of faraway Spencer Gulf. Along the way you may see galahs, black tiger snakes, euro kangaroos (most active at dawn or dusk), and a wide range of bird life.

*Camel trek, Flinders Ranges National Park.* PHOTO BY ERIC HOFFMAN.

Ask a ranger at the park headquarters at the southern end of the park about other walks. (However, the most spectacular part of the Flinders Ranges is farther north in Flinders and Gammon Ranges National Parks.)

*Accommodations.* Mount Remarkable encourages both car and bushcamping. Sites cost $A8. You must have a permit to camp. Contact the head ranger at the Mambray Creek office, 48 kilometers north of Port Pirie on Highway 1. No bushcamping is allowed during the fire season from November to May.

*Access.* There is no public transportation to the park. You can take a bus to Port Germein, which is roughly 30 kilometers short of the Mambray Creek campground. By car take the Princess Highway from Adelaide to Port Germein, and 19 kilometers past Port Germein turn east to the park. The trip takes about 4 hours from Adelaide.

## Flinders Ranges National Park and Wilpena Pound
### Wilpena Pound

Flinders Ranges National Park, featuring Wilpena Pound, the heart and focal point of the range, is about 180 kilometers north of Mount Remarkable National Park. Wilpena Pound is a huge natural amphitheater measuring 15 kilometers long and 5 wide. Its perimeter is a continuous oval-shaped ridge with peaks reaching 1,170 meters. The pound is the best-known geological feature in South Australia.

*Wilpena* is an Adnjamanthahna term meaning "bent fingers." If you cup your hand and bend your fingers upward, you'll get the picture. The fingers are the rugged peaks and your palm is the pound's sink-shaped middle.

Most activities start at Wilpena Pound Resort, where there's a motel, a large campground, and a small interpretive center. Several worthwhile walking tracks start here. The road to the pound is paved, though the rest of the roads in the park are dirt. The pound proper is for bushwalkers only. Vehicles are not allowed.

*Walks.* Starting at the parking area near the motel is the Mount Ohlssen Bagge (also known as Mount John) Trail and Nature Walk.

The round-trip is 4 to 5 kilometers and includes a 950-meter climb. The trail is well trodden and steep, but the view is worth it. To the west is the pound, to the northeast is Lake Frome. I did the walk in about 2 hours round-trip, but pushed to do it that fast. If you aren't up to the climb, there's a short loop called the Nature Walk that branches off the starting point of the Mount Ohlssen Bagge Trail. Throughout the walk examples of native flora have been labeled.

The Old Homestead Trail is another 4- to 5-kilometer round-trip stroll, but with very little change in elevation.

Climbing to the top of Saint Mary's Peak (1,170 meters) is probably the most popular long walk in the pound. From its summit you can look down into the oval of the pound and to the north to the Heysen and ABC ranges.

There are two trails to the summit. Both can be deceptively hazardous if you don't prepare properly. The heat can be excessive during the steep climbs, and inclement weather can roll in unexpectedly. The most direct route starts along Pound Road about 80 meters from the Wilpena campground. The first 4 kilometers of the trail are mostly level along the base of the north-facing escarpment of the pound. Then the trail turns steeply up toward Tanderra Saddle. Allow 5 to 7 hours round-trip from Wilpena campground to the peak. The other route to the peak is the Old Homestead Trail. This route is approximately 8 kilometers one way but it's less challenging than the route up the north face.

## The Heysen and ABC Ranges

Joined to the pound from the north are the Heysen and ABC Ranges. These are two parallel escarpments. The Aroona Valley separates the two ranges. From both ranges dramatic red-and-orange rock gorges lined with river red gums intersect the Aroona Valley.

Car camping sites, some with water, have been strategically placed throughout the Heysen and ABC Ranges. Contact the National Parks and Wildlife Services offices in Wilpena or Oraparinna for a list of their locations. Aside from school holidays, many of these campsites receive light use.

Much of the Aroona Valley is accessible by car on a sometimes narrow but usually well-maintained dirt road. Walking tracks branch off from the road at various junctures. From the south you can reach the Aroona Valley from Wilpena Pound. From the west, access is via Highway 47 between Hawker and Parachilna. Turn east from Highway 47 to Brachina Gorge. From the north, the Aroona Valley turnoff is on the road that connects Blinman and Parachilna.

*The Heysen Trail between Wilpena and Parachilna.* The Heysen Trail is probably the most ambitious walking trail in Australia. It will someday stretch 1,200 kilometers, from Kangaroo Island to the Flinders. The 55-kilometer stretch between Parachilna and Wilpena Pound is one of the most popular sections. Some of the day walks outlined above are on segments of this section of the Heysen Trail. The 55-kilometer north-south walk through the Heysen and ABC Ranges usually takes 3 days and goes through the heart of the Flinders.

The biggest challenge facing walkers on the Heysen Trail is finding surface water. There are only eight certain water sources. You should not walk extensively in the area without a topographic map. From the States, contact the Department of Industry and Trade, Recreation and Sport, 27 Valetta Road, Kidman Park, S.A. 5001; phone 08-8416-6677. Purchase the Heysen Trail (Parachilna Gorge to Wilpena) topographic map ($A6.50) in either Adelaide or Quorn. Locate the water sources before starting, and check with park rangers about the status of each water source when you reach the park.

The Heysen Trail is closed in the Flinders between November 1 and April 1 because of fire danger. The visitor prohibition can be extended if conditions merit. Be sure you understand and abide by the fire restrictions.

You need a permit to camp in Flinders Ranges National Park. The Oraparinna park headquarters is located on the Wilpena-Blinman Road; phone 08-8648-0017.

## Aboriginal Art Sites

There are several principal Aboriginal art sites near Wilpena Pound. Among them are examples of the full spectrum of yellow, red, and white ochre paintings and rock engravings of animals, animal tracks, abstract designs, human figures, and initiation ceremonies.

*Yourambulla.* Yourambulla is a clearly signposted site on Highway 47 a few kilometers south of the town of Hawker. There are two principal areas within a 20-minute walk from the parking area. The paintings were touched up by the Adnjamanthahna in 1947, the year of the last initiation ceremony in the region. *Yourambulla* is the Adn-jamanthahna word for "two men."

The first group of paintings is at the end of a short climb. You'll see stenciled hands, circles with lines through them, parallel lines, and concentric circles with lines running from and through them. There are columns of short line segments that look like a tally or count had been taken. Most of these symbols signify an initiation ceremony. The two lines and concentric circles are thought to symbolize lines of initiated and uninitiated people who attended ceremonies and sometimes faced and taunted one another before a rite. Emu tracks in a grouping or an individual emu track may mean the passing of a day. In the end your interpretation of some of the art may be as valid as anyone else's. "Some of it's a mystery," said Ranger Clifford Coultard, himself a Adnjamanthahna.

The first art site is surrounded by mesh to discourage vandalism. The second is similarly protected and can be reached only by a fixed ladder extending 10 meters up a rock face.

*Sacred Canyon.* You reach this site by turning east from the Hawker Road about 4 kilometers south of the Wilpena Pound turnoff. Both sides of the canyon have engravings that are predominantly abstract forms, but also contain recognizable kangaroo and animal tracks. Several techniques were used to make these engravings, so the site may have been used for many generations. Some work is thought to date back 20,000 years, but nobody knows for sure. The site has been vandalized.

## Tours

*By Air.* Billing their offerings as "local scenic flights," the Wilpena Pound Holiday Resort runs a single-engine aircraft that seats seven and busily takes people for 20-minute flights over Flinders Ranges National Park. The landing strip is a 10-minute drive from the resort, and it costs $A70–85 per person to go aloft; phone 08-8648-0004. Besides the scenic aspect of the flight, which is reason enough to purchase a ticket, I valued seeing the lay of the land I would be walking as well.

*By Camel.* Rex Ellis, owner of Flinders Camel Trek-Bush, runs some of his camels out of Blinman. His schedule varies from year to year. I signed on for a long-haul camel trek that encompassed 140 kilometers in a journey that entered the Flinders through the western end of Bunyeroo Gorge and went the length of the Aroona Valley to the Parachilna-Blinman Road and back along the western escarpment to our starting point. Ellis's camels are among the best mannered I experienced during my many forays into the bush on these amazing creatures. If you sign on, ask to ride Govenor, and avoid Cooper (alias Yoyo). Contact Rex Ellis, P.O. Box 53, Waikerie, S.A. 5330; phone 08-8543-2280. The cost of a five-day trip is $A685.

*By Car.* The route from Wilpena to Bunyeroo Gorge, Brachina Gorge, the Aroona Valley, and to Highway 47 via Brachina Gorge gives you the most in-depth look at the heart of the Flinders. The dirt roads in this region are maintained, but due to the terrain you'll average about 30 kilometers an hour over the 35- to-50-kilometer route.

*Accommodations.* The largest campground in the park is run by the Wilpena Pound Holiday Resort, which leases its land from the National Parks and Wildlife Service. The resort has 34 motel units ($A90 per twin share) and 400 caravan and camping sites. There's a nominal fee for camping. This is a good place to get started. Call the resort directly at 08-8648-0004.

There are camping areas throughout the park. Many of them are remote and are nestled in the heart of the Flinders. You can get a list of these places at the Wilpena and Oraparinna park facilities.

## The Town of Quorn

Traveling north on Highway 47 from Port Augusta you'll pass through Quorn. Established in 1878 as a railway hub, Quorn looks much like it did at the turn of the century. When a change in the gauge of the rails suddenly made this hub obsolete, the town emptied overnight. Its grand sandstone hotels, pubs, and railway station survived and are bunched around Railway Terrace. With a newfound purpose of serving increasing numbers of tourists, Quorn's old structures are assured of a bright future. There is a movement afoot to declare the entire town a "heritage town." There are about 20 structures, including the town hall, banks, churches, and hotels, that rate as historic structures. Everything you need to know can most likely be found at the Quorn Tourist Information Centre on Seventh Street; phone 08-8648-6419.

On Friday and Saturday nights the pubs and hotels on Railway Terrace come to life. During the week these pubs are quiet, sedate, and good refuges for a quiet talk, a beer, a counter meal, and a room for the night.

## The Pichi Richi Railroad

*Pichi Richi* is an Aboriginal term describing a local plant that was chewed to induce an "altered state of consciousness." Today the name lives on because of a collection of highly dedicated and skilled railroad aficionados whose only opiate is old trains. Quorn is the headquarters of the Pichi Richi Railway Preservation Society, which has established a remarkable railway workshop and museum here. Its membership is 600 strong and comes from all over Australia. Not only has the society restored many of Australia's grandest old steam locomotives and coaches but they actually put them to the test for the paying public on 43 kilometers of track between Quorn and Pichi Richi Pass, which is an intensively engineered and terraced bed laid down by Chinese labor and Welsh masons. The trains run mostly on holidays. A two-hour ride is $A22 for adults, $A11 for children.

*Accommodations Outside of Flinders Ranges National Park.* On the main drag of Quorn there are four old hotels. My favorite is the Transcontinental Hotel on Railway Terrace. You will never forget a Friday night in the pub. Everyone shows up and drinks for a long time. My visit was reminiscent of the bar scene in *Star Wars*—characters galore, but generally friendly to the freshly scrubbed, goggle-eyed tourists trying to fit in. Upstairs a double goes for about $A50, and a single rents for about half as much; phone 08-8648-6076. You can also try the Austral/Hotel, Railway Terrace, Quorn, S.A. 5433, for the moderate price of around $A45 per double; phone 08-8648-6016. The Andu Lodge on First Street is a laid-back, clean place. The owner and his staff are helpful in directing you to Aboriginal art and walks. They will also (for a low fee) take you to and from trailheads. They have both dorms and private rooms. A dorm bed costs $A14 per night, and a double in a private room goes for around $A40; phone 08-8648-6655. If Quorn fails you, there are four hotels in nearby Hawker and one hotel in Blinman.

## Gammon Ranges National Park

If you find Flinders Ranges National Park fascinating, you'll find Gammon Ranges National Park doubly so. Outdoor adventure expert and educator Joc Schmiechen, who has logged thousands of walking kilometers throughout Australia, describes the Gammons as "magical, mystical, and pure." Warren Bonython, a vanguard conservationist in South Australia for the last 40 years, fell in love with the Gammons in the 1940s when he pioneered the exploration of the labyrinth of narrow gorges and water holes. Bonython is largely responsible for the formation of the park.

At its inception in 1970, the park was 15,550 hectares. It has now grown to 128,000 hectares, making it the largest national park in South Australia.

The Gammons are unparalleled in their stark and stunning chasms, which are so narrow in some places that you can touch the opposing sides of 100-meter-high sheer rock walls. Expect twisted rock formations, sandy white riverbeds lined with river red gums, and a greater sense of remoteness than you experienced in the more often visited southern Flinders Ranges.

At sunrise and sunset the color of the red-rock cliffs changes from dull brown to hot red in moments. The day brings cobalt blue skies touched by red gorges and the screech and chatter of parrot-filled river red gums in the late afternoon. Near water, tiny zebra finches twitter and bathe. Colorful dragon lizards spy on you from rock outcrops, and wedge-tailed eagles vigilantly soar in search of a meal.

The Gammons' steep rock faces are home to yellow-footed rock wallabies. Red kangaroos are abundant in the flat open areas. Bulky euros reside in hilly areas and take refuge under overhangs during the day.

Birds, especially parrots, are plentiful. Besides the more common little corellas and galahs you may see the uncommon red-breasted, blue-winged Bourke's parrot or the more common scarlet-chested parrot. The cliff faces are used by nesting peregrine falcons, and brown falcons are common. In all, 67 bird species have been sighted in the park.

There are 60 species of lizards and 18 species of snakes in the park. Five kinds of dragon lizards occur in the park, including the luminously colored red-barred dragon.

The park's management is tied closely to the nearby Adnjaman-thahna Aboriginal community of Nepabunna. For a time the entire park staff was Aboriginal, including the chief ranger. Perhaps its remote majesty and the conspicuous Aboriginal presence gives Gammon Ranges National Park a mystical quality that I found only at Uluru and Kakadu in the Northern Territory and at Carnarvon Gorge in Queensland.

## Walks

From the park headquarters at Balcanoona the Weetootla Gorge is the closest place to get a look at chasms and yellow-footed rock wallabies. The road up the gorge has been blockaded and changed to a walking track. Within a half hour's walk you may see colorful wallabies around the springs. You may see euro kangaroos as well. Both species are most active in the mornings and evenings. Look for small, purple-flecked gudgeons in the permanent water holes.

Farther up the gorge is a shepherd's hut and the Loch Ness well. They sit near spectacular chasms. There's a wide range of possibilities from the hut. This is a stepping-off point for bushwalkers wanting to see chasms and mining ruins. Bunyip Chasm, a 4-hour walk from the hut, is a favorite: it's so narrow that you can touch both sides of the chasm by holding your arms out. "It's like walking in the mountain's heart," explained a young ranger who grew up in Nepabunna. To get the full splendor of Bunyip, you must scale an 18-meter precipitous wall that requires good balance. Some bushwalkers use rope. The walk to Bunyip Chasm is a cross-country excursion, which is the norm since there are few trails.

Italowie Gorge is about 10 kilometers west of the park headquarters on the road to Nepabunna. It's a naturally occurring cut passing through the park's main plateau. There is year-round water here. You'll see near-vertical red quartzite cliffs with river red gums lining the creek. If you wander along the creek and find clear water, sit still and chances are yellow-footed rock wallabies and colorful finches and parrots will come to drink. This is also a popular casual camping area. Depending on when you visit, dust kicked up by passing cars and the loss of solitude from the same can be annoying.

*Accommodations.* There are no formal campgrounds in the park. Most visitors car-camp next to riverbeds and bring their own water.

There are several excellent sites west of the park headquarters along Balcanoona Gorge. Many experienced bushwalker groups use water holes when they explore the interior of the park.

Arkaroola, on the park's northern boundary, is the nearest place with a bed. The Arkaroola Resort has a small store, restaurant, and gas. There are nine cabins; you may share one with strangers if it's too crowded. A night in a shearer's quarters and a campsite are $A10 per night. For a bed in a cabin it's $A29 per person per night. There are campsites, shearer's quarters, and lodge accommodations. The Arkaroola Travel Centre (50 Pirie Street, Adelaide, S.A. 5000; phone 08-8212-1366) books tours and accommodations at Arkaroola.

*Access.* Gammon Ranges National Park lies 610 kilometers north of Adelaide and about 230 kilometers north of Wilpena Pound. There is no public transportation to the park, but there is Ridgetop Tours, which takes you to the hardest-to-reach wonder spots. From Hawker there are two fairly good quality dirt roads leading to the park. The route with the most pavement is Highway 47 from Hawker to Leigh Creek South.

To check on conditions in the park, call the ranger at park headquarters in Balcanoona; phone 08-8648-4829.

# The Murray River

The Murray River has a rich Aboriginal and pioneer history. During the 1800s steam-driven paddle wheelers belched up and down the river, avoiding snags and persevering through drought and flood. Today the Murray is a much tamer river because of the dams and weirs designed to control it, largely for agriculture. Despite the Murray's burden of supporting the lion's share of Aussie agriculture, there are pockets of wild areas along its course that offer superb outdoor experiences for canoeists and houseboaters. For the couch potato who wants a pretend adventure, there are the highly promoted replication paddle wheelers that churn up and down the Murray with all the comforts and security of home.

The Murray River, with its tributaries the Darling, Murrumbidgee, Lachlan, Goulburn, Warrego, and scores of streams and rivers, makes up the largest river system in Australia, collecting water over an area the size of New Mexico and Texas. Rainwater accumulating in tropical Queensland can travel 2,000 kilometers to Encounter Bay in South Australia, where the Murray meets the sea. To the east the drainage includes Mount Kosciuszko, the nation's tallest mountain, and Canberra, the capital of Australia. The fact that a drainage area this size doesn't produce one of the world's major rivers is testimony to how arid Australia is. Compared in volume to the world's great river systems, the Murray is practically insignificant. It has 22,700 million cubic meters of annual runoff, while the Amazon has 5,840,000 million and the Mississippi 568,000 million.

## The Murray River in South Australia

In South Australia the Murray River is a sluggish, brown Sacramento River–sized channel that twists like a great snake through an immense floodplain defined by yellow and red sandstone and limestone cliffs. Besides the river's main channel, the floodplain contains a maze of interlocking channels, streams, and lagoons that are lined with gigantic river red gums. Black box gums dot the usually arid floodplain between watercourses. These floodplain waterways offer solitude, countless swimming holes, and varying amounts of wildlife. Many of these smaller channels are negotiable only by canoe.

## Canoeing and Camping on the Murray Waterways

The Murray River and its web of waterways are built to order for the novice canoeist. The current is usually weak or nonexistent. To enjoy camping from a canoe you will need camping gear, adequate food rations (we drank from the river, though you may want to bring a purifier), sunscreen, a hat, a compass, a map, and possibly a fishing line.

The Murray is usually sluggish. You should expect to paddle, not drift between points, which means you'll get plenty of exercise. During much of the year the Murray and its interconnecting streams stop moving, held in check by weirs that have been put in place to ensure sufficient water even in times of drought. The advantage of a near motionless river is that you can paddle in either direction, which makes loop routes possible. This eliminates the hassle of one-way trips that require returning a canoe to a rental shop when you don't have an automobile. If you're in reasonable shape, allow for a speed of about 4 kilometers per hour in these conditions.

## Murray River Canoe Guides

The Department of Recreation and Sport of South Australia has developed a series of Murray River Canoe Guides that highlight routes, campsites, cautions, regulations, Aboriginal and European history, and wildlife in different areas. These guides provide all the particulars, including permit requirements and a clearly marked river map to help you through the mazelike waterways.

## Canoe Camping on the Murray

Once you decide on an area, contact the nearest tourist information center, which will tell you which lands are public and private and give you phone numbers and names of land owners requiring permission. Your choices of campsites may depend on the conditions attached to the portion of the river you have chosen. If you're coming from overseas, procuring permission might be expedited by working through an adventure outfitter or an outdoor-travel consultant.

*Chambers Creek and Lake Bonney Region.* This can be a one-way or round-trip paddle between the town of Barmera and historic Overland Corner. There are 1-, 2-, and 3-day paddles encompassing as much as 40 kilometers. The route takes in historical ruins from the stagecoach era, islands, reed-lined creeks, river red gums, aquatic and arid-lands bird life, and probable sightings of gray kangaroo and goannas. There are also "canoe trees," where Aborigines cut bark from river red gums to make the original Murray River canoes.

Obtain the *Chambers Creek Canoe Guide* by contacting Mr. Terry Walker (Mannum Community Centre 51 Adelaide Road, Mannum, S.A. 5238; phone 08-8569-2534) or from outdoor outfitters in the large towns.

*Pike River Region.* This system at the Murray River town of Renmark has several routes that can encompass 30 kilometers in 1-, 2-, and 3-day paddles. There is greater variety in wildlife here than in

Chambers Creek and the Lake Bonney region. On Goat Island is a sanctuary for koalas introduced by conservationists in the 1960s. The animals escaped to a nearby paddock after the stream isolating them changed course. However, Goat Island has remained a sanctuary, and, with a little luck and a spotlight at night, you can get a look at echidnas and feather-tailed gliders.

For details contact the Department of Industry and Trade, Recreation and Sport and ask for the *Pike River Canoe Guide* (phone 08-8416-6677); you can also try the Mannum Community Centre (phone 08-8569-2534).

*Chowilla Country.* This may be the best place of all, though it is difficult to get to. Chowilla Country has pristine river red gum forests and watercourses with few signs of modern intrusions. Some conservation groups claim the wetlands have international importance. Maps of the area are available from the Department of Industry and Trade, Recreation and Sport, 27 Valetta Road, Kidman Park, S.A. 5001; phone 08-8416-6677 or 08-8569-2534.

## Houseboating on the Murray

If paddling and camping seem a little too spartan, you may find houseboating a more pleasant way to travel. Naturally, the costs are higher than canoeing. Many of the houseboats berth ten and come fully equipped—just like a house—though a few companies also rent small two-berthers. To rent a houseboat you need a valid driver's license and must attend a 15-minute on-the-spot instruction.

There are seasonal differences in houseboat rental prices: per person rates can range from $A20 to $A45 a day. In the off-season the full rental of an eight-berther for seven nights may be only $A600, but in the summer holidays (Christmas and New Year's in Australia) the price is close to $A1,000 for the same package. See contacts listed under "River Travel and Wine Tasting."

## Paddle Wheelers and Luxury Cruises

I must confess to a general bias against these modes of transportation on the Murray River. The large paddle wheelers I've seen miss the point of getting to know the Murray; the irony is readily apparent when one of these big boats steams past. Its coming is marked by birds fleeing the area. When the riverboat passes, it usually appears strangely devoid of people—even when fully boarded. "Where are the people?" I asked a 16-year-old in the next canoe. "They're inside playing games, like table tennis and bingo, and drinking."

The big boats' advertisements talk of bird-watching, target practice, bushwalking, canoeing, and visiting river towns, though they don't explain how well bird-watchers and target shooters get along. With the exception of the out-of-place pursuit of target practice, you can experience all big-boat nature-oriented activities without a big boat.

There are some fairly authentic smaller, older vessels plying the Murray, too. Some of these are supposed to be authentic, and are not sanitized to the point of sterility. The best of these operate out of Victoria. Check with the South Australia Tourism and Travel Centre for information: phone 08-8212-1505.

## River Travel and Wine Tasting

Many of the Riverlands wineries are near the Murray River. If the idea of combining boating and wine tasting appeals to you, read the section on the Riverlands wineries in the section entitled "South Australia's Wineries."

*Canoe Rentals.* Because proprietors change from year to year, the surest way to locate operative canoe-rental businesses is through the Renmark Paringa Visitor Information Centre, Murray Avenue, Renmark, S.A. 5341; phone 08-8582-3456; fax 08-8582-2513; E-Mail: bigriver@riverland.net.

*Houseboat Rentals.* Try Warriuka Houseboats (P.O. Box 74, Paringa, S.A. 5340; phone 08-8595-5324) or Riverland Holiday Booking Centre (151 Murray Avenue, Renmark, S.A. 5341; phone 08-8586-4444).

*Cruise Boats.* The P.S. *Murray Princess,* an authentic-looking three-deck paddle wheeler, operates out of Renmark and takes customers on 6-day river trips covering 700 kilometers. Inquire at Murray River Cruises; phone (toll-free inside Australia) 1-800-804-843.

*Overnight Hotel or Motel Accommodations.* Try the Ventura Motel (234 Renmark Avenue, Renmark; phone 08-8586-6841) or the Citrus Valley Motel (210 Renmark Avenue, Renmark; phone 08-8586-6717).

*Road Access to the Murray River.* You can get to the Riverlands towns of Renmark, Loxton, Barmera, and Berri by rental car or coach from Adelaide. The journey takes between 2 and 4 hours.

# The Coorong and Murray Mouth

Adventure travel consultant and outdoor educator Joc Schmiechen and I silently sat perched on a sandhill that spilled into the Coorong. Joc quietly spoke into my microcassette recorder: "In any sort of weather you can sit on these dunes and be treated to one of the great environmental light shows. Black rain squalls streaming across the channel, glowing fireball sun sinking over golden water, and stark dunes coloring everything in ever-changing hues of orange and pink. Myriad little bays and backwaters filled with waterbirds. Above them, wedge-shaped squadrons of Cape Barren geese and cormorants wing their way to their evening roosts. The Coorong is bird land and presents a kaleidoscope of constantly changing weather, light, and moods. It has a spiritual quality accentuated by bountiful signs of past Aboriginal occupation and eerie solitude. There is nowhere quite like it."

The unique ecology and physical characteristics of Coorong are the result of 6,000 years of silting action by the Murray River, earlier fluctuations in sea level due to ice ages dating back to the Pleistocene, and constant tidal turbulence from the Southern Ocean.

The Coorong is made up of a narrow tidal lagoon and associated inland waterways and is separated from the Southern Ocean by the narrow Younghusband Peninsula, which parallels the mainland for 140 kilometers. The shoestring-shaped Younghusband Peninsula is the unique geographic feature of the region and is the Coorong's ecological foundation.

The northern end of this waterway is the terminus of the Murray River, where it gently merges with the sea near the town of Goolwa. The point of the actual merger between Australia's longest river and the Southern Ocean is called the Murray Mouth. Goolwa, named for

an Aboriginal term meaning "elbow," is a small, historically signifi-
cant town that sits on the river's last bend before it enters the sea.
The inland waterway and the Younghusband Peninsula make up
Coorong National Park.

Though the ecology of the Coorong has been altered since European settlement of Australia, it remains a unique, seemingly pristine
wild place. There are 80 species of marine birds and nesting areas for
Australian pelicans and black swans. Here you can see impressive
concentrations of emus, shags, cormorants, darters, herons, egrets,
kites, ospreys, terns, oystercatchers, grebes, ducks, ibises, and the
once endangered Cape Barren geese.

A walk across the Younghusband Peninsula from the inland
shore's calm waters to the breakers pounding the endless beach is a
step back in time. The peninsula is rarely wider than 800 meters, but
in crossing it you tread through 6,000 years of Aboriginal history in
the form of huge middens often blown out by ocean storms. It's not
uncommon to find skeletons of Aborigines whose burial place has
been exposed by the constantly shifting dunes. On your wander
through time you'll come across emus sprinting through sandhills
and down beaches. The birds appear, then disappear, swallowed up
in dunes that tower around you, shaped like an angry sea storm that
has been frozen for an instant.

Climatically, the Coorong is exciting and unpredictable. South-
westerlies and storm conditions are common, but so are sun-
drenched calm days, in which the wakes of fleets of Australian
pelicans fishing in unison are the only ripples on the water. It's not
unusual to be basking in the sun while watching rain squalls move
over the Coorong a few kilometers away. The lighting at dawn and
dusk can be spectacular.

## Aboriginal Culture in a Land of Abundance

When Europeans arrived at the Coorong they found what may have
been the densest concentration of Aborigines in all of Australia.
These people, who called themselves Ngarrindjeri, had a sophisticated form of government that operated as a confederation of clans.
Unlike the "walkabout" way of life common to most Aboriginal
groups, the Ngarrindjeri stayed put in a settled community built
around their rich environment. The Ngarrindjeri built dome-shaped
houses framed with wood and walls woven of reeds.

# Camping and Exploring along the Coorong

Tauwitchere Point is the west end of a snub-nosed promontory that pokes into the Coorong from Younghusband Peninsula directly across from Tauwitchere Island. It is an excellent place to camp and a logical base of operation for exploring the rest of the Coorong. Look for a green shed and go ashore about 50 meters south of it. Inland you will find the oldest dwelling on the Coorong, a whitewashed colonial cottage known as the Snake Pit. This is old-timer Bernie Shipway's place and is one of the only structures you'll find in the area. The cottage is built from bricks that served as ballast on lightly laden windjammers that came to collect cargo for the return to England.

## Boat Camping on the Coorong

The Coorong is an exceptional wilderness camping spot. It's also a very fragile area and demands careful, minimum-impact camping. It is relatively easy to reach and is usually empty of people except on holidays. Before you visit the Coorong, keep in mind that you must go forth entirely self-contained, including an ample supply of fresh water. The usual means of access are light boats: canoe, centerboard or catamaran sailboat, and outboard-motor-powered aluminum dinghy.

The Coorong is not the place to learn how to skipper a small craft on your own. You must have reasonable skills in operating the boat of your choice. If you aren't proficient in the use of small craft, a local in Goolwa can deliver you to a camping place with an agreement to pick you up in a few days. You can also visit the Coorong under the supervision of Osprey Wildlife Expeditions (phone 08-8339-4899), a quality adventure-tour operator that runs organized trips to the area.

*Boat Hire.* This is a bigger problem than it should be, considering the riches of the Coorong. During my visit I was unable to find reasonably priced small boats in Goolwa, so I rented a boat in Adelaide and towed it to the Coorong. The Goolwa businesses renting small boats had jacked their prices up and were catering to half-day and day users, rather than overnight users. Check with the Tourist Information Service, 76 Princess Highway, Meningie; phone 08-8575-1698.

## Fishing

Most Australians frequenting the Coorong are fishermen, for the Channel is well known for its mullet, bream, garfish, and mulloway (a huge cannibalistic fish that can weigh up to 25 pounds). For details about fishing inquire at boat-rental businesses in Goolwa.

### Goolwa

Goolwa is 83 kilometers from Adelaide and is easy to locate on any road map. Stateliner and Ansett/Pioneer coaches regularly stop at Goolwa.

*Accommodations.* Goolwa Hotel, 7 Cadell Street, Goolwa, S.A. 5260; phone 08-8555-2012. Noonameena House and Lodge, P.O. Box 105, Meningie, S.A. 5264; phone 08-8575-6200.

*Access.* It takes about 90 minutes to reach Goolwa by car or bus from Adelaide.

# The Eyre Peninsula

The Eyre Peninsula is an immense triangular hunk of land that juts southward, separating Spencer Gulf from the Great Australian Bight. This pie-shaped, arid, and rolling landscape is outlined with three major roads: the Eyre, Lincoln, and Flinders Highways, all paved, straight, and fast. The connecting points of the triangle are Port Augusta in the northeast, Port Lincoln to the south, and Ceduna to the northwest. Port Augusta, the northeastern point of the triangle, is 317 kilometers from Adelaide. Mining, dryland agriculture, and fishing occupy most of the population. From Port Augusta the Lincoln Highway runs southwesterly 357 kilometers to its end at Port Lincoln.

Most of the Lincoln Highway is uneventful, but there are excellent stands of mallee that teem with lorikeets, honeyeaters, and other nectar-eating birds, especially during the bloom. Stop the car, roll down the window, and you'll be amazed at the noise level.

There aren't many towns along the Lincoln Highway. About 75 kilometers from Port Augusta you pass by the steel-producing town of Whyalla. Tumby Bay, just 49 kilometers from Port Lincoln, is the nearest mainland town to the wildlife-rich Joseph Banks Islands.

On the peninsula's west coast, the Flinders Highway stretches over 425 kilometers from Port Lincoln to Ceduna. Difficult-to-reach offshore islands dot the Southern Ocean along this route, much of which passes through dryland grain-growing areas. This highway is marked by Coffin Bay National Park, a half dozen small towns, a pioneer-vintage roadhouse and cemetery, several conservation parks, and Point Labatt, the only known Australian sea lion colony on the mainland (see details on the Australian sea lion in the Kangaroo Island section, above).

The Point Labatt Conservation Park can be reached by turning off the Flinders Highway 28 kilometers southeast of Streaky Bay at the Dalca turnoff. Head south until you reach the Dalca–Sceale Bay Road turnoff. After 8.5 kilometers look for a sign directing you to Point Labatt, 19 kilometers down a dirt road.

Running east and west, the Eyre Highway stretches 468 kilometers across the top of the peninsula to connect Port Augusta with Ceduna. The intermediate stops along the way—Iron Knob, Kimba, Poochera, and Wirrulla—have basic accommodations. This route also passes through Pinkawillinie and Lake Gilles Conservation Parks. If you're interested in what the native flora looked like before it was cleared, ask in Kimba for directions to Pinkawillinie Conservation Park. The turnoff is about 50 kilometers west of Kimba. The park has a wide variety of mallees and arid-land plants.

East of Kimba is Lake Gilles Conservation Park. Depending on when the last significant amount of rain fell, Lake Gilles is either a huge salt pan or a shallow salt lake. Mallee fowl and emus are common in the southern end of this park.

Both of these conservation parks are unimproved, other than dirt tracks that allow access for conventional vehicles most of the year. It is recommended that you bring ample water. If your car fails, you may wait a few days—or longer—for help.

If you're pushing down the Eyre Highway and need a convenient spot to stretch your legs, take in a view, and eat lunch, stop at Turtle Rock, a miniature Uluru (Ayers Rock) created by the same forces of nature that shaped Uluru.

The Eyre Highway is the fastest route across the Eyre Peninsula and has the least to offer in terms of scenery and parks. Cactus Beach, the treeless Nullarbor Plain, and Western Australia are your next stops west. Ceduna, where the Eyre and Lincoln Highways meet, is the stepping-off point to the Nullarbor. Ceduna has an attractive waterfront that is often plagued with drunk Aborigines, who usually appear more pathetic than threatening. The town has many types of accommodations. From Ceduna it's a short drive to Penong and the turnoff to Cactus Beach, which you must see if you're in this neck of the woods. It has huge waves and is a hangout for surfers from all over Australia.

## Sailing to Wilderness Isles

The Eyre Peninsula, a rare combination of absolute solitude and easily accessible spectacular wild areas, hasn't received the fanfare of other regions of Australia, which is your good fortune. I found the peninsula's offshore islands a rich and unspoiled Galápagos-type natural laboratory. The islands, with mainland stops at two national parks, are definitely worth the extra effort to visit.

On the islands you can see a variety of unspoiled habitats, rare wallabies, kangaroos, multitudes of seabirds and waterfowl, many species of parrots, wombats, two or more species of pinnipeds, penguins, mutant races of tiger snakes, geckos, great white sharks, dolphins, and dozens of other creatures.

Sailing among the offshore islands is an experience etched vividly in my memory. I rate adventure sailing here in the top four accessible coastal cruising areas in all Australia (the other three places being the Cobourg Peninsula, the Kimberley region, and the Whitsunday Islands, all of which are in the tropics). This is the least-known region in my top four, and is the only one in a temperate climate.

The islands along the Eyre Peninsula's exposed west coast are difficult to visit. With the exception of Flinders Island, reaching them requires an expedition-style commitment because of the pounding surf, exposed anchorages, and hazardous landing areas. Many of these islands are entirely pristine environments and worth the visit, if you're up to the challenge of procuring a skipper who'll deliver and pick you up. A few of the islands are off-limits because they are the last stronghold of endangered rat-size marsupials. Visitors to these islands usually hire a fishing boat in the off-season from Venus Bay, Streaky Bay, or Ceduna. Flinders Island is the only island regularly visited. This 3,500-hectare island sits in the Great Australian Bight about 30 kilometers west of Elliston. Much more difficult to reach is

Pearson Island, a huge granite outcrop teeming with bird life and rock wallabies.

Flinders Island has a small airstrip and a shearer's quarters for accommodation, and over 30 beaches and safe swimming areas. Aside from a few islands tucked away in bays, the rest of the west coast islands can be approached only across the open ocean. You can obtain more information on these islands at the Far West District Office of the National Parks and Wildlife Service in Streaky Bay.

The more protected Spencer Gulf side of the Eyre Peninsula is easier to get to. There are both charter and "bare boat" (skippering your own yacht) businesses that provide a means to reach these islands. The Joseph Banks Islands, islands of the Thorny Passage, and Dangerous Reef have the most to offer. In all, there are more than 30 islands and the coastline of Lincoln National Park to explore. Most of the islands are parks, but some are privately owned.

My original purpose for visiting these islands was simply to observe the wildlife, which was accomplished easily enough, but I came away awed by the total experience. There were many magic moments: the sunsets, dolphins cruising along the bow and an albatross gliding effortlessly past, and bumping ashore in our rubber dinghy on tiny islands with chirping rock parrots buzzing everywhere and marbled geckos perched on granite boulders. Every morning we were greeted by vistas of a smooth ocean dotted with shimmering islands.

At one point we shared a beach with sea lions who swam and sunbathed with us while a sea eagle circled overhead. We sailed from one island to the next under light-to-moderate breezes. Sometimes we'd fish with a hand-held line, baited with Polish sausage. Usually, within an hour we'd catch whitings and Tommy roughs for the evening meal.

Port Lincoln and Tumby Bay are the stepping-off places for most of the islands.

## Port Lincoln

For a tourist or adventurer Port Lincoln is the most appealing town on the peninsula. It has good restaurants and an assortment of accommodations, including an 1840 vintage hotel. Campgrounds are close by—key mainland and island parks—and a fledgling tourist industry is ready to provide access to islands and mainland wild areas.

Port Lincoln is a town in transition. It has a tree-lined esplanade on Boston Bay with a row of 1940s-style storefronts facing the ocean. Large grain silos and a pier large enough for oceangoing ships dominate the commercial waterfront. In 1987 a $A50 million harbor was completed primarily for the tuna fishing fleet that, 20 years earlier, claimed only one fishing boat. That boat, the *Tacoma*, was built from an American design and is still owned by the Haldane family, who started South Australia's tuna industry. Port Lincoln now supplies 90 percent of Australia's tuna. The new harbor has begun to attract pleasure boats.

*Parks in the Region.* There are 2 national parks and 11 conservation parks on the mainland of the Eyre Peninsula. Most of the offshore islands are conservation parks as well. Before visiting any of the parks you should check with the Port Lincoln Visitor Information Centre, 66 Tasman Terrace, Port Lincoln, S.A. 5606; phone 08-8683-3544.

# Coffin Bay National Park

Coffin Bay is an extremely rich and varied coastal environment with a large protected bay, secondary bays, fresh- and saltwater swamps, lakes, massive destabilized and stabilized dune systems, islands, limestone cliffs, and ancient granite formations. There are beaches without people and a wide range of plant communities that include the dryland tea tree, drooping she-oaks, and other semiarid plants, salt- and wind-tolerant coastal shrubs, and lichens, as well as dune system shrubs like velvet bush, sandhill daisies, and wattles.

*Getting to Coffin Bay.* Coffin Bay National Park is 50 kilometers northwest of Port Lincoln on the Flinders Highway. At the town of Coffin Bay follow signs to Coffin Bay National Park. Proceed to the ranger station.

*Camping, Swimming, and Cautions.* Bushcamping is the rule in Coffin Bay. Your optimum campsite can be found by first describing to the ranger on duty the kind of campsite you want. He'll direct you to secluded beaches or to specific kinds of wildlife habitats that your vehicle is able to reach. Also, tell the ranger if you plan to swim or snorkel. The underwater visibility is generally excellent, and the water comfortable, but keep in mind that the plentiful pinnipeds may attract great white sharks. Also, in some areas undertows may be dangerous. Play it safe—ask first.

*Coffin Bay's Bird Life.* More than most coastal areas on the mainland, Coffin Bay is rich in bird life. Over 148 bird species have been recorded here, among them rare rock parrots, the once-endangered Cape Barren geese, white-breasted sea eagles, many species of lorikeets, honeyeaters, egrets, pelicans, albatrosses, and petrels.

*Southern Hairy-Nosed Wombats and Kangaroos.* Around dusk you may be lucky enough to see a southern hairy-nosed wombat. This is a burly, land-dwelling, tunnel-making, marsupial relative of the koala that is larger than its tree-dwelling relative. Wombats look like a cross between a basset hound and a small bear, and amble along at a slow pace. The southern hairy-nosed is the rarest of the two wombat species and, due to rough treatment by Europeans, it exists in only a few arid areas along the southern coast of Australia. If you wait quietly at dusk near one of their freshly dug burrows (looks like a gopher hole, but with a meter-wide opening), one may come out to forage.

*Accommodations.* You can stay outside the park at the small town of Coffin Bay in caravan parks and motels. For a motel with a dining room try the Coffin Bay Hotel/Motel, Coffin Bay, S.A. 5607; phone 08-8685-4334.

## Offshore Islands

Of the Eyre Peninsula's 70 offshore islands, the most accessible are the islands of the Thorny Passage, about 20 kilometers southeast of Port Lincoln, and the Joseph Banks Islands, about 40 kilometers east of Port Lincoln and 20 kilometers from Tumby Bay. The islands are either privately owned or are conservation parks; in either case you need permission to go ashore. If you plan to skipper your own boat, talk with park personnel at 90 Tasman Terrace in Port Lincoln for details. Usually going over the ground rules is all that is required.

Ross Haldane, the owner of a charter sailboat company in Port Lincoln, calls these islands "an accessible wilderness sailing experience that offers safety, complete solitude, and unique animals, islands, and beaches as extras." I found the animals interesting. The islands are home to a great number of birds, such as migratory shearwaters (locally known as muttonbirds), fairy penguins, sea eagles, ospreys, rock parrots, gulls, oystercatchers, Cape Barren geese, and open-ocean species of gannets and albatrosses. There are mammals, as well, probably the most attractive of which is the rare Pearson Island rock wallaby, which hops along sandy beaches and rock out-crops on Thistle Island. Australian sea lions and New Zealand fur seals are plentiful and, if you know where to look, you'll find great white sharks.

Boston Island is 5 kilometers across Boston Bay from Port Lincoln. This privately owned island, cleared in decades past for sheep grazing, acts as a breakwater for the bay and is the first island you pass on your way to the Thorny Passage. You can rent a farmhouse on the island. It has a very inviting sandy beach on the back side and a fair number of tammar wallabies that were transplanted from Kangaroo Island.

## Islands of the Thorny Passage

The islands of the Thorny Passage are 25 kilometers southeast of Boston Island. Coves, beaches, and the differences in ecosystems from one island to the next make this a rich area to explore. If you enjoy sailing, the conditions are ideal.

The islands' appearances vary from native scrub to heavily cleared barren grasslands once used for sheep. The shorelines are a combination of pocket beaches, tortured limestone cliffs, and granite out-crops. Generally the islands that have been cleared for grazing are starker in initial appearance, but not necessarily at a loss for wildlife. Most of the islands are from 2 to 200 acres in size. The three biggest, Boston (not part of Thorny Passage), Taylor, and Thistle Islands, are privately owned, which means going ashore should be arranged through your boat operator. The rest of the islands are conservation parks. When in doubt about going ashore, keep in mind that, even on privately owned islands, landing is always permissible as far up as the high-water mark, which means you can use the beach.

Snake-free Thistle Island may be the richest in wildlife. It measures 17 kilometers long and 4 kilometers wide, making it by far the largest island of the Thorny Passage. The nearly extinct Pearson Island rock wallaby can be found in plentiful numbers along the cliffs on the southwest coast. This is an attractively marked creature that is unafraid of people. Sea eagles and ospreys nest here, and Australian sea lions and New Zealand fur seals haul out on many places around the island. Goannas are easy to find, and there are two resident emus. The sheep population is vocal, 2,000 strong, and in evidence near the farmhouse.

Hopkins Island is nearest Thistle, but its ecology is entirely different. On Hopkins the coves are often heavily populated with sea lions whose curiosity about you is equal to yours about them. They will usually move off if approached on land, but will come within a meter in the water.

Millions of shearwaters engulf Hopkins Island and many nearby islands from November to March. However, the casual observer may not notice the birds because of their secretive ways. They raft together offshore and wait for darkness before flying to their nests to feed their young. Sitting on a promontory on one of these nesting islands during a moonlit night provides an unforgettable sight of a sky filled with frenzied wings. It's surreal as birds disappear into the ground and return a short time later to contribute to the din of thousands of wingbeats.

The tiger snakes on Hopkins Island are handsome, robust creatures with glistening black bodies and rounded heads. They are unusually large, some measuring 1.5 meters. Although they are retiring by nature, their venom can kill humans. Your chief risk is stepping on a tiger snake when your weight caves in a shearwater burrow where a snake may be resting.

Owens Island, directly north of Taylor Island, is a tiny pristine granite outcrop covered with vegetation. It is home to rock parrots. Dozens and dozens of them flit every which way, rapidly calling to one another. We wandered around the island and saw a half dozen Cape Barren geese, a pair of shy albatrosses, some marble geckos, skinks, and no tiger snakes. It felt as if no more than a dozen people had ever set foot on Owens Island. The abundance of wildlife and the rare solitude made Owens Island my favorite of these islands.

## Joseph Banks Islands

The Joseph Banks Islands are much like the Thorny Passage group in appearance. However, in terms of wildlife there are differences. Splisby Island is the year-round stronghold and nesting grounds for the once endangered Cape Barren geese. The world population of these colorful geese is about 6,000. Splisby and Flinders Chase National Park on Kangaroo Island are the best places to see them.

Eight hundred sheep are grazed on Splisby. If you want this 400-hectare island to yourself, the island has a small landing strip and renovated farmhouse that sometimes doubles as a vacation rental.

## Dangerous Reef

This is billed as a stronghold for great white sharks. It's an isolated rock outcrop and not a reef at all. Located midway between Taylor Island in the Thorny Passage and Splisby Island at the southern end of the Joseph Banks group, Dangerous Reef is world famous for its high concentrations of great white sharks (called white pointers in Australia) that prey on sea lions. Chances are that any film footage you've seen of the great white's ferocious feeding behavior was shot here. This is where underwater shark freaks come to chum the water with buckets of blood and dismembered livestock to attract a monster or two, so they will bite at the bars of their submerged diver cages—reputedly giving the caged diver the thrill of a lifetime. Divers from around the world pay top dollar to sit in these suspended cages while the ultimate eating machine frustrates itself on the bars.

The biggest recorded great white measured 7 meters and weighed over 3,500 kilograms (7,000 pounds). They always come equipped with rows of replaceable spoon-size serrated teeth. To too many people they have been cast as the ultimate villains of the ocean, worthy of purging. This attitude has resulted in their alarming scarcity in recent years.

Your chances of seeing a great white are still fairly good, according to Rodney Fox, an acknowledged great white expert in Adelaide. Fox has the distinction of once being grabbed and spit out by a great white. Photographs of Fox exposing his scarred torso have appeared in *National Geographic*. But Fox doesn't hold a grudge: he now runs diving expeditions of three days or longer to the Dangerous Reef and has become a foremost proponent of a ban on hunting the sharks. "Their numbers, especially the large ones, have dropped drastically," he says. To meet a great white shark through a charter expedition, contact Rodney Fox, 22 Argyle Walk, Bellview Heights, S.A. 5050; phone 08-8227-1694.

### Key Contacts on the Eyre Peninsula

Camping permits and requirements: permits and fees (only a few dollars) are required for camping. The advice alone is worth it. Keep in mind that many parks are harsh environments and are constantly changing with regard to availability of water, road conditions, and fires.

There are three National Parks and Wildlife Service offices on the Eyre Peninsula: Port Lincoln District Office (90 Tasman Terrace, Port Lincoln, S.A. 5606; phone 08-8682-3936), Coffin Bay District Office (Coffin Bay National Park, Coffin Bay, S.A. 5607; phone 08-8685-4047), and the Far West District Office (15 Bay Road, Streaky Bay, S.A. 5680; phone 08-8626-1008).

## Motel and Hotel Accommodations

Port Lincoln has 13 motels and hotels. One of the most fully equipped is the Hilton Motel; phone 08-8682-1144. A more modestly priced place is the Kingscourt Motel; phone 08-8682-6951.

In Ceduna accommodations include Ceduna Community Hotel/Motel (phone 08-8625-2008), which is on the ocean. On the highway out of town is the East West Motel; phone 08-8625-2101. There are a number of caravan parks with onsite vans. Try Ceduna Caravan Park, south of the post office; phone 08-8678-2290.

For more details on accommodations, obtain a free copy of *Secrets of Eyre Peninsula*, available in any business catering to tourists. This booklet is produced by the Eyre Peninsula Tourism Association.

## Boat Hire

Port Lincoln: For a big-boat charter try Yachtaway (phone 08-8684-4240) and ask for Charlie Rigg. Rigg skippers his 54-foot Quasar for groups, and also has a 33-foot sailboat. Other possibilities in Port Lincoln are Sea Charter (phone 08-8682-2935), Spencer Gulf Charters (phone 08-8682-2843), and Investigator Cruises (phone 08-8682-2741).

From Tumby Bay you have one choice: Tumby Bay Charters (phone 08-8688-2811) has a small cabin cruiser that will take you to the Joseph Banks Islands.

*Small Airlines.* For daily flights between Adelaide and Port Lincoln call Kendall Airlines at 08-8682-1933 or Whylla Airlines at 08-8645-8922.

*Bus Service.* For Stateliner in Adelaide, phone 08-8415-5555; in Port Lincoln, phone 08-8682-1734.

*Rental Cars in Port Lincoln.* Budget (phone 08-8684-3668), Hertz (phone 08-8682-1933), Avis (phone 08-8682-1072). Most of these companies allow one-way rentals between Adelaide and Port Lincoln with no extra charge for not returning the vehicle to your starting point. Inquire to make sure.

# Coober Pedy

Seemingly in the middle of nowhere, about halfway between Adelaide and Alice Springs on the Stuart Highway, sits opal-rich Coober Pedy. It is one of the weirdest places on earth. Its stark environment and social mix make it the perfect setting for a sci-fi thriller, and indeed, *Mad Max: Beyond Thunderdome* was filmed here.

You'll know you're nearing Coober Pedy before you see anything resembling civilization. The flat desert with shimmering mirages, salt pans, and occasional patches of mallee and mulga gives way to a scarred and cratered landscape that looks as if a squadron of B-52s regularly bombs the area. Signs along the road show a human figure falling down a mine shaft with the caption "Deep Shaft."

The contrast between the barren, hostile environment and the people who live here is compelling. Dennis Wentiro describes the social climate of Coober Pedy from his dugout 20 meters below the parched earth surface. "I'm bold enough to say that there's no place like it in the world. There's no racial tension. Mining partnerships may consist of an Aborigine, a Greek, a white Australian, and a Hungarian all working together. We have medical doctors, electricians, schoolteachers, mechanics, and dentists who have given up their professions for opal mining. You may be a millionaire and ride a push-bike in tattered shorts and thongs and drink beer with everybody else at the bar. It doesn't matter whether you're drinking with a pauper today because tomorrow . . ."

Wentiro knows the town's spell well. He arrived as a social worker assigned to grapple with the family problems of the town's 40 nationalities. He soon caught the opal bug, quit his job, and joined the ranks of opal miners. That was ten years ago. He still mines while running the Umoona Opal Mine Museum.

Australia produces 80 percent of the world's opals, and Coober Pedy accounts for 70 percent of that national output—$A40 to $A60 million annually.

Seventy-five percent of the town's inhabitants live beneath the surface in the burrows they've carved into the lunarlike landscape. Churches, motels, a bookstore, a museum, and a drugstore are underground. Only a few gaudy opal shops and assorted other buildings are aboveground.

Many of the subterranean homes have all the modern conveniences, including tile or carpeted floors, built-in bookcases, chandeliers, and private bars. The rooms are a variety of shapes with rounded, Moorish-looking ceilings. They're gouged out of dense sandstone with the same tunneling machines used to mine opals.

The Underground Church of Saint Peter and Paul on Hutchinson Street is perhaps the easiest dugout to visit. The orange vinyl-covered chairs are a bit of an eyesore and the decor is stark and bright. The Saturday evening mass at 6:30 and the Sunday morning mass attract an international mix of locals and tourists.

The church gives you a feel for subterranean living, but the essence of Coober Pedy is in the dugout homes. Visitors often grapple mentally for suitable associations; some of the interiors could be catacombs in medieval Europe, a burial chamber in an Egyptian pyramid, or the home of cartoon characters Wilma and Fred Flintstone.

Coober Pedy comes from the Aboriginal term *kupa piti,* meaning "white man in hole." People live underground in dugouts because it's no Garden of Eden on the surface. Even when it's 130°F outside and the school's swimming pool is standing room only, the underground temperatures rarely creep above 78 degrees.

Unlike most rich mineral deposits in Australia, Coober Pedy's opals are not controlled by large mining companies. It's a free-enterprise system open to anyone taking out a Precious Stones Prospecting Permit from the Department of Mines and Energy in South Australia. Usually individuals form partnerships of two to four miners.

Until recently, a strong back and mental toughness were the primary ingredients for success in the opal fields. A few sticks of dynamite, a pick, shovel, and screwdriver were used to extract opals. In recent years, new technologies have been adopted; you can learn more about these innovations if you take a mine tour.

## Buying Opals

Buying opals in Coober Pedy can save you plenty. You can deal directly with miners or with shops that buy directly from miners. Some shops have their own mines. Overseas travelers can avoid sales tax by showing their passports and airline tickets.

It takes just a little knowledge to "talk" opals. After chips and cracks, the chief factors affecting price are carat, radiance, color, color pattern, quality of the cut and polish, and presentation. How these factors combine to set a price is subjective as well as objective. An opal's weight is measured in carats; most opals sell for between $A50 and $A250 per carat. Coober Pedy produces mostly clear or light-colored stones, so black opals are more valuable than clear, and the more radiant an opal, the greater its value.

The best final advice may simply be to have the seller identify an opal you're interested in buying. When you know what you're looking at, shop comparatively before making your choice.

## Transportation to Coober Pedy

Even by Australian standards, Coober Pedy is in the middle of nowhere: 600 kilometers south of Alice Springs and 840 kilometers north of Adelaide. From Adelaide you pass through Port Augusta at the top of the Spencer Gulf. Port Augusta is a mere 570 kilometers south of Coober Pedy. (Port Augusta is an important terminus; a trip through the Nullarbor Plain, Eyre Peninsula, and the Flinders Ranges starts here.)

The Stuart Highway, the only vehicular access route, is straight, fast, and empty during the day. Cars commonly travel at 140 kilometers an hour or faster (the legal limit is 110 kilometers per hour).

Night driving is a different story. Locals try to avoid it altogether. At night, wild cattle, horses, and donkeys wander onto the Stuart Highway, especially on the stretch between Coober Pedy and Alice Springs.

*Taking the Bus.* Buses run regularly along the Stuart Highway. In South Australia you can book with Stateliner in Adelaide; phone 08-

8415-5555. If you're coming from the Northern Territory, book a seat in Alice Springs. The ride from Port Augusta to Coober Pedy is the least expensive way to travel. If you hitchhike, carry plenty of water. If you're a woman hitchhiker, keep in mind that many of the miners in Coober Pedy are young and single and come from other countries, where notions about hitchhiking women may be entirely different from yours.

*Air Travel.* Kendall Airlines flies a 16-seat turboprop to Coober Pedy from Adelaide three times a week. Make bookings with Ansett in Adelaide; phone 08-8231-9567. The flight is about two hours, with an intermediate stop at the uranium mine at Olympic Dam.

*Accommodations.* Any night spent in Coober Pedy should be underground. The best deal in town is the Umoona Opal Mine and Museum, which has seven rooms to rent. It's Coober Pedy in a nutshell, because you can also buy opals and Aboriginal art and go on a mine tour. Write to Umoona Opal Mine and Museum, P.O. Box 372, Coober Pedy, S.A. 5723, or phone 08-8672-5288. The rooms are neat and have basic amenities just down the hall.

You can also rent a room at the Underground Hotel, P.O. Box 375, Coober Pedy, S.A.; phone 08-8672-5324. If you're traveling by car, turn north from Stuart Highway onto Hutchinson Street (the main street) and turn right when the business section ends.

The closest thing to an opulent cave experience may be the Desert Cave Hotel, which, like almost everything else, is on Hutchinson Street. Owner Robert Croco is hoping the Stuart Highway's paved surface will deliver more and more tourists. The Cave Hotel is the "world's only underground luxury hotel," with 44 suites, 5 shops, a buffet bar, a convention room, galleries, and a coffee shop. It's the biggest thing on Hutchinson Street; phone 08-8672-5688.

For aboveground accommodation there is the Opal Inn Motel/Hotel; phone 08-8673-5054. The Opal Inn Motel/Hotel also has underground units.

Economical places to stay include Radekas Dugout, with moderate-priced underground rooms and a youth hostel; phone 08-8672-5223. There are also three caravan parks.

*Eateries.* Coober Pedy has several good restaurants. Try Trace's for seafood; phone 08-8672-5147. A filling, balanced meal at Opal Inn

Hotel costs about $A15, and there are Greek and Italian restaurants on Hutchinson Street.

*When Not to Visit.* Avoid school holidays (see calendar of events for South Australia), and try to avoid summer, because it's often incredibly hot. Even Coober Pedyites retreat to the coast during the peak heat months of December and January.

# PART VIII

# Western Australia

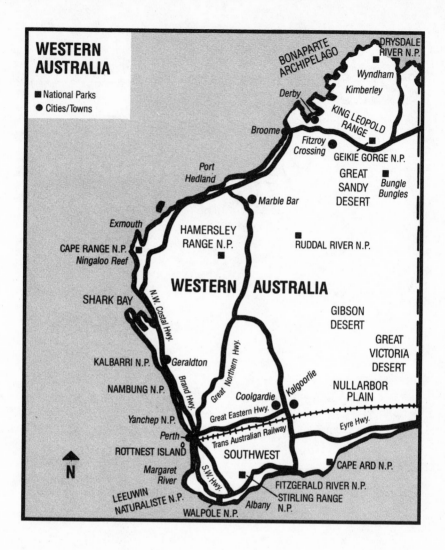

# WESTERN AUSTRALIA

■ National Parks
● Cities/Towns

BONAPARTE ARCHIPELAGO

DRYSDALE RIVER N.P.

Wyndham
Kimberley

Derby

KING LEOPOLD RANGE

Broome

Fitzroy Crossing

GEIKIE GORGE N.P.

Port Hedland

GREAT SANDY DESERT

Bungle Bungles

Marble Bar

Exmouth

HAMERSLEY RANGE N.P.

RUDDAL RIVER N.P.

CAPE RANGE N.P.
Ningaloo Reef

WESTERN AUSTRALIA

SHARK BAY

GIBSON DESERT

N.W. Coastal Hwy.

GREAT VICTORIA DESERT

KALBARRI N.P.

Geraldton

NULLARBOR PLAIN

Great Northern Hwy.

Brand Hwy.

NAMBUNG N.P.

Coolgardie
Kalgoorlie

Yanchep N.P.

Great Eastern Hwy.

Perth

Trans Australian Railway

Eyre Hwy.

ROTTNEST ISLAND

SOUTHWEST

CAPE ARD N.P.

Margaret River

S.W. Hwy.

FITZGERALD RIVER N.P.

LEEUWIN NATURALISTE N.P.

Albany

STIRLING RANGE N.P.

WALPOLE N.P.

N

# Overview

Western Australia is the island continent's largest state, claiming one-third of the Australian land mass. It encompasses more than 2.5 million square kilometers, making it nearly four times bigger than Texas. Its shores are lapped by the Southern Ocean, the Indian Ocean, and the Timor Sea. The eastern side of the state borders the Northern Territory and South Australia. It also has two outstanding scenic regions: the exotic Kimberley and the Southwest near Perth. The Kimberley, in the northern tropics, is largely uninhabited and is typified by boab trees; two-meter-tall cane grass; monsoons; Aboriginal communities; mesalike ridgelines; unexplored river systems with crashing waterfalls, crocodiles, flocks of black cockatoos, and dramatic gorges; the colorfully sculpted Bungle Bungles; and the wonderfully laid-back and multicultural town of Broome. The Southwest is known for its wildflowers, towering karri forests, and dramatic coastal parks. Aside from these two regions, other points of interest include the Hamersley Ranges; Monkey Mia, where wild dolphins greet people on a daily basis; Kalbarri and the Murchison River; the surreal landscape known as the Pinnacles; and the goldfields centered around Kalgoorlie and Coolgardie. Deserts occupy a great deal of the center of the state, and the Nullarbor Plain fills in the bottom along the Bight. Much of the state is uninhabited. There are only 1.6 million Western Australians, and 1.1 million of those live in the capital, Perth.

The Australian predicament known as the "tyranny of distance" is nowhere more apparent than between Perth and Broome, the two gateway cities to the state's most attractive regions. Broome and Perth are 2,200 kilometers apart, connected by a seemingly endless ribbon of pavement known as the North West Coastal and Brand Highways. If you're primarily interested in the Kimberley, consider doing it via Darwin—it's closer than Perth and therefore is a less expensive and time-consuming departure point—providing you've cut a ticket with an international carrier that includes Darwin.

In spring (August to November) people from around the globe come to Western Australia to view the wildflowers. Much of the coast and the southern part of the state becomes an endless amalgamation of blues, pinks, reds, yellows, and whites that appear in subtly changing patterns as you travel along the roadways. Western Australia boasts more than 8,000 species of flowering plants as well as 75 kinds of ferns and 5 different cycads. Many of the plants are found only in Western Australia because for millions of years vast oceans or deserts have isolated their evolution. About 75 percent of the flowering plants are found in the Southwest.

The trees are no less unique. In the north are boabs with steel-colored bulbous trunks. In the Southwest between the towns of Pemberton and Walpole are karri forests. These straight trees are often 75 meters high. Jarrah gums are a tad shorter but are often part of a striking plant community that includes an understory of grass trees.

# Perth

Perth is advertised in Japanese travel brochures as the safest and cleanest large city in the world. I've been there three times. Twice I arrived by air and asked the cab drivers, "What's good about Perth?" Each answered as if on cue, "It's the best city in the world!"

"The best city in the world" captures the slightly provincial and superior attitude you'll find among the relaxed citizenry. As for the Japanese observation that Perth is trouble-free, I haven't experienced anything to prove that wrong. The consensus in Perth is "we've got it made compared to the rest of the world," and they may be right. For starters, Perth is the sunniest Australian capital, averaging eight hours of sunshine a day, with average high temperatures of 86°F in the summer and 66°F in the winter.

Perth is a cosmopolitan city built around the Swan River, where its founders laid out the city grid in 1829. The city is easy to figure out for a first-time visitor. Hay Street, William Street, and Saint Georges Terrace are the primary streets and main hubs for transportation, shopping, travel booking, and information. These streets are within a block of one another. Fremantle, of 1986–87 America's Cup fame, is Perth's port. It lies 19 kilometers south of the downtown and can be reached on a 20-minute bus ride from the city's center.

## Transportation

*Air.* Perth Airport is about 20 kilometers east of the city. The international terminal is a fair distance from the domestic terminal. If you're arriving on a domestic flight you may arrive at Jandakot Airport, which is a few kilometers south of the city and about 30 minutes away from the international terminal at Perth Airport. For airport information phone 08-9478-8888. The busiest large carriers that can connect you to any other state capital are Qantas (phone 13-13-13) and Ansett (phone 13-13-00). Skywest flies regularly to Broome; phone 08-9334-2288. Getting to Perth by air is expensive. From most places (Cairns, Sydney, Melbourne) on the east coast a ticket runs about $A1,400 one way. If you're Perth-bound from outside Australia, book the flight overseas as part of a package to get a reduced fare.

There is an airport shuttle that sometimes is a little slow to show at the international terminal. The interval between buses is often about 50 minutes; phone 08-9479-4131. The one-way fare to the city from the international terminal is $A9; from the domestic terminal it's $A7. If you're headed to Fremantle there is a separate shuttle, for a fare of around $A12; phone 08-9383-4115. A cab from the international terminal to the city runs around $A25. Try Swan Taxis; phone 08-9444-4444.

*Bus.* The East Perth Terminal, on West Parade, handles interstate bus traffic from other parts of Australia. Greyhound is the volume carrier; phone 13-20-30. Fares from Sydney are about $A340, and the trip takes about 23 hours. Perth has a good internal bus system. For route information, phone Transperth, 13-22-13. There is a free CAT bus that runs a downtown loop for shoppers.

*Train.* The *Indian Pacific,* thoroughly described as the world's most boring train ride in the coverage of South Australia, arrives at the East Perth Terminal on Summers Street. From Sydney the trip takes three days, from Adelaide *only* 39 hours. The Adelaide-Perth leg

costs about $A530 for the economy sleeper; it's about $A850 from
Sydney. If you're a masochist you can buy a seat and try to sleep sitting up and arrive as a back-sore zombie; from Sydney it'll cost
$A400, from Adelaide $A250. For train schedules phone Westrail,
13-10-53.

*Rental Cars.* The major car companies have booths in the international and domestic terminals: Budget (phone 08-9277-9277), Hertz
(phone 08-9479-4788), and Thrifty (phone 08-9277-9281). Cottesloe Car Hire in Swanbourne (a suburb) undercuts the big companies;
phone 08-9383-3057. Also try Bayswater Rentals, 160 Adelaide Terrace, for a good price; phone 08-9325-1000. If you're planning to
use a car to tour the Southwest and head north to Monkey Mia and
beyond, make sure your contract is for unlimited mileage and that
the insurance covers cracked windshields.

## Information Sources

The Western Australian Tourist Centre, 469 Wellington Street, has
maps, brochures, and stacks of tourist information; phone 08-9483-
1111. The Department of Conservation and Land Management
(CALM) has an information-disseminating office at 50 Hayman
Road, Como, W.A. 6152 (phone 08-9334-0333), and operates the
Western Australia Naturally Outdoor Information Centre in Fremantle (phone 08-9430-8600). Ask about *Landscapes,* a high-
quality informative magazine put out by CALM. They also have a
great deal of specialized outdoor material on parks and activities
such as kayaking, bird-watching, and plant identification, as well as
many details about the unique natural history of Western Australia.
CALM is the most reliable source I found in Western Australia.
CALM has regional outlets throughout Western Australia, often
sharing an office with the Western Australia Tourism Commission's
offices. Find one and you may find both. The Royal Automobile
Club, 228 Adelaide Street, is an excellent source for touring maps,
road conditions, and statewide emergency services.

## Tours

I've traveled extensively in Western Australia in rental cars and spent
time shopping to get the best deal. But depending on your budget and

inclination to take on long driving hours in sometimes hazardous conditions, a bus or 4WD tour may make better sense. Your tour choices and selections need to be coordinated with the seasons. For example, August to November is the traditional season for blooms in Western Australia. Literally miles of landscape become an explosion of color as nearly everything blooms. The entire rainbow is represented—there are even green and blue flowers. More than 7,000 plant species, including many unusual ones, such as the immense conelike banksia flowers, will be entirely new to most visitors.

The large tour companies operate out of Perth. There are numerous aerial tours that either do flyovers or deliver you to an in-state destination, such as York, Exmouth, Monkey Mia, or Broome. Check with the tourist center at 469 Wellington; phone 08-9483-1111.

*Tour Companies.* Here are some of the better-known tour companies and their specialties: Australian Pinnacle Tours goes north to the Pinnacles and other parks. This is a good bet during the bloom months, when plant life becomes an array of colors; phone 08-9221-5411. Australia Pacific Tours offers large coach tours of regions and parks throughout Western Australia. These are informative and popular with retired folks; phone 13-13-04. For a varied, multiday experience that may include some tent camping try West Coast Safaris (phone 08-9401-0031) or Overland 4WD Safaris (phone 08-9358-3588).

The most authentic hands-on experience is offered by Landscope Expeditions, which is part of the Department of Conservation and Land Management (CALM). The trips go to remote wild areas, where "inductees" help scientists with wildlife studies and natural history projects. These trips involve living together in bunkhouses and tents, plus stays in regular roadside motels. For details contact CALM's office at 50 Hayman Road, Como, W.A. 6152; phone 08-9334-0498.

*Schooner Tours.* These tour packages are so unique that they deserve mention. The *Leeuwuwin II* is a huge three-masted schooner that takes paying passengers up and down the Western Australian coastline. The ship is moored in Fremantle and leaves for trips of one day to two weeks. Students pay about $A90 a day and nonstudents, around $A100. The trips often include anchorages well away from road access. For details phone 08-9430-4105.

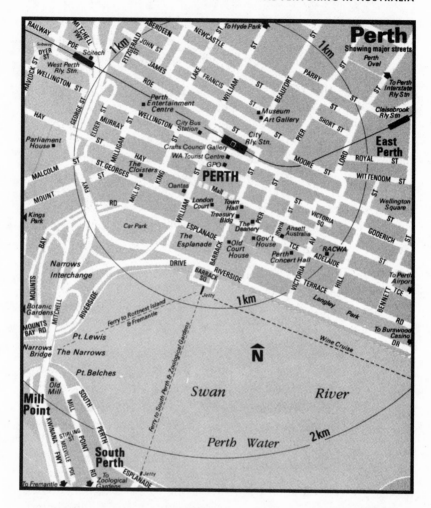

*Air Service Tours.* Western Australia is a big place, and if your budget allows it you may want to take advantage of a quicker method of transportation. There are small air services that have designed trips to remote areas stretching from Perth to the Kimberley. Some of these trips are 20-day-plus affairs taking in a dozen stops and minitours. Two of the companies offering this kind of touring are: Kookaburra Air (phone 08-9354-1158) and Complete Aviation (phone 08-9414-1044).

*Ferry Tours.* Several companies run ferries to Rottnest Island. The *Rottnest Express* departs Victoria Quay in Fremantle several times daily. Round-trip on the same day is $A32 for adults; phone 08-9225-6406. Oceanic Cruises leaves from Pier 2 on the Barrack Street Jetty in Perth. Round-trip on the same day for adults is $A40. Phone 08-9325-1191.

*Bicycle Tours.* Perth and its outlying areas are relatively flat and suitable for bike riding. Visit the Western Australian Tourist Centre at 469 Wellington Street for maps; phone 08-9483-1111. For a good-quality bicycle call on Bikewest, at 441 Murray Street; phone 08-9320-9301.

## Accommodations

*Economy.* Try Shiralee, 107 Brisbane Street, Northbridge, W.A. 6000, phone 08-9227-7448, which is friendly and clean. Doubles go for $A40 and dorm beds for $A16. Also in the Northbridge district are several other economy-priced accommodations. The Rainbow Lodge Backpacker, 133 Summers Street, Northbridge, W.A. 6000, with a low dorm fare of $A14 per night, has free pickup from bus and train arrivals; phone 08-1792-7529. There is also North Lodge Central City Backpacker, 225 Beaufort Street, Northbridge, W.A. 6000, which offers free train, airport, and bus pickup. Dorms are $A14, twins $A33; phone 08-9227-7588.

*Moderate.* Sullivan's, 166 Murray Street, sits near tranquil and usually flowering Kings Park. It's a small hotel with a casual atmosphere near the heart of the city. Rooms start at around $A125; phone 08-9321-8022. The Criterion Hotel, 560 Hay Street, Perth, W.A. 6000, is a modernistic structure in downtown. Rooms start at around $A150; phone 08-9325-5155. The Radisson Observation City Hotel on the Esplanade at Scarborough Beach, Perth, W.A. 6019, puts you on the doorstep of the "sandgroper" culture with all the amenities. Rooms start at around $A150; phone 08-9340-5555.

*Upmarket.* Expensive hotels can go as high $A380 per night, so ask. The Burswood Resort and Casino is a luxury hotel with extensive gardens facing the Swan River. Rooms are $A250 and higher; phone 08-9362-7777. There's also the Rendezvous Observation City Hotel on the Esplanade at Scarborough Beach. This is the top end and was built by the famous entrepreneur Alan Bond, or "Bondy," who is bet-

ter known for his financial support of past America's Cup boat building. If you are willing to fork over the $A350 a night, make sure you
get a room with a balcony looking down on the beach; phone 08-
9245-1000.

## Restaurants

For less than $A25 per meal, try the Moon on 323 William Street.
This is a "happening" place with good light dishes and salads; phone
08-9328-7474. In this same price range is the Canton Restaurant at
532 Hay Street; phone 08-9221-1501. For not a whole lot more try
L'Escargot, at 71 Bennett Street, for French cuisine; phone 08-9325-
1660. Vultures, on the corner of Francis and Williams Streets, wins it
for ghoulish name and offbeat atmosphere. You can dine on a Balinese bed or at a low table with large cushions for chairs. The food is
mostly from the sea but creatively put together. Main entrées start at
around $A15; phone 08-9227-9087. One of the best view restau-
rants is the Moorings Café, located on the Barrack Street Jetty. It has
a great view across the Swan River and fairly standard meals, including Aussie bush cuisine such as kangaroo. Meals start at around $A35
per meal; phone 08-9325-4575. Like the revolving restaurants in the
United States and elsewhere, Perth has its answer in the Hilite 33
Revolving Restaurant, at 778 Hay Street. Look up and you'll see the
restaurant perched above you, nearly 185 meters (or roughly 600
feet) up. You can't argue about the view and the ease with which it
changes. It's expensive though, with a full-course meal usually more
than $A70 per head; phone 08-9325-4844.

## Things to Do

Amid the shiny new skyscrapers, Perth has a collection of Edwar-
dian, Victorian, and colonial buildings that date back to the 1830s.
Some of the more impressive structures and districts are: His
Majesty's Theatre (Edwardian, 1904); the Cloisters (1836); the Old
Gaol (1856); the Government House (1859); the Old Courthouse in
Stirling Gardens (1836); the Old Mill in South Perth; and in Freman-
tle, the Maritime Museum, the Round House, and the Art Centre.
The Art Gallery adjacent to the Western Australian Museum has a
fine collection of traditional and contemporary works. The Perth
zoo, in South Perth, has a particularly impressive nocturnal house.

Many of Perth's best sights are within one kilometer of the city's downtown.

For information about concerts and live plays, phone Westac-comm, 08-9277-9199, or consult the daily or weekend edition of *The Sunday Times* or *The West Australian*.

## The Beaches

Western Australians are called sandgropers because so many of their social and recreational activities are centered on beaches. The Perth metropolitan area has 19 beaches spread over 30 kilometers, from the southern suburb of South Fremantle to the northern suburb of Mullaloo. These beaches have something for everyone. They usually have public toilets and a green lawn area for picnics. When Prince Charles came to Perth in his younger days, he made for North Cottesloe Beach to go bodysurfing. Right next door is Swanbourne, a beach that underwent an $A300,000 improvement in the 1980s that included an expanded parking facility. The idea of improvements, not the expenditure, kicked off a hot debate in Perth. Swanbourne has long been an au naturel swimmers' and tanners' beach. The debate centered around the possibility that easier access and more people might attract a "kinky" crowd. The parking facility went in, and the civic fathers were relieved—the kinky crowd didn't materialize. City Beach is one of the safest swimming beaches because of the puny surf and the usually wimpy undertow. City, Cottesloe, and Scarborough are the most popular beaches.

From south to north, here is what you'll find. In the area of North Fremantle are Port and Leighton Beaches. Both are considered safe for swimming. Cottesloe, City, and Floreat are also considered good swimming beaches. Scarborough is a surfing beach that's popular with young people and is fronted on by swank hotels and a casino complex. Farther north is Trigg Island Beach, a favorite of surfers. From Trigg through Sorrento are coves and bays that are used by people avoiding crowds. Mullaloo is the safest beach in this area and usually has no surf at all. Sailboarding, surfing, volleyball, and tanning are the four pastimes here. Just south of Mullaloo at Hillary is a fully developed beach marina that sprang up with the America's Cup. It's used primarily by families.

Beach culture is at its zenith in Perth. All of Perth goes to the beach. You'll see pensioners sitting under trees reading the paper, young mums with their "ankle biters," and youthful water-sports freaks. On some beaches there are vendors who'll spray you (for a price) with suntan lotion, so you don't have to coerce a friend into applying the goo. There are surf clubs patrolling most of the beaches, windsurfing rental shops, and volleyball nets at irregular intervals.

## Kings Park

Kings Park is the best city park in Australia. It features many of the botanical wonders of Western Australia. The 1912 *Official Handbook of Western Australia* claimed that there was "no prettier landscape under the Southern Cross than this great park." The park remains much as it was in 1912, although annual visitors now exceed three million and its largely pristine appearance contains an impressive collection of memorials, statues, playgrounds, botanical gardens, fountains, restaurants, and an information center to enhance your visit. Since so much of Western Australian flowering fauna decorates the park, it's wise to get a copy of *A Guide to 101 Wildflowers of Western Australia,* so you'll know what you're looking at.

Kings Park is a lunch-hour retreat for businesspeople from Perth's downtown skyscrapers, and it's a favorite haunt of birders, walkers, and joggers. Weekends are busy—everything from family reunions to romancing couples and weddings can be found. The park can be reached in 30 minutes from the city's center by walking west on Saint Georges Terrace and left on Mount Street to the park.

## Rottnest Island

Rottnest Island is 19 kilometers from Fremantle. The island's name comes from the quokkas, the pint-sized kangaroolike animals that inhabit the island in great numbers. In 1696 Dutch explorer Wilhelm de Vlaming landed on the island looking for fresh water and assumed that the quokkas were some kind of huge hopping rat, and thus "rat's nest" island was named. The quokkas are plentiful and handsome creatures, often eager for handouts, and not adverse to pillaging an unguarded picnic.

Now usually called "Rotto," the island is promoted as the best day trip from Perth. Except for a few tourist buses, it's free of vehicular traffic. People travel by bicycle or foot. Much of the island is parklike, and there are 40 kilometers of coastline. Some of the beaches are more suitable for swimmers; others are primarily used by surfers or scuba divers. There's a small museum that chronicles the island's past as a penal settlement, an area of numerous shipwrecks, and an army post during World War II. The *Under Water Explorer,* a semisubmersible, operates from Rotto's pier. If the visibility is good, this ride will give you a good look at the more than 150 kinds of sea life around the island. There's a hamburger joint and the more formal Restaurant. You can stay overnight in hotels (one was a prison), cottages, or campsites.

Much of the charm of Rotto is getting there—you can choose a helicopter, light aircraft, or high-speed or low-speed ferry. For more information on ferries, see "Ferry Tours," above.

## Whale Watching

Whale watching has caught on in the last several years in Perth. Humpbacks and southern right whales are often in the area, most reliably between September and December, when humpback females arrive offshore with their calves. Depending on the length of the cruise (usually a half or a full day), whale watching costs between $A20 and $A40 per adult. There are also Swan River cruises, which take in the sights, including the homes of wealthy people. Try Captain Cook Cruises (phone 08-9325-3341), Boat Torque 2000 (phone 08-9221-5884), and Oceanic Cruises (phone 08-9325-1191). This last outfit whale watches with a schooner.

## Fremantle

Despite Fremantle's multimillion-dollar "face lift" and "identity crisis" brought on by the 1987 America's Cup, it's charming and dominated by classic old pub-hotels and buildings that date back to the convict labor that built them. The town can be explored easily on foot. If you hang around a pub and strike up a conversation with the natives, you'll probably still hear some grumbling about Fremantle's sudden surge in rents, food, and even beer—all 14 kinds of tap and the 45 bottled varieties.

There is plenty do in Fremantle. The Fremantle Tourist Bureau at the Town Hall is a good place to get started. There is also the Tourist Information Centre in the park along the Esplanade where Essex Street and Marine Terrace meet; phone 08-9336-6952. If you like walking tours, arrive before 10:00 A.M., so you can join a tour with a guide from the Maritime Museum. I happened onto the Fremantle Art Centre at 1 Finnerty Street in the afternoon and listened to a wonderful jazz concert for free. This wasn't a fluke. The center has a free concert every Sunday starting around 2:00 P.M. and usually lasting a couple of hours. The art is good quality and the exhibits change regularly; phone 08-9335-8244. The Fremantle History Museum is part of the Fremantle Art Centre. It's worth a visit. There are a series of themes and old photographs to tell much of the story of settlement, including the displacement of Aborigines. There are two maritime museums. The Maritime Museum on Cliff Street tells the story of shipwrecks dating to the ill-fated Dutch ship *Batavia* and other Dutch who found Australia in the 1600s, about 160 years before the British arrived; phone 08-9431-8444. At the same phone number but located at Victoria Quay is the Historic Boats Museum, which has all kinds of small boats (powered by both sail and motor) plus isolated features, such as the winged keel that allowed Australia to run away with the America's Cup in 1983. The old gaol is also a popular tour. Known as the Fremantle Prison, it is located at 1 The Terrace. The escape story of a daring Irishman is a true epic; phone 08-9430-7966. Set aside about an hour.

*Accommodations.* Fremantle is a comfortable place with many old hotels, pubs, and shops. Lodging costs can be prohibitive, but there are still places with good atmosphere and reasonable prices. Try Fremantle Hotel, at the corner of High and Cliff Streets. This is an attractive Victorian structure with a long and colorful history. Rooms start at $A85; phone 08-9430-4300. At the other end of the pecking order is the Esplanade Hotel, on the corner of Marine Terrace and Essex Street. This hotel is heavy on spas and is centrally located. Rooms start at around $A200 per night; phone 08-9432-4000.

## Restaurants

Restauranting is a competitive undertaking in Perth. There are at least 1,300 restaurants for the one million residents—nearly the same number of restaurants as in Melbourne, a city three times more populous. Malaysian, French, Dutch, Indonesian, Chinese, Mexican, Portuguese, and American are well represented. Eating out is obviously popular in Perth. The city's newspapers have regular columns about cuisines. Among the top-flight Chinese restaurants are the Golden Eagle and Emperors Court, found within 100 meters of each other in Perth's Northridge area. (Northridge is the unofficial restaurant center, featuring mostly Italian eateries.) The best seafood restaurants are in Fremantle and the coastal suburbs. Zita's, in central Perth, is tops for Portuguese food, and the River Room at the Sheraton continually wins "Gold Plate" awards. There are lots of fast-food places. Of these, the Chinese ones offer the best quality. The best way to satisfy your palate is to buy *Cheap Eats in Perth,* a review of more than 280 restaurants throughout Perth, Fremantle, and other suburbs.

In Fremantle, the George Street Café Club, 73 George Street, has good vegetarian dishes, light meals, and a myriad of deserts. Locarnos, at the corner of Norfolk Street and Marine Terrace, has both inside and outside dining with good seafood. Meals run around $A35 a plate.

# East of Perth: Kalgoorlie and the Golden Mile

In 1893 Patrick Hannan and two fellow Irishmen found gold in the middle of the desert hundreds of kilometers east of Perth.

The find was on an unimpressive mound called Mount Charlotte. As more discoveries were made, the area around Mount Charlotte became known as the Golden Mile, and the towns of Kalgoorlie, Coolgardie, and Boulder sprang up around it. The towns were built with material from the coast hauled on the backs of camels. The area is rich in history and classic architecture, still actively mined, and a society unto itself. There's the Two-Up School, where this Australian form of gambling is practiced daily. A block from the police station is a famous house of prostitution, technically illegal but sanctioned by the police as has been done since the first houses opened their doors in the 1890s. The woman in the tourist bureau described the town's institutionalized brothels this way: "There are four houses, each with six girls. The houses are structured for incomes from the very lowest to the elite. The girls are required to undergo medical checkups once a week, and they must follow safe sex practices because of AIDS. It's an institution here, like a drugstore or barbershop. There are strict rules, and the girls follow them or they're asked to leave. The system has worked a long time, and most citizens feel it makes the streets safer."

Kalgoorlie reached its peak in 1903, and the town's classic pub-hotel architecture dominates the streets.

*Information Sources.* Visit the Kalgoorlie-Boulder Tourist Centre at 250 Hannan Street (phone 08-8202-5400) to get details about mine tours, the Two-Up School, camel tours, accommodations, and places to eat.

## Things to Do

### The Golden Mile Museum

This homey museum reflects the history of the area. Curator Jill Moffett describes the museum as "an accurate and complete depiction of the social history of Europeans in the area. We plan to expand the museum a great deal to include Aboriginal and natural history." The museum is housed in an attractive brick building built in 1898, near the corner of Hannan Street and Outridge Terrace.

### Goldrush Tours

Allan Young runs Goldrush Tours and zips people around Kalgoorlie, visiting everything from the Two-Up School to the brothels (just a drive by), the mines, the radio station, the grand old hotels, places to fossick on your own, and the historic sites. Some of his tours include visiting the nearby towns of Coolgardie, Boulder, and Kambalda. These towns are typified by classic old sandstone buildings with wide verandas and exceptionally wide streets—so that camels pulling mining equipment could turn around. (The only camels in the area now are feral or those belonging to the camel farm near Coolgardie that offers rides of varying lengths to the public.)

Goldrush Tours is located on Maritana Street between Egan and Hannan Streets; phone 08-9021-2954. Pick a tour that includes going to Hainault Mine and the Two-Up School. You'll be shown the former residence of Herbert Hoover, the eventual U.S. president who spent time here as a mining engineer at the turn of the century. The trip to Coolgardie is also worthwhile.

## Yamatji Bitja Aboriginal Bush Tours

Aborigine Geoffery Stokes takes tourists on a 4WD "bush" outing in which he shows his guests how to track emus, prepare kangaroo meat, eat witchetty grubs, and learn the ways Aborigines survived in the bush. On the evening tours Stokes tells Dreamtime stories over a campfire that boils billy tea. The outing does a good job at putting people in touch with the land and shows how centuries of survival were possible because the inhabitants knew it well; phone 08-9035-3745.

## The Hannan's North Tourist Mine

The Hannan's North Tourist Mine has received national tourist awards as one of the most unique tourist attractions in Australia. I'll never forget it. You are outfitted as a miner and taken by cage elevator deep into an active mine, where you creep down narrow passages held up by timbers. John Yellant, one of the two docents, was a retired miner with a dramatic gift that was enhanced by his gravelly voice. He told stories of debilitating diseases and horrible tragedies and demonstrated equipment used over the years. Have you ever heard a steam-powered jackhammer in a tunnel and contemplated what it would be like to work one day after day? He also imparted the camaraderie between miners that erased social and racial barriers. He received an enthusiastic ovation from the group I was on. The mine is open daily. Tours run at 9:00, 11:00, and 2:30 daily. There is a nominal fee, but the tour's well worth it. Phone 08-9091-4074 for more information.

## The Two-Up School

The Two-Up School is located 7 kilometers north of Kalgoorlie on Broad Arrow Road. It's a circular structure made of rusting corrugated iron with a ring in the middle. Gambling begins at 1:30 P.M. daily. Two-up is a form of gambling invented in Australia by the early convicts. It involves flipping two coins and betting on the outcome. Two pennies are used. The heads' side is usually polished, and the tails' side is marked with white paint. A "ring keeper" selects a "spinner," who tosses the coins from a flat stick called a "kip." If the coins don't spin properly the ring keeper will "bar 'em," which voids the throw. If the spinner "ones 'em," which means one tail and one head, he throws the coins again; one of each doesn't decide a bet. If the spinner gets two tails, he loses his money and the right to spin. If he "heads" them, he collects from those who bet against him and can spin again or pass the kip to a new spinner. The spinner pays the ring keeper 10 percent of the winnings. Most players bet "on the side," which leaves the ring keeper and commission out of it. When the coins are in the air you'll hear a player yell an amount (usually between $A20 and $A40) and either "tails" or "heads." While the coins are still airborne someone else will take up the challenge and yell back "betcha," and the bet is on. Gamblers like the game because the odds are fifty-fifty each time—which gives every participant an equal chance of winning or losing. The betting is fast and furious. On busy afternoons thousands of dollars will change hands in minutes. Allan Young, who took me to the school, won $A100 in the ten minutes we were there, but don't try it unless you've watched for a while and are sure how to go about it. Taking photographs is considered offensive—don't do it. Children and alcohol are not allowed.

*Accommodations.* In Kalgoorlie you should stay in a grand old historical pub-hotel. The York Hotel, 259 Hannan Street, Kalgoorlie, W.A. 6430, phone 08-9021-2337, is a nicely preserved pub-hotel with spacious rooms and it's in the center of town (rooms are $A80 and up). The Mercure Inn, on Lower Hannan, is three kilometers out of town, but clean and quiet; phone 08-9021-1121. Other hotels are clustered around Hannan and Maritana Streets.

*Access.* Kalgoorlie is 600 kilometers east of Perth. Rail is the most interesting way to get there. The *Indian Pacific* stops here on its transcontinental run from Sydney to Perth. The *Prospector,* a fast, comfortable train, makes the run from Perth regularly. If you're driving from Perth, the Eastern Highway connects Kalgoorlie to Perth. Regularly scheduled air travel also connects Kalgoorlie to the rest of Australia.

# The Southwest

The region known as the Southwest is a favorite vacation area with a great natural beauty. Every town and park in the region can be reached by a day's drive south from Perth. The area has spectacular spring blooms of myriads of peculiar flowers. Aside from flowers, it has vineyards, limestone caves, towering forests, brushlands, and river systems. There are over a dozen national parks. And there are numerous caravan parks, campgrounds, and motel accommodations throughout the area.

## The Beach Towns

The towns of Rockingham, Mandurah, Bunbury, and Busselton have wide beaches, sweeping bays, surf—and numerous surf and recreational-equipment rental shops. Windsurfing, swimming, and sun worship go on in this area with a vengeance. I didn't find great differences among these towns, though I wasn't in them for long. Rockingham has calm waters. You can reach it on city buses from Fremantle or Perth. Mandurah enjoys great popularity because of its calm-water beaches and convenient distance to Perth (80 kilometers). Bunbury is Western Australia's second-largest city. The Dolphin Discovery Centre is here. This center is dedicated to dolphins. You can swim with them or watch films about them; phone 08-9791-3088. Busselton was my favorite. It has calm-water beaches in Geographe Bay, the oldest church (Saint Mary's) in Western Australia, and the only natural tuart forest in the world. The southern Darling Range behind these towns contains a unique plant community called a jarrah forest. The jarrahs are towering, yellow-barked gums that often have an understory of grass trees. Rock Forest Park on the road from Armadale to Brookton is representative of this attractive environment, as are many sections of the roads cutting inland from Mandurah to Bunbury. From Perth the Brand Highway takes you to Bunbury.

## The Margaret River Area

The Margaret River area has some of the most spectacular limestone caves in Australia. You won't be disappointed with the guided tours of the Jewel, Lake, Yallingup, and Mammoth Caves. In my opinion, Lake Cave is the best of the bunch. To sign on to a guided tour, visit the tourist information center in Margaret River. You must be part of a tour to visit them. Margaret River is also known for its wine, green pastures, and stud farms. Nearby Cowaramup is the heart of the wine area. Cape Naturaliste, the northern end of Cape Leeuwin–Naturaliste National Park, is north of Margaret River. The nearby town of Yallingup and the small park of the same name are known for big-wave surfing. The entire section of coast between Capes Naturaliste and Leeuwin is popular with bushwalkers. It's possible to walk the 100-kilometer coastline (or portions of it) that connects these two capes. Visit the Augusta/Margaret River Tourism Association on Bussell Highway in Margaret River. They have maps for self-guided winery tours; phone 08-9757-2911.

## Denmark

Denmark is a scenic town on a rugged green coastline. There are farms amid the mighty karri forests, which reminded me of California's coastal redwoods. Karri trees are indigenous to the Southwest, and the area between Denmark and Manjimup contains the only stretch of pure karri forests. There are also numerous inlets and waterways suitable for canoeing or investigating in an aluminum dinghy with an outboard. The Wilson Inlet and the Denmark River have a wide range of light boat possibilities in an abundantly green setting. Visit the tourism office behind Strickland Street; phone 08-9848-2055.

## Walpole-Nornalup National Park

The park and the Avenue of the Giants (huge karri trees) are near Denmark. Walpole-Nornalup is best known for its spring wildflower bloom. The Avenue of the Giants is as impressive as any grove of California redwoods. There is a signed interpretive walk through the heart of the biggest grove. On the day I visited I had the grove entirely to myself. It's excellent for a picnic stop, but camping is not allowed. The road to the Giants is an 18-kilometer loop off Highway 1. The western end of the loop is the most scenic and allows the most direct access. The turnoff is 13 kilometers from Walpole and 53 kilometers from Denmark. In this area I saw quite a few emus and kookaburras, the latter not native but introduced from the eastern states. For more information call the Walpole tourist center: 08-9840-1111.

## Albany

Albany is a sizable town and was the first settlement in Western Australia. It has a beautiful natural harbor and rows of historic buildings, including some classic pubs. The Royal George Hotel and White Star Hotel are grand old structures. The Penny Post Restaurant is in an attractively converted train depot. The Pancake House is another good eatery. There's an ample sprinkling of bed-and-breakfast places in the town's many old colonials. The tourist office is located at the southern end of York Street and a block east inside the train depot; phone 08-9841-1088.

## Porongorup

Porongorup is both the name of a small town and a national park located 50 kilometers north of Albany off the Albany Highway. The park is an interesting combination of eroded granite domes surrounded by deep valleys filled with jarrah and karri forests. There are several short walks, and wildlife is plentiful. Camping is allowed, but the Karribank Lodge is the real place to sleep. Built in 1897, it's the oldest resort lodge in Western Australia. Fully modernized with plumbing and electricity, the lodge's meter-thick rammed-earth walls are a testimonial to how long-lasting a low-budget construction technique can be. For information, phone 08-9851-1163.

*Accommodations in the Southwest.* All of the areas covered thus far can be visited from Perth in less than a day's driving time. There are a variety of places to stay, and this is a good area for car camping. Here are some of the possibilities: Heritage Trail Lodge, 31 Bussell Street, Margaret River, is a series of secluded cabins in a karri forest not far from town. This is a romantic place to stay. Cabins rent for around $A160 per night; phone 08-9757-9595. 1885 Hotel, Farrelly Street, Margaret River, is a series of cabins on an original homestead. The decor is both Victorian and casual. Cabins are in the $A80 range; phone 08-9757-3177. Karri Valley Resort, Vasse Highway, 17 kilometers north of Pemberton, is a sort of nature camp for grown-ups. The lodge is in Beedelup National Park on a beautiful tree-lined lake. The daily activities include fishing, mountain biking, and possibly helping rangers conduct a wildlife study. Cabins go for around $A190 a night; phone 08-9776-2020. In Norseman try the Norseman Hotel on Robert Street. This is a charming two-story colonial structure in the middle of town. Rooms go for about $A80 a night; phone 08-9039-1023.

## Stirling Range National Park

Stirling Range is a striking, sharply jutting range known for its bushwalks, vistas, rock climbs, and wildflowers. The park is about 80 kilometers inland from Albany. Despite the range's rather puny elevation of only 1,073 meters at the highest point, the Stirling Range looks much bigger than it actually is. The dark jagged appearance creates a foreboding silhouette that can be seen 100 kilometers away. Camping is allowed in the park. There's also the Stirling Range Caravan Park, located 89 kilometers north of Albany and 31 kilometers south of Borden. It's a full-amenities caravan park, with powered campsites and chalets ($A70 per night).

The Stirlings are about 330 kilometers southeast of Perth. For information, contact the Stirling Range Retreat at 08-9827-9229.

## Fitzgerald River National Park

East of Albany are Bremer Bay and Hopetoun, the stepping-off places for immense, mostly undeveloped 254,000-hectare Fitzgerald River National Park. The park was set aside because of its variety of plant life, which numbers in excess of 1,700 species. Bremer Bay is the western access point and has a camping area and kiosk. Ian Maley, owner of Wilderness Equipment in Fremantle, says there are many excellent beach walks at the park's western end. However, there are no clearly marked walking tracks other than 4WD tracks left behind by fishermen and doggers (dingo trappers) before the park was set aside. The Fitzgerald River cliffs are colorful reds, yellows, and oranges. They are composed of a material called spongelite, which was created from millions of dead, spongelike organisms impregnated with clay. The combination creates bright colors. Walks of more than a couple of kilometers in length should be discussed with rangers, who can be found at either end of the park. The Twertup Field Study Centre is the easiest place to see spongelite. It can be reached by a dirt road. The flowers in this region are radiant from September through October.

*Royal hakea, Fitzgerald River National Park.* PHOTO BY ERIC HOFFMAN.

Fitzgerald River National Park is roughly 550 kilometers from Perth and the farthest extent of the region known as the Southwest.

There are rangers stationed at each end of the park, in Bremer Bay and in Hopetoun. Write to Ranger in Charge, Fitzgerald River National Park, P.O. Box 33, Jerramungup, W.A. 6337. If a response isn't forthcoming, contact the Department of Conservation and Land Management, 50 Hayman Road, Como, W.A. 6152; phone 08-9430-8699.

## North of Perth

### Nambung National Park

Nambung National Park is best known for its unusual formation, the Pinnacles. The Pinnacles look like huge stalagmites poking out of the earth in otherwise fairly nondescript and barren coastal sand-dune country.

*Access.* Nambung National Park is 244 kilometers north of Perth on the Brand Highway. The turnoff is signposted to Cervantes. The last 26 kilometers of road are rough dirt and not advisable when wet. If you don't have a way to visit the park but have made it to Cervantes, inquire at Pinnacles Beach Backpackers, Seville Street (phone 08-9652-7377). They can put you on to a shuttle service.

### Kalbarri and the Murchison River

Kalbarri has emerged into a "get away from it all" resort town in the last 15 years. The Murchison River ends its long journey to the Indian Ocean here, 600 kilometers north of Perth. The gorges created by the Murchison cut dramatically into an undulating sand plain through tumblagooda sandstone, exposing millions of years of the geological record. The combination of the town, sea, and gorges is an attractive package.

Kalbarri claims an important historic footnote: Wouter Loos and Jan Pelgrom, two mutinous Dutch seamen, were put ashore here in 1629. Against their will they became the first white men to live in Australia. They arrived 141 years before Captain Cook, but no European settlement followed and no one knows what happened to them. Kalbarri's streets are named after other misfortunate seamen who were shipwrecked here during the last century.

When you get into town, visit the Kalbarri Travel Office on Grey Street; phone 08-9937-1104. For canoes and sailboards, look for the Murchison Caravan Park and inquire; phone 08-9937-1005.

## Shark Bay and the Dolphins of Monkey Mia

Monkey Mia is proof that dolphins can always draw a crowd, even in the middle of nowhere. Monkey Mia is unique because a population of wild dolphins seems to have decided that people can be trusted. This optimism started 35 years ago when local fishermen befriended a pod of local dolphins. Ever since, ensuing generations have come to shore at Monkey Mia to visit with any human who wades into the water. The dolphins will actually park themselves a few feet offshore and poke their beaks skyward. Perhaps it's their upturned mouths that makes them look as if they're smiling, but what happens next is quite a sight. Older people who haven't worn a bathing suit for 25 years abandon their shoes, pull their dresses and pant legs up, and wade into the water. Tiny tots barely able to walk are led into the water by their parents, bikini-clad teenage girls and lithe muscled boys forget about each other, and whole families wade in to be with the dolphins. The dolphins are nonchalant. They cruise through the legs of all these humans, occasionally stopping to lift their heads aloft to survey this odd human phenomenon from above water as well as from below.

Monkey Mia is on a desolate section of coast in Shark Bay far from a city, but still the campground is full most of the year. The dolphins are at Monkey Mia throughout the year, though their numbers sometimes decrease in November during the breeding season. May through October are the best months for reasonable temperatures.

If you want to wake up and go to sleep with the dolphins, stay a stroll away at the Monkey Mia Dolphin Resort; phone 08-9948-1320. Dorm-type sleeping arrangements go for $A12 a night; for sheets add $A10 more.

*A wild but friendly dolphin from Monkey Mia.* PHOTO BY ERIC HOFFMAN.

## Denham

Denham (population 400), the Peron Peninsula's only township, is on the opposite side of the peninsula from Monkey Mia. Visit the Shark Bay Tourist Centre at 71 Knight Street; phone 08-9948-1253. Denham has a restaurant and hotels built of shell block. You'll be able to top off your gas tank and sip a tap beer with a hot meal. The town consists of a set of parallel streets and a half dozen businesses. The pub in the Shark Bay Hotel could pass for a setting in the *Crocodile Dundee* films. The Old Pearler Restaurant is the best-built shell-block building in Denham—it even has solid buttresses holding the walls up. To rent sailboards, rowboats, and powerboats, drop by the Shark Bay Service Station.

*Access.* Shark Bay is 838 kilometers north of Perth (130 of those kilometers are off the main highway). There is no regular public transportation. The trip takes about 8 hours by car and 3 hours in a light plane. For information about buses, check with Greyhound Pioneer in Perth (phone 13-20-30) with information outlets in Geraldton, or with the Western Australia Tourist Centre in Perth (phone 08-9483-1111).

# North of Shark Bay

## The Towns: Carnarvon and Exmouth

Carnarvon (population 7,000) has all the basic necessities and 323 sunny days a year. The area is also the hub of a prawn industry. The Blowholes, 70 kilometers north of town, are dramatic. Exmouth (population 2,800) is 184 kilometers off the North West Coastal Highway and about 320 kilometers north of Carnarvon. Contact Carnarvon Tourism Centre, 11 Robinson Street; phone 08-9941-1444.

## Cape Range National Park and Ningaloo Reef

The park is known for its gorges and pristine beaches. The west coast tracks lead to superb camping spots near the northern Ningaloo Reef, Western Australia's most accessible and biggest coral reef. In several areas the reef is close to shore and can be easily reached by snorkelers. The variety of creatures under the surface includes 460 species of fish. Dugongs and dolphins are common offshore, and the beaches are nesting rookeries for sea turtles. Yardie Creek is a scenic area with a conspicuous population of wallabies and red kangaroos.

Ningaloo Reef is an immense reef system stretching 260 kilometers from Coral Bay to Exmouth. It has increased in popularity as a dive destination in recent years. In part this is because of the high number of whale sharks sighted in the waters out past the reef. Boats with snorkelers spot these immense plankton eaters with the help of a light plane. The boat then races to the sharks so that snorkelers can jump in and swim next to these spotted, bus-sized fish. The majority of the dive operations accessing the reef are in Exmouth. Some dive outfits offer both diving and snorkeling in shallow water. Turquoise Bay is a popular snorkeling site. If you are a diver or game to snorkel contact: Ningaloo Deep (phone 08-9949-1663) or Village Dive (phone 08-9949-1101). Ningaloo Ecology Cruises offers glass-bottomed boat rides over parts of the reef; phone 08-9949-2255.

## Hamersley Ranges National Park

The Hamersley Ranges National Park is inland from Nanutarra, which is 148 kilometers north of the Exmouth turnoff on the North West Coastal Highway. From the north the park can also be reached from Port Hedland. The roads in this region are often dirt. Hamersley covers 617,600 hectares and has deep, colorful gorges and an eerie beauty. There are several camping areas, but no guaranteed water. Hamersley is only for the hardiest campers. During the summer months it is usually too hot for even reasonable comfort. Desert wildlife is common, especially reptiles, birds, and red kangaroos. Seek advice in Port Hedland, Carnarvon, Broome, or Perth before attempting to reach this park by car. Write to Ranger in Charge, P.O. Box 119, Karratha, W.A. 6714.

*Cautions.* On the North West Coastal Highway gas stations are far apart. As a general rule you should top off your tank whenever you see a pump. Night driving is hazardous because of kangaroos, livestock, and trucks.

# The Kimberley

The Kimberley region is often referred to as Australia's last frontier. Located at the northern end of the state, 2,200 kilometers north of Perth and 875 kilometers west of Darwin, the Kimberley takes up an area three times the size of the British Isles. It is a land of extremes. In the summer, monsoons pound the landscape and bring forth an explosion of greenery that includes immense plains of 3.5-meter-high spear grass. River systems become churning torrents, and low areas become floodplains. With winter comes the dry season, a period when the landscape browns and watercourses shrink and often become intermittent large pools. In both the wet and the dry season the area is striking: huge twisted orange-rock gorges, boab trees, wild cattle, basking crocodiles, flocks of black cockatoos, spectacular waterfalls, Aboriginal art, and one of the remotest and most spectacular coastlines in the world. The Kimberley is mostly an untamed wilderness. There are two gateway towns: Broome (2,200 kilometers from Perth) on the west coast and Kununurra (875 kilometers from Darwin) in the east near the Northern Territory. Broome, Derby, and Kununurra have jet airports linking them to Darwin and Perth.

## Broome

In 1987 Broome was the most charming town I visited in Australia. Since then longtime resident John Braithwaite tells me that the word is out and Broome is changing fast. "I hear talk of an international airport, mate. It looks like the rest of the world finally found out about us. We're overflowing with tourists."

Any description of Broome starts with its rich history and casual ambience. It is probably the most culturally diverse small town in Australia. Japanese, Chinese, Malaysians, Filipinos, Aborigines, and Europeans all played major roles in the town's development, which is still reflected in the town's polyglot racial makeup and acceptance of different cultures. There is a refreshing live-and-let-live attitude in Broome.

Broome has shiny white broad beaches and sparkling aqua blue water. Australians from cooler regions visit it during the winter (July through September). Winter rain is scarce, and the beachside temperature is usually 80°F.

The biggest annual event is the Shinju Matsuri Festival (August 11 through 20) celebrating the town's historical roots as the world's pearling capital at the turn of the century. The town got its start in the 1880s as a source of natural pearls. At the peak of pearling, 3,200 men and 400 luggers (pearling boats) worked from Broome, supplying 80 percent of the world's pearls. Most of the divers were Japanese, but Malaysians and Filipinos also crewed on the luggers. The life expectancy of the pearl divers was not long, as the town's large and well-kept Japanese cemetery attests (see "Things to Do," below). The Chinese ran the town's businesses during the pearling bonanza, and today they run pearl shops and restaurants. Broome's corrugated iron mini-Chinatown is a charming place.

## Information Sources

For an overview of Broome and the entire Kimberley, contact Kimberley Tourism Association; phone 08-9193-6660; E-mail: kimbtour@tpgi.com.au. KTA represents most of the tour operators in the Kimberley. The Broome Tourist Bureau, on the corner of Broome Highway and Bagot Street, is also an excellent contact. They are open seven days a week and can put you in touch with sources for accommodations, tour operators, and what's happening in the town; phone 08-9192-2222; E-mail: tourism@broome.wt.com.au.

## Things to Do

*Cable Beach.* Located 7 kilometers out of town, this 22-kilometer stretch of beautiful sand is the most popular beach in the Broome area. It's an excellent swimming and windsurfing beach. Usually both the beach and the water are amazingly smooth (past the breakers). Beach activities include surfing, windsurfing, camel trekking, Jet Skiing, massage, and, of course, sunbathing. Though the beach is one continuous stretch of sand, the parking area serves as the division between south and north Cable Beach. You are allowed to drive your car onto the northern beach, which allows access to beaches much farther up the coast. Nude bathing is the norm on the northern beach, but not on the southern. On the southern beach you can rent a windsurfer.

*Malcolm Douglas's Broome Crocodile Farm.* The croc farm has a collection of both freshwater and saltwater crocodiles. There are some particularly impressive large salties. The crocs are fed in the morning and afternoon. Docents do a good job of explaining the biology of these modern-day dinosaurs. $A6 per adult at feedings.

*Camel Treks.* Two outfits run camel strings on the northern end of Cable Beach. These camels are among the best trained and managed of the many camels I've ridden in Australia. The rides can take most of the day; cover 15 kilometers of beach, dune, and wet brushland; and include fishing and lunch. Or they can be one-hour outings. There are also twilight rides. You should book at least a day in advance. A taxi can deliver you from the tourism bureau or your motel to the camels. Contact Red Sun Camel Safaris; phone 08-1600-1745. They operate Monday–Saturday, year-round. Also try Ships of the Desert; phone 08-1600-1730.

*Exploring the Kimberley by Sea.* Broome's Deep Water Jetty (not the historic Streeters Jetty, where pearl luggers once unloaded) is a hub of activity. This is the departure point for charter boats that explore the spectacular coastline. Between Broome and Wyndham, a distance of 1,000 kilometers, the tiny town of Derby and the Kalumburu Aboriginal Mission are the only human populations. Boat charters vary from the superdeluxe high-powered seagoing catamarans to the 90-foot motor sailers; for the spartan-class adventurer, there are restored pearl luggers that will chug up the coast for four- to ten-day trips.

These boats will take you to a world few people have seen. Charts in use today haven't been improved on since the 1800s. In fact, charts made by the *Beagle*, which carried Charles Darwin around the world, are still in use. The coastline is a series of dramatic fjordlike inlets and immense vertical-faced stone fortresses adorned with tropical and subtropical vegetation. River systems often crash into the sea in dramatic waterfalls. The Buccaneer Archipelago, Lacepede Islands, Koolan Islands, Bonaparte Archipelago, and Bigge Island are just some of the offshore areas of interest that contain everything from turtle rookeries to dense populations of rare wallabies.

*Boat Operators Serving Visitors to Broome and the Kimberley.* After the publication of the first edition of *Adventuring in Australia* I learned a valuable lesson about the Kimberley. The natural beauty and wildness of the area attract people wanting to make a living here, but a ripple through the Australian transportation infrastructure can be economically unsettling to a place as remote as Broome, especially to its boat operators, who must rely on tourists in order to survive. Right after the first edition of *Adventuring in Australia* was published, in 1990, most Australian domestic air carriers quit flying because of a pilots strike that lasted months. The result in Broome was that a year after the book was published, all the operators plying the coastal waters were out of business. You should sort through the list of operators below knowing that in times of a fickle economy they may be hard-pressed to weather the storm. The beautiful pearl lugger *DMcD*, which had been meticulously restored by its then skipper, Dave Jackson, who took me up the coast, is now a museum piece in Roebuck Bay, alongside its sister ship, *Sam Male*. Visitors can tour both vessels.

Coral Princess Cruises is a high-end operator that works out of both Townsville and Cairns in Queensland, as well as Darwin and Broome. They run two boats. The *Coral Princess* does the "across-the-top cruise," taking in 1,000 kilometers of one of the remotest, least-inhabited coastlines in the world. The *Coral Princess* has the capacity to sleep 54 people in luxury-type accommodation; there is a biologist on board, and the ship stops periodically along the way so that passengers can go ashore or photograph coastal areas. Contact: Kimberley Coral Princess Cruises, Breakwater Terminal, Sir Leslie Thiess Drive, Townsville, Queensland 4810; phone 07-4721-1673; E-mail: cruisecp@coralprincess.com.au.

Most of the other operators in Broome offer one- to four-day outings that explore the coast north of Broome. Many of them design an outing after covering the possibilities with a client. Try the following: Broome Hovercraft, P.O. Box 5473, Cable Beach, W.A. 6726; phone 08-9193-5025; E-mail: broomeacv@wn.com.au. Broomtime Charters, P.O. Box 229, Broome, W.A. 6726; phone 08-9192-2458. Willie Lugger Cruises, P.O. Box 5211, Cable Beach, W.A. 6726; phone 08-0418-9191.

*Land and Air Operators Serving the Kimberley.* Numerous small airplanes and 4WD operators offer trips into the Kimberley, which stretches between Broome and Kununurra. On the ground the busiest and most often recommended is Safari Treks, 11 Foundry Street, Maylans, W.A. 6061; phone 08-9271-1271; E-mail: info@safaritreks. com.au.

Safari Treks travels to Windjana Gorge, the Gibb River Road, Tunnel Creek, King Edward River, Mitchell Plateau, Bungle Bungles, Fitzroy Crossing, Geikie Gorge, and other remote areas. They operate out of Kununurra and Broome. They also tackle the Canning Stock route and other multiday 4WD wilderness experiences.

There are several air businesses operating throughout the Kimberley. Most of them have fly-in tours and will also tailor tours to a client's desires. Try: Seair Broome, P.O. Box 3234, Broome, W.A. 6725; phone 08-9192-6208. Alligator Airways, P.O. Box 10, Kununurra, W.A. 6743; phone 08-9168-1333. Heliwork W.A., P.O. 165, Kununurra, W.A. 6743; phone 08-9168-1811. For a more complete list of aviation offerings, contact the Kimberley Tourism Association; phone 08-9193-6660.

*The Japanese Cemetery.* This is an artistic, traditional Japanese cemetery. It's filled with the graves of 919 young men, mostly Japanese, who perished while pearl diving in the region. The epitaphs are moving. About 30 men died annually from the bends (a misunderstood disease then called "diver's paralysis"), and larger numbers were lost when the fleet was caught at sea during a cyclone.

*Restaurants in Broome.* Fong Sam's Cafe (near the theater), phone 08-9192-1030, and Murray's Pearler (on Dampie Terrace), phone 08-9192-2049, received enthusiastic accolades from friends living in Broome. The Old Zoo Café, built in an immense former aviary, is an interesting place to eat and has good seafood dishes. It is located on Lullfitz near Cable Beach; phone 08-9193-6366.

*Accommodations in the Kimberley.* Broometime Lodge, P.O. Box 1632, Broome, W.A. 6725; phone 08-9193-5957. Merecure Inn Continental, P.O. Box 79, Broome, W.A. 6725; phone 08-9192-1002. Spinifex Hotel, P.O. Box 9, Derby, W.A. 6728; phone 08-9191-1031. King Sound Resort Hotel, P.O. Box 75, Derby, W.A. 6728; phone 08-9193-1044. Kununurra Lakeside Resort, P.O. Box 1129, Kununurra, W.A. 6743; phone 08-9169-1092. Kimberley Backpackers Adventure, P.O. Box 1119, Kununurra, W.A. 6743; phone 08-8960-9168.

## Derby

Derby is the other coastal town in the western Kimberley. Its 3,000 residents live on the shores of King Sound. It's a nicely laid out small town with all the basic necessities, including a number of good motels on the main drag. (See "Accommodations in the Kimberley," above.) Derby is 232 kilometers northeast of Broome on a good-quality paved road that I remember mostly for its boab trees and wild cattle on the roadway. In fact, there's an immense boab tree a few kilometers outside of Broome that was hollowed out and used to imprison Aborigines. The tree is still living. Buses run regularly between Derby and Broome. For the adventure-minded traveler, Derby is significant because it's the starting point for the Gibb River Road and the Devonian Reef National Parks. To learn more about the area contact the Derby Tourist Centre, Clarendon Street, Derby, W.A. 6728; phone 08-9191-1426.

## The Gibb River Road

The Gibb River Road runs 650 kilometers from Derby to Wyndham. It is a rugged dirt track cutting through the center of the Kimberley. It's impassable during the monsoon season and is suitable only for 4WD vehicles. But along the road you can visit Windjana and Chamberlain Gorges; the King Leopold, Pentacost, and Napier Ranges; and a series of huge cattle stations. You purchase your fuel from the stations, and they sometimes charge fees for camping. Fires are forbidden and campsites must be left free of litter. The area has pristine valleys, mesalike escarpments, savannah plains, river systems (and many crossings) suitable for swimming and fishing, wild cattle, wallabies, and bird life of all kinds. The Gibb River Road takes you into the frontier Australia of the last century, with the automobile being the only visible change. You may get glimpses of cattle drives supervised by Aboriginal jackeroos and a style of life that revolves around self-contained stations. This road should be taken only by a properly provisioned driver who is hardy and will accept a long bumpy ride. The Department of Conservation and Land Management has installed several campsites with showers and toilets in response to the ever-increasing use of the road. For more information, contact the Derby Tourist Centre, Clarendon Street,

Derby, W.A. 6728; phone 08-9191-1426. Or, in Kununurra (the road ends/starts in nearby Wyndham), contact the Kununurra Visitors Centre, Coolibah Drive, P.O. Box 446, Kununurra, W.A. 6743; phone 08-9168-1177.

## Devonian Reef National Parks

The parks include Geikie and Windjana Gorges and Tunnel Creek, which can be reached by the Gibb River Road (dirt) or the Great Northern Highway (paved until the final turnoff). The gorges were once part of a huge coral reef measuring 1,000 kilometers long and 25 kilometers wide. Layers of fossils are exposed in the strata of these gorges. It's not usually possible to visit these parks during the wet season. The best time to visit is in the dry season, between April and November. At this time days are hot but nights are cool. The gorges are surrounded by savannah country typical of much of the Kimberley. There are freshwater mangroves and paperbarks along the banks and streaked red and orange rock cliffs towering above the dramatic river courses.

Freshwater crocodiles are common in both gorges. When alarmed they sometimes sprint to the water en masse—a herd of sprinting crocodiles. They are harmless fish eaters, but expect to be bitten if you pick one up. In the Fitzroy River, which runs through Geikie Gorge, you may be lucky enough to see freshwater stingrays and sawfish, species that have been cut off from the sea for millions of years. Archerfish are active in the gorge and a joy to watch. Agile wallabies are common around dusk. The gorges are also home to thousands of birds.

There are numerous Aboriginal art sites. The art often contains Windjana men that were drawn without mouths and with rounded headpieces. One theory has it they represent beings from another galaxy. According to the Worora Aborigines, Windjanas came from the wind and made the earth.

There's excellent swimming in Geikie Gorge at the confluence of the Margaret and Fitzroy Rivers. For a dramatic sunset, take the walk along the west wall of the gorge. The reflection off the brightly colored walls is spectacular. There's a 3.5-kilometer walk up Windjana Gorge and Tunnel Creek that features a 750-meter walk through solid rock in a tunnel created by the creek. To get through the tunnel you must walk or swim down the creek, which is 3 to 12 meters deep. This should be attempted only during the dry season.

*Accommodations.* There are campgrounds with toilets, water, and showers (cold only at Windjana) at Geikie and Windjana Gorges. Camping is not allowed at Tunnel Creek.

*Access.* Windjana and Geikie Gorges are 30 kilometers apart on a 160-kilometer dirt track that connects the Gibb River Road to the Great Northern Highway. Geikie Gorge is easily reached from the Great Northern Highway (paved) at Fitzroy Crossing. If you must pick one gorge to visit, make it Geikie.

*Caution.* Check on road conditions and the weather forecast. The entire area around Fitzroy Crossing is subject to flooding during the monsoon season.

## Kununurra and the Eastern Kimberley

Kununurra, founded in 1963, is the only town built in the Kimberley this century. It houses workers for the Ord River–Lake Argyle irrigation scheme. It's a nondescript, clean town that serves as the eastern gateway to the Kimberley. It's an hour from Darwin by air and a day away (875 kilometers) by car (it's 480 kilometers from Katherine and 1,148 kilometers from Broome). The Kununurra Visitors Centre (75 Coolibah Drive, P.O. Box 446, Kununurra, W.A. 6743; phone 08-9168-2598) is the place to find out about accommodations, tours, and eateries, and to plan itineraries. The tourism center has videos of the Bungle Bungles, the northern coastline, and other areas of interest; it's also geared for the adventure traveler. The Kimberleyland Holiday Park on Duncan Highway is a full-amenities (including a washer and dryer) caravan camp. The camping area is on the shore of Lake Kununurra. For details on national parks in the area, contact Regional Manager Kimberley, Department of Conservation and Land Management, P.O. Box 242, Kununurra, W.A. 6743. If you're equipped and ready for a "real adventure," talk to the staff about the Mitchell Plateau or Drysdale River. There are a great number of adventure possibilities originating in and around Kununurra. Some of the most attractive include using light aircraft, which is relatively inexpensive.

## Day Trips from Kununurra

*Hidden Valley.* Hidden Valley is 2 to 3 kilometers out of town and has several short walking tracks. The area contains strikingly layered sandstone, a mini–Bungle Bungles rich in birds.

*Lake Kununurra.* The lake (7 kilometers from town) is a diversion dam. It has an extensive wetlands and bountiful bird life. There's a good-quality boat tour that will show you everything from flocks of red-tailed black cockatoos and brolgas to freshwater crocodiles. More than 200 species of birds frequent the area, some of them indigenous just to this area.

*The Argyle Diamond Mine.* In 1979 the world's largest diamond deposit was discovered south of Kununurra. The mine can't be visited from the ground because of security reasons, but scenic flights to the Bungle Bungles go directly over the huge pits and active mining operations. The mine now accepts tour groups.

*Lake Argyle.* Located about 70 kilometers from Kununurra, Lake Argyle is an immense man-made lake covering more than 740 square kilometers—nine times the size of Sydney's harbor. Lake Argyle Holiday Village, a self-contained town, serves the lake. While one would expect the lake to be a boater's paradise, it's usually empty! But there are many islands suitable for camping.

## The Bungle Bungles

The Bungle Bungles are timeworn, brightly layered formations that rival Uluru and the Olgas as Australia's most striking rock formations. Because they are in the remote Kimberley, they did not come to the attention of most Australians until 1983, when several articles were written about them. When I visited them I had vowed to use only one roll of film. Instead, I shot five—the place is that unique.

The Bungle Bungles are a maze of domelike formations with hundreds of horizontal layers of exposed strata that are called tiger stripes because they alternate between black and orange. From a distance the formations look like immense sculpted layer cakes. In reality the plateau is made of an uncommon kind of siliceous sandstone that is very fragile and should not be climbed on. Much of the area

around the Bungles is spinifex country. You'll find a few ponds and
water at Piccaninny Creek. There are fair numbers of reptiles and
amphibians in the wetter areas of what is an otherwise hot and hostile environment. The area around the Bungle Bungles is overgrazed,
and you may come across wild bulls; remember that they can be dangerous.

*Access.* Several light aircraft leave Kununurra daily for low-altitude
flying over the Bungle Bungles. On the ground the trip consists of
197 kilometers on the Great Northern Highway from Kununurra
and another 65 kilometers on a bone-jarring dirt road that can be
negotiated only in a 4WD vehicle by an experienced driver.

# Glossary of Aussie Slang

When the English language arrived in Australia it adapted to the new land and took on an identity of its own. Words were created to name the wildlife and the landscape: words like *kangaroo, kookaburra, Nullarbor,* and *platypus*. The male-dominated egalitarian frontier culture added *matemanship* and *fair go*. Aboriginal names of places and things were added too. Often sheer inventiveness mixed with irreverence created words such as *squatocracy* (for today's landed gentry). Cockney rhyming slang came ashore with the prison gangs, as did the king's English of the wealthy settlers. The written language that emerged follows British spelling and is entirely understandable to Americans. However, the spoken language contains colloquialisms and slang that can put you up a gum tree. To avoid being labeled a drongo, study some of the more common Aussie words.

**Abo**  offensive term for Aborigine

**Aborigine (Aboriginal)**  the generic word for the first inhabitants of Australia, who now make up 1.1 percent of the continent's population. Each Aboriginal group has its own regional identity: Danggadi, Ngaanyatjarra, Wadi-Wadi, and so on

**(the) *Alice***  the train that runs from Sydney to Alice Springs

**amber fluid**  beer

**ankle biter**  a young child

**Anzac**  a soldier from Australia or New Zealand

**aryo**  afternoon

**Aussie**  Australian

**Australian salute**  passing one's hand over your face to brush flies away

**Back of Bourke**   Outback:
Back of Beyond
**bag of fruit**   man's suit (rhyming slang)
**ball and chain**   wife
**banana bender**   Queenslander
**bathers**   swimwear
**beaut**   fine, perfect, just right
**billabong**   a freshwater pond
or swamp
**billy**   a metal container used
for boiling water over an
open fire, usually for tea
**bitumen**   pavement
**Blinky Bill**   fool (rhyming
slang)
**bloke**   man; also, boss
**bludger**   one who lives off
others; also, on the dole
**blue**   a violent argument or
fight
**bog**   a soft surface where a
vehicle might get stuck
**bonnet**   car's hood
**boot**   car's trunk
**booze bus**   mobile police unit
where drivers with blood
alcohol higher than .05 are
incarcerated
**bottle shop**   liquor store
**bowser**   petrol (gasoline) pump
**brumby**   wild horse
**bugger-all**   to do very little
**buggered**   tired, exhausted,
failed
**bugger off**   depart
**bull dust**   deep dust on dirt
roads that can be deceptive
and dangerous

**bush**   Outback, camping
**bush bashing**   cross-country
hiking in challenging country
**bushman (bushie)**   a person at
home in the outdoors
**bushranger**   road bandit (historic); unscrupulous person
(today)
**bush tucker**   food collected
and prepared in the out-
doors
**BYO**   a restaurant without a
liquor license: *b*ring *y*our
*o*wn bottle

**chalkie**   teacher
**chemist's shop**   drugstore
**china plate**   mate; friend
(rhyming slang)
**(the) Coathanger**   Sydney
Harbour Bridge
**coolamon**   an Aboriginal
woman's all-purpose con-
tainer, usually made of soft
wood and measuring about
three feet
**corroboree**   Aboriginal term
used by Europeans to
describe all ceremonial Aboriginal dancing and songs
**crook**   sick, broken
**crooked on**   angry
**crystal highway**   a section of
road constantly littered with
windshield glass from acci-
dents
**cultural cringe**   a sense of infe-
riority about one's culture

**damper** bread made on a campfire

**Deep North** Queensland (same sense as *Deep South* in the United States)

**didgeridoo** eerie-sounding wind instrument made from a hollow eucalyptus branch and played by Aborigines in the tropics

**digger** an Aussie soldier; also, miner

**dingo** wild dog with 10,000-year history in Australia

**dinky-di** true, honest

**Down Under** the name for Australia, New Zealand, and South Pacific islands from the perspective of the Northern Hemisphere; not especially appreciated in Australia

**Dreamtime (dreaming)** Aboriginal legends that contain their cultural beliefs, rules for living, and creation myths

**drongo** fool, dummy

**dunny** an outhouse, toilet

**dunny budgie** a fly

**Earbasher** a talkative bore

**esky** a portable ice box

**fair dinkum** genuine

**fair go** being given an equal chance

**flog** attempt to sell something

**footie** football Aussie style

**galah** a common pink and gray cockatoo; also, a stupid person

**g'day** good day (common greeting)

**(the)** *Ghan* the railroad that runs between Alice and Adelaide

**greenie** a conservationist or environmentalist

**gum tree** any of hundreds of species of eucalyptus

**higgledy piggledy** confused

**jackeroo** a novice male station hand

**jilleroo** a novice female station hand

**joey** a baby kangaroo

**jumpbuck** a sheep

**Kiwi** a New Zealander

**larrikin** an irreverent tough guy with some likable qualities

**lollies** candy

**loo** toilet

**maggoty** angry

**mate** comrade, friend, equal

**meat pie** an Australian culinary concoction made of meat in a pie crust

**middy** a medium-sized glass of beer

**moke** a small open-air vehicle

**mozzie** mosquito

**Ned Kelly**   a notorious outlaw, often used in comparison, as in "as fearless as Ned Kelly"

**New Australian**   an immigrant after World War II from somewhere other than England, usually southern Europe

**nick, in good nick**   in good physical condition
> **in the nick**   nude
> **nick off**   leave

**no-hoper**   a meritless person

**no worries**   everything is fine

**ochre**   naturally occurring pigment used by Aborigines in ceremonial rock and body art

**ocker**   a stereotypical boorish, chauvinistic Australian workingman—like *redneck* in the United States

**pommy or pom**   Englishman (can be offensive) from *pris*oner *of* Mother England

**poofter**   male homosexual (offensive)

**postie**   mailman

**prang**   car crash

**pub**   a public house, a beer hall or tavern

**pub crawl**   drinking at a succession of pubs

**raging**   partying

**Rainbow Serpent**   a mystical Dreaming entity

**ratbag**   an oddball, a jerk

**sanger**   a sandwich

**sheila**   a girl or woman (can be offensive)

**she'll be right**   everything is fine

**shoot through**   to leave in a hurry

**shout**   to buy a round of drinks

**stubby**   a small beer bottle

**suss out**   to figure out

**swag**   a large bedroll and personal belongings

**Tassie**   the island state of Tasmania

**tea**   the herbal drink or dinner, depending on the context

**tellie**   television

**tinnie**   a can of beer

**Top End**   the northern central region of Australia around Darwin

**track**   a dirt road (possibly for 4WD) or walking trail

**tucker**   food

**two-bob**   poor quality

**two-up**   a popular Australian gambling game involving flipping two coins

**up (a gum tree)**   confused, helpless

**ute**   pickup truck

**Vegemite**   a foul-tasting sandwich spread made of yeast

**walkabout**  to wander about nomadically

**wallaby**  any of scores of species of middle-sized kangaroos

**wallaroo**  the euro kangaroo, a mountain kangaroo

**walloper**  a policeman

**wanker**  a self-important fool

**warrigal**  Aboriginal for *dingo*, now used for anything wild

**whinger**  a constant complainer

**wowser**  an uptight prude; synonymous with censorship

**yabber**  talk

**yachtie**  a yachtsman or yachtswoman

**yakka**  work (derived from an Aboriginal word)

**yank tank**  a large American car

**you-beaut country**  Australia

# Index

# About the Author

ERIC HOFFMAN is a professional writer with a special interest in the natural world. A former college journalism instructor, he has written more than two hundred feature stories for many magazines, including *Wildlife Conservation, International Wildlife, Outside, Animals, Pacific Discovery, Fine Homebuilding,* and the Sunday magazines for the *San Jose Mercury News* and *San Francisco Chronicle*. He is the author of books on a wide range of subjects, including contemporary architecture (*Renegade Houses*) as well as books on South American cameloids. He is co-author of *The Alpaca Book* and is a recognized expert on llamas, alpacas, vicunas, and guanacos in both South and North America. He has written sophisticated animal registries utilizing DNA technology to preserve rare breeds of livestock. For Sierra Club Books he also wrote *Adventuring in Belize*.

For research on *Adventuring in Australia* Eric visited Australia 12 times, often on assignment for wildlife magazines. He traveled more than 60,000 kilometers internally in Australia, utilizing camels, trains, a variety of watercraft, light aircraft, and rental cars. He has been assigned articles on everything from how U.S. farm subsidies affect wheat farmers in Australia to stories on how to best manage maneating saltwater crocodiles in the Northern Territory to explaining the unique evolution and adaptations of the platypus, which allowed it to survive in Australia's waterways for thousands of years. When he's not traveling Eric lives on his alpaca ranch near Santa Cruz, California.